Firm Competitive Advantage Through Relationship Management

Bartosz Deszczyński

Firm Competitive Advantage Through Relationship Management

A Theory for Successful Sustainable Growth

Bartosz Deszczyński
Poznań University of Economics and Business
Poznań, Poland

ISBN 978-3-030-67337-6   ISBN 978-3-030-67338-3 (eBook)
https://doi.org/10.1007/978-3-030-67338-3

© The Editor(s) (if applicable) and The Author(s) 2021. This book is an open access publication.

Open Access This book is licensed under the terms of the Creative Commons Attribution 4.0 International License (http://creativecommons.org/licenses/by/4.0/), which permits use, sharing, adaptation, distribution and reproduction in any medium or format, as long as you give appropriate credit to the original author(s) and the source, provide a link to the Creative Commons licence and indicate if changes were made.

The images or other third party material in this book are included in the book's Creative Commons licence, unless indicated otherwise in a credit line to the material. If material is not included in the book's Creative Commons licence and your intended use is not permitted by statutory regulation or exceeds the permitted use, you will need to obtain permission directly from the copyright holder.

The use of general descriptive names, registered names, trademarks, service marks, etc. in this publication does not imply, even in the absence of a specific statement, that such names are exempt from the relevant protective laws and regulations and therefore free for general use.

The publisher, the authors and the editors are safe to assume that the advice and information in this book are believed to be true and accurate at the date of publication. Neither the publisher nor the authors or the editors give a warranty, expressed or implied, with respect to the material contained herein or for any errors or omissions that may have been made. The publisher remains neutral with regard to jurisdictional claims in published maps and institutional affiliations.

Cover pattern © Melisa Hasan

This Palgrave Macmillan imprint is published by the registered company Springer Nature Switzerland AG.
The registered company address is: Gewerbestrasse 11, 6330 Cham, Switzerland

*To my Father for encouraging me to write
and to Saint Joseph the Labourer for his intercession for
my peace of mind while writing.*

Preface

Although common sense would suggest relationships are an inherent and vital aspect of any human social activity, the actual effectiveness of relationship management (RM) as a business model seems to be very individual- and case-specific. This observation is reflected in the extraordinary richness of relationship-oriented research (Payne and Frow 2017; Zineldin and Philipson 2007). Moreover, the number of one-shot studies and the semantic voluntarism of conceptual models is well beyond the capacity to test and establish them, which makes vast parts of the research on RM 'practically phenomenological' (Niemczyk 2015; Ward and Webster 1991). Such a state of affairs echoes a general problem of insufficient programmatic research in management science (Reid et al. 2004) and the increase in the theory-practice gap (Bratnicka-Myśliwiec et al. 2018). However, instead of classifying RM research as irrevocably highly context-sensitive, in this book I intend to take a nometic course and follow the promising logic of theory simplification, completion and bridging (Strużyna 2015).

The way to achieve this and simultaneously to close a fundamental gap in the contemporary body of research is to define what characterizes the state of achieving maturity in RM (Lichtarski 2015). More precisely, there is a need to determine the activities and approaches of truly RM-oriented (RM-mature) companies (Mumuni and O'Reilly 2014), that is, the companies who are capable of implementing RM processes to a higher degree than others (Reinartz et al. 2004). However, the superficial and/or fragmented understanding of the RM business model makes it hard to separate these firms from those that declare relationships as their priority but in fact prefer transactional short-termism. Consequently, studying the correlation between the RM business model and firm competitive advantage is impaired. This systemic problem also has a methodological dimension, which is about founding research more on firm declarative attitudes towards relationships in general and/or on temporary proficiency in particular relational tactics than on a concrete and coherent set of dedicated decisions that validate a long-term and value-oriented reciprocal cooperation.

Meanwhile, another way to achieve more clarity in RM research is by developing a simple and workable mid-range theory (Brodie 2017; Gummesson 2017; Guo et al. 2017). This theory level offers much more potential for generalization than idiosyncratic micro-theories and is intermediate to grand theories, which themselves are too remote to account for what is observed (Merton 1968). Nonetheless, there are doubts as to whether it is possible to merge all relational research streams (including business networks, channel relationships, customer relationship marketing, interactive marketing and services marketing) into one actionable theory (Möller and Halinen 2000; Möller 2013). However, a successful conceptualization of RM maturity could possibly facilitate this process and contribute to closing another research gap.

With the intention to explore this synergistic potential, the first objective of this book is to refine the understanding of the RM business model by conceptualizing and testing the notion of RM maturity and to verify if RM-mature firms possess the ability to achieve sustainable competitive advantage over their transaction-oriented rivals. The second related objective is to use the theoretical and empirical insights gained in the process of developing this new concept to propose a robust framework for an RM mid-range theory.

Owing to the adopted logic it is premature to propose any set of detailed hypotheses before the conceptualization of RM maturity is accomplished. It would have to take the form of listing dozens of tactical positivistic propositions or their allocation to several unobservable constructs arbitrarily perceived as being relevantly linked. Therefore, in this book only one twin theory-methodic (H1tm) and empiric (H1e) – hypothesis is proposed:

H1tm: Delimitation of truly RM-oriented firms (RM-mature firms) from superficially relationship-oriented ones (which are actually transaction-oriented) is necessary to determine whether the RM business model is a source of sustainable competitive advantage.

H1e: The RM business model is a source of sustainable competitive advantage for RM-mature firms only.

In order to accomplish the set objectives and to verify the twin-hypotheses, this book is divided into five chapters and applies a hypothetico-deductive theory confirmation method (Doty and Glick 1994). This method serves as the underlying framework for the research design model (Fig. 1).

Chapter 1 introduces the notion of competitive advantage in multiple research perspectives of the dominant strategic management schools and references the academic discourse on the fundamental issue of the locus of competitive advantage.

STEP #1: Set the boundaries of the envisioned RM mid-range theory
> define the domain of RM and the RM business model
> propose and articulate the epistemic isolating mechanism for the RM mid-range theory
> draft the position of RM mid-range theory in the system of theories of competitive advantage

STEP #2: Conceptualize RM maturity
> define the notion of maturity
> review the RM literature and discuss RM-related themes
> propose preliminary RM maturity model

STEP #3: Empirically test preliminary RM model
> set the methodology
> carry out quantitative field research
> apply machine learning techniques to propose and discuss the ultimate RM maturity model

STEP #4: Propose the underlying framework for RM mid-range theory
> incorporate the notion of RM maturity into RM theory development
> illustrate the applicability of RM business model with practical examples
> formulate normative guidelines for RM business practice

Fig. 1 Research design model

In Chap. 2 the domain of relationship management is discussed, including its socio-economic duality and the diversity of partly overlapping relational constructs. Following this, the theoretical boundaries of the envisioned RM mid-range theory in a hypothetical system of theories for competitive advantage are drafted (step 1 of the research design model). In the course of this epistemological ideation process, an isolating mechanism is applied to delimit the research field of the new theory by focusing on fewer but universally observable organizational phenomena. This procedure reflects the author's preference for pragmatism as the guiding epistemic virtue (Ketokivi and Mantere 2010) and helps in maintaining high generalizability of a theory without losing its workability, since isolation, as opposed to straight abstraction, does not significantly distort the observed phenomena, but extracts them intact from more variable environments (Mäki 2006).

Chapter 3 presents the consequent steps of the conceptualization of RM maturity within a systematic literature review procedure (step 2 of the research design model). Its product is a flexible preliminary model with a wide palette of options (RM activities and approaches) incorporated from all streams of RM-related literature, provided they fit into the broad definitional basis of RM (Morgan and Hunt 1994). In particular, a discussion on 12 RM-related themes grouped into 3 dimensions is given, as well as a separate theory-integrative discourse on RM and Service-Dominant Logic as permeable paradigms (Gummesson and Mele 2010).

The preliminary deductively elaborated RM maturity model is operationalized into a 40-question-strong research tool in Chap. 4. Then, the methodology of the quantitative research is described. The empirical test is designed to assess both proficiency in RM and firm sustainable competitive advantage. It encompasses the self-reporting of business respondents based on telephone interviewing and machine learning analytical techniques, which aim to identify a 'basket' of critical RM activities and approaches constituting the notion of RM maturity, as described in step 3 of the research design model. It assumes that only a fraction of these will be found highly relevant, however, without any harm to the final model of RM maturity, which is presented and discussed in the concluding section of the chapter. Thus, the twin-hypotheses will be verified, and the first main goal of this book will be achieved.

In the last chapter, Chap. 5, according to step 4 of the research design, the deductive and inductive arguments resulting from the previous discussions are brought together and synthetized into an underlying framework for the RM mid-range theory of higher order. In particular, the newly empirically tested concept of RM maturity is incorporated into the normative discourse of theory development, thus contributing to the accomplishment of the second main goal of this book. In addition, the chapter presents empirical examples showing diverse challenges in managing relationships elaborated from direct interviews with interlocutors from eight different companies. They serve as a supplementary qualitative method illustrating different facets of RM 'in motion'. In addition to the five chapters, the book encompasses this Preface and the Final Note.

Poznań, Poland					Bartosz Deszczyński

References

Bratnicka-Myśliwiec, K., M. Kulikowska-Pawlak, and M. Bratnicki. 2018. Contemporary Thinking About Theory Building: A Review of the Concept with Application to Organisational Politics Researching. *Organizacja i Zarządzanie: Kwartalnik Naukowy* 2. https://doi.org/10.29119/1899-6116.2018.42.1.

Brodie, Roderick J. 2017. Enhancing Theory Development in the Domain of Relationship Marketing: How to Avoid the Danger of Getting Stuck in the Middle. *Journal of Services Marketing* 31 (1): 20–23.

Doty, D. Harold, and William H. Glick. 1994. Typologies as a Unique Form of Theory Building: Toward Improved Understanding and Modeling. *The Academy of Management Review* 19 (2): 230–251. https://doi.org/10.2307/258704.

Gummesson, Evert. 2017. From Relationship Marketing to Total Relationship Marketing and Beyond. *Journal of Services Marketing* 31 (1): 16–19. https://doi.org/10.1108/JSM-11-2016-0398.

Gummesson, Evert, and Cristina Mele. 2010. Marketing as Value Co-Creation Through Network Interaction and Resource Integration. *Journal of Business Market Management* 4 (4): 181–198. https://doi.org/10.1007/s12087-010-0044-2.

Guo, Lin, Thomas Gruen, and Chuanyi Tang. 2017. Seeing Relationships Through the Lens of Psychological Contracts: The Structure of Consumer Service Relationships. *Journal of the Academy of Marketing Science* 45 (3): 357–376.

Ketokivi, Mikko, and Saku Mantere. 2010. Two Strategies for Inductive Reasoning in Organizational Research. *Academy of Management Review* 35 (2): 315–333. https://doi.org/10.5465/amr.35.2.zok315.

Lichtarski, Jan. 2015. *Praktyczny Wymiar Nauk o Zarządzaniu.* Warszawa: Polskie Wydawnictwo Ekonomiczne.

Mäki, Uskali. 2006. On the Method of Isolation in Economics. *Recent Developments in Economic Methodology* 3: 3–37.
Möller, Kristian. 2013. Theory Map of Business Marketing: Relationships and Networks Perspectives. *Industrial Marketing Management*, Theoretical Perspectives in Industrial Marketing Management, 42 (3): 324–335. https://doi.org/10.1016/j.indmarman.2013.02.009.
Möller, Kristian, and Aino Halinen. 1999. Business Relationships and Networks. *Industrial Marketing Management* 28 (5): 413–427. https://doi.org/10.1016/S0019-8501(99)00086-3.
Morgan, Robert M., and Shelby D. Hunt. 1999. Relationship-Based Competitive Advantage: The Role of Relationship Marketing in Marketing Strategy. *Journal of Business Research* 46 (3): 281–290. https://doi.org/10.1016/S0148-2963(98)00035-6.
Mumuni, Alhassan G., and Kelley O'Reilly. 2014. Examining the Impact of Customer Relationship Management on Deconstructed Measures of Firm Performance. *Journal of Relationship Marketing* 13 (2): 89–107. https://doi.org/10.1080/15332667.2014.910073.
Niemczyk, Jerzy. 2015. Metodologia Nauk o Zarządzaniu. In *Podstawy Metodologii Badań w Naukach o Zarządzaniu*, ed. Wojciech Czakon, 3rd ed. Warszawa: Oficyna a Wolters Kluwer business.
Payne, Adrian, and Pennie Frow. 2017. Relationship Marketing: Looking Backwards towards the Future. *Journal of Services Marketing* 31 (1): 11–15. https://doi.org/10.1108/JSM-11-2016-0380.
Reid, David Alan, Richard E. Plank, and J. David Lichtenthal. 2004. *Fundamentals of Business Marketing Research*. New York: Haworth Press.
Reinartz, Werner, Manfred Krafft, and Wayne D. Hoyer. 2004. The Customer Relationship Management Process: Its Measurement and Impact on Performance. *Journal of Marketing Research*. https://doi.org/10.1509/jmkr.41.3.293.35991.
Strużyna, Janusz. 2015. Oryginalność w Badaniach Naukowych w Dyscyplinie Nauk o Zarządzaniu. In *Podstawy Metodologii Badań w Naukach o Zarządzaniu*, ed. Wojciech Czakon, 3rd ed. Warszawa: Oficyna a Wolters Kluwer business.
Ward, Scott, and Frederick E. Webster. 1991. Organizational Buying Behavior. In *Handbook of Consumer Behavior*, Ellis Horwood Series in Analytical, ed. T.S. Robertson and H.H. Kassarjian. Upper Saddle River: Prentice-Hall. https://books.google.pl/books?id=dz0fAQAAIAAJ
Zineldin, Mosad, and Sarah Philipson. 2007. Kotler and Borden Are Not Dead: Myth of Relationship Marketing and Truth of the 4Ps. *Journal of Consumer Marketing* 24 (4): 229–241. https://doi.org/10.1108/07363760710756011.

Acknowledgements

This book was prepared as a result of research project 2015/19/ D/ HS4/01956 funded by the Polish National Science Centre.

Contents

1. **Research on the Competitive Advantage of the Firm** — 1
   1.1 *Dominating Schools of Strategic Management* — 1
   1.2 *The Discourse on the Locus of Competitive Advantage* — 5
   References — 14

2. **Theoretical Foundations of the Relationship Management Mid-Range Theory** — 21
   2.1 *The Domain of Relationship Management* — 21
   2.2 *The Boundaries of RM Mid-Range Theory* — 35
   References — 46

3. **Relationship Management Maturity** — 67
   3.1 *The Design and Introductory Steps of RM Maturity Conceptualization* — 67
   3.2 *The Strategic Dimension of RM Maturity* — 81
   3.3 *The Processual and ICT Dimensions of RM Maturity* — 94
   References — 103

4. **Validating the Relationship Management Maturity Concept** — 121
   4.1 *The Design of a Research Tool on RM Maturity* — 121
   4.2 *Analytical Strategy* — 135
   4.3 *The Empirical Results on RM Maturity and Competitive Advantage* — 141
   References — 150

5	Developing the Relationship Management Upper Mid-Range Theory	159
	5.1 The Final Proposal of the RM Maturity Model and Its Practical Interpretation	161
	5.2 Relational Niche	166
	5.3 Illustrative Examples of RM Practice	181
	References	209

Final Note — 217

References — 221

Index — 275

ABBREVIATIONS

BPM	Business Process Management
CMM	Capability Maturity Model for software
CRM	Customer Relationship Management
CSR	Corporate Social Responsibility
ERM	External Relationship Management
H-D	Hypothetico-deductive theory confirmation method
HRM	Human Resources Management
ICT	Information and Communication Technologies
IMP	Industrial Marketing and Purchasing Group
IRM	Internal Relationship Management
KM	Knowledge Management
NPS	Net Promoter Score
IOE	Industrial Organization Economics
R-A	Resource-Advantage Theory of Competition
RBV	Resource-Based View
RM	Relationship Management
SCM	Supply Chain Management
SCP	Structure Conduct Performance paradigm
SDL	Service-Dominant Logic
SEM	Structural Equation Models
SET	Social Exchange Theory
VRIO	Valuable, Rare, Inimitable, Organized resources

List of Figures

Fig. 1.1	Causal chain of interdependencies in M. Porter's dynamic theory of strategy. (Source: Adapted from Porter 1991, p. 100; van den Bosch 1997, p. 95)	9
Fig. 1.2	Strategic assets and strategic industry factors. (Adapted from Amit and Schoemaker (1993, p. 37))	13
Fig. 2.1	RM factors and the capital of the firm. Note: This figure does not attempt to enumerate all components of the listed upper-range constructs. Its role is to provide a common understanding of the expressions used later in this book. 'Partner' can be understood as any actor (whether individual or institutional) a company has a relation to	29
Fig. 2.2	Content of RM mid-range theory. Note: The proposed content of the envisioned RM mid-range theory is marked by the bold text. (Inspired by: Obłój (2007, pp. 22–40); Williamson (1993, pp. 3–17))	39
Fig. 2.3	The isolating mechanism-based delimitation of the RM mid-range theory. Note that this figure illustrates the management sciences focus of R-A theory and excludes its macroeconomic focus. If the full research agenda of R-A theory were to be visualized, the other theories would have to go further right on the X axis. (Adapted from: Hedström and Udehn (2011, p. 29))	42
Fig. 2.4	Hypothetical system of theories for competitive advantage. (Adapted from Pinder and Moore (1980, p. 197), inspired by Möller (2013, pp. 324–325))	43

LIST OF FIGURES

Fig. 3.1	Design of RM maturity conceptualization. (Source: Adapted from Fink (2010))	71
Fig. 3.2	Descriptive analysis of RM-related content	77
Fig. 3.3	Co-citation density by authors in the reviewed literature. (Source: VOSviewer, version 1.6.14)	80
Fig. 3.4	Most cited papers in the reviewed literature. (Source: VOSviewer, version 1.6.14)	81
Fig. 3.5	CRM strategy framework. (Source: Adapted from Payne and Frow (2005, p. 171))	82
Fig. 3.6	The interplay between RM and SDL	86
Fig. 3.7	Strategic dimension in preliminary RM maturity model	93
Fig. 3.8	Processual dimension in preliminary RM maturity model	99
Fig. 3.9	Preliminary RM maturity model	102
Fig. 4.1	Mean results for every item in the dataset broken down by competitive advantage groups	142
Fig. 4.2	Comparison of differences in the mean results between the 'extremely high competitive advantage' and 'no competitive advantage' groups of companies	143
Fig. 4.3	Companies' characteristics across groups of achieved competitive advantage. Note: For decoding the results on the X axis, please refer to section E of the questionnaire	144
Fig. 4.4	The network of association rules. Note: For decoding the item subsets composing the rules, please refer to sections A, C and D of the questionnaire	146
Fig. 5.1	Final proposal of the RM maturity model	163
Fig. 5.2	Model of transactional rivalry. Note: The picture has an indicative character and does not show oligopoly. The actual number of companies does not matter as long as customers have a choice of comparable alternatives	171
Fig. 5.3	The coexistence of RM-mature and transaction-oriented companies. Note: The picture has an indicative character. There could me more RM-mature companies in the market, which would isolate their relational niches. There could be cross-sections of these niches; however, the modus operandi of RM-mature companies would remain the same	172
Fig. 5.4	Factors influencing the size of relational niche. Note: The more intense gradient in the triangle, the more likely a substantial relational niche can be built	179

List of Tables

Table 3.1	Google Scholar search results on RM	72
Table 3.2	Search criteria applied to scientific databases	73
Table 3.3	List of journals and number of referred articles	74
Table 3.4	Overview of the thematic literature review	84
Table 4.1	The questionnaire on RM maturity	125
Table 4.2	Response statistics in CATI survey	136
Table 4.3	Companies of different competitive advantage in the dataset	141
Table 4.4	Association rules computed for the 'extremely strong competitive advantage' group of companies	145
Table 5.1	Overview: Home décor retailer	183
Table 5.2	Overview: Large FMCG manufacturer	187
Table 5.3	Overview: Pamapol S.A.	189
Table 5.4	Overview: Chemicals' manufacturer	193
Table 5.5	Overview: Konimpex-Invest Sp. z o.o.	195
Table 5.6	Overview: Termy Maltańskie Sp. z o.o.	198
Table 5.7	Overview: Sugar-refining group	202
Table 5.8	Overview: Aquanet S.A.	206

CHAPTER 1

Research on the Competitive Advantage of the Firm

1.1　Dominating Schools of Strategic Management

The shortest definition of a good strategy can be boiled down to 'passion and discipline' (Obłój 2013). Passion means to retain an entrepreneurial spirit (eagerness for progress, flexibility, courage and optimism) — however old and extensive an organization may be. Discipline means to build a professional method for interpretation of the signals from the inside and outside of an organization and to retain a coherent logic of decision making. No less passionate and disciplined should be the work of researchers on strategic management, who—just like the business practitioners—try to find out how to create and run a perfect company. The answers they propose add to a highly diversified body of knowledge, which is often criticized for being too broad, unstructured and lacking identity (Lichtarski 2015; Sobczyk 2010; Trocki 2005). Still, given the applicable character of strategic management and management science in general, a wide range of proposals makes it more likely for business practitioners to find inspiration in a theory relating to a particular situation of a given company and its market environment (Krupski 2009a; Romanowska 2018).

The richness of ideas and concepts in strategic management does not mean they are all totally random. On the contrary, there are several streams of research (often called schools), which each integrate a distinctive way of thinking about the firm in the context of its strategy (Czakon 2014). This

© The Author(s) 2021
B. Deszczyński, *Firm Competitive Advantage Through Relationship Management*, https://doi.org/10.1007/978-3-030-67338-3_1

means that they try to provide a synoptic picture of the following areas of corporate activities (Obłój 1998, pp. 34–35):

- mission;
- business domain;
- competitive advantage;
- strategic goals;
- functional programmes.

Although these five build a consistent system of interdependencies, in this book the focus is on the origins of competitive advantage understood as the (relatively) stable generation of economic rents by the company (Czakon 2005). Strategic management is in essence the theory of corporate effectiveness (Obłój 2019), and the question of how firms achieve and sustain competitive advantage lies at the heart of its research agenda (Rumelt et al. 1995). Moreover, it seems the problem of competitive advantage is the only field that offers a chance to formulate possibly universal directives at the intersection of business practice and theory building. It is also the analysis of competitive advantage that initiates the creation of a business model, which transforms an abstract image of a company into its real operations (Banaszyk 2014; Obłój 2002). Hence, at least in terms of management science, the theory of competitive advantage has the potential to remain simultaneously actionable and generalizable.

The other four elements of strategy formulation described by Obłój (1998) need more specific studies in the context of a particular company or a group of companies, taking into account their size, structures, network embeddedness, industries or technologies. And thus, corporate mission describes the identity of an organization. Business domain answers the questions 'how', 'where' and 'when' a company should enter or leave a particular market. Strategic goals roughly reflect a company's response to a SWOT analysis. Functional programmes operationalize particular business activities (Krupski 2009b). Although useful, such studies largely deal with positivist or phenomenological descriptions, which are usually too idiosyncratic in nature to enable inductive enumeration and normative inference. As the normative significance of a theory depends on the fit between its assumptions and reality, the applicability of such models is most likely restricted to a small subgroup of firms whose characteristics fit the model's assumptions (Porter 1991).

There have been numerous attempts to organize the body of knowledge on the theory of the firm, including strategic management as an associated theory. They are only partly compatible, because of their background, analytical cross-section, attention to detail and the passage of time (Zimniewicz 2014). As this book concerns relationship management underpinned by resource-based and dynamic capabilities theories, a comprehensive review of all possible classifications is not intended. However, some examples are chosen to gradually build a theoretical context of the envisioned relationship management (RM) mid-range theory in the context of sustainable competitive advantage creation.

K. Conner distinguishes six research streams in the theory of the firm: five of these take the whole industry as the unit of analysis and are embedded in economic science (Industrial Organization Economics—IOE); the sixth concentrates on the firm level (Resource Based View—RBV) and is explicitly embedded in management science. She briefly characterizes these schools as followings (1991, pp. 121–132):

- neoclassical perfect competition theory: firms as combiners of inputs;
- E. Mason and J. Bain's structure-conduct-performance (SCP) school: firms as output restrainers;
- J. Schumpeter's entrepreneurial school: firms as seekers of new ways of competing;
- Chicago school: firms as seekers of production and distribution efficiencies;
- R. Coase and O. Williamson's transaction cost economics: firms as avoiders of the cost of market exchange;
- RBV: firms as seekers of costly-to-copy inputs for production and distribution.

Conner's analysis illustrates, inter alia, how subsequent theories were dealing with gradual restructuring and concentration in many American industries, linking the mechanism of company growth with an attempt to achieve abnormal profits thanks to monopolistic rents. What is important in the context of this book is that her classification illuminates the similarities (apart from key distinctive features) between all IOE schools and the RBV. For example, the RBV sees a company as an input combiner (neoclassical view), which can achieve abnormal profits (J. Bain's view) thanks to new ways of competing based on innovations (J. Schumpeter's view) and efficiencies in acquiring, combining and deploying resources

(Chicago school view). In turn, the specificity of resources constrains a company's strategic options (R. Coase and O. Williamson's view; Conner 1991, pp. 132–133). Thus, although intra-organizational analysis is central to the RBV, its proponents do not place the company in a total vacuum. The bridges between the RBV and some of the IOE theories have become even more evident since the notion of dynamic capabilities has enriched the original concept (Teece et al. 1997). A Schumpeterian style of evolutionary competition by adopting and creating innovations instead of price competition over existing products, or structuring relationships and posting 'performance bonds' as a mechanism for safeguarding business agreements in transaction cost economics, serves as a good example (Klein and Leffler 1981; Schumpeter 2010 (1950); Williamson 1983).

Reflecting on the strategy process formation, H. Mintzberg and J. Lampel initially proposed ten research streams in strategic management, which are given below with a brief description (Niemczyk 2009, pp. 13–14; Mintzberg and Lampel 1999, pp. 23–24):

- Design School: strategy as a project;
- Planning School: strategy as a long-term plan;
- Positioning School: strategy as taking positions towards competitors;
- Entrepreneurial School: strategy as a vision;
- Cognitive School: strategy making as a mental process;
- Learning School: strategy as an emergent incremental process;
- Power School: strategy making as a process of negotiations;
- Cultural School: strategy as a team process;
- Environmental School: strategy as a reaction to external situation;
- Configuration School: strategy as a transformation process.

What these authors highlight are different base disciplines, which build the original perspectives and the inspiration for strategy making: inter alia, anthropology, biology, economics, military science, politic science and psychology. They also indicate that blending different theories is a more fruitful process than erecting borders between them. And therefore H. Mintzberg and J. Lampel, for example, see the resource- and dynamic capabilities-based approach as a blend of the Design, Learning and Culture schools, whereas the work of M. Porter and his followers connects the Positioning and Power schools (1999, p. 26).

The highlighted theoretical intersections show that none of the theories are entirely outdated or can prove their superiority in every market/

industry/company situation. In fact, a comprehensive grand theory of the firm or a grand theory of competitive advantage cannot be based on one single school of strategic management. In order to better illustrate how competitive advantage is created in a given market context (e.g. B2B versus B2C, contractual versus non-contractual, quality-oriented market segments versus price-oriented market segments), more specialized mid-range theories are needed. These mid-range theories will inherit some general assumptions from their parenting grand theory. There are three such underlying options, which deal with the locus of competitive advantage:

- the locus of competitive advantage is external to the firm;
- the locus of competitive advantage lies inside of the firm;
- a hybrid approach.

The following section explains the essence of the dispute between the two principal external/internal approaches.

1.2 The Discourse on the Locus of Competitive Advantage

The notion of competitive advantage reveals a wide variety of approaches in measurement and application (Buckley et al. 1988). A general definition of competitiveness, "the above industry average manifested exploitation of market opportunities and neutralization of competitive threats" (Sigalas 2013, p. 324), indicates that it is a relative phenomenon. In order to fully assess whether a company possesses a competitive advantage, it has to be compared to its rivals (Peteraf and Barney 2003). As, because of practical reasons, the verification of competitive advantage takes place predominately in the market, the notion of business performance and its (usually) financial measures arises. However, the potential to generate positive business results cannot, in the longer run, be detached from the individual situation of the firm. The resounding examples of Enron and more recently Lehman Brothers, who suddenly went bankrupt amid public scandal, remind us that competitive advantage is not only about today's results, but also about their sustainability.

Obviously, the sustainability of competitive advantage is not only endangered by speculative actions. For example, a company can successfully operate by applying functionally based marketing and by concentrating on the acquisition of random customers. If the number of floating customers who are not emotionally bound to any brand, company or individual employee is high enough, this strategy will temporarily pay off. Simultaneously, the results of such firms are a function of generic tactical activities, which do not build any insurmountable gap for competitors who have financial capacities to launch an extensive market expansion strategy (Bass et al. 2004; Coyne 1986). In this respect, their competence in making a profit through servicing the market is not comparable in terms of sustainability to those companies who have built their advantage on more idiosyncratic hard-to-imitate factors (Bharadwaj et al. 1993; Mawdsley and Somaya 2018). In other words, sustainable competitive advantage is achieved when it rests upon factors that resist erosion by simple duplication or replacement and that are updated in a timely manner to reflect the pace of technological change, natural business cycles, environmental constraints and emerging business opportunities (Barney 1986b; Bingham and Eisenhardt 2008).

The issue of time is reflected in the differences between the IOE and the RBV, which can be synthetized as a pair of contradictory approaches: short-term strategizing (IOE) versus long-term economizing (RBV). Strategizing means that the company particularly deeply analyses the behaviour and relative positions of its rivals (Williamson 1991). Moreover, it involves deliberate actions to influence the industry structure, for example by acquiring its competitors and enhancing the economies of scale cost reduction effect, or by creating entry barriers like industry standards and irreversible commitments (Porter 1980; Shapiro 1989). The more favourable its position, the more likely it is that a company will try to maximize profits by consciously restricting its output and setting prices far above the marginal cost and thereby securing a monopolistic rent (Teece 1984).

Economizing in the resource-based sense reflects the superiority of resources that the company possess. A familiar interpretation of D. Ricardo's concept of rent indicates that some production factors (resources) are more effective than the rest, and their owners can generate rents either through lower costs or by catering to customers' needs in a distinctively better way, or both (Montgomery and Wernerfelt 1988). The difference between monopolistic and Ricardian rents lies in the nature of limited supply. In a monopoly, supply is intentionally kept low to curb the price above equilibrium. The Ricardian rent is generated at maximum output because the uniqueness of the resources implies their limited character. The elastic expansion of supply is almost impossible, however high the price would be (Peteraf 1993).

A classic synthesis of the strategizing approach is represented in Porter's first article published in *Harvard Business Review* (1979; repeatedly cited elsewhere). It asserts the following assumptions:

- the environment determines the behaviour of a company;
- a strategy is the act of aligning a company and its environment;
- the success of a company (business unit) results from the rivalry in a particular industry;
- there are three generic ways of achieving competitive advantage: cost leadership, differentiation and focus (a combination of one of these two with a narrow specialization within an industry or an isolated niche).

In addition, Porter's familiar five forces model and diamond model of international competitiveness, as well as dozens of other concepts (e.g. decision-making matrices and methods of strategic analysis), have delivered an effective managerial toolbox that is useful in strategizing to achieve an above-average performance (compared to an industry level). This feature is clearly distinctive and explains why the Positioning School has enjoyed, and still does, so much resonance with researchers, business consultants and managers (Obłój 2007).

However, there is another side to the coin. In his early work, Porter builds up his concepts on the SCP paradigm (Bain 1968). A crucial aspect of the SCP reasoning is that because '(S)tructure' determined '(C)onduct', which in turn determined '(P)erformance', the mediating variable could be ignored, because the industry structure alone explained performance. Although in the updated version of SCP (with a reverse feedback effect added) Porter does not omit 'conduct', his interest focuses on fundamental structural parameters of an industry rather than on companies' intrinsic choices, which (if rational) should fall in the schema of a five-forces-game (Porter 1981).

Another issue is the examples of companies that Porter frequently uses, which suggest an ethnocentric American way of looking at the world or at least a triad-nations (USA, UE, Japan) dominated lens (Dunning 1993; Rugman and Cruz 1993): Microsoft and Intel showing how the superior bargaining power of a supplier influences the margins of PC assemblers; e-Bay explaining the demand side of economies of scale; and SAP having an effective customer switching costs strategy (Porter 2008). These are giant companies that have nearly monopolized their industries, or at least occupy vast segments of respective markets. Again, this is a strong reference to the tradition of IOE research, where so-called oligopoly theory (studying competitive interactions in those markets where a few firms' actions directly affect each other) has always been a prominent convention (Caves and Porter 1978; Chamberlin 1962; Phillips 1960). Under this premise, not only competitors but also suppliers and customers are perceived as rivals in rent appropriation, which simplifies the analysis but does not reflect the whole spectrum of business activities (Czakon 2005).

Porter's five-forces model is also usually criticized for being based on the assumption of perfect factor markets, which implies that firms' resources are homogenous (Wang 2014). The RBV proponents argue that the position of market leaders could not be explained if the value they offer was entirely the result of factors obtained from external markets (Barney 2014). Interestingly, if one analyses Porter's work without prejudice, multiple references can be found to firms' unique strengths as well. As he personally notes: "Simple observation clearly revealed that firms differed a great deal in performance even though they competed in the same industry. Therefore, while IO[E] is useful for determining the likely average profitability of an industry, in its traditional form it clearly is not very useful for sorting out the different performances of different companies" (Porter 1981, p. 612).

In his dynamic theory of strategy framework (reproduced in Fig. 1.1), Porter does not exclude the idiosyncrasy of companies. On the contrary, he points out that what longitudinally impacts performance is the managerial choices that brought a company to a specific position (and determined initial conditions with reference to the starting point of analysis). Moreover, he indicates that there exists an interdependency loop between them and firm resources and 'activities'. The latter are "basic units of competitive advantage", which can also create other assets in the form of skills, organizational routines and knowledge (Porter 1991, p. 102). Also the notion of 'drivers' includes both internal and external "structural determinants of differences in the cost or buyer value of activities or groups of actions" (p. 100), such as economies of scale, government regulations, timing, localization and firm policy choices (p. 104). The core difference between his analysis and the RBV is the answer to the question: "to what extent the environment shapes initial conditions and choice, in contrast to idiosyncratic, creative decision-making process within the firm" (1991, p. 101).

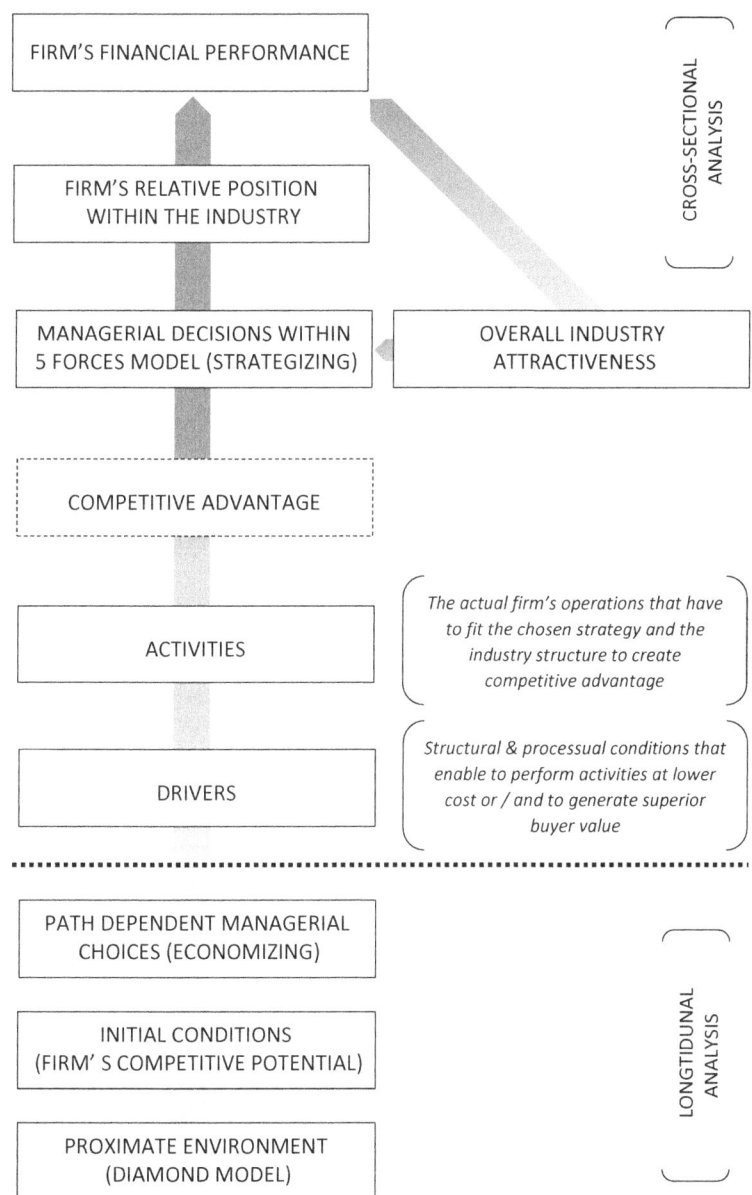

Fig. 1.1 Causal chain of interdependencies in M. Porter's dynamic theory of strategy. (Source: Adapted from Porter 1991, p. 100; van den Bosch 1997, p. 95)

In search of "the origins of the origins", Porter builds his analysis upon the notion that the initial firm conditions are determined by past managerial choices, which, however, reflect the environmental pressure at that time (1991, p. 106). This is a typical economic perspective that sees the company from the outside, and its main theoretical goal is to provide a systematic understanding of differences and sustainability of profits in given industry environments (Wiktor 2019). Nonetheless, although in his model Porter situates the locus of competitive advantage in the market, he explains it as a consequence of a firm's own competitive drivers and activities. Only a firm's short-term financial performance is directly influenced by the overall industry attractiveness.

The RBV, in turn, clearly locates its interest inside a company. Traditionally, the origins of this school are placed in the work of E. Penrose (2009 (1959); 1960), at least at the descriptive level (the crucial role of resources and specialization determining the expansion of a firm; Rugman and Verbeke 2004). However, the idea of studying how a single business entity works is much older. For example, in the nineteenth century, J. Say developed A. Smith's definition of productive labour, pointing out the role of an entrepreneur, who can effectively make use of their own organizational and management skills and borrowed capital to create added value (Kunasz 2006).

The basic assumptions of the RBV (related to the earlier excerpted IOE assumptions) are as follows (Andrews 1971; Barney 1997; Peteraf 1993; Teece et al. 1997; Wernerfelt 1984):

- the differences in firm performance are a function of their internal heterogeneity;
- competitive advantage is built on VRIO resources (valuable, rare, difficult to imitate, organized);
- a strategy is the act of aligning and developing what the company can do particularly well with environmental opportunities;
- the success of a company results from the deployment of resources so that they produce value that can be monetized in the market, while preserving their unique character;
- the three generic ways of achieving a competitive advantage are based on non-generic strategic assets.

The fundamental notion of the RBV is its definition of a company as a "bundle of resources and capabilities" (Amit and Schoemaker 1993,

p. 37). Some of them are extraordinarily valuable, as well as rare; difficult to imitate, substitute and trade; durable; well organized (appropriable) and complementary (co-specialized; Barney 1986a; Ciszewska-Mlinarič and Wąsowska 2015; Teece 1986). Because of their unique character they can be labelled 'strategic assets'—assets that have the potential to generate a sustainable competitive advantage for the company (Amit and Schoemaker 1993).

Analogous to the industry entry barriers in the IOE, the RBV distinguishes 'isolating mechanisms', which can be understood as knowledge-based, physical or legal barriers that prevent competitors imitating and undoing the competitive advantage of a successful company (Lepak et al. 2007). Some of them are even shared with the IOE: patents, trademarks, consumer switching and search costs, producer sunk costs and so on (Rumelt 1997, p. 141). But more specifically, the RBV-style isolating mechanisms refer to path-dependent asset specificity based on causal ambiguity, social complexity, time compression diseconomies, hard-to-reverse commitments and partner asset interconnectedness (Barney 1991; Dierickx and Cool 1989; Dyer and Singh 1998; Ghemawat 1991; Lippman and Rumelt 1982; Teece 2007). In turn, such intangible assets emerge as, for example, reputation, trust and commitment, effective corporate culture, unique knowledge and partner-specific absorptive capacity. They are not traded in the factor markets, nor can they be quickly replicated. In fact, these resources are not only perfectly immobile and of highly limited supply, but their strong tacit and history-dependent dimension, which is a function of successive decisions affected by managerial bounded rationality (inward-oriented choices that underestimate some facts while overestimating others; Bratnicki and Dyduch 2020; Mahoney and Pandian 1992), makes them hardly definable even by the companies they belong to, let alone would-be imitating competitors (Teece et al. 1994). Many of them may even be too idiosyncratic to retain the same value outside of the host company or business network (Rumelt 1987). This implies that their value in a native state (ex ante cost of acquisition) was well below their value once appropriated and developed by the firm (ex post value); or alternatively, the company was far better at accumulating and developing these classes of resources than its competitors, even if they had recognized them early and anticipated their potential ex post value (Peteraf 1993). These two conditions decide on the prospects of a company to generate a sustainable competitive advantage and the consequent above-average rents.

The heterogeneity of companies is especially present in their activities. As some resources can be obtained in the factor markets, companies may be, to some extent, comparable in this respect (Amit and Schoemaker 1993). Moreover, a company may have a unique understanding, for example, of a technically complex process (technical competence), but this does not mean it has the capability to effectively market it at a profit (Dyduch and Bratnicki 2015). Just as in the Parable of Talents, even precious resources are unproductive if not used. Meanwhile, the notion of company-specific 'resource conversion activities' has always been present in the resource-based way of thinking (Rumelt 1984, p. 561). But it was not until D. Teece et al.'s seminal article (1997) followed by many other scholars (Eisenhardt and Martin 2000; Winter 2003) that 'dynamic capabilities' were advanced as a fundamental extension of RBV. These authors locate the most important activities of a company in learning processes, as well as in the continuous integration and reconfiguration of internal and external resources (Teece et al. 1997). The missing link between these resources and company performance is processes of complex interactions (Wu 2007), which prolifically deal with the competitive business environment (Shams 2016). Dynamic capabilities are therefore managerial and organizational processes that refer to the way coordination, learning and transformation are done in the company. They are, in turn, manifested in organizational routines, which are group and individual patterns of behaviour that represent successful solutions to particular problems (Mitręga et al. 2012; Teece et al. 1997).

Dynamic capabilities link the internal environment of the company with the outer world, which by definition implies that industry analysis remains a vital part of research in management. This reflects the dual nature of competitive advantage and suggests that the dichotomist approaches of the IOE and the classic RBV on the roots of competitive advantage are matters of analytical focus and of methodological convenience. There were (and still are) attempts being made to combine both views into one coherent approach. For example, G. Hooley et al. (2001) developed a concept of strategic positioning, which they define as the combination of competitive advantage (how the firm will compete) and choice of target market (where the firm will compete). Figure 1.2 depicts the interactions between the key firm and industry constructs in R. Amit and P. Shoemaker's model of strategic assets and organizational rent (1993). These scholars incorporate the IOE tradition in the form of 'strategic industry factors', which include Porter's five-forces model

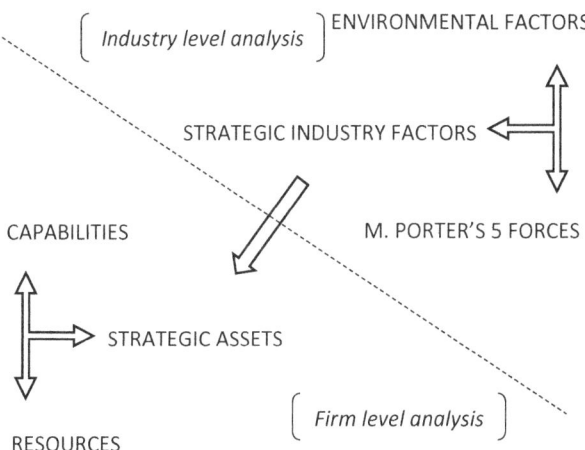

Fig. 1.2 Strategic assets and strategic industry factors. (Adapted from Amit and Schoemaker (1993, p. 37))

supplemented by 'environmental factors' (changes in technology, regulation, etc.). They insist that, to be useful, the company's strategic assets have to overlap with the strategic industry factors (1993, p. 37). Perhaps the most comprehensive theory, which simultaneously builds on the IOE and RBV research traditions, is the Resource-Advantage Theory of Competition (R-A theory; Hunt and Morgan 1996). A more detailed reference to R-A theory will be made in the next chapter during the discussion on the scope of the envisioned RM mid-range theory.

What the IOE and RBV theories undoubtedly have in common is that they mainly depict a market situation of competing entities. However, companies can appropriate substantial rents not only generated from their own resources but also resulting from the resources of their business partners, provided within a long-lasting joint venture or even during a temporal project (Gołębiowski and Lewandowska 2015). A network rent (or in a narrower sense a relational rent) will depend, inter alia, on the value of these resources, the absorptive capability of cooperating partners and the relationship governance model (Dyer and Singh 1998). The same mechanism can be reflected in a B2C setting or in any other situation where synergies exist that create conditions for an exchange based on a non-zero sum game (Deszczyński 2016). However, provided both partners stay as independent subjects of a relationship, volatile 'coopetition' behaviours are possible (more/less cooperation/competition; Bengtsson and Kock 2000). On one hand, this reflects the RBV style of economizing based on strategic resources and capabilities. On the other, it resembles the IOE style of strategizing in the way companies adjust their positions in an inherently unbalanced partnership or a network setting (Birkinshaw et al. 2001; Jankowska 2009). This creates a situation of a unique relationship dynamism and the necessity to manage multiple relationships.

References

Amit, Raphael, and Paul J.H. Schoemaker. 1993. Strategic Assets and Organizational Rent. *Strategic Management Journal* 14 (1): 33–46. https://doi.org/10.1002/smj.4250140105.

Andrews, Kenneth R. 1971. The Concept of Corporate Strategy. In *Historical Evolution of Strategic Management*, 18–46. Homewood: Dow-Jones Irwin. https://doi.org/10.4324/9781315253336-11.

Bain, Joe Staten. 1968. *Industrial Organization*. 2nd ed. New York: John Wiley & Sons Inc.

Banaszyk, Piotr. 2014. Model Biznesu Jako Podstawa Zarządzania Strategicznego Przedsiębiorstwem. *Zeszyty Naukowe Akademii Ekonomicznej w Poznaniu* 43: 7–27.

Barney, Jay B. 1986a. Organizational Culture: Can It Be a Source of Sustained Competitive Advantage? *The Academy of Management Review* 11 (3): 656–665. https://doi.org/10.2307/258317.

———. 1986b. Strategic Factor Markets: Expectations, Luck, and Business Strategy. *Management Science* 32 (10): 1231–1241. https://doi.org/10.1287/mnsc.32.10.1231.

———. 1991. Firm Resources and Sustained Competitive Advantage. *Journal of Management* 17 (1): 99–120. https://doi.org/10.1177/014920639101700108.

———. 1997. *Gaining and Sustaining Competitive Advantage*. Reading: Addison-Wesley Publishing Company.

———. 2014. How Marketing Scholars Might Help Address Issues in Resource-Based Theory. *Journal of the Academy of Marketing Science* 42 (1): 24–26. https://doi.org/10.1007/s11747-013-0351-8.

Bass, Frank M., A. Krishnamoorthy, Ashutosh Prasad, and Suresh P. Sethi. 2004. Advertising Competition with Market Expansion for Finite Horizon Firms. *Journal of Industrial and Management Optimization*. https://utd-ir.tdl.org/handle/10735.1/3643.

Bengtsson, Maria, and Sören Kock. 2000. "Coopetition" in Business Networks – to Cooperate and Compete Simultaneously. *Industrial Marketing Management* 29 (5): 411–426. https://doi.org/10.1016/S0019-8501(99)00067-X.

Bharadwaj, Sundar G., P. Rajan Varadarajan, and John Fahy. 1993. Sustainable Competitive Advantage in Service Industries: A Conceptual Model and Research Propositions. *Journal of Marketing* 57 (4): 83–99. https://doi.org/10.2307/1252221.

Bingham, Christopher B., and Kathleen M. Eisenhardt. 2008. Position, Leverage and Opportunity: A Typology of Strategic Logics Linking Resources with Competitive Advantage. *Managerial and Decision Economics* 29 (2–3): 241–256. https://doi.org/10.1002/mde.1386.

Birkinshaw, Julian, Omar Toulan, and David Arnold. 2001. Global Account Management in Multinational Corporations: Theory and Evidence. *Journal of International Business Studies* 32 (2): 231–248. https://doi.org/10.1057/palgrave.jibs.8490950.

Bratnicki, Mariusz, and Wojciech Dyduch. 2020. Understanding Cognitive Biases in Strategic Decisions for Value Creation and Capture. In *Contemporary Challenges in Cooperation and Coopetition in the Age of Industry 4.0*, Springer Proceedings in Business and Economics, ed. Agnieszka Zakrzewska-Bielawska and Iwona Staniec, 359–373. Cham: Springer International Publishing. https://doi.org/10.1007/978-3-030-30549-9_19.

Buckley, Peter J., Christopher L. Pass, and Kate Prescott. 1988. Measures of International Competitiveness: A Critical Survey. *Journal of Marketing Management* 4 (2): 175–200. https://doi.org/10.1080/0267257X.1988.9964068.

Caves, R.E., and Michael E. Porter. 1978. Market Structure, Oligopoly, and Stability of Market Shares. *The Journal of Industrial Economics* 26 (4): 289–313. https://doi.org/10.2307/2098076.

Chamberlin, E. H. (1962). *The theory of monopolistic competition-a reorientation of the theory of value.* Cambridge: Harvard University.

Ciszewska-Mlinarič, Mariola, and Aleksandra Wąsowska. 2015. Resource-Based View (RBV). In *Wiley Encyclopedia of Management*, 1–7. American Cancer Society. https://doi.org/10.1002/9781118785317.weom060174.

Conner, Kathleen R. 1991. A Historical Comparison of Resource-Based Theory and Five Schools of Thought Within Industrial Organization Economics: Do We Have a New Theory of the Firm? *Journal of Management* 17 (1): 121–154. https://doi.org/10.1177/014920639101700109.

Coyne, Kevin P. 1986. Sustainable Competitive Advantage-What It Is, What It Isn't. *Business Horizons* 29 (1): 54.

Czakon, Wojciech. 2005. Ku Systemowej Teorii Przewagi Konkurencyjnej Przedsiębiorstwa. *Przegląd Organizacji* 5: 5–8.

———. 2014. Szkoły a Mody w Zarządzaniu Strategicznym. *Prace Naukowe WWSZIP* 27 (2): 47–55.

Deszczyński, Bartosz. 2016. The Impact of Opportunity Management on the Relationship Business Model (A Study in the Polish Housing Industry). *Journal of Eastern European and Central Asian Research (JEECAR)* 3 (2): 1–10. https://doi.org/10.15549/jeecar.v3i2.137.

Dierickx, Ingemar, and Karel Cool. 1989. Asset Stock Accumulation and Sustainability of Competitive Advantage. *Management Science* 35 (12): 1504–1511. https://doi.org/10.1287/mnsc.35.12.1504.

Dunning, John H. 1993. Internationalizing Porter's Diamond. *MIR: Management International Review* 33: 7–15.

Dyduch, Wojciech, and Mariusz Bratnicki. 2015. Tworzenie i przechwytywanie wartości w organizacjach współdziałających w sieci. *Prace Naukowe Wałbrzyskiej Wyższej Szkoły Zarządzania i Przedsiębiorczości* 32 (2): 77–93.

Dyer, Jeffrey H., and Harbir Singh. 1998. The Relational View: Cooperative Strategy and Sources of Interorganizational Competitive Advantage. *The Academy of Management Review* 23 (4): 660–679. https://doi.org/10.2307/259056.

Eisenhardt, Kathleen M., and Jeffrey A. Martin. 2000. Dynamic Capabilities: What Are They? *Strategic Management Journal* 21 (10–11): 1105–1121. https://doi.org/10.1002/1097-0266(200010/11)21:10/11<1105::AID-SMJ133>3.0.CO;2-E.

Ghemawat, Pankaj. 1991. *Commitment: The Dynamic of Strategy*. New York/Toronto: Free Press.

Gołębiowski, Tomasz, and Małgorzata Stefania Lewandowska. 2015. Influence of Internal and External Relationships of Foreign Subsidiaries on Innovation Performance. Evidence from Germany, Czech Republic and Romania. *Journal of East European Management Studies* 20 (3): 304–327.

Hooley, Graham, Gordon Greenley, John Fahy, and John Cadogan. 2001. Market-Focused Resources, Competitive Positioning and Firm Performance. *Journal of Marketing Management* 17 (5–6): 503–520. https://doi.org/10.1362/026725701323366908.

Hunt, Shelby D., and Robert M. Morgan. 1996. The Resource-Advantage Theory of Competition: Dynamics, Path Dependencies, and Evolutionary Dimensions. *Journal of Marketing.* 107–114.

Jankowska, Barbara. 2009. Competition or Cooperation? (Konkurencja czy kooperacja?). *Ekonomista (The Economist)* 1: 67–89.

Klein, Benjamin, and Keith B. Leffler. 1981. The Role of Market Forces in Assuring Contractual Performance. *Journal of Political Economy* 89 (4): 615–641. https://doi.org/10.1086/260996.

Krupski, Rafał. 2009a. Strategia Jako System UC. In *Koncepcje Strategii Organizacji*, ed. Rafał Krupski, Jerzy Niemczyk, and Ewa Stańczyk-Hugiet, 23–44. Warszawa: Polskie Wydawnictwo Ekonomiczne.
———. 2009b. *Teleologiczny Kontekst Elastyczności Strategii*. Ed. Rafał Krupski, Jerzy Niemczyk, and Stańczyk-Hugiet, 155–68. Warszawa: Polskie Wydawnictwo Ekonomiczne.
Kunasz, Marek. 2006. Zasoby przedsiębiorstwa w teorii ekonomii. *Gospodarka Narodowa* 211 (10): 33–48. https://doi.org/10.33119/GN/101446.
Lepak, David P., Ken G. Smith, and M. Susan Taylor. 2007. Value Creation and Value Capture: A Multilevel Perspective. *Academy of Management Review* 32 (1): 180–194. https://doi.org/10.5465/amr.2007.23464011.
Lichtarski, Jan. 2015. *Praktyczny Wymiar Nauk o Zarządzaniu*. Warszawa: Polskie Wydawnictwo Ekonomiczne.
Lippman, Steven A., and Richard P. Rumelt. 1982. Uncertain Imitability: An Analysis of Interfirm Differences in Efficiency Under Competition. *The Bell Journal of Economics* 13 (2): 418–438. https://doi.org/10.2307/3003464.
Mahoney, Joseph T., and J. Rajendran Pandian. 1992. The Resource-Based View within the Conversation of Strategic Management. *Strategic Management Journal* 13 (5): 363–380. https://doi.org/10.1002/smj.4250130505.
Mawdsley, John K., and Deepak Somaya. 2018. Demand-Side Strategy, Relational Advantage, and Partner-Driven Corporate Scope: The Case for Client-led Diversification. *Strategic Management Journal* 39 (7): 1834–1859.
Mintzberg, Henry, and Joseph Lampel. 1999. Reflecting on the Strategy Process. *Sloan Management Review* 40 (3): 21–30.
Mitręga, Maciej, Sebastian Forkmann, Carla Ramos, and Stephan C. Henneberg. 2012. Networking Capability in Business Relationships Concept and Scale Development. *Industrial Marketing Management*, IMP 2011 The Impact of Globalization on Networks, 41 (5): 739–751. https://doi.org/10.1016/j.indmarman.2012.06.002.
Montgomery, Cynthia A., and Birger Wernerfelt. 1988. Diversification, Ricardian Rents, and Tobin's q. *The RAND Journal of Economics* 19 (4): 623–632. https://doi.org/10.2307/2555461.
Niemczyk, Jerzy. 2009. Filozofie i Szkoły Strategii. In *Koncepcje Strategii Organizacji*, ed. Rafał Krupski, Jerzy Niemczyk, and Stańczyk-Hugiet, 11–23. Warszawa: Polskie Wydawnictwo Ekonomiczne.
Obłój, Krzysztof. 1998. *Strategia Sukcesu Firmy*. Warszawa: Polskie Wydawnictwo Ekonomiczne.
———. 2002. *Tworzywo Skutecznych Strategii*. Warszawa: Polskie Wydawnictwo Ekonomiczne.
———. 2007. *Strategia Organizacji*. Warszawa: Polskie Wydawnictwo Ekonomiczne.

———. 2013. *The Passion and Discipline of Strategy*. London: Palgrave Macmillan UK. https://doi.org/10.1057/9781137334947_1.

———. 2019. *Pasja i Dyscyplina Strategii. Jak z Marzeń i Decyzji Zbudować Sukces Firmy*. Warszawa: Poltext.

Penrose, Edith T. 1960. The Growth of the Firm – A Case Study: The Hercules Powder Company. *Business History Review (Pre-1986)* 34 (000001): 1.

———. 2009. *The Theory of the Growth of the Firm*. Oxford: Oxford University Press.

Peteraf, Margaret A. 1993. The Cornerstones of Competitive Advantage: A Resource-Based View. *Strategic Management Journal* 14 (3): 179–191. https://doi.org/10.1002/smj.4250140303.

Peteraf, Margaret A., and Jay B. Barney. 2003. Unraveling the Resource-Based Tangle. *Managerial and Decision Economics* 24 (4): 309–323. https://doi.org/10.1002/mde.1126.

Phillips, Almarin. 1960. A Theory of Interfirm Organization. *The Quarterly Journal of Economics* 74 (4): 602–613. https://doi.org/10.2307/1884355.

Porter, Michael E. 1979. How Competitive Forces Shape Strategy. *Harvard Business Review*, March 1. https://hbr.org/1979/03/how-competitive-forces-shape-strategy

———. 1980. Industry Structure and Competitive Strategy: Keys to Profitability. *Financial Analysts Journal* 36 (4): 30–41. https://doi.org/10.2469/faj.v36.n4.30.

———. 1981. The Contributions of Industrial Organization to Strategic Management. *Academy of Management Review* 6 (4): 609–620. https://doi.org/10.5465/amr.1981.4285706.

———. 1991. Towards a Dynamic Theory of Strategy. *Strategic Management Journal* 12 (S2): 95–117. https://doi.org/10.1002/smj.4250121008.

———. 2008. The Five Competitive Forces That Shape Strategy. *Harvard Business Review*, January 1. https://hbr.org/2008/01/the-five-competitive-forces-that-shape-strategy.

Romanowska, Maria. 2018. Idea spójności w zarządzaniu strategicznym. *Przegląd Organizacji* 6: 3–9. https://doi.org/10.33141/po.2018.6.1.

Rugman, Alan M., and Alain Verbeke. 2004. A Final Word on Edith Penrose. *Journal of Management Studies* 41 (1): 205–217. https://doi.org/10.1111/j.1467-6486.2004.00429.x.

Rumelt, Richard P. 1984. Towards a Strategic Theory of the Firm. *Competitive Strategic Management* 26 (3): 556–570.

———. 1987. Theory, Strategy, and Entrepreneurship. In *The Competitive Challenge.*, ed. David Teece, 137–158. Cambridge, MA: Ballinger.

———. 1997. Towards a Strategic Theory of the Firm. In *Resources, Firms, and Strategies: A Reader in the Resource-Based Perspective*, ed. Nicolai J. Foss, 137–145. Oxford: Oxford University Press.

Rumelt, Richard P., D. Schendel, and David J. Teece. 1995. *Fundamental Issues in Strategy: A Research Agenda*. Cambridge, MA: Harvard Business School Press. https://books.google.pl/books?id=rttTzECN9_YC.

Schumpeter, J.A. 2010 (1950). *Capitalism, Socialism and Democracy: 1st Edition (Paperback)*. Abingdon: Routledge.

Shams, S.M. Riad. 2016. Capacity Building for Sustained Competitive Advantage: A Conceptual Framework. *Marketing Intelligence & Planning* 34 (5): 671–691. https://doi.org/10.1108/MIP-08-2015-0161.

Shapiro, Carl. 1989. The Theory of Business Strategy. *The RAND Journal of Economics* 20 (1): 125–137. https://doi.org/10.2307/2555656.

Sigalas, Christos. 2013. Developing a Measure of Competitive Advantage. *Journal of Strategy and Management* 6 (4): 320–342. https://doi.org/10.1108/JSMA-03-2013-0015.

Sobczyk, Janusz R. 2010. Kryzys podstaw metodologicznych nauk o zarządzaniu – kryzysem powinowactwa z naukami społecznymi. *Acta Universitatis Lodzensis – Folia Oeconomica* 234: 335–345.

Teece, David J. 1984. Economic Analysis and Strategic Management. *California Management Review (Pre-1986); Berkeley* 26 (3, Spring): 87.

———. 1986. Profiting from Technological Innovation. *Research Policy* 15: 285–305.

———. 2007. Explicating Dynamic Capabilities: The Nature and Microfoundations of (Sustainable) Enterprise Performance. *Strategic Management Journal* 28 (13): 1319–1350. https://doi.org/10.1002/smj.640.

Teece, David J., Richard Rumelt, Giovanni Dosi, and Sidney Winter. 1994. Understanding Corporate Coherence: Theory and Evidence. *Journal of Economic Behavior & Organization* 23 (1): 1–30. https://doi.org/10.1016/0167-2681(94)90094-9.

Teece, David J., Gary Pisano, and Amy Shuen. 1997. Dynamic Capabilities and Strategic Management. *Strategic Management Journal* 18 (7): 509–533. https://doi.org/10.1002/(SICI)1097-0266(199708)18:7<509::AID-SMJ882>3.0.CO;2-Z.

Trocki, Michał. 2005. Točsamość nauk o zarządzaniu. *Przegląd Organizacji* 1: 7–10.

van den Bosch, Frans A.J. 1997. Porter's Contribution to More General and Dynamic Strategy Frameworks. In *Perspectives on Strategy: Contributions of Michael E. Porter*, ed. F.A.J. van den Bosch and A.P. De Man, 91–100. Boston: Springer US. https://doi.org/10.1007/978-1-4615-6179-8_10.

Wang, Hui-Ling. 2014. Theories for Competitive Advantage. In *Being Practical with Theory: A Window into Business Research*, ed. H. Hasan, 33–43. Wollongong: THEORI. https://ro.uow.edu.au/buspapers/408.

Wernerfelt, Birger. 1984. A Resource-Based View of the Firm. *Strategic Management Journal* 5 (2): 171–180. https://doi.org/10.1002/smj.4250050207.

Wiktor, Jan. 2019. Koncepcja Konkurencji M.E. Portera a System Ochrony Rynku Wewnętrznego Unii Europejskiej. *Przegląd Organizacji* 6: 9–16. https://doi.org/10.33141/po.2019.6.1.

Williamson, Oliver E. 1983. Credible Commitments: Using Hostages to Support Exchange. *The American Economic Review* 73 (4): 519–540.

———. 1991. Strategizing, Economizing, and Economic Organization. *Strategic Management Journal* 12 (S2): 75–94. https://doi.org/10.1002/smj.4250121007.

Winter, Sidney G. 2003. Understanding Dynamic Capabilities. *Strategic Management Journal* 24 (10): 991–995. https://doi.org/10.1002/smj.318.

Wu, Lei-Yu. 2007. Entrepreneurial Resources, Dynamic Capabilities and Start-Up Performance of Taiwan's High-Tech Firms. *Journal of Business Research* 60 (5): 549–555. https://doi.org/10.1016/j.jbusres.2007.01.007.

Zimniewicz, Kazimierz. 2014. *Teoria i Praktyka Zarządzania: Analiza Krytyczna.* Warszawa: Polskie Wydawnictwo Ekonomiczne.

Open Access This chapter is licensed under the terms of the Creative Commons Attribution 4.0 International License (http://creativecommons.org/licenses/by/4.0/), which permits use, sharing, adaptation, distribution and reproduction in any medium or format, as long as you give appropriate credit to the original author(s) and the source, provide a link to the Creative Commons licence and indicate if changes were made.

The images or other third party material in this chapter are included in the chapter's Creative Commons licence, unless indicated otherwise in a credit line to the material. If material is not included in the chapter's Creative Commons licence and your intended use is not permitted by statutory regulation or exceeds the permitted use, you will need to obtain permission directly from the copyright holder.

CHAPTER 2

Theoretical Foundations of the Relationship Management Mid-Range Theory

2.1 The Domain of Relationship Management

Since the 1980s, the dissatisfaction with the perception of, in particular, industrial marketing as a set of isolated dyadic transactions between completely unrelated business actors has caused numerous scholars to form groups developing studies on relationship marketing (Sheth and Parvatiyar 2000). One of the earliest contributions was the book co-authored by the founders of the Industrial Marketing and Purchasing Group (IMP; Håkansson 1982), which contested the familiar microeconomic paradigm and instead promoted the network approach to business marketing (Ford 2011). The representatives of other research traditions, such as the North American (e.g. Dwyer et al. 1987), Anglo-Australian (e.g. Christopher et al. 1991) and Nordic traditions (e.g. Gummesson 1987), followed the same logic and, although they highlighted various foci, centred their interest on the conditions shaping the buyer–seller relational exchange process (relationships with other stakeholders were added to the research agenda later).

In their seminal article J. Dyer and H. Singh introduced the relational view to the theory of strategic management (1998), thereby giving new vitality to the IOE/RBV dispute on the locus of competitive advantage. By placing the emphasis not purely on a single company but on its business network, they highlighted four sources of a relationship rent-based

© The Author(s) 2021
B. Deszczyński, *Firm Competitive Advantage Through Relationship Management*, https://doi.org/10.1007/978-3-030-67338-3_2

advantage: relationship-specific assets, knowledge-sharing routines, complementary resources and capabilities, and effective governance (1998, pp. 662–663).

The overall message of this approach is that because competition is not the only mechanism of market coordination, some of a firm's critical resources and capabilities do not have to be owned but can be shared and co-developed with its cooperating partners (Sepulveda and Gabrielsson 2013; Sulejewicz 1997). In consequence, the relational view of strategic management is a vital extension of the RBV (Lavie 2006; Rudny 2014). On the basis of RBV logic, the search for business partners can be perceived as looking to improve one's own imperfect assets or to create new capabilities faster and/or at lower cost, thus achieving competitive advantage (Czakon 2011; Sopińska 2019).

However, the relational approach to strategic management does not only address the issue of the locus of competitive advantage. It also contributes to a major debate that has been sparking among strategic management scholars from the 1990s onward on a no less fundamental issue: the balance between the strategic planning horizon and the strategy implementation cycle (Prahalad and Hamel 1994). The dominant product–market focus of the IOE suggests taking predominately short-term positions. In contrast, the development of VRIO resources and dynamic capabilities, which are highlighted by the RBV, takes some time, but it also occurs in the more controllable environment of the firm's strategic networks, as well as with regard to its own human and processual infrastructure (Krupski 2012; Lichtarski 2015). The unit of analysis in the relational approach to strategic management is therefore, by definition, not solely the market or a company per se, but a company in relation to its external and internal stakeholders. Hence, the relational view enables the planning range to be somewhat longer than the standard planning horizon adopted in the given industry. This is because it is stabilized by the system of multiple interdependencies, which, in turn, can be decomposed into sets of human-to-human relationships.

Certainly, the overall view of a firm as a social construct is not new. For instance, the Evolutionary School presumes that companies grow both when they accomplish planned goals and when they exploit opportunities with the help of the ad hoc strategies emerging as a result of internal bargaining processes (Krupski 2009). In the RBV, path dependency has a clearly behavioural context embedded in the experiential and cultural dimensions of socialization processes influencing the mindset of managers and other internal stakeholders (Hooley et al. 1998). In addition, dynamic capabilities are viewed as intensely entrepreneurial, so long as they involve shaping (and not just adapting to) the environment (Teece 2007). In business network studies, which have traditionally analysed the formal relationships of the focal company and its partners (Dymitrowski et al. 2019; Ford and Håkansson 2006), the analysis nowadays includes the social exchange perspective—that is, the informal relations among individuals representing companies (Burt 2009; Chetty and Blankenburg Holm 2000; Deszczyński et al. 2017). The bedrock of relationship management is therefore of sociological origin.

Among all management disciplines that involve human relationships, social exchange theory (SET) is probably the most prominent source of inspiration. It is based on a central premise that the fundamental form of human interaction is an exchange and that the voluntary actions of individuals in social contexts are motivated by the returns (social and material) they are expecting to get in the course of such exchanges (Blau 1986). These exchanges can take the form of (Fiske 1991, p. 42):

- communal sharing (sharing resources as required by all community members irrespective of their individual contribution);
- authority ranking (accessing resources according to restricted priorities and only secondly according to the individual contribution);
- equality matching (balancing the number of resources in an exchange so that the individual contribution equals the return);
- market pricing (regulating the exchange based on a supply and demand mechanism).

In contrast to an economic exchange per se, social exchange goes beyond what was explicitly contracted—it focuses on the actors of exchange and their relations and only secondly on the resources and benefits being the subjects of a transaction (Shore et al. 2006). Therefore, social exchange is not necessarily governed by the principle of immediate maximization of profit as it is founded upon personal ties (of varying strength) that are, in turn, the result of successful interactions over time that produce trust, commitment and reciprocity of rewards (Gouldner 1960; Granovetter 1977).

By combining the economic and social perspectives, Adler and Kwon propose a three-dimensional model of relationships, which includes (2002, p. 20):

- market relationships;
- hierarchical relationships;
- social relationships.

In classic form, market relationships involve mainly sellers and buyers and come as transactional interactions—so-called arm's length relationships. However, in B2B markets and in some B2C markets (e.g. where contractual forms of purchase exist accompanied by relatively high transaction value), these relationships can take a durable form and involve multiple stakeholders (Deszczyński 2008; Fonfara et al. 2012). Hierarchical relationships belong to the intra-organizational human resource management perspective, as they involve employees and their principles. Social relationships highlight the individual dimension of interactions. They include exchanging favours and gifts, which can be a part of private life but also emerge over time in any social context.

It is clear that managing relationships by definition spans both social and economic perspectives. This duality is reflected in the broad definitional basis of the relational phenomena given by Morgan and Hunt, who explain that managing relationships is "all marketing activities directed towards establishing, developing, and maintaining successful transactions" (1994, p. 22). This definition indicates that the company's response to the need to manage relationships is materialized in marketing activities, which marketing scholars call 'relationship marketing'. In turn, strategic management scholars tend to use the expression 'relationship management'. This apparent double voice has been accompanying the academic discourse on managing relationships from the early beginning. Even in 1983, which marks the starting point of the major interest in studying relationships in management (Payne and Frow 2017), L. Berry at an American Marketing Association conference spoke about 'relationship marketing' (1983), whereas T. Levitt, in his pioneering article published by *Harvard Business Review*, used the expression 'relationship management' (1983). However, the relationship between marketing and other disciplines of management is, in the end, only a matter of perspective (Gummesson 1999; Zineldin and Philipson 2007). For example, so-called market orientation, which is an original marketing contribution to business strategy that explicitly draws on the marketing concept, is considered to be both: as a 'bridge' between corporate strategy and the organization's business culture/philosophy, but also as a measure of the implementation of a marketing concept's components (Hunt and Lambe 2000; Slater and Narver

1995). Hence, both terms—relationship management and relationship marketing—may be used interchangeably and should be understood as closely related components of the same phenomenon, which can be labelled 'marketing-oriented management'. Nonetheless, in this book, relationship management (RM) works as a basic term, while relationship marketing will only be used to reflect the original work of a particular author.

RM is not a monolith, as it is a theoretical-methodological direction in management science that draws upon almost all orientations of management, including market, strategic, process, human, change and knowledge orientation (to mention only the most important; Lichtarski 2010). To be effective, it requires a coordination of the main building blocks of a company: strategy; organizational structure and culture; human, knowledge, financial and IT resources; and processes (Gordon 2001). Hence, RM can also be defined as 'strategic management of relationships with all relevant stakeholders' (Payne and Frow 2013, p. 4), which is a part of the incremental strategic management process reflected in the corporate business model (Deszczyński 2011; Tvede and Ohnemus 2001).

K. Möller and A. Halinen argue that the main demarcation line between different traditions in RM research corresponds to the basic division of B2C and B2B markets (2000). According to their meta-theoretical analysis, market-based relationships (B2C) are fairly simple and substitutive connections immersed in the market exchange context, whereas network-based relationships (B2B) have much more complex, idiosyncratic and context-rich natures (2000). The differences between these two main approaches are not only of semantic incommensurability (Tadajewski 2008). Research streams focused on the exchange of mass-type products and services, such as CRM (Customer Relationship Management), behaviourally driven relationship research and services research, apply reductionist causal structural equation models to identify the antecedent factors that shape (predominately) dyadic customer–supplier relationships and to explain how relationship characteristics influence relational outcomes (Anderson and Narus 1990; Cho 2006). The network-based approach takes a fuller view of relationships and tries to incorporate the IOE theory of competition, albeit changing the unit of analysis from a single company in an industry setting to a network (or a focal network) and the method of industry statistical analysis to (preferably) longitudinal case study research (Ford et al. 2011; Hunt and Lambe 2000; Möller 2013). According to K. Möller, the ontological and epistemological premises of these two approaches to RM are so distinctive that "blending or combining these approaches [in a single theory is] untenable or at least useless in any pragmatic sense" (2013, p. 331). As the aim of this book is to contribute to the development of the RM mid-range theory, such a statement demands further comment. I will address this in the section 'The boundaries of RM mid-range theory' in this chapter. First, however, it is necessary to get a more comprehensive perspective of RM by introducing the RM business model and RM factors.

A business model is the representation of a firm's underlying logic and its strategic choices for creating and capturing value (Shafer et al. 2005), a general construct explaining how a firm interacts with its customers, suppliers and other important partners (Zott and Amit 2010). S. Nenonen and K. Storbacka specify 12 building blocks of business models (in a 4×3 matrix: market, offering, operations and management matrixed against design principles, resources and capabilities; 2010, p. 50). Hence, the RM business model can be perceived as an organizational philosophy oriented to value creation (Piercy 2016; Rudawska et al. 2016), a managerial process aimed at meeting shareholders' goals by reinforcing relations with selected stakeholders (Doyle 2000; Grönroos 1996), and, more specifically, a bundle of strategies and methods devoted to strengthening customer loyalty and reducing the operating costs of sales, promotion and acquisition (Reichheld and Markey 2011). The core characteristics of the RM business model, which should be addressed by every relationship-oriented company, are (Chen and Popovich 2003; Grönroos 2004; Kumar et al. 2018):

- dialogical communication;
- long-term perspective;
- orientation to the value creation process.

Relationships are built from continuing and meaningful interactions. In this respect, a company is not only a broadcaster of a marketing message but has to 'listen' to what customers (and the other stakeholders) have to say. A dialogue necessitates interactive communication tools and planning, but also a corporate memory (Shukla and Pattnaik 2019). This can be generated by an information management process, which connects all customer contact points and shares customer insight to all responsible corporate units, thus facilitating appropriate marketing responses (Payne and Frow 2005). Such a systemic approach to all transactional and non-transactional interactions with customers is a distinctive feature of RM, which enables a continuum of events to be encompassed without treating them as discrete, separate contacts (as is the case in mass marketing; Dwyer et al. 1987).

Seeing beyond the horizon of a single, immediate transaction enables a company to take more intelligent decisions, which take into account the relationship economics represented by precise measures, such as CLV (Customer Lifetime Value) and cost-to-serve customer scoring (Venkatesan and Kumar 2004). Such a strategic view of marketing redirects company focus from simply attracting new consumers to the development of closer relationships with selected existing customers and giving them reasons to remain loyal (Berry 1983). Especially in a B2B setting, a long-term strategic partnership is not a simple extension of a long-term contractual relationship, in which both parties maintain their initial bargaining positions and look for better prices or conditions. On the contrary, a long-term partnership is a philosophy of trust and cooperation based on a mutual expectation that coordinated activities will enable better understanding, creation and delivery of value for the end markets (Anderson et al. 2009; Dwyer et al. 1987).

At this point all three basic elements of the RM business model are forming a circle. If marketing in a relational context should contribute to the superior delivery of perceived customer value, some time is needed to understand customers and to engage in their value creating processes (Eggert et al. 2006; Grönroos 2009). This is achieved by a dialogical exchange and fulfilment of promises that, if the company is doing its job well, makes it possible to maintain and enhance relationships with customers at a profit (Grönroos 1990). In other words, the RM business model only works if the customers' investment (e.g. of money and time) is balanced by the value they get in the form of products/services satisfying their needs (Pluta-Olearnik 2017). This creates a win-win situation—the customer value creation is coupled with the corporate value creation (Reichheld 2001). Hence, under the premise of RM, customer relationships are the 'raison d'etre' of the firm (Sheth and Parvatiyar 2000). This may sound familiar to economic historians, as in the early beginnings of corporatism, corporations were founded only to coordinate joint efforts in meeting an important goal for the community (e.g. building a bridge), and once this goal was met, they were dissolved (Davis 2016). Hence, relationship management is not so much a discovery as a re-discovery (Payne and Frow 2017).

The discussion on the RM business model will be further continued in Chap. 3, where the notion of RM maturity is conceptualized. Now, however, comes the time to synthetize what the literature has to say about the varied effects of relationship management.

In the course of a successful relationship, something more than financial results or utility value is being produced. Relationships are based on mutual trust and commitment (Morgan and Hunt 1999). Trust can be perceived in two dimensions: as the credibility of a partner and as their benevolence (the degree of interest in their partner's success; Ganesan 1994; Doney and Cannon 1997). Commitment means, in turn, the allocation of one's own resources that are impossible or hard to recover (e.g. because of time or the idiosyncrasy of produced effects) and a partial sacrifice of the freedom of choice (Morgan and Hunt 1999). Trust and commitment are simultaneously the key characteristics and mediating variables of a successful relationship (1999). However, although these two remain the central constructs of RM, over the years RM research began to diverge extensively (Sheth 2017). A clear example is the plethora of studies trying to identify differently conceptualized dimensions of a relationship, including relationship quality, outcomes, benefits or assets. To ensure the clarity of further narration, this diverse relational taxonomy will be discussed in the following paragraphs. Figure 2.1, in contrast, represents the uniform taxonomy that will be used later in this book.

The term 'relationship quality' was first coined by L. Crosby et al. to reflect how a salesperson can positively influence customer behaviour by utilizing relational selling techniques (1990). From the corporate perspective, it can be conceptualized as the ability of a firm to identify, select and retain highly profitable customers and also to effectively manage the processes of converting potentially highly profitable customers into corporate accounts (Lau et al. 2016). In the original proposal, relationship quality was regarded as a higher-order construct composed of two core variables: trust in the salesperson and satisfaction with the salesperson (Crosby et al. 1990, p. 70). Other researchers supplemented relationship quality with additional elements, such as: conflict and continuity (Kumar et al. 1995); customer commitment (Geyskens et al. 1996); cooperative norms (Baker et al. 1999); opportunism and customer orientation (Dorsch et al. 1998); and relationship-specific investments (Nyaga and Whipple 2011).

A slightly different approach is taken by the authors who focus on relational outcomes. They generally try to position them as mediating variables between more complex constructs (such as relationship quality) and

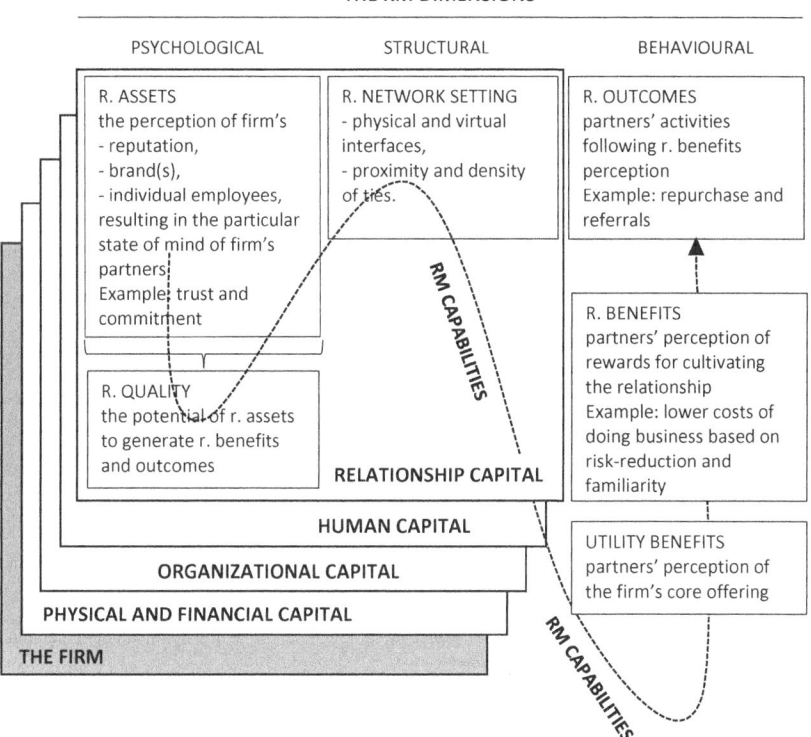

Fig. 2.1 RM factors and the capital of the firm. Note: This figure does not attempt to enumerate all components of the listed upper-range constructs. Its role is to provide a common understanding of the expressions used later in this book. 'Partner' can be understood as any actor (whether individual or institutional) a company has a relation to

company financial performance. However, in the absence of a generally accepted definition of relationship quality, it is a common praxis to mix relationship quality and relational outcomes together, for example by incorporating some building blocks of the relationship quality construct as separate relationship outcomes (Wong and Zhou 2006).

The definitional problems also remain at the level of relational outcomes. Since, at first glance, the term seems to be obvious and self-definable (as the outcomes/consequences/effects of a relationship), some misunderstandings arise in the classification of particular RM factors as relational outcomes (understood as phenomena that directly influence the bottom line; Azza and Norchene 2017). For example, loyalty is in fact a psychological outcome (a state of mind), while repurchase activities are its behavioural manifestation (Blodgett et al. 1997). Hence, loyalty does not produce financial results per se, while repeatable purchases do. In the psychological context, the relational outcomes should be defined as "the feelings, thoughts and perceived relationships arising from the social interaction" (Butcher et al., p. 314), while in the behavioural understanding, they are the activities that directly produce the payoff of a relationship (Lacey et al. 2007). However, psychological and behavioural RM factors are relatively freely applied in various models as changing constellations of antecedents, mediators or effects of each other; as meta-constructs or as stand-alone factors; and as alternatives ignoring the existence of each other. Examples of these include benevolence, bonding, co-creation, communication, customer competence, customer empathy, customer feedback, integrity, idiosyncratic investment, increasing current purchase levels, preferential treatment, reciprocity, customer retention, customer satisfaction, service quality, shared values and word-of-mouth referrals (different cross-matches can be found, inter alia, in: Franklin and Marshall 2019, p. 170; Hennig-Thurau et al. 2002, p. 235; Jones et al. 2007, p. 337; Lacey et al. 2007, p. 244; Macintosh 2007, p. 151; Prior 2012, p. 100; Sin et al. 2005, p. 38).

The positive problem of the rich and diversified approaches to RM factors also exists in the case of so-called relational benefits. The authors who focus on relational benefits mainly (but not exclusively) have a service marketing background. They predominately take the customer perspective on relational exchange, looking for relationship-specific reasons for customers to stay loyal. Therefore, they generally define relational benefits as benefits that "exist above and beyond the core service provided" (Hennig-Thurau et al. 2002, p. 234). In the original study on relational benefits, K. Gwinner et al. quote three types of such factors (1998, p. 109):

- confidence benefits (perceived risk reduction in interactions with the company—what is known to be expected);
- social benefits (personal recognition by front-line personnel, familiarity or friendship);

- special treatment benefits (structured or unstructured financial and non-financial rewards that are unavailable to the average customer).

These are believed to be antecedents of customer loyalty, satisfaction and positive word-of-mouth communication, which, in this research tradition, are not labelled 'relational outcomes' but 'relational consequences' (Gremler and Gwinner 2015). Sometimes they are causally linked with alternative 'relational consequences' including customer active voice (e.g. willingness to complain), customer feedback (e.g. willingness to cooperate with the company), customer value clusters and share of customer (Lacey et al. 2007, p. 244; Spake et al. 2003, p. 323).

Although the original three relational benefits are widely accepted by the authors who followed Gwinner et al., a gradual fragmentation of the concept has distended its compact form, just as in the case of relational outcomes and relational quality. The examples of additionally proposed benefits include advice, confidence, comfort (including psychological comfort), convenience, customization, identity-enhancement, relation to history and structural time-saving (different cross-matches can be found, inter alia, in: Colgate et al. 2007, p. 217; Hennig-Thurau et al. 2000, p. 377; Hennig-Thurau 2005, p. 14; Paul et al. 2009, p. 222; Reynolds and Beatty 1999, p. 13; Spake et al. 2003, p. 328). Some scholars extend the original construct of relational benefits to all kinds of benefits that a customer may generate in the course of a relationship and adopt very broad definitions (such as the following one in a B2B setting): "benefits and rewards manufacturers have perceived from doing business with L[ogistic] S[ervice] P[roviders]" (Li et al. 2012, p. 5445). In turn, new relational benefits are proposed, sometimes structured as components of a higher-order benefit including economic, functional and quality benefits (Hennig-Thurau 2005, p. 14; Lin et al. 2003, p. 112; Marzo-Navarro et al. 2004, p. 427; Ruiz et al. 2008, p. 5). This makes studying them an even more challenging endeavour.

Quite similar is the case of relational assets, which are the other side of the same coin. While relational benefits can be regarded as the payoff of a relationship, relational assets are more a stock of possibilities to generate such a payoff, which has been traditionally studied from the corporate perspective (Dunning 2003). In the course of any balanced relationship, a company will generate some intangible resources in the form of positive associations with the organization, its brand(s) and its representatives, as well as useful knowledge. This, in turn, should bring benefits to particular individuals working for the company (e.g. due to salesperson preference) and reinforce its overall competitive position (due to company/brand preference; Chen et al. 2011; Deszczyński 2014; Hsu and Wang 2012). This makes relational assets a similar concept to relational outcomes, with all the associated consequences of psychological versus behavioural definitional problems. Accordingly, relational assets seem to have more of a psychological nature (e.g. trust). However, it is hard to measure an amount of trust, while the customer preferences it produces can be empirically captured. Therefore, the behavioural/practical manifestation/outcome of relational assets (e.g. referrals or mutual alignment) is sometimes regarded as a part of the same phenomenon (Ng et al. 2013) and technically comes as, for example, 'customer assets', which are a part of the intangibles and goodwill section in financial accounting reporting (Lusch et al. 2011). Nevertheless, conventional accounting is far behind the needs of the precise measurement of relational economics (Håkansson and Ford 2010).

A natural extension of the notion of relational assets is the concept of relational (social, relationship) capital. As a higher-order construct, this can be defined as some kind of network structure that facilitates certain actions of partners, which mobilize and enhance assets embedded within the network (Burt 2009; Coleman 1988). Relationship capital therefore comprises a network setting, individual relationships (known as 'actor bonds' in the B2B research tradition; Håkansson and Snehota 1995) and their characteristics (e.g. trust, respect, friendship; Nahapiet and Ghoshal 1998). Hence, it generally relies upon interaction at a personal level (Kale et al. 2000), although some institutional frameworks, such as formal contracts, also facilitate the relationship network (Hoetker and Mellewigt 2009).

From the SET perspective, the strength or value of relationship capital depends on the durability of obligations arising from the feeling of reciprocity, which is immersed in an environment of complex informal social interdependencies and formal norms, guaranteed rights and sanctions (Bourdieu 1986; Coleman 1988). From the economic point of view, relationship capital is an idiosyncratic investment in the socialization processes that produces efficiency in the form of goodwill between the partners and a stock of other intangible benefits, which have the potential to generate financial benefits (Cousins et al. 2006; Crawford 1990). Hence, the existence of relationship capital may precede a successful collaboration, but in the longer run a business relationship cannot be fed only on future expectations (Deszczyński 2019). Therefore, the technical and organizational competences/potential of partners should be comparable in scale and scope before the cooperation begins, and benefits consumption should be maintained in relation to the partners' contribution and degree of dependence, as well as the sense of fairness (Mowery et al. 1998; Urbańczyk 2012).

Relationship capital is, by definition, dormant unless it is used to produce an interaction and dialogue, and this always generates some knowledge (Gummesson 2004). Therefore, besides its apparent cost-effectiveness, the most important function of relationship capital is the diffusion of information through minimizing redundancy (Burt 2009). Hence, in the relationship context, a firm can be understood as "a social unit specializing in speed and efficiency in the creation and transfer of knowledge" (Kogut and Zander 1996, p. 503).

The notion of knowledge links relationship capital with a broader concept of the intellectual capital of a firm (Bontis 1998; Stewart 2007) and other conceptualizations of its intangible resources (Falkenberg 1996; Gummesson 1999). Sticking to the terminology proposed in intellectual capital research, it refers to the explicit and implicit knowledge and knowing capability of individual employees, the whole firm-wide collective wisdom, and the overall knowledge governance manifested in the organizational structures, processes, systems and other intangibles (Spender 1996). Therefore, its three base building blocks—human capital, relationship capital and organizational capital—outweigh the importance of the firm's financial and physical resources, which they precede in the value creating mechanism (Roos et al. 2001).

The interaction between relationship capital and the other two building blocks of intellectual capital indicates that organizations develop some particular capabilities which enable them to transform individual action into a collective endeavour, which in a given organizational setting and market situation underpins organizational advantage (Nahapiet and Ghoshal 1998). The resemblance to the RBV enhanced by the notion of dynamic capabilities is, at this juncture, very clear. Therefore, relationship capital may be viewed as an upper-range VRIO resource and, from a processual perspective, as a competence or capability aimed at maintaining a balance between relationship exploration, cultivation and exploitation (Loufrani-Fedida et al. 2019; Mitręga and Pfajfar 2015).

Meanwhile, in strategic management, there is an ongoing trend to describe almost every activity of a company in the context of relationship management capabilities. Examples include absorptive capability (Cohen and Levinthal 1990), customer agility (Roberts and Grover 2012), customer response capability (Jayachandran et al. 2004), dynamic marketing capability (Mitręga 2019), employee capability (Kim & Kim 2009), network capability (Mitręga et al. 2012), portfolio management (Möller and Halinen 1999), relationship learning and renewal capability (Jarratt 2008), social media capability (Wang et al. 2017) and supplier relationship management capability (Forkmann et al. 2016). However, the view of a company from the RM capabilities perspective faces the same prescriptive limits as the traditional RBV (Pukas 2019). If there are so many causally ambiguous resources/capabilities, which of them actually generated the advantage (Barney and Arikan 2017)?

Finding a satisfactory answer to this question may be a matter of finding a proper context. For example, there seems to be less room for relational exchange in stable markets with well-known players and standardized value creating activities and processes than in more volatile markets (Möller 2006). Within the consumer market, high-contact customized service providers are able to generate more relational benefits for their consumers than standardized commodity manufacturers (Kinard and Capella 2006). Unfortunately, the more detailed the focus, the less transparent the theory (Scott and Davis 2015). The body of strategic management research is full of conceptualizations which seem to be important in a given context on the strategic, functional or even operational level (Hooley et al. 1998). This high context-sensitivity even affects the work of individual researchers. For example, in their comparative longitudinal analysis of the theoretical perspectives of inter-organizational relationship performance, R. Palmatier et al. found that trust, commitment and relationship-specific investment are the key drivers behind the relational outcomes directly and indirectly mediating financial performance (2007, p. 186). A year later, based on a different sample of companies and research method, R. Palmatier published a paper in which he only confirmed the roles of trust and commitment, without mentioning relationship-specific investment at all. Instead, he added the number and decision-making authority of inter-firm contacts and (in specific circumstances) the overall contact density as important relational factors (2008, p. 76). Unfortunately, in economics, there has traditionally been a problem of only reaching partial answers with limited reproducibility (Zawiślak 2010). Hence, it seems the promise of multidimensional profiling and typologies to better uncover the roots of competitive advantage has to be confronted with the fact that the identification of all such micro-foundations will always be incomplete (if not opaque) and implausible to communicate and implement (Barney 2001; Teece 2007).

Or perhaps one just has to look for a different kind of context? A context that is stable enough to offer some room for generalization, but still meaningful enough to avoid oversimplification.

2.2 The Boundaries of RM Mid-Range Theory

Finding a context in which a new theory can be embedded is a matter of setting its boundaries in relation to the already established one(s). This applies especially to mid-range theories, which are always subsets of a grand theory with more specific, narrower boundaries (Pinder and Moore 1980). As the focus in this book is on whether and how RM can improve a firm's sustainable competitive advantage, the most appropriate grand theory to relate to will be a theory of competition. Further on, as RM is embedded in the RBV's logic of primarily endogenous growth, a corresponding grand theory of competition should explain firm diversity, be genuinely dynamic and accommodate path dependencies in a Lamarkian sense. All these conditions are met by S. Hunt and R. Morgan's Resource-Advantage Theory of Competition (1996; R-A theory).

To justify its claims as a grand theory of competition, the R-A theory has a dual macroeconomic and management focus. Therefore, it goes beyond the research agenda of strategic management and the theory of the firm embedded in management sciences and includes such problems as institutional economics, public policy making and economic growth (Hunt 2000). However, it will only be briefly introduced to sketch the broad context in which the envisioned RM mid-range theory should be located.

The R-A theory is congruent with the IOE in stating that the market position of a firm directly influences its financial performance. In turn, a range of external factors, such as the activities of competitors, suppliers, distributors and customers, as well as the availability of societal resources and the 'rules of the game' set by societal institutions, affect this position (Hunt and Morgan 1996). Nonetheless, R-A theory takes the relationship-based view that the fundamental source of competitive advantage is situated inside the firm (Hunt and Morgan 1995). The best companies are simply the best combiners of heterogeneous, imperfectly mobile resources, and both—the firms and their resources—are historically situated entities (Hunt and Lambe 2000). Thus, competitive advantage is a dynamic, disequilibrium-provoking category, which may be periodically achieved within the realm of segments of rather high granularity (Hunt and Morgan

2005). The sustainability of the market position of a firm is, in turn, a function of the learning processes and the purposeful investment in resources and capabilities, which enable a firm to capitalize on (relative) innovations, bringing better value for customers, or lower prices, or both (Hunt 1997a). Importantly for RM, the R-A theory permits that not all of the applied resources and capabilities are directly owned by the company. It is enough that the company can gain access to them, which is true in the case of many relational assets. As these assets are heterogeneous and immobile, they can potentially result in achieving the position(s) of (sustainable) competitive advantage (Hunt 1997b), which implies that RM should be encompassed in the process of strategic planning.

Placing the envisioned RM mid-range theory in the context of the R-A theory and in congruence with the RBV necessitates positing two assumptions, which delimit and direct its focus. Since external factors influence the competitiveness of a firm to some extent but, in a market economy, their influence should not have a systematic discriminatory effect (e.g. the availability of basic resources which are being transformed into heterogeneous resources, such as inexperienced into experienced employees, is relatively freely granted), it is the firm itself that decides on its success. Accordingly, to establish a relationship, a company needs a partner, but as external partners are potentially available to any market player, it is the relationship capability of the player that decides their competitive advantage generated through relationships (relationship-based competitive advantage). Of course, any well-established business or social network is not freely accessible for a newcomer, and in that sense a market for relational assets in the neoclassical understanding of perfect competition could only serve as a 'special case' (Hunt 2000). Thus, the structural dimension of RM and the so-called fit (strategic, operational and personal) among business partners (Shi et al. 2005; Toulan et al. 2006) does matter and differentiate among firms. However, under the core premise of the RBV, these are only second-order, resulting factors in essence, external to the firm. Therefore, fully incorporating studies on the quality and diversity of a firm's external partners into the RM mid-range theory would unnecessarily add to the complexity of the analysis. Moreover, this would require blending the environmental conditions of the B2C and B2B markets together, which, according to the earlier quoted argument of K. Möller, would deprive such a theory of any pragmatic utility (2013, p. 331).

Of course, such an epistemological self-restraint may be criticized. Nonetheless, the potential critique would, *nolens volens*, have to adopt the

IOE's ontological basis and assume (after M. Porter) that the external environmental conditions determine managerial choices in a decisive way and therefore push further back in the 'chain of causality' of the origins of competitive advantage (Porter 1991, p. 106). The view embedded in the RBV takes a different vantage point: it is the managerial reactions that are primarily decisive in studying the roots of competitive advantage, not the external conditions which trigger them (Barney and Arikan 2017; Hansen and Wernerfelt 1989; Hunt and Morgan 2005; Obłój 2007). Given a hypothetical situation of a brand new beginning of a given economy or market, similar initial conditions cannot explain the likely differences in firm growth rates or financial performance that will occur as time goes by. Therefore, the position of the firm in a given market or network is first and foremost the function of its own capabilities and attractiveness to potential partners. Ergo, the RM mid-range theory should primarily not concentrate on the structural dimension of a firm's relationships.

Note that whether to grant the dominant position to the endogenous or to the exogenous perspective in studying the roots of competitive advantage will always remain in dispute (De Wit and Meyer 2010). Moreover, the research on competitive advantage (indifferent to the principal position of the authors) usually reports mixed but not unilateral results, mainly arguing about the proportions of industry-, segment-, network- or intra-firm-specific factors, or the research methodology, or only focusing on a specific performance trait (Ciszewska-Mlinarič et al. 2015; Coyne and Dye 1998; Datta et al. 2005; Gulati et al. 2011; Ma 1999; McGahan and Porter 1997; Robins and Wiersema 1995; Powell 1996; Rumelt 1991). Thus, staying in line with K. Möller and A. Halinen's meta-theoretical analysis excerpted in this chapter, provided that the universal principles applicable to all RM-oriented firms are given, the RM mid-range theory should not completely ignore the particularities of market segments or clusters. Within the same segment, the general rules of market activity remain the same, but between segments they may not. Thus, studying the ability of RM-oriented firms to adequately respond to specific market circumstances may be interesting and practical. However, first the principles for managing market, hierarchical and social relationships by such entities have to be determined (for further details on levels of granularity of the RM mid-range theory, please refer to Fig. 2.4 and the accompanying discussion).

To be successful, the RM mid-range theory will also have to navigate between two extreme approaches in studying human relationships in the business context. First is the reductionist transactional approach of 'homo economicus', inherited from the classical economy, stating that human decisions are solely a function of economic stimulus (Romanow 1997). The other assumes that human behaviour is extremely complex and therefore that developing a theory with broad applicability would require identifying and specifying countless variables and linkages among them and still many exceptions would potentially remain unaddressed (Johnson et al. 2019). Nonetheless, there exist some distinct features of human culture, society and behaviour which are universally found among all peoples (Brown 2004). In a business setting, the relational roots of competitive advantage can be examined by transposing such human universals as the admiration of trustworthiness into a model of business practices which potentially foster relationships, and by searching for their occurrence among the most successful companies. Incorporating some stable rules that govern human social behaviour can help to establish the principal forms of RM theory and may provide it with an epistemological and normative power, while leaving room for the countless possibilities for its firm-specific reinterpretations and reconfigurations. Ergo, the starting point of analysis for the RM mid-range theory development should be internal relationship management (IRM) and its direct impact on the ability to execute effective external relationship management (ERM).

Note that to avoid overloading the RM mid-range theory its content should be focused on meaningful but individual company context-free (widely replicable) relational factors, activities and approaches distilled from idiosyncratic product-service contexts, such as the marketing-mix or employee remuneration schemes. Hence, at this level of theorizing, it is not so important what kind of utility benefits the company provides (as a supplier, employer or business partner), but how it can boost the quality of its relationships in general and whether this affects the bottom line.

Again, this assumption may well be criticized, this time by the proponents of the RBV. Setting apart the idiosyncratic product-service factors seems to be partly leaving the company out of its internal context. However, for theory building purposes in management sciences, it is more important to search for the quantum that immutably transpires to be essential in all business realities, as well as to explain and predict its occurrence, even if the theory does not encompass all particularities of the studied phenomenon (Czakon 2018; Hunt 1991). The essence of strategic management research, by contrast, is not exactly to propose an all-weather strategy, but more importantly to illuminate how to make good strategy

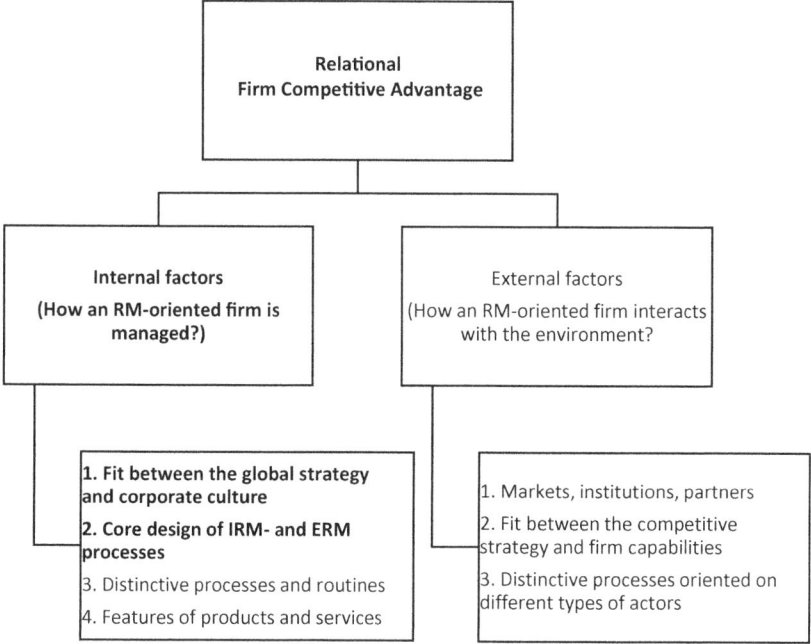

Fig. 2.2 Content of RM mid-range theory. Note: The proposed content of the envisioned RM mid-range theory is marked by the bold text. (Inspired by: Obłój (2007, pp. 22–40); Williamson (1993, pp. 3–17))

choices and how to implement them (Porter 1991). Therefore, for the generic activities which form the core of RM strategy one should look not towards products and markets, but towards qualified management of internal interactions, which directly impacts the quality of ERM (Ballantyne 2000). The content of the envisioned RM mid-range theory amid the other basic questions on the nature of an RM-oriented firm is depicted in Fig. 2.2.

Of course, if all firms were to simultaneously and effectively implement the envisioned generic RM strategy, it would eventually lose its competitive leverage. J. Barney calls this paradox a 'rule for riches' and states that even if such a rule existed and "created economic value, that value would be fully appropriated by those who invented and marketed [it]" (2001, p. 50). P. Schoemaker notes in the same vein that rent seeking is creativity seeking, and voices doubts as to whether organizations can be systematically creative, adding that if there were a general formula for this, it would soon vanish through diffusion (1990). However, as to hierarchical and intra-organizational social relationships, which are proposed to constitute the bulk of RM mid-range theory, the rules for successful human resources management have been easily accessible in various forms for decades. This body of knowledge includes general theories directly drawing on psychology and behavioural studies, such as the already mentioned SET, and diverse human content and processual, intrinsic and extrinsic motivation theories (Hackman and Oldham 1976, 1980; Frey and Osterloh 2001), or more tactical Human Resource Management (HRM) techniques. Despite this tremendous pool of knowledge, it is estimated that many frequent modern toxic management practices which neglect the well-being of employees may cost up to 120,000 excess deaths a year and produce more than $300 billion in losses annually for American business alone (Pfeffer 2018, pp. 1–2). It seems, therefore, that management is widely ignoring what is, at least theoretically, right, and creates an environment of active employee disengagement (Bonner et al. 2016; Deszczyński 2016; Kelleher 2011). A partial reason for this could be managerial temporal myopia (Miller 2002), a consequence of the more general phenomenon of economic short-termism (a short-term transactional approach to business; Laverty 1996), which obscures plain greed (Haynes et al. 2015). The other factor is that human relationships are hard to master in practice because to be sustainably successful, the partners need to constantly show relational humility and readiness for progression of their own self (Davis et al. 2011, 2013; Van Tongeren et al. 2014; Wirzba 2008). This implies that, in case of hierarchical and intra-organizational social relationships, to ensure the high quality of a supervisory alliance, especially in managing conflicts, the supervisors need to demand more from themselves than from the supervisees and take responsibility for their reportees' well-being at work (Watkins et al. 2016). Drawing on W. Kim and R. Mauborgne's 'blue ocean leadership' concept, the overall RM formula would therefore be to distribute authentic leadership at senior, middle and frontline level to unlock the dormant talent and energy deposits that stretch deep into a company (2014). More concretely, the content/research programme for the RM mid-range theory delimited by the two basic assumptions discussed up to this point aims to define the systemic links among:

- the general relationship business model;
- the key IRM activities and the resulting ERM activities; and
- the economic stimulus for RM-related investment in the form of a direct repeatable positive feedback loop between the RM activities and approaches and business performance.

Having defined the content of the envisioned RM mid-range theory, this is the time to locate the theory in the formal system of theories. Theories, in general, are "a series of logical arguments that specify a set of relationships among concepts, constructs or variables" (Doty and Glick 1994, p. 231). Their purpose is to parsimoniously organize a complex empirical world, to raise non-trivial questions of 'how' and 'why', and to clearly communicate the proposed answers (Bacharach 1989). The boundaries of a theory (e.g. spatial or temporal) dictate its general empirical generalizability. Hence, there exist different levels on which one can theorize (1989). Mid-range theories lie at the intersection of axiomatic positivism and phenomenological empiricism, which implies that they simultaneously embody abstraction and groundedness (Shott 1998). According to R. Merton, whose critique of 'totalism' of abstract universal theories prompted him to enunciate his programme for middle-range theories in sociology, they "lie between the minor but necessary working hypotheses that evolve in abundance during day-to-day research and the all-inclusive systematic efforts to develop a unified theory that will explain all the observed uniformities of social behaviour, social organization and social change" (1968, p. 39). Being an intermediate body of theory, the role of mid-range theories is to link the macro and micro theoretical levels by explaining the relationships between some delimited important constructs without, however, falling into an extreme reductionism (Haynes et al. 2015; Hedström and Udehn 2011). Further on, they should also guide the empirical research, highlighting theoretical problems and gaps in knowledge, and integrating separated theoretical generalizations from interrelated domains of research (Kaidesoja 2019; Merton 1968).

To preserve its utility, a mid-range theory has to be focused on certain elements and intentionally ignore others (Merton 1968). Such an isolating mechanism consolidates the research field by choosing the explanatory factors and defining the phenomenon explained (Mäki 2006). Figure 2.3 positions the envisioned RM mid-range theory against other types of theories based on these two dimensions.

R-A theory attempts to comprehensively define the roots of competitive advantage of any firm, and a hypothetical single entity case study does

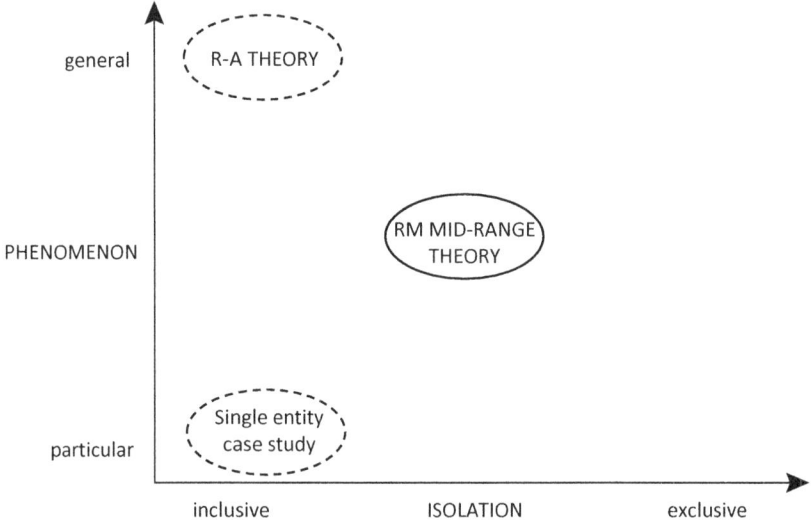

Fig. 2.3 The isolating mechanism-based delimitation of the RM mid-range theory. Note that this figure illustrates the management sciences focus of R-A theory and excludes its macroeconomic focus. If the full research agenda of R-A theory were to be visualized, the other theories would have to go further right on the X axis. (Adapted from: Hedström and Udehn (2011, p. 29))

so in terms of a particular RM-oriented one. The RM mid-range theory concentrates on the universal conditions for relationship-based sustainable competitive advantage. Moreover, the exclusion of the structural dimension of a firm's relationships and the idiosyncrasy of its product-service offer concentrates the theory's focus mainly on the firm's internal relationship management landscape, whereas the other two depicted types of theories are more inclusive at their respective phenomenological levels: R-A theory attempts to include all the internal and market factors that matter as far as the competition is concerned (Hunt 2000), whereas the hypothetical single entity case study would encompass all the factors relevant for a particular RM-oriented firm in a given market situation.

Certainly, the design of RM mid-range theory could be more inclusive. However, the choice made was inspired by S. Bacharach's definition of a good theory, which should be both falsifiable and of high utility (1989). Falsifiability is achieved when a theory is "coherent enough to be refuted", while high utility implies that a theory establishes a substantive meaning of constructs, which it explains and enables the prediction of by comparing them to empirical evidence (1989, p. 501). The earlier discussion on the variety of relational factors and the fluidity in creating different relational constructs shows that we are currently suffering from an overabundance rather than from a scarcity of ideas. In the light of the eclectic character of RM research, the pursuit of greater theoretical clarity is therefore most welcome (Möller 2013). Moreover, as one might expect, after establishing the essence of RM-related competitive advantage, a relatively exclusive RM mid-range theory can pave the way for grounding the whole network of RM theories. Figure 2.4 shows the gradual descent from grand theory and mid-range theories of higher order to mid-range theories of a

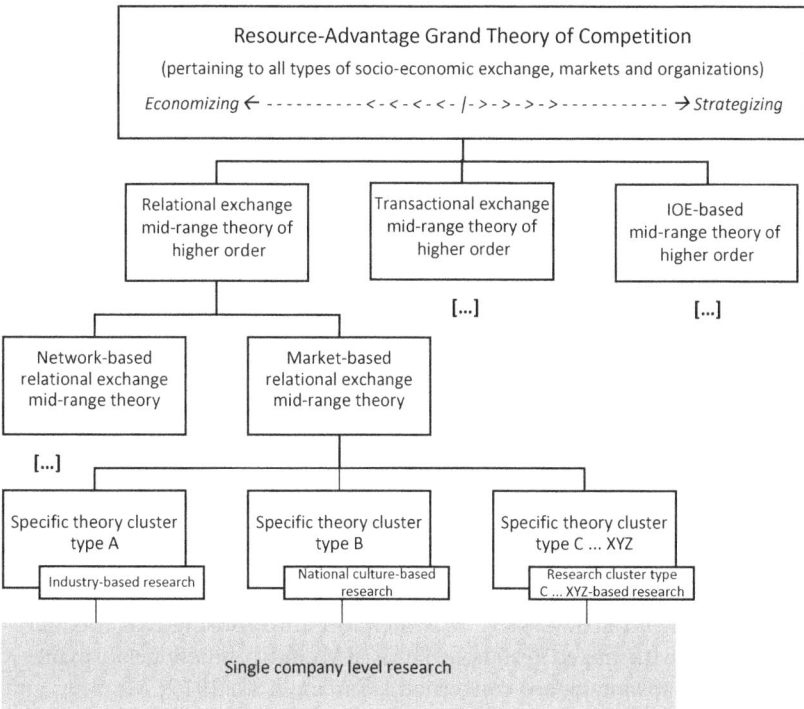

Fig. 2.4 Hypothetical system of theories for competitive advantage. (Adapted from Pinder and Moore (1980, p. 197), inspired by Möller (2013, pp. 324–325))

particular relational exchange type and lower-order specific theories in a hypothetical system of theories of competitive advantage. The practical difference between the two levels of RM mid-range theories will be manifested in the number of constructs and their generalizability. The envisioned higher-order RM mid-range theory (stronger mid-range theory; Möller 2013, p. 332) should operate on fewer constructs (or even on one construct) applicable to all types of companies and markets. Some constructs and factors used at the levels of network-based and market-based relational exchange mid-range theories will incorporate the specificity of ERM in these markets and thus will be disjunctive. Simultaneously, according to the definition of a mid-range theory, both theoretical levels have to remain empirically testable and actionable.

Meanwhile, the testability of the existence of a causal link between the relational approach to business and competitive advantage or market performance is uncertain, or, more accurately, not given. As J. Barney remarks, economic performance depends on both, whether corporate strategies create imperfectly competitive markets (where a company can best execute its competitive advantage) and on the costs of creating such markets (1986). By introducing their Commitment–Trust Theory of RM, R. Morgan and S. Hunt clearly emphasized that not all business relationships will flourish over time and specified some conditions partners have to fulfil in order to cooperate successfully. These include providing superior resources, maintaining high standards of corporate values, communicating valuable information and avoiding malevolent activities (1994; p. 34). Without the strategic and structural fit of partners, their relationship will tend to be unbalanced and non-reciprocal, which will likely result in its failure (Morgan and Hunt 1999; Toulan et al. 2006). Hence, the interactive nature of relationships posits that they are always multifaceted and 'incomplete' and impedes causally linking them with company performance metrics (Harvey et al. 2003). Moreover, some very costly and sophisticated ICT issues only add to the complexity of the relational business endeavour, highlighting the problem of proper implementation and tooling of the RM business model (Baran and Galka 2017; Deszczyński 2011; Payne and Frow 2013). It is therefore unsurprising that the literature comes with mixed results as far as RM and business performance/competitive advantage are concerned (Fonfara et al. 2019; Mumuni and O'Reilly 2014; Palmatier et al. 2007; Pillai and Sharma 2003; Reinartz et al. 2004; Wang and Feng 2012), including some very disappointing results (Bernd 2005; Coltman 2007; Keramati et al. 2010).

Some researchers have looked for the reasons for such an ambiguity and found that there can be severe differences in the ability to generate relational rents, depending upon the type of firm and its environment (Coltman et al. 2011). For example, N. Paparoidamis et al. found that smaller firms are more likely to be successful with RM by exploiting the trust–loyalty effect (2019); J. Zhang et al. highlighted the varied effects of RM mechanisms on customers in different relational states (transactional, transitional, communal and damaged; 2016); while J. Hoppner et al. and Ł. Małys et al. argued that the key mediating relational factors may not hold across all cultures as far as business performance is concerned (2015; 2017). A. Mumuni and K. O'Reilly took a different approach by deconstructing the measures of performance and checking which of them are positively affected by RM, claiming that in the overall composite measure of performance these correlations could be lost (2014).

Indeed, the devil may be in the detail. For the RM mid-range theory, it will be of utmost importance to define what it really means for a company to be relationally oriented. Even if one presumes, by deduction, that the RM business model is reasonably linked with sustainable competitive advantage, its partial imitation or unskilful replication may (as in the case of any business model) yield zero benefits (Teece et al. 1997; Witek-Crabb 2012). Moreover, as maintaining relationships is generally a positive concept, most companies can believe that they are already 'customer-centric', provided they are essentially trustworthy, even though their employees and customers might disagree (Peppers and Rogers 2013). This means in practical terms that, when managers fill in research questionnaires, they may, for example, interpret arm's length market relationships as truly relational, even if, in fact, they are incapable of producing relational rents (Dyer and Singh 1998). It is also highly unlikely that a particular company possesses a superior position in every single aspect of its relational activities and operations (Ray et al. 2004). Hence, no company can be labelled totally relationship-oriented; there must be some 'shades of grey' among them.

Drawing on the notion that all sound empirical research necessitates an adequate definition of the maturity level of the implemented concept (Lichtarski 2015), there is also a need for an adequate definition of RM maturity. This, in short, translates into answering the question: What exactly does a company have to do in terms of RM to achieve a sustainable competitive advantage? The specificity of a mid-range theory as an actionable theoretical concept that offers simplification and focuses on decisions and results (Gummesson 2017) implies that the RM mid-range theory will use the RM maturity concept in a dual way. First, it will constitute the central theoretical construct addressing the complexity of relational strategies, resources, processes and ICT systems. Second, this construct, operationalized and tested through empirical research, will enable truly relationship-oriented companies to be distinguished from transactionally oriented ones (who only *perceive* themselves as relationship-oriented). In turn, the practices and approaches of such a purified group of companies who have achieved sustainable competitive advantage will define what exactly it means to successfully implement an RM business model. Since the development of the RM maturity concept is itself a serious task, it deserves an exclusive chapter.

References

Adler, Paul S., and Seok-Woo Kwon. 2002. Social Capital: Prospects for a New Concept. *Academy of Management Review* 27 (1): 17–40. https://doi.org/10.5465/amr.2002.5922314.

Anderson, James C., and James A. Narus. 1990. A Model of Distributor Firm and Manufacturer Firm Working Partnerships. *Journal of Marketing* 54 (1): 42–58. https://doi.org/10.1177/002224299005400103.

Anderson, James C., James A. Narus, and Das Narayandas. 2009. *Business Market Management: Understanding, Creating, and Delivering Value*. 3rd ed. New York: Pearson Prentice Hall. https://www.amazon.com/Business-Market-Management-Understanding-Delivering/dp/0136000886.

Azza, Temessek Behi, and Ben Dahmane Mouelhi Norchene. 2017. Social and Physical Aspects of the Service Encounter: Effects on Trust and Customer Loyalty to the Service Provider. *Advances in Economics and Business* 5 (1): 1–10. https://doi.org/10.13189/aeb.2017.050101.

Bacharach, Samuel B. 1989. Organizational Theories: Some Criteria for Evaluation. *The Academy of Management Review* 14 (4): 496–515. https://doi.org/10.2307/258555.

Baker, Thomas L., Penny M. Simpson, and Judy A. Siguaw. 1999. The Impact of Suppliers' Perceptions of Reseller Market Orientation on Key Relationship Constructs. *Journal of the Academy of Marketing Science* 27 (1): 50–57. https://doi.org/10.1177/0092070399271004.

Ballantyne, David. 2000. Internal Relationship Marketing: A Strategy for Knowledge Renewal. *International Journal of Bank Marketing* 18 (6): 274–286. https://doi.org/10.1108/02652320010358698.

Baran, Roger, and Robert Galka. 2017. *Customer Relationship Management: The Foundation of Contemporary Marketing Strategy.* 2nd ed. Abingdon: Routledge Publications.

Barney, Jay B. 1986. Strategic Factor Markets: Expectations, Luck, and Business Strategy. *Management Science* 32 (10): 1231–1241. https://doi.org/10.1287/mnsc.32.10.1231.

———. 2001. Is the Resource-Based "View" a Useful Perspective for Strategic Management Research? Yes.

Barney, Jay B., and Asli M. Arikan. 2017. The Resource-Based View: Originse and Implications. In *The Blackwell Handbook of Strategic Management*, ed. Michael A. Hitt, R. Edward Freeman, and Jeffrey S. Harrison, 123–182. Oxford: Blackwell Publishing Ltd. https://doi.org/10.1111/b.9780631218616.2006.00006.x.

Bernd, Heinrich. 2005. Transforming Strategic Goals of CRM into Process Goals and Activities. Edited by Ilia Bider and Paul Johannesson. *Business Process Management Journal* 11 (6): 709–723. https://doi.org/10.1108/14637150510630873.

Berry, Leonard. 1983. *Relationship Marketing*, 25–80. Chicago: American Marketing Association.

Blau, Peter M. 1986. *Exchange and Power in Social Life*. 2nd ed. New Brunswick: Routledge.

Blodgett, Jeffrey G., Donna J. Hill, and Stephen S. Tax. 1997. The Effects of Distributive, Procedural, and Interactional Justice on Postcomplaint Behavior. *Journal of Retailing* 73 (2): 185–210. https://doi.org/10.1016/S0022-4359(97)90003-8.

Bonner, Julena M., Rebecca L. Greenbaum, and David M. Mayer. 2016. My Boss Is Morally Disengaged: The Role of Ethical Leadership in Explaining the Interactive Effect of Supervisor and Employee Moral Disengagement on Employee Behaviors. *Journal of Business Ethics* 137 (4): 731–742. https://doi.org/10.1007/s10551-014-2366-6.

Bontis, Nick. 1998. Intellectual Capital: An Exploratory Study That Develops Measures and Models. *Management Decision* 36 (2): 63–76. https://doi.org/10.1108/00251749810204142.

Bourdieu, Pierre. 1986. The Forms of Capital. In *Handbook of Theory and Research for the Sociology of Education*, ed. J. Richardson, 241–258. Westport/New York: Greenwood Press. http://www.socialcapitalgateway.org/content/paper/bourdieu-p-1986-forms-capital-richardson-j-handbook-theory-and-research-sociology-educ.

Brown, Donald E. 2004. Human Universals, Human Nature & Human Culture. *Daedalus* 133 (4): 47–54. https://doi.org/10.1162/0011526042365645.

Burt, Ronald S. 2009. *Structural Holes: The Social Structure of Competition*. Cambridge: Harvard University Press.

Chen, Injazz, and Karen Popovich. 2003. Understanding Customer Relationship Management (CRM): People, Process and Technology. *Business Process Management Journal* 9 (5): 672–688. https://doi.org/10.1108/14637150310496758.

Chen, Tser-Yieth, Tsai-Lien Yeh, and Hsin-Chun Yeh. 2011. Trust-Building Mechanisms and Relationship Capital. *Journal of Relationship Marketing* 10 (3): 113–144. https://doi.org/10.1080/15332667.2011.596471.

Chetty, Sylvie, and Desiree Blankenburg Holm. 2000. Internationalisation of Small to Medium-Sized Manufacturing Firms: A Network Approach. *International Business Review* 9 (1): 77–93. https://doi.org/10.1016/S0969-5931(99)00030-X.

Cho, Jinsook. 2006. The Mechanism of Trust and Distrust Formation and Their Relational Outcomes. *Journal of Retailing* 82 (1): 25–35. https://doi.org/10.1016/j.jretai.2005.11.002.

Christopher, Martin, Adrian Payne, and David Ballantyne. 1991. *Relationship Marketing: Bringing Quality Customer Service and Marketing Together*. Oxford: Butterworth Heinemann.

Ciszewska-Mlinarič, Mariola, Krzysztof Obłój, and Aleksandra Wąsowska. 2015. Zasobowe i brančowe uwarunkowania wyników polskich małych i średnich przedsiębiorstw. *Marketing i Rynek* 9 (CD): 78–88.

Cohen, Wesley M., and Daniel A. Levinthal. 1990. Absorptive Capacity: A New Perspective on Learning and Innovation. *Administrative Science Quarterly* 35 (1): 128–152. https://doi.org/10.2307/2393553.

Coleman, James S. 1988. Social Capital in the Creation of Human Capital. *American Journal of Sociology* 94: S95–S120. https://doi.org/10.1086/228943.

Colgate, Mark, Vicky Thuy-Uyen Tong, Christina Kwai-Choi Lee, and John U. Farley. 2007. Back From the Brink: Why Customers Stay. *Journal of Service Research* 9 (3): 211–228. https://doi.org/10.1177/1094670506295849.

Coltman, Tim. 2007. Why Build a Customer Relationship Management Capability? *The Journal of Strategic Information Systems* 16 (3): 301–320. https://doi.org/10.1016/j.jsis.2007.05.001.

Coltman, Tim, Timothy M. Devinney, and David F. Midgley. 2011. Customer Relationship Management and Firm Performance. *Journal of Information Technology*, September 1. https://doi.org/10.1057/jit.2010.39.

Cousins, Paul D., Robert B. Handfield, Benn Lawson, and Kenneth J. Petersen. 2006. Creating Supply Chain Relational Capital: The Impact of Formal and Informal Socialization Processes. *Journal of Operations Management*,

Incorporating Behavioral Theory in OM Empirical Models, 24 (6): 851–863. https://doi.org/10.1016/j.jom.2005.08.007.
Coyne, Kevin P., and Renée Dye. 1998. The Competitive Dynamics of Network-Based Businesses. *Harvard Business Review.* https://hbr.org/1998/01/the-competitive-dynamics-of-network-based-businesses
Crawford, Vincent P. 1990. Relationship-Specific Investment. *The Quarterly Journal of Economics* 105 (2): 561–574. https://doi.org/10.2307/2937801.
Crosby, Lawrence A., Kenneth R. Evans, and Deborah Cowles. 1990. Relationship Quality in Services Selling: An Interpersonal Influence Perspective. *Journal of Marketing* 54 (3): 68–81. https://doi.org/10.2307/1251817.
Czakon, Wojciech. 2011. Paradygmat Sieciowy w Naukach o Zarządzaniu. *Przegląd Organizacji* 11 (5): 3–6.
———. 2018. Consultation on the applicability of theories during the 24th Nordic Workshop on Interorganizational Research organized by the Vaasa University, Finland, 25–27.04.2018.
Datta, Deepak K., James P. Guthrie, and Patrick M. Wright. 2005. Human Resource Management and Labor Productivity: Does Industry Matter? *Academy of Management Journal* 48 (1): 135–145. https://doi.org/10.5465/amj.2005.15993158.
Davis, Joseph Stancliffe. 2016. *Essays in the Earlier History of American Corporations.* Clark: The Lawbook Exchange Ltd.
Davis, Don E., Joshua N. Hook, Everett L. Worthington Jr., Daryl R. Van Tongeren, Aubrey L. Gartner, David J. Jennings II, and Robert A. Emmons. 2011. Relational Humility: Conceptualizing and Measuring Humility as a Personality Judgment. *Journal of Personality Assessment* 93 (3): 225–234. https://doi.org/10.1080/00223891.2011.558871.
Davis, Don E., Everett L. Worthington Jr., Joshua N. Hook, Robert A. Emmons, Peter C. Hill, Richard A. Bollinger, and Daryl R. Van Tongeren. 2013. Humility and the Development and Repair of Social Bonds: Two Longitudinal Studies. *Self and Identity* 12 (1): 58–77. https://doi.org/10.1080/15298868.2011.636509.
de Wit, Bob, and Ron Meyer. 2010. *Strategy: Process, Content, Context: An International Perspective.* 3rd ed. Andover: Cengage Learning EMEA.
Deszczyński, Bartosz. 2008. Customer Relationship Management Gwarantem Bezpieczeństwa Konsumenta. In *Bezpieczeństwo Państw a Procesy Migracyjne*, ed. L. Kacprzak and J. Knopek, 157–167. Piła: Wydawnictwo Państwowej Wyższej Szkoły Zawodowej (PWSZ) w Pile.
———. 2011. *CRM. Strategia. System. Zarządzanie zmianą: Jak uniknąć błędów i odnieść sukces wdrożenia.* Warszawa: Wolters Kluwer.
———. 2014. Zasoby relacyjne – konceptualizacja pojęcia w świetle zasobowej teorii przedsiębiorstwa. *Studia Oeconomica Posnaniensia* 2 (11): 25–44.

———. 2016. The Maturity of Corporate Relationship Management. *Gospodarka Narodowa* 283 (3): 73–104. https://doi.org/10.33119/GN/100777.

———. 2019. The Determinants of Global Account Management (Gam). A Relationship Decision-Making Model. *Argumenta Oeconomica* 2 (43): 233–253. https://doi.org/10.15611/aoe.2019.2.10.

Deszczyński, Bartosz, Krzysztof Fonfara, and Adam Dymitrowski. 2017. The Role of Relationships in Initiating the Internationalization Process in B2B Markets. *Entrepreneurial Business and Economics Review* 5 (4): 91–109.

Doney, Patricia M., and Joseph P. Cannon. 1997. An Examination of the Nature of Trust in Buyer–Seller Relationships. *Journal of Marketing* 61 (2): 35–51. https://doi.org/10.1177/002224299706100203.

Dorsch, Michael J., Scott R. Swanson, and Scott W. Kelley. 1998. The Role of Relationship Quality in the Stratification of Vendors as Perceived by Customers. *Journal of the Academy of Marketing Science* 26 (2): 128–142. https://doi.org/10.1177/0092070398262004.

Doty, D. Harold, and William H. Glick. 1994. Typologies as a Unique Form of Theory Building: Toward Improved Understanding and Modeling. *The Academy of Management Review* 19 (2): 230–251. https://doi.org/10.2307/258704.

Doyle, Peter. 2000. Value-Based Marketing. *Journal of Strategic Marketing* 8 (4): 299–311. https://doi.org/10.1080/096525400446203.

Dunning, John H. 2003. Relational Assets, Networks and International Business Activity. In *Alliance Capitalism and Corporate Management*, ed. John H. Dunning and Gavin Boyd. Cheltenham: Edward Elgar Publishing. https://ideas.repec.org/h/elg/eechap/2550_1.html.

Dwyer, F. Robert, Paul H. Schurr, and Sejo Oh. 1987. Developing Buyer-Seller Relationships. *Journal of Marketing* 51 (2): 11–27. https://doi.org/10.1177/002224298705100202.

Dyer, Jeffrey H., and Harbir Singh. 1998. The Relational View: Cooperative Strategy and Sources of Interorganizational Competitive Advantage. *The Academy of Management Review* 23 (4): 660–679. https://doi.org/10.2307/259056.

Dymitrowski, Adam, Krzysztof Fonfara, and Bartosz Deszczyński. 2019. Informal Relationships in a Company's Internationalization Process. *Journal of Business & Industrial Marketing* 34 (5): 1054–1065. https://doi.org/10.1108/JBIM-11-2018-0363.

Eggert, Andreas, Wolfgang Ulaga, and Franziska Schultz. 2006. Value Creation in the Relationship Life Cycle: A Quasi-Longitudinal Analysis. *Industrial Marketing Management* 35 (1): 20–27. https://doi.org/10.1016/j.indmarman.2005.07.003.

Falkenberg, Andreas Wyller. 1996. Marketing and the Wealth of Firms. *Journal of Macromarketing* 16 (1): 4–24. https://doi.org/10.1177/027614679601600102.

Fiske, Alan Page. 1991. *Structures of Social Life: The Four Elementary Forms of Human Relations: Communal Sharing, Authority Ranking, Equality Matching, Market Pricing*, Structures of Social Life: The Four Elementary Forms of Human Relations: Communal Sharing, Authority Ranking, Equality Matching, Market Pricing. New York: Free Press.

Fonfara, Krzysztof, Miłosz Łuczak, Łukasz Małys, Milena Ratajczak-Mrozek, Robert Szczepański, Marcin Soniewicki, Adam Dymitrowski, and Bartosz Deszczyński. 2012. *The Development of Business Networks in the Company Internationalisation Process*. Wydawnictwo Uniwersytetu Ekonomicznego w Poznaniu.

Fonfara, Krzysztof, Łukasz Małys, and Milena Ratajczak-Mrozek. 2019. *The Internationalisation Maturity of the Firm: A Business Relationships Perspective*. Cambridge: Cambridge Scholars Publishing.

Ford, David. 2011. IMP and Service-Dominant Logic: Divergence, Convergence and Development. *Industrial Marketing Management*, Special issue on Service-Dominant Logic in Business Markets, 40 (2): 231–239. https://doi.org/10.1016/j.indmarman.2010.06.035.

Ford, David, and Håkan Håkansson. 2006. IMP – Some Things Achieved: Much More to Do. Edited by Judy Zolkiewski and Peter Turnbull. *European Journal of Marketing* 40 (3/4): 248–258. https://doi.org/10.1108/03090560610648039.

Ford, David, Lars-Erik Gadde, Håkan Håkansson, and Ivan Snehota. 2011. *Managing Business Relationships*. 3rd ed. Chichester: John Wiley. https://www.wiley.com/en-us/Managing+Business+Relationships%2C+3rd+Edition-p-9780470721094.

Forkmann, Sebastian, Stephan C. Henneberg, Peter Naudé, and Maciej Mitrega. 2016. Supplier Relationship Management Capability: A Qualification and Extension. *Industrial Marketing Management* 57: 185–200. https://doi.org/10.1016/j.indmarman.2016.02.003.

Franklin, Drew, and Roger Marshall. 2019. Adding Co-Creation as an Antecedent Condition Leading to Trust in Business-to-Business Relationships. *Industrial Marketing Management* 77: 170–181. https://doi.org/10.1016/j.indmarman.2018.10.002.

Frey, Bruno S., and Margit Osterloh. 2001. *Successful Management by Motivation: Balancing Intrinsic and Extrinsic Incentives*. Springer.

Ganesan, Shankar. 1994. Determinants of Long-Term Orientation in Buyer-Seller Relationships. *Journal of Marketing* 58 (2): 1–19. https://doi.org/10.1177/002224299405800201.

Geyskens, Inge, Jan-Benedict E.M. Steenkamp, Lisa K. Scheer, and Nirmalya Kumar. 1996. The Effects of Trust and Interdependence on Relationship Commitment: A Trans-Atlantic Study. *International Journal of Research in Marketing* 13 (4): 303–317. https://doi.org/10.1016/S0167-8116(96)00006-7.

Gordon, Ian H. 2001. *Relacje z Klientem. Marketing Partnerski*. Warszawa: Polskie Wydawnictwo Ekonomiczne. https://eki.pl/index.php?br1=30000&page=74&detailed=PWE375&.

Gouldner, Alvin W. 1960. The Norm of Reciprocity: A Preliminary Statement. *American Sociological Review* 25 (2): 161–178. https://doi.org/10.2307/2092623.

Granovetter, Mark S. 1977. The Strength of Weak Ties. *American Journal of Sociology* 78 (6): 1360–1380. https://doi.org/10.1016/B978-0-12-442450-0.50025-0.

Gremler, Dwayne D., and Kevin P. Gwinner. 2015. Relational Benefits Research: A Synthesis. *Handbook on Research in Relationship Marketing*, January 30. https://www.elgaronline.com/view/edcoll/9781848443686/9781848443686.00007.xml

Grönroos, Christian. 1990. Marketing Redefined. *Management Decision* 28 (8). https://doi.org/10.1108/00251749010139116.

———. 1996. Relationship Marketing: Strategic and Tactical Implications. *Management Decision* 34 (3): 5–14. https://doi.org/10.1108/00251749610113613.

———. 2004. The Relationship Marketing Process: Communication, Interaction, Dialogue, Value. *Journal of Business & Industrial Marketing* 19 (2): 99–113. https://doi.org/10.1108/08858620410523981.

———. 2009. Marketing as Promise Management: Regaining Customer Management for Marketing. *Journal of Business & Industrial Marketing* 24 (5/6): 351–359. https://doi.org/10.1108/08858620910966237.

Gulati, Ranjay, Dovev Lavie, and Ravindranath (Ravi) Madhavan. 2011. How Do Networks Matter? The Performance Effects of Interorganizational Networks. *Research in Organizational Behavior* 31: 207–224. https://doi.org/10.1016/j.riob.2011.09.005.

Gummesson, Evert. 1987. The New Marketing – Developing Long-Term Interactive Relationships. *Long Range Planning* 20 (4): 10–20. https://doi.org/10.1016/0024-6301(87)90151-8.

———. 1999. Total Relationship Marketing: Experimenting With a Synthesis of Research Frontiers. *Australasian Marketing Journal (AMJ)* 7 (1): 72–85. https://doi.org/10.1016/S1441-3582(99)70204-1.

———. 2004. Return on Relationships (ROR): The Value of Relationship Marketing and CRM in Business-to-Business Contexts. *Journal of Business &*

Industrial Marketing 19 (2): 136–148. https://doi.org/10.1108/08858620410524016.

———. 2017. From Relationship Marketing to Total Relationship Marketing and Beyond. *Journal of Services Marketing* 31 (1): 16–19. https://doi.org/10.1108/JSM-11-2016-0398.

Gwinner, K.P., D.D. Gremler, and M.J. Bitner. 1998. Relational Benefits in Services Industries: The Customer's Perspective. *Journal of the Academy of Marketing Science* 26 (2): 101–114. https://doi.org/10.1177/0092070398262002.

Hackman, J. Richard, and Greg R. Oldham. 1976. Motivation Through the Design of Work: Test of a Theory. *Organizational Behavior and Human Performance* 16 (2): 250–279. https://doi.org/10.1016/0030-5073(76)90016-7.

———. 1980. *Work Redesign*. Reading: Addison-Wesley.

Håkansson, Håkan. 1982. *International Marketing and Purchasing of Industrial Goods: An Interaction Approach*. Nowy Jork: Wiley. https://books.google.pl/books?id=DEd1AAAACAAJ.

Håkansson, Håkan, and David Ford. 2010. *Accounting in Networks*. Ed. Kalle Kraus, Johnny Lind, and Håkan Håkansson. London: Routledge.

Håkansson, Håkan, and I. Snehota. 1995. *Developing Relationships in Business Networks*. London/New York: Routledge. /paper/Developing-relationships-in-business-networks-H%C3%A5kansson-Snehota/d23b990b4914ac25b889d0cb02c9ec0213038e40

Hansen, Gary S., and Birger Wernerfelt. 1989. Determinants of Firm Performance: The Relative Importance of Economic and Organizational Factors. *Strategic Management Journal* 10 (5): 399–411.

Harvey, Michael, Matthew B. Myers, and Milorad M. Novicevic. 2003. The Managerial Issues Associated with Global Account Management: A Relational Contract Perspective. *Journal of Management Development* 22 (2): 103–129. https://doi.org/10.1108/02621710310459685.

Haynes, Katalin Takacs, Michael A. Hitt, and Joanna Tochman Campbell. 2015. The Dark Side of Leadership: Towards a Mid-Range Theory of Hubris and Greed in Entrepreneurial Contexts. *Journal of Management Studies* 52 (4): 479–505. https://doi.org/10.1111/joms.12127.

Hedström, Peter, and Lars Udehn. 2011. *The Oxford Handbook of Analytical Sociology*. Oxford: OUP.

Hennig-Thurau, Thorsten. 2005. Managing Service Relationships in a Global Economy: Exploring the Impact of National Culture on the Relevance of Customer Relational Benefits for Gaining Loyal Customers. In *Research on International Service Marketing: A State of the Art*. Ed. P. Gwinner Kevin, K. de Ruyter, and P. Pauwels, Trans. Paul Michael, Advances in International

Marketing, 15, 11–31. Emerald Group. https://doi.org/10.1016/S1474-7979(04)15002-3.

Hennig-Thurau, Thorsten, Kevin P. Gwinner, and Dwayne D. Gremler. (2000). Why Customers Build Relationships with Companies—And Why Not. In T. Hennig-Thurau & U. Hansen (Eds.), *Relationship Marketing: Gaining Competitive Advantage Through Customer Satisfaction and Customer Retention* (pp. 369–391). Springer. https://doi.org/10.1007/978-3-662-09745-8_21.

———. 2002. Understanding Relationship Marketing Outcomes: An Integration of Relational Benefits and Relationship Quality. *Journal of Service Research* 4 (3): 230–247. https://doi.org/10.1177/1094670502004003006.

Hoetker, Glenn, and Thomas Mellewigt. 2009. Choice and Performance of Governance Mechanisms: Matching Alliance Governance to Asset Type. *Strategic Management Journal* 30 (10): 1025–1044. https://doi.org/10.1002/smj.775.

Hooley, Graham, Amanda Broderick, and Kristian Möller. 1998. Competitive Positioning and the Resource-Based View of the Firm. *Journal of Strategic Marketing* 6 (2): 97–116. https://doi.org/10.1080/09652549800000003.

Hoppner, Jessica J., David A. Griffith, and Ryan C. White. 2015. Reciprocity in Relationship Marketing: A Cross-Cultural Examination of the Effects of Equivalence and Immediacy on Relationship Quality and Satisfaction with Performance. *Journal of International Marketing*, December 1. https://doi.org/10.1509/jim.15.0018

Hsu, Li-Chang, and Chao-Hung Wang. 2012. Clarifying the Effect of Intellectual Capital on Performance: The Mediating Role of Dynamic Capability. *British Journal of Management* 23 (2): 179–205. https://doi.org/10.1111/j.1467-8551.2010.00718.x.

Hunt, Shelby D. 1991. *Modern Marketing Theory: Critical Issues in the Philosophy of Marketing Science*. Cincinnati: South-Western Pub. Co.

———. 1997a. Competing Through Relationships: Grounding Relationship Marketing in Resource-Advantage Theory. *Journal of Marketing Management* 13 (5): 431–445. https://doi.org/10.1080/0267257X.1997.9964484.

———. 1997b. Resource-Advantage Theory: An Evolutionary Theory of Competitive Firm Behavior? *Journal of Economic Issues* 31 (1): 59–78. https://doi.org/10.1080/00213624.1997.11505891.

———. 2000. A General Theory of Competition: Too Eclectic or Not Eclectic Enough? Too Incremental or Not Incremental Enough? Too Neoclassical or Not Neoclassical Enough? *Journal of Macromarketing* 20 (1): 77–81. https://doi.org/10.1177/0276146700201010.

Hunt, Shelby D., and C. Jay Lambe. 2000. Marketing's Contribution to Business Strategy: Market Orientation, Relationship Marketing and Resource-Advantage Theory. *International Journal of Management Reviews* 2 (1): 17–43. https://doi.org/10.1111/1468-2370.00029.

Hunt, Shelby D., and Robert M. Morgan. 1995. The Comparative Advantage Theory of Competition. *Journal of Marketing* 59 (2): 1–15. https://doi.org/10.2307/1252069.

———. 1996. The Resource-Advantage Theory of Competition: Dynamics, Path Dependencies, and Evolutionary Dimensions. *Journal of Marketing*: 107–114.

Hunt Shelby, D., and M. Morgan Robert. 2005. The Resource-Advantage Theory of Competition. In *Review of Marketing Research*, Review of Marketing Research, ed. Naresh K. Malhotra, vol. 1, 153–206. Emerald Group Publishing Limited. https://doi.org/10.1108/S1548-6435(2004)0000001008.

Jarratt, Denise. 2008. Testing a Theoretically Constructed Relationship Management Capability. *European Journal of Marketing* 42 (9/10): 1106–1132. https://doi.org/10.1108/03090560810891172.

Jayachandran, Satish, Kelly Hewett, and Peter Kaufman. 2004. Customer Response Capability in a Sense-and-Respond Era: The Role of Customer Knowledge Process. *Journal of the Academy of Marketing Science* 32 (3): 219–233. https://doi.org/10.1177/0092070304263334.

Johnson, Janet Buttolph, H.T. Reynolds, and Jason D. Mycoff. 2019. *Political Science Research Methods*. Thousand Oaks: CQ Press.

Jones, Michael A., Kristy E. Reynolds, David L. Mothersbaugh, and Sharon E. Beatty. 2007. The Positive and Negative Effects of Switching Costs on Relational Outcomes. *Journal of Service Research* 9 (4): 335–355. https://doi.org/10.1177/1094670507299382.

Kaidesoja, Tuukka. 2019. Building Middle-Range Theories from Case Studies. *Studies in History and Philosophy of Science Part A* 78: 23–31. https://doi.org/10.1016/j.shpsa.2018.11.008.

Kale, Prashant, Harbir Singh, and Howard Perlmutter. 2000. Learning and Protection of Proprietary Assets in Strategic Alliances: Building Relational Capital. *Strategic Management Journal* 21 (3): 217–237. https://doi.org/10.1002/(SICI)1097-0266(200003)21:3<217::AID-SMJ95>3.0.CO;2-Y.

Kelleher, Bob. 2011. Engaged Employees Equals High-Performing Organizations (Achieving Successful Employee Engagement). *Human Resource Management International Digest* 19 (6). https://doi.org/10.1108/hrmid.2011.04419faa.011.

Keramati, Abbas, Hamed Mehrabi, and Navid Mojir. 2010. A Process-Oriented Perspective on Customer Relationship Management and Organizational Performance: An Empirical Investigation. *Industrial Marketing Management, Selling and Sales Management* 39 (7): 1170–1185. https://doi.org/10.1016/j.indmarman.2010.02.001.

Kim, Hyung-Su, and Young-Gul Kim. 2009. A CRM Performance Measurement Framework: Its Development Process and Application. *Industrial Marketing*

Management, Impact of Outsourcing on Business-to-Business Marketing, 38 (4): 477–489. https://doi.org/10.1016/j.indmarman.2008.04.008.

Kim, W. Chan, and Renee Mauborgne. 2014. *Blue Ocean Strategy, Expanded Edition: How to Create Uncontested Market Space and Make the Competition Irrelevant.* Boston: Harvard Business Review Press.

Kinard, Brian R., and Michael L. Capella. 2006. Relationship Marketing: The Influence of Consumer Involvement on Perceived Service Benefits. *Journal of Services Marketing* 20 (6): 359–368. https://doi.org/10.1108/08876040610691257.

Kogut, Bruce, and Udo Zander. 1996. What Firms Do? Coordination, Identity, and Learning. *Organization Science* 7 (5): 502–518. https://doi.org/10.1287/orsc.7.5.502.

Krupski, Rafał. 2009. Wstęp. In *Koncepcje Strategii Organizacji*, ed. Rafał Krupski, Jerzy Niemczyk, and Stańczyk-Hugiet, 7–9. Warszawa: Polskie Wydawnictwo Ekonomiczne.

———. 2012. Dwie koncepcje strategii organizacji – razem czy osobno? *Przegląd Organizacji* 1: 3–4.

Kumar, Nirmalya, Lisa K. Scheer, and Jan-Benedict E.M. Steenkamp. 1995. The Effects of Supplier Fairness on Vulnerable Resellers. *Journal of Marketing Research* 32 (1): 54–65. https://doi.org/10.2307/3152110.

Kumar, V., Avishek Lahiri, and Orhan Bahadir Dogan. 2018. A Strategic Framework for a Profitable Business Model in the Sharing Economy. *Industrial Marketing Management* 69: 147–160. https://doi.org/10.1016/j.indmarman.2017.08.021.

Lacey, Russell, Jaebeom Suh, and Robert M. Morgan. 2007. Differential Effects of Preferential Treatment Levels on Relational Outcomes. *Journal of Service Research* 9 (3): 241–256. https://doi.org/10.1177/1094670506295850.

Lau, Henry, Dilupa Nakandala, Premaratne Samaranayake, and Paul K. Shum. 2016. BPM for Supporting Customer Relationship and Profit Decision. *Business Process Management Journal* 22 (1): 231–255. https://doi.org/10.1108/BPMJ-04-2015-0039.

Laverty, Kevin J. 1996. Economic "Short-Termism": The Debate, the Unresolved Issues, and the Implications for Management Practice and Research. *The Academy of Management Review* 21 (3): 825–860. https://doi.org/10.2307/259003.

Lavie, Dovev. 2006. The Competitive Advantage of Interconnected Firms: An Extension of the Resource-Based View. *Academy of Management Review* 31 (3): 638–658. https://doi.org/10.5465/amr.2006.21318922.

Levitt, Theodore. 1983. After the Sale Is Over. *Harvard Business Review* 62 (1): 87–93.

Li, Ling, John B. Ford, Xin Zhai, and Li Xu. 2012. Relational Benefits and Manufacturer Satisfaction: An Empirical Study of Logistics Service in Supply Chain. *International Journal of Production Research* 50 (19): 5445–5459. https://doi.org/10.1080/00207543.2011.636388.

Lichtarski, Jan. 2010. Profile Orientacji w Zarządzaniu Przedsiębiorstwem i Kształtujące Je Czynniki. In *Kierunki i Dylematy Rozwoju Nauki i Praktyki Zarządzania Przedsiębiorstwem*, ed. Henryk Jagoda and Jan Lichtarski, vol. 169. Wrocław: Wydawnictwo Uniwersytetu Ekonomicznego we Wrocławiu.

———. 2015. *Praktyczny Wymiar Nauk o Zarządzaniu*. Warszawa: Polskie Wydawnictwo Ekonomiczne.

Lin, Neng-Pai, James C.M. Weng, and Yi-Ching Hsieh. 2003. Relational Bonds and Customer's Trust and Commitment – A Study on the Moderating Effects of Web Site Usage. *The Service Industries Journal* 23 (3): 103–124. https://doi.org/10.1080/714005111.

Loufrani-Fedida, Sabrina, Valérie Hauch, and Djamila Elidrissi. 2019. The Dynamics of Relational Competencies in the Development of Born Global Firms: A Multilevel Approach. *International Business Review* 28 (2): 222–237. https://doi.org/10.1016/j.ibusrev.2018.09.001.

Lusch, Robert F., James R. Brown, and Matthew O'Brien. 2011. Protecting Relational Assets: A Pre and Post Field Study of a Horizontal Business Combination. *Journal of the Academy of Marketing Science* 39 (2): 175–197. https://doi.org/10.1007/s11747-010-0197-2.

Ma, Hao. 1999. Anatomy of Competitive Advantage: A SELECT Framework. *Management Decision* 37 (9): 709–718. https://doi.org/10.1108/00251749910299129.

Macintosh, Gerrard. 2007. Customer Orientation, Relationship Quality, and Relational Benefits to the Firm. *Journal of Services Marketing* 21 (3): 150–159. https://doi.org/10.1108/08876040710746516.

Mäki, Uskali. 2006. On the Method of Isolation in Economics. *Recent Developments in Economic Methodology* 3: 3–37.

Małys, Łukasz, Justyna Światowiec-Szczepańska, and Michał Zdziarski. The Quality of Business Relationships in the Automotive Industry and the Company Performance: The Case of Polish and Brazilian Markets. *Problemy Zarządzania* 3/2017 (70), t.2 (2017): 76–87.

Marzo-Navarro, Mercedes, Marta Pedraja-Iglesias, and Ma Pilar Rivera-Torres. 2004. The Benefits of Relationship Marketing for the Consumer and for the Fashion Retailers. *Journal of Fashion Marketing and Management: An International Journal* 8 (4): 425–436. https://doi.org/10.1108/13612020410560018.

McGahan, Anita M., and Michael E. Porter. 1997. How Much Does Industry Matter, Really? *Strategic Management Journal* 18 (S1): 15–30. https://doi.

org/10.1002/(SICI)1097-0266(199707)18:1+<15::AID-SMJ916>3. 0.CO;2-1.
Merton, Robert King. 1968. *Social Theory and Social Structure*. New York: Simon and Schuster.
Miller, Kent D. 2002. Knowledge Inventories and Managerial Myopia. *Strategic Management Journal* 23 (8): 689–706. https://doi.org/10.1002/smj.245.
Mitręga, Maciej. 2019. Dynamic Marketing Capability – Refining the Concept and Applying It to Company Innovations. *Journal of Business & Industrial Marketing* 35 (2): 193–203. https://doi.org/10.1108/JBIM-01-2019-0007.
Mitręga, Maciej, and Gregor Pfajfar. 2015. Business Relationship Process Management as Company Dynamic Capability Improving Relationship Portfolio. *Industrial Marketing Management* 46: 193–203. https://doi.org/10.1016/j.indmarman.2015.02.029.
Mitręga, Maciej, Sebastian Forkmann, Carla Ramos, and Stephan C. Henneberg. 2012. Networking Capability in Business Relationships Concept and Scale Development. *Industrial Marketing Management*, IMP 2011 The Impact of Globalization on Networks, 41 (5): 739–751. https://doi.org/10.1016/j.indmarman.2012.06.002.
Möller, Kristian. 2006. Role of Competences in Creating Customer Value: A Value-Creation Logic Approach. *Industrial Marketing Management*, Creating Value for the Customer Through Competence-Based Marketing, 35 (8): 913–924. https://doi.org/10.1016/j.indmarman.2006.04.005.
———. 2013. Theory Map of Business Marketing: Relationships and Networks Perspectives. *Industrial Marketing Management*, Theoretical Perspectives in Industrial Marketing Management, 42 (3): 324–335. https://doi.org/10.1016/j.indmarman.2013.02.009.
Möller, Kristian, and Aino Halinen. 1999. Business Relationships and Networks. *Industrial Marketing Management* 28 (5): 413–427. https://doi.org/10.1016/S0019-8501(99)00086-3.
———. (2000). Relationship Marketing Theory: Its Roots and Direction. Journal of Marketing Management, 16(1–3), 29–54. https://doi.org/10.1362/026725700785100460.
Morgan, Robert M. 1994. The Commitment-Trust Theory of Relationship Marketing. *Journal of Marketing* 58 (3): 20–38. https://doi.org/10.1177/002224299405800302.
Morgan, Robert M., and Shelby D. Hunt. (1994). The Commitment-Trust Theory of Relationship Marketing. *Journal of Marketing* 58 (3): 20–38. https://doi.org/10.1177/002224299405800302.
———. 1999. Relationship-Based Competitive Advantage: The Role of Relationship Marketing in Marketing Strategy. *Journal of Business Research* 46 (3): 281–290. https://doi.org/10.1016/S0148-2963(98)00035-6.

Mowery, David C., Joanne E. Oxley, and Brian S. Silverman. 1998. Technological Overlap and Interfirm Cooperation: Implications for the Resource-Based View of the Firm. *Research Policy* 27 (5): 507–523. https://doi.org/10.1016/S0048-7333(98)00066-3.

Mumuni, Alhassan G., and Kelley O'Reilly. 2014. Examining the Impact of Customer Relationship Management on Deconstructed Measures of Firm Performance. *Journal of Relationship Marketing* 13 (2): 89–107. https://doi.org/10.1080/15332667.2014.910073.

Nahapiet, Janine, and Sumantra Ghoshal. 1998. Social Capital, Intellectual Capital, and the Organizational Advantage. *Academy of Management Review* 23 (2): 242–266. https://doi.org/10.5465/amr.1998.533225.

Nenonen, Suvi, and Kaj Storbacka. 2010. Business Model Design: Conceptualizing Networked Value Co-Creation. *International Journal of Quality and Service Sciences* 2 (1): 43–59. https://doi.org/10.1108/17566691011026595.

Ng, Irene C. L., David Xin Ding, and Nick Yip. 2013. Outcome-Based Contracts as New Business Model: The Role of Partnership and Value-Driven Relational Assets. *Industrial Marketing Management*, Business Models – Exploring Value Drivers and the Role of Marketing, 42 (5): 730–743. https://doi.org/10.1016/j.indmarman.2013.05.009.

Nyaga, Gilbert N., and Judith M. Whipple. 2011. Relationship Quality and Performance Outcomes: Achieving a Sustainable Competitive Advantage. *Journal of Business Logistics* 32 (4): 345–360. https://doi.org/10.1111/j.0000-0000.2011.01030.x.

Obłój, Krzysztof. 2007. *Strategia Organizacji*. Warszawa: Polskie Wydawnictwo Ekonomiczne.

Palmatier, Robert W. 2008. Interfirm Relational Drivers of Customer Value. *Journal of Marketing* 72 (4): 76–89. https://doi.org/10.1509/jmkg.72.4.076.

Palmatier, Robert W., Rajiv P. Dant, and Dhruv Grewal. 2007. A Comparative Longitudinal Analysis of Theoretical Perspectives of Interorganizational Relationship Performance. *Journal of Marketing* 71 (4): 172–194. https://doi.org/10.1509/jmkg.71.4.172.

Paparoidamis, Nicholas G., Constantine S. Katsikeas, and Ruben Chumpitaz. 2019. The Role of Supplier Performance in Building Customer Trust and Loyalty: A Cross-Country Examination. *Industrial Marketing Management* 78: 183–197. https://doi.org/10.1016/j.indmarman.2017.02.005.

Paul, Michael, Thorsten Hennig-Thurau, Dwayne D. Gremler, Kevin P. Gwinner, and Caroline Wiertz. 2009. Toward a Theory of Repeat Purchase Drivers for Consumer Services. *Journal of the Academy of Marketing Science* 37 (2): 215–237. https://doi.org/10.1007/s11747-008-0118-9.

Payne, Adrian, and Pennie Frow. 2005. A Strategic Framework for Customer Relationship Management. *Journal of Marketing* 69 (4): 167–176. https://doi.org/10.1509/jmkg.2005.69.4.167.

Payne, A., & Frow, P. (2013). *Strategic Customer Management: Integrating Relationship Marketing and CRM*. Cambridge University Press.
———. 2017. Relationship marketing: Looking backwards towards the future. *Journal of Services Marketing* 31(1), 11–15. https://doi.org/10.1108/JSM-11-2016-0380.
Peppers, Don, and Martha Rogers. 2013. Extreme Trust: The New Competitive Advantage. *Strategy and Leadership* 41 (6): 31–34. https://doi.org/10.1108/SL-07-2013-0054.
Pfeffer, Jeffrey. 2018. *Dying for a Paycheck: How Modern Management Harms Employee Health and Company Performance—and What We Can Do About It*. New York: Harper Business.
Piercy, Nigel. 2016. *Market-Led Strategic Change | Transforming the Process of Going to Market | Taylor & Francis Group*. London: Routledge. https://www.taylorfrancis.com/books/9780203507766.
Pillai, Gopalakrishna Kishore, and Arun Sharma. 2003. Mature Relationships: Why Does Relational Orientation Turn into Transaction Orientation? *Industrial Marketing Management* 32 (8): 643–651. https://doi.org/10.1016/j.indmarman.2003.06.005.
Pinder, Craig C., and Larry F. Moore. 1980. The Resurrection of Taxonomy to Aid the Development of Middle Range Theories of Organizational Behavior. *Middle Range Theory and the Study of Organizations*: 187–211. https://doi.org/10.1007/978-94-009-8733-3_16.
Pluta-Olearnik, Mirosława. 2017. Usługi a wartość poszerzona dla klienta na przykładzie rynku wyposaċenia i dekoracji wnętrz. *Marketing i Zarządzanie* 48 (2): 397–405.
Porter, Michael E. 1991. Towards a Dynamic Theory of Strategy. *Strategic Management Journal* 12 (S2): 95–117. https://doi.org/10.1002/smj.4250121008.
Powell, Thomas C. 1996. How Much Does Industry Matter? An Alternative Empirical Test. *Strategic Management Journal* 17 (4): 323–334. https://doi.org/10.1002/(SICI)1097-0266(199604)17:4<323::AID-SMJ803>3.0.CO;2-5.
Prahalad, C.K., and Gary Hamel. 1994. Strategy as a Field of Study: Why Search for a New Paradigm? *Strategic Management Journal* 15 (S2): 5–16. https://doi.org/10.1002/smj.4250151002.
Prior, Daniel D. 2012. The Effects of Buyer-supplier Relationships on Buyer Competitiveness. *Journal of Business & Industrial Marketing* 27 (2): 100–114. https://doi.org/10.1108/08858621211196976.

Pukas, Anetta. 2019. *Zarządzanie relacjami z klientem w tworzeniu przewagi konkurencyjnej przedsiębiorstwa: ujęcie dynamiczne.* Wydawnictwo Uniwersytetu Ekonomicznego we Wrocławiu.

Ray, Gautam, Jay B. Barney, and Waleed A. Muhanna. 2004. Capabilities, Business Processes, and Competitive Advantage: Choosing the Dependent Variable in Empirical Tests of the Resource-Based View. *Strategic Management Journal* 25 (1): 23–37. https://doi.org/10.1002/smj.366.

Reichheld, Frederick. 2001. *Loyalty Rules!: How Today's Leaders Build Lasting Relationships.* Boston: Harvard Business School Press. https://books.google.pl/books?hl=pl&lr=&id=oT3lL0QdWiwC&oi=fnd&pg=PP1&dq=reichheld+2001+loyalty&ots=zD3RjjPbTW&sig=cYD89k0tVodkW2Tc1HhiTuZhacc&redir_esc=y#v=onepage&q=reichheld%202001%20loyalty&f=false.

Reichheld, Frederick, and Rob Markey. 2011. *The Ultimate Question 2.0: How Net Promoter Companies Thrive in a Customer.* Boston: Harvard Business Publishing. https://books.google.pl/books?hl=pl&lr=&id=e8jhiYjQrU0C&oi=fnd&pg=PR7&dq=reichheld+markey&ots=CC1eQacr8I&sig=iSgh_lWq6TPhrVgOpVEfeP3Hnzw&redir_esc=y#v=onepage&q=reichheld%20markey&f=false.

Reinartz, Werner, Manfred Krafft, and Wayne D. Hoyer. 2004. The Customer Relationship Management Process: Its Measurement and Impact on Performance. *Journal of Marketing Research.* https://doi.org/10.1509/jmkr.41.3.293.35991.

Reynolds, Kristy E., and Sharon E. Beatty. 1999. Customer Benefits and Company Consequences of Customer-Salesperson Relationships in Retailing. *Journal of Retailing* 75 (1, Spring): 11–32. https://doi.org/10.1016/S0022-4359(99)80002-5.

Roberts, Nicholas, and Varun Grover. 2012. Investigating Firm's Customer Agility and Firm Performance: The Importance of Aligning Sense and Respond Capabilities. *Journal of Business Research* 65 (5): 579–585. https://doi.org/10.1016/j.jbusres.2011.02.009.

Robins, James, and Margarethe F. Wiersema. 1995. A Resource-Based Approach to the Multibusiness Firm: Empirical Analysis of Portfolio Interrelationships and Corporate Financial Performance. *Strategic Management Journal* 16 (4): 277–299. https://doi.org/10.1002/smj.4250160403.

Romanow, Zbigniew. 1997. *Historia Myśli Ekonomicznej w Zarysie.* Poznań: Wydawnictwo Akademii Ekonomicznej w Poznaniu.

Roos, Göran, Alan Bainbridge, and Kristine Jacobsen. 2001. Intellectual Capital Analysis as a Strategic Tool. *Strategy & Leadership* 29 (4): 21–26. https://doi.org/10.1108/10878570110400116.

Rudawska, Edyta, Ewa Frąckiewicz, and Małgorzata Wiścicka. 2016. Sustainable Marketing as a Response to Contemporary Challenges Facing Companies in Poland. *International Journal of Management Cases* 18 (4): 15–29.

Rudny, Włodzimierz. 2014. Zasoby sieciowe a strategia przedsiębiorstwa. *Studia Ekonomiczne* 202: 23–33.

Ruiz, David Martín, Dwayne D. Gremler, Judith H. Washburn, and Gabriel Cepeda Carrión. 2008. Service Value Revisited: Specifying a Higher-Order, Formative Measure. *Journal of Business Research*, Formative Indicators, 61 (12): 1278–1291. https://doi.org/10.1016/j.jbusres.2008.01.015.

Rumelt, Richard P. 1991. How Much Does Industry Matter? *Strategic Management Journal* 12 (3): 167–185. https://doi.org/10.1002/smj.4250120302.

Schoemaker, Paul J.H. 1990. Strategy, Complexity, and Economic Rent. *Management Science* 36 (10): 1178–1192. https://doi.org/10.1287/mnsc.36.10.1178.

Scott, W. Richard, and Gerald F. Davis. 2015. *Organizations and Organizing: Rational, Natural and Open Systems Perspectives*. New York: Routledge.

Sepulveda, Fabian, and Mika Gabrielsson. 2013. Network Development and Firm Growth: A Resource-Based Study of B2B Born Globals. *Industrial Marketing Management*, Business Models – Exploring Value Drivers and the Role of Marketing, 42 (5): 792–804. https://doi.org/10.1016/j.indmarman.2013.01.001.

Shafer, Scott M., H. Jeff Smith, and Jane C. Linder. 2005. The Power of Business Models. *Business Horizons* 48 (3): 199–207. https://doi.org/10.1016/j.bushor.2004.10.014.

Sheth, Jagdish N. 2017. Revitalizing Relationship Marketing. *Journal of Services Marketing* 31 (1): 6–10. https://doi.org/10.1108/JSM-11-2016-0397.

Sheth, Jagdish N., and Atul Parvatiyar. 2000. *Handbook of Relationship Marketing*. London: SAGE.

Shi, Linda H., Shaoming Zou, J. Chris White, Regina C. McNally, and S. Tamer Cavusgil. 2005. Executive Insights: Global Account Management Capability: Insights from Leading Suppliers. *Journal of International Marketing* 13 (2): 93–113. https://doi.org/10.1509/jimk.13.2.93.64858.

Shore, Lynn M., Lois E. Tetrick, Patricia Lynch, and Kevin Barksdale. 2006. Social and Economic Exchange: Construct Development and Validation. *Journal of Applied Social Psychology* 36 (4): 837–867. https://doi.org/10.1111/j.0021-9029.2006.00046.x.

Shott, Michael J. 1998. Status and Role of Formation Theory in Contemporary Archaeological Practice. *Journal of Archaeological Research* 6 (4): 299–329. https://doi.org/10.1007/BF02446082.

Shukla, Mahendra Kumar, and Pinaki Nandan Pattnaik. 2019. Managing Customer Relations in a Modern Business Environment: Towards an Ecosystem-Based

Sustainable CRM Model. *Journal of Relationship Marketing* 18 (1): 17–33. https://doi.org/10.1080/15332667.2018.1534057.

Sin, Leo Y.M., Alan C.B. Tse, Oliver H.M. Yau, Raymond P.M. Chow, and Jenny S.Y. Lee. 2005. Market Orientation, Relationship Marketing Orientation, and Business Performance: The Moderating Effects of Economic Ideology and Industry Type. *Journal of International Marketing* 13 (1): 36–57. https://doi.org/10.1509/jimk.13.1.36.58538.

Slater, Stanley F., and John C. Narver. 1995. Market Orientation and the Learning Organization. *Journal of Marketing* 59 (3): 63–74. https://doi.org/10.1177/002224299505900306.

Sopińska, Agnieszka. 2019. Wybór partnerów współdziałania jako jeden z elementów treści strategii relacyjnej. *Przegląd Organizacji* 4: 10–17. https://doi.org/10.33141/po.2019.4.2.

Spake, Deborah F., Sharon E. Beatty, Beverly K. Brockman, and Tammy Neal Crutchfield. 2003. Consumer Comfort in Service Relationships: Measurement and Importance. *Journal of Service Research* 5 (4): 316–332. https://doi.org/10.1177/1094670503005004004.

Spender, J.-C. 1996. Making Knowledge the Basis of a Dynamic Theory of the Firm. *Strategic Management Journal* 17 (S2): 45–62. https://doi.org/10.1002/smj.4250171106.

Stewart, Thomas A. 2007. *The Wealth of Knowledge: Intellectual Capital and the Twenty-First Century Organization*. New York: Crown Publishing Group.

Sulejewicz, Aleksander. 1997. *Partnerstwo Strategiczne: Modelowanie Współpracy Przedsiębiorstw*. Warszawa: Szkoła Główna Handlowa.

Tadajewski, Mark. 2008. Incommensurable Paradigms, Cognitive Bias and the Politics of Marketing Theory. *Marketing Theory* 8 (3): 273–297. https://doi.org/10.1177/1470593108093557.

Teece, David J. 2007. Explicating Dynamic Capabilities: The Nature and Microfoundations of (Sustainable) Enterprise Performance. *Strategic Management Journal* 28 (13): 1319–1350. https://doi.org/10.1002/smj.640.

Teece, David J., Gary Pisano, and Amy Shuen. 1997. Dynamic Capabilities and Strategic Management. *Strategic Management Journal* 18 (7): 509–533. https://doi.org/10.1002/(SICI)1097-0266(199708)18:7<509::AID-SMJ882>3.0.CO;2-Z.

Toulan, Omar, Julian Birkinshaw, and David Arnold. 2006. The Role of Interorganizational Fit in Global Account Management. *International Studies of Management & Organization* 36 (4): 61–81. https://doi.org/10.2753/IMO0020-8825360403.

Tvede, Lars, and Peter Ohnemus. 2001. *Marketing Strategies for the New Economy*. Hoboken: Wiley. https://books.google.pl/books?id=z_wonQEACAAJ.

Urbańczyk, Tomasz. 2012. *Rozwój sieci dostaw poprzez wdraćanie koncepcji łańcucha solidarności*. Poznan University of Economics and Business.

Van Tongeren, Daryl R., Jeffrey D. Green, Timothy L. Hulsey, Cristine H. Legare, David G. Bromley, and Anne M. Houtman. 2014. A Meaning-Based Approach to Humility: Relationship Affirmation Reduces Worldview Defense. *Journal of Psychology and Theology* 42 (1): 62–69. https://doi.org/10.1177/009164711404200107.

Venkatesan, Rajkumar, and Vita Kumar. 2004. A Customer Lifetime Value Framework for Customer Selection and Resource Allocation Strategy. *Journal of Marketing* 68 (4): 106–125. https://doi.org/10.1509/jmkg.68.4.106.42728.

Wang, Yonggui, and Hui Feng. 2012. Customer Relationship Management Capabilities: Measurement, Antecedents and Consequences. *Management Decision* 50 (1): 115–129. https://doi.org/10.1108/00251741211194903.

Wang, Yun, Michel Rod, Shaobo Ji, and Qi Deng. 2017. Social Media Capability in B2B Marketing: Toward a Definition and a Research Model. *Journal of Business & Industrial Marketing* 32 (8): 1125–1135. https://doi.org/10.1108/JBIM-10-2016-0250.

Watkins, C. Edward, Jr., Joshua N. Hook, Joey Ramaeker, and Marciana J. Ramos. 2016. Repairing the Ruptured Supervisory Alliance: Humility as a Foundational Virtue in Clinical Supervision. *The Clinical Supervisor* 35 (1): 22–41. https://doi.org/10.1080/07325223.2015.1127190.

Williamson, Oliver E. 1993. Introduction. In *The Nature of the Firm: Origins, Evolution, and Development*, 3–17. Oxford: Oxford University Press.

Wirzba, Norman. 2008. The Touch of Humility: An Invitation to Creatureliness. *Modern Theology* 24 (2): 225–244. https://doi.org/10.1111/j.1468-0025.2007.00443.x.

Witek-Crabb, Anna. 2012. Sustainable Strategic Management and Market Effectiveness of Enterprises. *Procedia – Social and Behavioral Sciences* 58: 899–905. https://doi.org/10.1016/j.sbspro.2012.09.1068.

Wong, Amy, and Lianxi Zhou. 2006. Determinants and Outcomes of Relationship Quality. *Journal of International Consumer Marketing* 18 (3): 81–105. https://doi.org/10.1300/J046v18n03_05.

Zawiślak, Andrzej. 2010. *Ekonomia. Nauka Praw Tymczasowych*. Warszawa: Oficyna Wydawnicza Warszawskiej Szkoły Zarządzania.

Zhang, Jonathan Z., George F. Watson, Robert W. Palmatier, and Rajiv P. Dant. 2016. Dynamic Relationship Marketing. *Journal of Marketing* 80 (5): 53–75.

Zineldin, Mosad, and Sarah Philipson. 2007. Kotler and Borden Are Not Dead: Myth of Relationship Marketing and Truth of the 4Ps. *Journal of Consumer Marketing* 24 (4): 229–241. https://doi.org/10.1108/07363760710756011.

Zott, Christoph, and Raphael Amit. 2010. Business Model Design: An Activity System Perspective. *Business Models* 43 (2): 216–226. https://doi.org/10.1016/j.lrp.2009.07.004.

Open Access This chapter is licensed under the terms of the Creative Commons Attribution 4.0 International License (http://creativecommons.org/licenses/by/4.0/), which permits use, sharing, adaptation, distribution and reproduction in any medium or format, as long as you give appropriate credit to the original author(s) and the source, provide a link to the Creative Commons licence and indicate if changes were made.

The images or other third party material in this chapter are included in the chapter's Creative Commons licence, unless indicated otherwise in a credit line to the material. If material is not included in the chapter's Creative Commons licence and your intended use is not permitted by statutory regulation or exceeds the permitted use, you will need to obtain permission directly from the copyright holder.

CHAPTER 3

Relationship Management Maturity

3.1 THE DESIGN AND INTRODUCTORY STEPS OF RM MATURITY CONCEPTUALIZATION

When building a theory, two strategies are generally available to management scholars: the interpretative–symbolistic contextualization and the neo-positivistic functionalistic–systemic idealization strategy (Czakon 2015). In the contextualization strategy, the inference and explanation are an interrelated, context-dependent process. The researcher is an active "interrogator of the data" who seeks to find the best theoretical explanation based on empirical evidence and preferred epistemic virtues (Easterby-Smith et al. 2012; Strauss and Corbin 1998). In consequence, the primary mode of reasoning is induction, and the developed theory is grounded in empirical data (Charmaz 2004).

The idealization strategy assumes the opposite direction of scientific inquiry. By appealing to deductive reasoning, theoretical propositions are formed and then empirically verified in search of objective, universally observable causal rules (Czakon 2015). These inductive arguments are reinforced by normative guidelines. The latter, in turn, rely on the hypotheses which were earlier analytically derived from the theory (Sprenger 2011). A specific product of such a hypothetico-deductive (H-D) theory confirmation method is so-called ideal organizational types and profiles. Ideal types are complex theoretical constructs, which describe a model

© The Author(s) 2021
B. Deszczyński, *Firm Competitive Advantage Through Relationship Management*, https://doi.org/10.1007/978-3-030-67338-3_3

organization that, if it existed, would enjoy the highest possible values of dependent variables. Ideal profiles, in turn, describe real organizations resembling different variants of the given ideal type (Doty and Glick 1994). According to H-D logic, if empirical data give credit to theoretical generalizations represented by the ideal type reflected in its associated profiles, the underlying theory can also be credited and qualified as valid (Ketokivi and Mantere 2010).

The theoretical ideal type resembles the notion of 'maturity', which, in general, can be understood as the state of being complete/perfect in implementing, or being ready to implement, something (e.g. a given strategic approach to management; Wendler 2012). Modelling of organizations' maturity has been applied in various ways, especially in project, process and quality management (Lichtarski 2015; Rosemann and de Bruin 2005). A good example is the ISO certification system or the Capability Maturity Model for software (CMM). The latter was developed in the period 1986–1991 by the Software Engineering Institute at Carnegie Mellon University to help organizations (firms and US governmental bodies) in successful deployment of their software projects (Paulk et al. 1993).

CMM is a widely adopted underlying framework in Business Process Management (BPM) research. It is unsurprising then that the very concept of maturity has also been extensively developed by BPM scholars (Mettler 2011; Röglinger et al. 2012; Tarhan et al. 2016). According to this research tradition, maturity models help to assess at what development stage an organization is situated by defining and arranging key descriptive management-related concepts and constructs. Further on, maturity models contain some prescriptive elements. Finally, they are used as a platform for disseminating research findings to the broader business audience (Kazanjian and Drazin 1989).

Clearly, the position of RM mid-range theory between R-A theory and empirical research amplifies the need for an unambiguously defined supporting RM maturity model (grounded in both theory and practice) that would demonstrate the identity of companies truly implementing the relational business model. However, the wide application of maturity models has also raised some criticism, especially highlighting their focus on a predefined sequence of maturity levels towards an imagined 'end state' and neglecting equifinal maturation paths (De Bruin et al. 2005). In response to this criticism several guidelines for the development of a successful maturity model have been proposed, including the following (Pöppelbuß and Röglinger 2011; Rosemann 2006):

- offering clear information about the model application domain, the proposed constructs and their theoretical underpinning;
- defining its key success factors to a high level of granularity (providing concrete answers to detailed questions concerning firm management);
- disseminating best practices in adoption methodology and improvement measures.

In summary, as the model of RM maturity should define the 'ideal type' of a truly relationship-oriented organization and because the model is intended for empirical testing, the H-D logic seems to be an appropriate methodological framework for this research. However, the soundness of an inductive argument requires that all (relevant) evidence is reflected in the sample (Maher 1996). Therefore, even if the inductive part of the research will rely on the deductive theoretical foundations, there still exist some risks: (1) the theory may turn out to be too vague to gain relevance in field research and (2) the empirical data may potentially turn out to be too ambiguous to provide a clear theoretical interpretation (Ketokivi and Mantere 2010). To mitigate these risks, the following principles for conducting theoretical and empirical research on RM maturity were adopted:

- reflect not only the core characteristics of the RM business model but also all of its reasonable extensions and bordering concepts (risk 1);
- define and illustrate the RM activities and approaches in a feasible, concrete way (risk 1);
- allow differentiation among firms to uncover possible distinctive profiles of the proposed ideal type (risk 2);
- employ a wide grading scale, which enables nuances to be detected between respondents' narrowing perceptions of their RM activities and approaches (risk 2).

The design of the RM maturity conceptualization process displayed in Fig. 3.1 acknowledges the systematic approach to literature review. In contrast to traditional narrative reviews, the systematic approach is a replicable and transparent scientific process helpful in unbiased identification of the conceptual content available in the research field, as well as in identifying emerging trends, themes and topics (Gough and Richardson 2018; Vural 2017).

In line with the first adopted research principle, in step 1 of the RM maturity conceptualization the following three groups of tactical, broadly set questions were defined:

- Are there any existing RM maturity models? What is their design? Were they empirically tested against achieving sustainable competitive advantage?
- What are the main streams of research in RM? Are they contradictory, cumulative or supplementary?
- Is there clear guidance over distinctive RM activities and approaches which lead to achieving sustainable competitive advantage?

These questions will be addressed later in this section.

In step 2, the choice of the scientific sources reflecting the contemporary state of high-quality research on RM has to be made, which is not a trivial one because the body of scientific work concerning RM is extensive. Table 3.1 shows Google Scholar results based on different syntaxes of the terms 'relationship management' and 'relationship marketing'. However, obviously they are very popular in scientific English, and therefore these raw Google Scholar results are not a dependable indicator of the real number of relevant scholastic RM contributions.

However, even browsing through the several thousands of papers in databases with more advanced search options, such as ProQuest, EBSCO and the databases of the main publishing houses, is neither feasible nor effective. On the other hand, narrowing the search criteria would contradict principle 1 of the RM maturity conceptualization and would pose the risk of ignoring a potentially valuable stream of RM-related research.

A promising alternative is to concentrate on the most recognizable scientific resources only (Czakon 2011). A good starting point in the search for these resources is the 'List of scientific journals and reviewed materials from international conferences', which is published by the Polish Ministry of Science according to article 267 paragraph 3 of the Act 'Law on Higher Education and Science' of 20 July 2018. The version dated 2 August 2019 contains 29,040 journals and conference publications from all over the world that are recognized as having a notable scientific impact. Their authority is reflected in a points system, starting with 20 points for

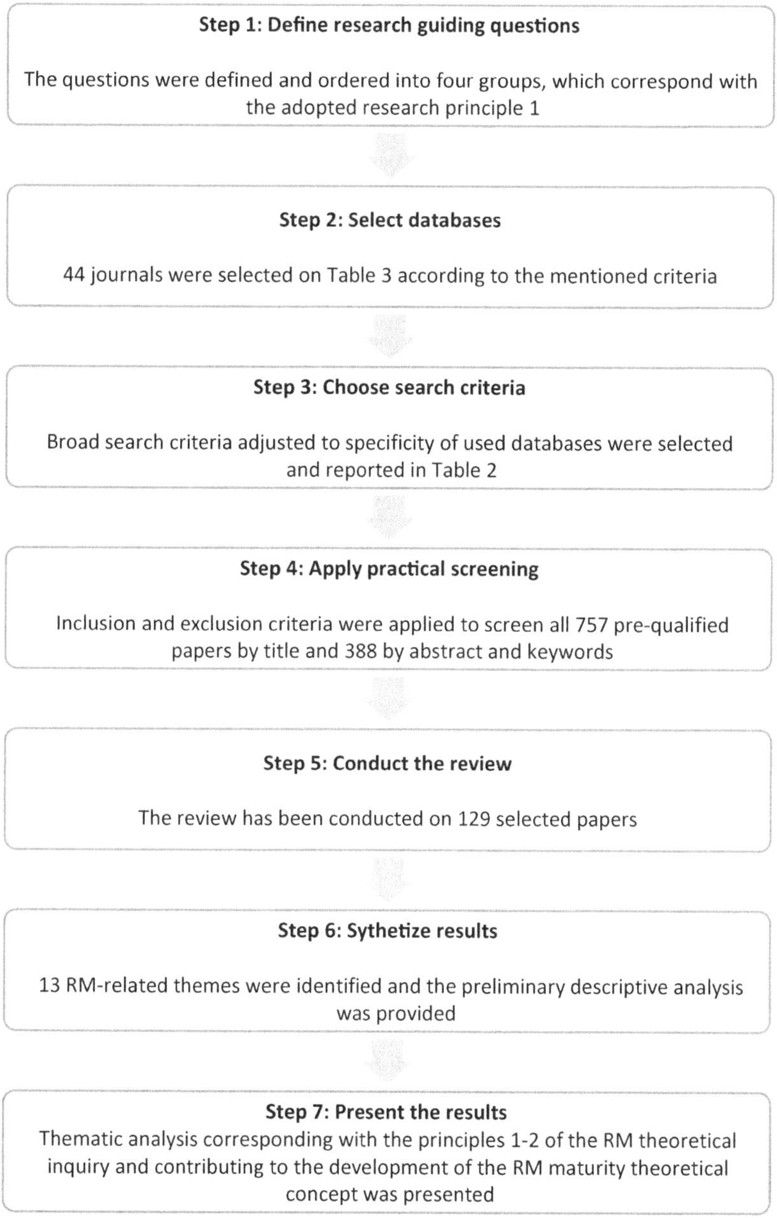

Step 1: Define research guiding questions

The questions were defined and ordered into four groups, which correspond with the adopted research principle 1

Step 2: Select databases

44 journals were selected on Table 3 according to the mentioned criteria

Step 3: Choose search criteria

Broad search criteria adjusted to specificity of used databases were selected and reported in Table 2

Step 4: Apply practical screening

Inclusion and exclusion criteria were applied to screen all 757 pre-qualified papers by title and 388 by abstract and keywords

Step 5: Conduct the review

The review has been conducted on 129 selected papers

Step 6: Sythetize results

13 RM-related themes were identified and the preliminary descriptive analysis was provided

Step 7: Present the results
Thematic analysis corresponding with the principles 1-2 of the RM theoretical inquiry and contributing to the development of the RM maturity theoretical concept was presented

Fig. 3.1 Design of RM maturity conceptualization. (Source: Adapted from Fink (2010))

Table 3.1 Google Scholar search results on RM

Search terms	Total number of scientific contributions without time restrictions	+ 'competitive advantage'	+ 'business performance'
'relationship management'	622,000	69,300	31,000
'relationship marketing'	235,000	44,300	14,900
Search terms	Total number of scientific contributions 2010 – 2020	+ 'competitive advantage'	+ 'business performance'
'relationship management'	162,000	25,400	16,900
'relationship marketing'	63,500	17,900	11,100

Source: Own enquiry carried out on 18th February 2020; results approximated by search engine

publications with noticeable but still relatively limited impact only and rising within the levels of 40, 70, 100 and 140 points to 200 points for highly prestigious periodicals such as *Nature* and the *Strategic Management Journal*. The list does not include books; however, their content is likely to repeat and summarize the ideas addressed and discussed earlier by their authors in journal publications.

In order to extract the most qualitative, factual RM-related journals, the following search criteria were applied (the number of journals cumulatively meeting the quoted criteria is given in parentheses):

- journals which are reported to be situated in the realm of management and quality science discipline (3532);
- journals which were granted at least 70 points and which contain one of the following terms in their title: 'management', 'marketing' or 'business' (315);
- journals devoted to strategic management or broadly positioned (e.g. B2B/B2C markets or service markets (44)).

Excluded from the final group were those journals having a specific focus on one industry (e.g. *Journal of Hospitality Industry*), management/marketing function (e.g. *Journal of Interactive Marketing*) or region (e.g. *Australasian Journal of Management*). It was assumed that specific insights published by these focused journals would diffuse to the mainstream management, marketing and business journals if they reached a certain level of relevance and acceptance. Then, elaborated and confronted with the experiences from multiple research areas, they could potentially qualify to build the RM maturity model. In addition, because it is a periodical exclusively devoted to RM, the *Journal of Relationship Marketing* (rated with 20 points) was included in the final group.

In step 3, the mix of search criteria (given in Table 3.2) was applied across scientific databases which host the content of selected journals. As papers in management are usually extensive publications, which may easily contain numerous terms used occasionally or referring to their peripheral meaning, to direct attention to the key RM research, the query was generally limited to the following search fields: title, abstract and keywords (Czakon et al. 2019). Only where this was not technically possible were wider criteria applied. In addition, the query was limited to papers from 2010 and after because, as time goes by, some concepts may turn out to be fads or passing fashions (Abrahamson 1991) and as such they should not be qualified for contemporary analysis. On the other hand, there are also numerous seminal papers on RM that are dated earlier than 2010. They build the core identity of RM research, including its links to the RBV,

Table 3.2 Search criteria applied to scientific databases

Publishing house	Main query 'relationship management' OR 'relationship marketing'	Anywhere	Title	Abstract	Keywords	Other than main text	Date: 2010 and newer
Academy of Management	•			•	•		•
Cambridge University	•	•	•			•	
Cracow University of Economics	•	•	•				
Elsevier	•			•	•		•
Emerald (via ProQuest)	•					•	•
Harvard Business School Publishing	•		•				•
Informs (Management Science)	•			•	•		
Informs (via ProQuest)	•					•	•
Sage (Marketing Theory via Ebsco)	•			•	•		•
Sage (via Proquest)	•					•	•
Springer	•					•	
Taylor Francis	•			•	•		•
Wiley & Sons	•		•				•

dynamic capabilities and the R-A theory. These were, however, explicitly addressed in Chap. 2. More operationalized concepts that are embedded in this theoretical backbone only emerged after the year 2000 (Gummesson 2017a) and were only developed and tested even later (e.g. the potential and risk of implementing CRM technology; Payne and Frow 2013).

Table 3.3 includes the list of 44 journals qualified for detailed RM maturity conceptualization. Columns 'A', 'B' and 'C' refer to the numbers of papers verified in subsequent review stages. They include step 4—practical screening by title (A), abstract and keywords (B)—and step 5—full paper

Table 3.3 List of journals and number of referred articles

Journal	Publishing house	Points	A	B	C
Academy of Management Annals	Academy of Management	200	0	0	0
Academy of Management Discoveries	Academy of Management	100	0	0	0
Academy of Management Journal	Academy of Management	200	1	0	0
Academy of Management Perspectives	Academy of Management	140	0	0	0
Academy of Management Review	Academy of Management	200	0	0	0
Business Economics	Springer	100	4	0	0
Business Horizons	Elsevier	100	16	11	8
Entrepreneurial Business and Economics Review	Cracow University of Economics	70	4	1	1
Harvard Business Review	Harvard Business School Publishing	70	0	0	0
Industrial Marketing Management	Elsevier	140	112	91	38
International Business Review	Elsevier	100	6	5	1
International Journal of Management	Wiley & Sons	200	23	11	2
International Journal of Research in Marketing	Elsevier	100	7	1	1
International Marketing Review	Emerald	100	0	0	0
Journal of Business and Industrial Marketing	Emerald	70	64	26	5
Journal of Business Economics and Management	Taylor & Francis	70	0	0	0
Journal of Business Research	Elsevier	140	63	37	20
Journal of Consumer Marketing	Emerald	70	11	9	1
Journal of Economics and Business	Elsevier	70	0	0	0
Journal of Economics and Management	Wiley & Sons	100	0	0	0

(*continued*)

Table 3.3 (continued)

Journal	Publishing house	Points	A	B	C
Journal of International Management	Elsevier	100	1	0	0
Journal of International Marketing	Sage	140	12	3	2
Journal of Management	Sage	200	0	0	0
Journal of Management and Governance	Springer	70	11	0	0
Journal of Management and Organization	Cambridge University	70	1	0	0
Journal of Marketing	Sage	200	18	12	1
Journal of Marketing Management	Taylor & Francis	70	3	2	1
Journal of Marketing Research	Sage	200	9	4	1
Journal of Marketing Theory and Practice	Taylor & Francis	70	0	0	0
Journal of Relationship Management	Taylor & Francis	20	20	17	2
Journal of Service Management	Emerald	140	23	12	2
Journal of Services Marketing	Emerald	100	61	33	13
Journal of Strategic Marketing	Taylor & Francis	70	11	6	3
Journal of the Academy of Marketing Science	Springer	140	157	62	18
Management and Organization Review	Cambridge University	70	1	0	0
Management Research Review	Emerald	70	15	6	2
Management Science	INFORMS	200	0	0	0
Marketing Letters	Springer	100	20	10	3
Marketing Science	INFORMS	100	9	6	0
Marketing Theory	Sage	100	2	2	0
Omega - International Journal of Management Science	Elsevier	140	4	2	0
Service Business	Springer	100	50	15	3
Strategic Management Journal	Wiley & Sons	200	18	4	1
Strategic Organization	Sage	100	0	0	0
Total number of papers examined:			757	388	129

review (C) (Czakon 2011; Fink 2010). Some of the journals did not publish any paper referring to the search terms in the specified period of time ('0' in column 'A'). To ensure transparency in the 'A'/'B' screening process among the remaining journals, several guiding exclusion and inclusion criteria were adopted (Vural 2017). The exclusion criteria were as follows:

- auxiliary/random use of the searched keywords: keywords were not reflected in the abstract;
- business network structure: papers devoted to an issue that lies beyond the boundaries of the envisioned RM (upper) mid-range theory;
- highly aggregated upper-range constructs: papers exploiting in a general way the impact of familiar relational constructs such as trust and commitment;
- industry- or firm-specific studies: papers with narrowed perspectives without aspirations to provide more general findings (e.g. critical CRM factors in the hospitality industry);
- national- or regional-specific studies: papers which explored the impact of national culture on their findings (e.g. the impact of guanxi on RM) or were presenting results of empirical research based on small samples of firms situated in a peripheral economy (e.g. lessons from Iranian social media businesses);
- management/marketing function-specific studies: papers which exhibited an interest in particular operational tools and techniques without aiming to examine their impact on overall company-wide RM (e.g. micro-solutions such as how to build a successful mobile application).

The inclusion criteria were as follows:

- RM-related models: papers showing how RM-related capabilities affect firm bottom line;
- RM-related activities: papers showing the impact of distinct firm activities and approaches on the quality of its relationships;
- stakeholder value: papers focusing on value created at the intersection of different firm stakeholders from the perspectives of these stakeholders and the firm.

Step 6—preliminary descriptive analysi—revealed 13 main themes which constitute the core of contemporary RM research. As many of them are interconnected, typically each reviewed paper was thoroughly addressing two or three of them, while simultaneously dealing with some others in the background. The statistical values presented in Fig. 3.2 show the topical share of voice based on the main paper narratives.

It comes as no surprise that the most popular theme in the literature is customer relationship management (CRM). These papers were usually

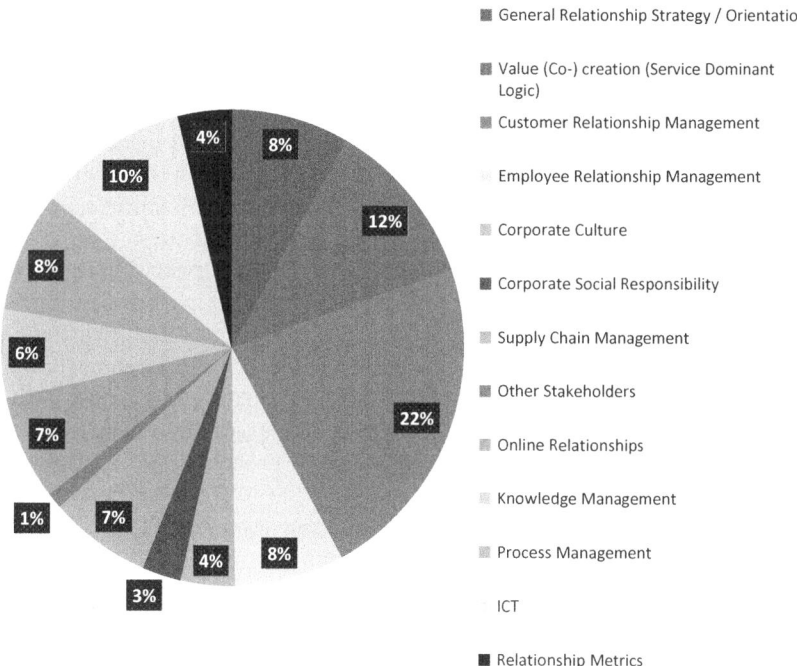

Fig. 3.2 Descriptive analysis of RM-related content

trying to arrange some processes, tools or techniques and link them with aggregated constructs—for example, distinctive customer-related capabilities. In turn, the impact of these capabilities on broadly understood business performance was examined.

The position of value co-creation as a stand-alone marketing paradigm, and Service-Dominant Logic (SDL) as its underlying theory, is notable in the reviewed literature. Numerous papers related various RM factors to the principles of SDL or to capabilities descending from the notion of customer value co-creation, in a similar manner as earlier in the case of SET-based trust and commitment. Owing to the distinctive characteristics of the service perspective, such as customer-centrism, process orientation, emphasis on dialogue and mutually beneficial cooperation, synergic effects between RM and SDL are frequently highlighted.

Employee management and corporate culture together attracted similar attention to the value co-creation/SDL theme. The corporate culture theme was presented as the invisible but decisive factor in securing employee commitment in hard-to-control areas like tacit knowledge management (KM) and empathic customer encounter. At a more operational level, the impact of employee management on successful CRM implementations was examined in the form of, for example, internal marketing and HRM techniques. A supervisor–supervisee relationship was highlighted as the most important single factor affecting employee satisfaction transferable into customer satisfaction, especially in service industries.

The ICT-related literature had a dual focus. Some papers examined the role of ICT-related capabilities in the effectiveness of other business areas, including CRM. Others emphasized the limited impact of ICT investment on company performance if not properly anchored in the organizational context. This included having clear strategic relationship orientation, demonstrated in top management priorities and appropriate project management. The latter took the form of business process optimization and implementation.

Online relationships were another significant topic, related simultaneously to a technological tool and a communication channel. Again the issue of the supportive role of technology was highlighted. However, developing engaged brand communities in social media, frequently given as the main goal of online relationship management, was positioned more as a marketing capability.

Among customers and employees, the third most important group of stakeholders emerging from the examined literature was suppliers. Again, as in the case of CRM and HRM, Supply Chain Management (SCM) was presented as a dynamic capability aggregate and as a natural area for implementing value co-creation strategies. However, a distinctive feature of the SCM-related papers was the significant impact of supplier relationships on innovativeness.

The notion of innovativeness was also visible in the KM-focused papers. However, this was not as breakthrough discoveries but rather as the capability to integrate knowledge—especially customer knowledge—into interactive and analytical processes. As a specific solution to this issue, some papers evaluated the role of various relational metrics in assessing and predicting future customer value. Finally, Corporate Social Responsibility and the relationships with other stakeholders were discussed in a few of the papers.

Following the classic systematic approach to literature review, the descriptive literature analysis usually captures the statistical distribution of papers across time, featured industries, applied research methods and geographical regions covered. However, given the goal of this inquiry (defining the preliminary RM maturity model), the appropriateness of such an additional analysis is limited. What *does* impact the way the detailed thematic review will be conducted is providing the answers to the tactical research questions of this literature review (step 1).

Although varied theoretical or empirically verified models were featured, there were no RM maturity models per se proposed in any of the reviewed papers. The presented frameworks were usually focused on customers or CRM only (by adding the technological dimension to, e.g., a customer-centricity approach) and often continued to apply wide-ranging research constructs such as trust and commitment as organizational ends of RM activities. In consequence they only indirectly examined the impact of the presented models on sustainable competitive advantage by defining additional non-monetary performance constructs, for example relational value. Moreover, most of them operationalized the applied constructs by forming research tools based on general questions prone to ambiguous interpretations and/or focused on a narrow aspect of RM tactics.

Nonetheless, the richness of the identified, predominately specific low-range approaches based on the dynamic capabilities framework proves the general importance and omnipresence of relationships. This polyphony, although not orchestrated, produced a non-contradictory but supplementary, sometimes cumulative body of research, which is a fairly good starting point for the development of the preliminary RM maturity model. However, two shortfalls make it necessary to adopt the 'snowballing approach' to literature review—that is, to further broaden the thematic literature review (step 7) by locating and exploring some additional scientific sources not appearing in the selected database (Zhang and Banerji 2017). First is the aforementioned scarcity of complex models integrating varied RM-related dimensions/capabilities, which could be potentially published in thus far unidentified sources. Second is the scant evidence on the direct impact of a concrete set of RM activities and approaches on sustainable competitive advantage, which continues to be disguised by various mediating RM constructs on the one hand and by indirect business performance metrics (e.g. customer satisfaction or customer loyalty) on the other.

To facilitate the application of the 'snowballing' procedure in the thematic literature review (step 7), which is offered in the remaining two sections of this chapter, bibliometric software was applied. Figure 3.3

Fig. 3.3 Co-citation density by authors in the reviewed literature. (Source: VOSviewer, version 1.6.14)

shows the co-citation density analysis carried out with VOSviewer, which is a shareware tool for constructing and visualizing bibliometric networks provided by the Centre for Science and Technology Studies at Leiden University, Holland. The relatedness of items shown is based on the number of times they are cited together, thus indicating the importance of the particular author in the scientific field. The relative importance of an author is indicated by the colour (the brighter the better) and by the size of the spot (the bigger the better) behind the name. The minimum number of citations was set at 20.

Figure 3.4 shows a network visualization of the bibliometric coupling analysis focused on paper citations. The relatedness of items is determined by the number of references they share. Both graphs are interactive (the static figures do not fully illustrate overlapping items) and help researchers to guide their attention in the most promising directions. In this thematic

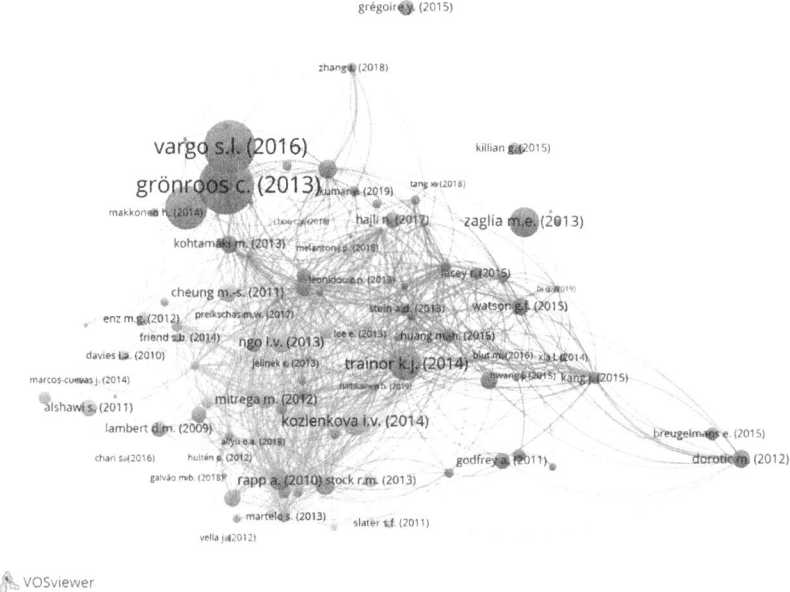

Fig. 3.4 Most cited papers in the reviewed literature. (Source: VOSviewer, version 1.6.14)

literature review (step 7), the 'snowballing' procedure will be applied within the selected group of academic sources cited in the most influential papers and within the extended body of papers authored by the most influential scholars.

3.2 The Strategic Dimension of RM Maturity

The 13 themes identified in the body of RM literature constitute a diversified constellation of theories and empirical material. To reach more clarity and to effectively facilitate the narration of the thematic literature review, they will not be analysed separately. Instead a constructive synthesis is proposed based on the insights from the process-oriented CRM literature, as most, if not all, of these themes can be brought down to a single process or a set of interrelated processes.

In this literature usually three- or four-dimension analytical frameworks are proposed. For example, G. Day insists CRM is predicated on addressing the following areas: strategy, technology, people and processes (2003).

I. Chen and K. Popovich (2003) describe CRM as an integrated approach to people, processes and technology orchestrated by a "cross-functional, customer-driven, technology-integrated business process management strategy" (2003, p. 673). V. Kumar and W. Reinartz differentiate between four CRM dimensions: organizational alignment, customer management, technology and CRM strategy implementation (2006). D. Lambert, by contrast, highlights the interfaces between the strategic and operational CRM processes and the remaining important corporate processes, such as supplier relationship management, demand management or revenue management (2008; 2010). Arguably the most comprehensive model integrating a strategic approach to RM and CRM, found thanks to the 'snowballing' extension of the reviewed literature, is A. Payne and P. Frow's 'CRM strategy framework' (2005; 2013) depicted in Fig. 3.5. In this model the central focus is placed on the strategic dimension that governs the so-called enabling processes (value co-creation, multichannel customer dialogue and IT-powered information management), whose effectiveness is measured within the performance assessment process.

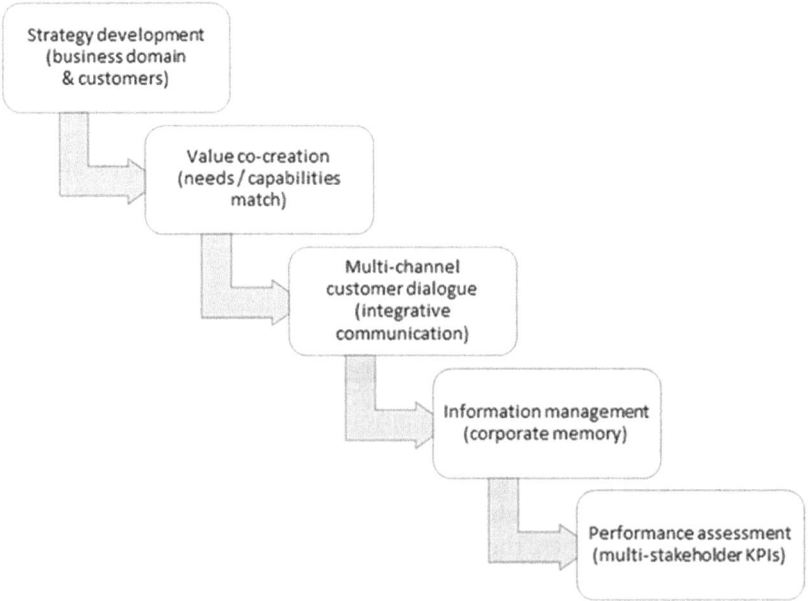

Fig. 3.5 CRM strategy framework. (Source: Adapted from Payne and Frow (2005, p. 171))

Given the diversity of proposed analytical frameworks and approaches, the choice of a particular one will always leave some room for controversy. Nonetheless, it seems that a framework that describes the RM maturity should take a slightly more strategic view than the models focused on CRM only, not least because of the necessity to take a whole-company perspective and to facilitate a multi-stakeholder approach. Therefore, the envisioned preliminary RM maturity model will consist of the following dimensions (the indicative placement of the alternative labels found in the evoked conceptualizations is given in parentheses):

- strategic (including people, organizational alignment, strategic processes and value co-creation),
- processual (including customer management, operational processes and multichannel customer dialogue),
- technical (ICT).

As the division between the strategic and processual dimensions is somewhat blurred, some of the themes are simultaneously discussed in these two dimensions, which reflects the dual focus of the literature.

More than one fifth of the analysed papers deal with CRM. However, it is value co-creation and its theoretical foundations (Service-Dominant Logic—SDL) that build the biggest consistent group of RM-related concepts. Therefore, the thematic review of the strategic dimension starts with the SDL and SDL-oriented RM literature, with special focus on the impact of SDL on the overall strategy and the balance between IRM and ERM. In a similar corporate strategy-oriented vein, the issues concerning stakeholder portfolio management will be presented, with emphasis placed on customers and employees as the most important classes of stakeholders. In the case of the latter, the discussion is highly concentrated on the prerequisites of an effective, RM-supportive corporate culture. The processual dimension of the preliminary RM maturity model exemplifies concrete activities and approaches resulting from an RM strategy. The technical dimension includes a general discussion on IT governance, project management and specific instances of ICT systems, with a dominant focus on CRM systems. The dimensions and themes represented in the preliminary RM maturity model are listed in Table 3.4.

The basic foundation of SDL laid out by S. Vargo and R. Lusch in their award-winning article (2004) is that the success of a company is determined by the extent to which it can offer value propositions to its

Table 3.4 Overview of the thematic literature review

Dimension	Theme	Section	Characteristic
Strategic	Value co-creation/SDL	3.2	• SDL view on the goals of a firm • value co-creation in a broad SDL-sense and in an RM-sense • interplay between SDL, RM, RBV and dynamic capabilities
Strategic	KM*	3.2	• importance of relational learning
Strategic	General relationship strategy / orientation	3.2	• complexities in simultaneously addressing different stakeholder interests • alignment of business strategy and ethics
Strategic	CSR	3.2	• external/internal focus of CSR initiatives
Strategic	CRM*, SCM & other stakeholders	3.2	• customer portfolio management and relationship economics • reciprocity to preferential treatment • customer quality definition
Strategic	Corporate culture & employee management*	3.2	• cognitive culture types • emotional culture types • culture values matching relational approach • employee management policies resulting from RM-supportive culture
Processual	Employee management*	3.3	• employee motivation • supervisor–supervisee interactions • employee empowerment • internal market orientation
Processual	CRM*	3.3	• relational communication & relational selling
Processual	Process management & KM*	3.3	• lead management • loyalty management • process enrichment by customer knowledge • complaint management
Processual	Relationship metrics	3.3	• RFM, CLV, NPS • importance of measuring the health of relationships
Processual	Online relationships	3.3	• principles of relational social media dialogue
ICT	ICT	3.3	• potential benefits • areas of application (CRM, HRM, KM) • project management

Themes and their characteristics given in order of appearance. '*'-marked themes are related both to strategy and processual instances customers. Moreover, it is not the company that creates value but the customers (beneficiaries) themselves. The company may get an opportunity to engage in the customer's value creation process as a co-creator, and to collaborate in resource integration that both parties bring as they interact, but always it is only the customer who is the value creator (Vargo and Lusch 2008). The main SDL idea is brilliant and simple: companies should focus on the customer, not on themselves, because the more individual the result of the co-creation process, the more favourable the assessment of value by the customers and their intentions to spend more with the firm (Ngo and O'Cass 2013). Even hardline manufacturers can leave the area of tangible product delivery and concentrate on the process of value co-creation, as service is the basis of any exchange in all industries. It is also a proven way to become meaningful to customers and differentiate the value proposition (Grönroos 2016; Vargo and Lusch 2004).

However, here is the problem. The co-creation process occurs by definition when a company processes the body, mind or possessions of the customer cooperatively (Wirtz and Lovelock 2016). It can take the form of value co-ideation, co-design, co-production, co-test or co-launch (Ramani and Kumar 2008; Russo-Spena and Mele 2012). But what if, for example, an individual fast-moving consumer goods (FMCG) customer or a business customer ordering stationery is not willing to actively collaborate because the area where the company offers its competences is beyond their core interest, or the perceived additional value this process could produce does not correspond to the costs (e.g. time devotion)? After the definition of S. Vargo and R. Lusch, the 'service economy' is embodied in the processes of using resources of partners for their benefit (2008, p. 7). Therefore, value co-creation is "simply a positive statement that, at least in human systems, which are characterized by specialization and thus interdependency, value is always co-created" (2016, pp. 8–9). In other words, if broadly defined, value can be co-created even without an active company–customer interaction, because the resources embedded in the offer can be autonomously integrated by the customer.

RM does not go that far. Although, given the available technology, customers do not necessarily need human-to-human contacts to interact with the company (e.g. they can use self-service at the website), the company should still analyse automated contacts and (if necessary) instantly react by proactively sparking dialogue. In consequence, no relational-based value co-creation can take place unless interactions between the company and the customer or other stakeholders occur (Gummesson 2017a). By contrast, when an individual customer applies moisturizing

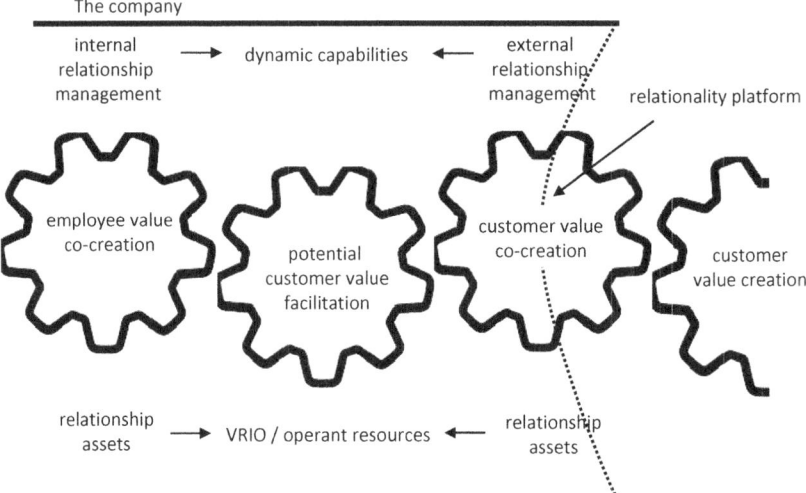

Fig. 3.6 The interplay between RM and SDL

cream to their face or the employees of a business client use a flipchart in a meeting, they do integrate these resources and they do generate some services upon them (value co-creation in a broadly defined SDL sense), but in a way that leaves the company involved in a dormant position (no value co-creation in an RM sense).

In general, however, the relational and value co-creation paradigms overlap (Preikschas et al. 2017). For instance, key concepts in SDL (value co-creation, collaboration, resource integration, interactivity and value creation networks) are relational (FitzPatrick et al. 2015). Service is also relational, and at the same time relationships are based on service (Grönroos 2017). Therefore, RM and SDL are believed to have the potential to be integrated into a single and relatively coherent conceptual structure (Gummesson and Mele 2010). Although it is not the intention of this book to provide such a framework, in Fig. 3.6 a brief overview of the interplay between RM and SDL embedded in the resource-based and dynamic capabilities theories is proposed. The RBV acts here as a general theory for value creation from the perspective of a company, stating that VRIO resources will give a company a sustainable competitive advantage in a particular area. In SDL, VRIO resources are labelled 'operant resources' and draw on the notion that intangibles, especially knowledge, are the fundamental source of 'strategic benefit' (as Vargo and Lusch now call competitive advantage; 2016). This can be monetized thanks to dynamic capabilities, which are essentially relational capabilities (e.g. network competence, alliance competence, internal market orientation, customer response capability, interaction orientation and relationship management capability; Jayachandran et al. 2004; Madhavaram et al. 2014).

To make this happen, all corporate functions must learn to collaborate with each other and across the customer and supplier organizations (Enz and Lambert 2012). In this context, the key managerial concern should be the development of a "relationality platform" (Grönroos 2016) or a "co-creation framework" (Sheth 2017). The RM-mature company should therefore coordinate multiple human and machine-assisted physical, mental or virtual communication channels to offer meaningful interactions that provide emotional engagement and positive surprise and—which is so essential to the co-creation process—integrate customer knowledge (Kaski et al. 2018; Payne et al. 2009). The latter comes in the form of relational learning (information sharing, joint sense-making and knowledge integration) and is an inalienable part of any customer-facing process (Cheung et al. 2011; Martelo et al. 2013).

Such a persistent dynamism also requires continuous coordination of internal and external relationship management processes (IRM and ERM). IRM is directed at co-creating value with employees, thereby enhancing VRIO/operant resources. ERM is directed at co-creating value with customers (external beneficiaries) and ultimately reflects the dynamic capabilities of a company.

The interplay between IRM and ERM is as follows. To create an attractive value proposition for external customers, the value facilitation process that takes place inside the company has to be built around and within the VRIO/operant resources. These resources can be used in the value facilitation process, but do not have to be. They are dormant in the employees, unless they become activated by proper HRM techniques (acknowledging individual skills, preferences and ambitions of employees) and an overall partnership between the workforce and the management team (effective corporate culture). The activation of VRIO/operant resources requires that the employees become internal customers of management and that they are invited to participate in an internal value facilitation process as co-creators and important co-beneficiaries (Grace and Lo Iacono 2015). Only by perceiving their work as a relationship in which they have a stake will employees directly and indirectly support relational selling strategies and techniques and believe they will enjoy greater personal benefits the more they try (Arli et al. 2018). By contrast, a purely transactional approach to work (time vs. pay) incentivizes employees to mediocrity, because the less effort they put into their work, the better outcome they get out of this exchange (Grandey 2003). Therefore, the odds for successful ERM are linked to successful IRM (Chomiak-Orsa 2016), because employees are the ones who, by creatively participating in the utility value facilitation process and by empathetically helping customers in the application of the resources their company provides, make such a relationship truly beneficial (Delpechitre et al. 2018). Hence, one can reframe RM maturity and value co-creation and converge them into a unified process and system for enhancing customer value, firm relational assets, competitive advantage and societal well-being (Lusch et al. 2010).

To sum up, in the light of SDL, a practical implementation of the RM business model is based on making interactions more meaningful to customers and other stakeholders. Therefore, the goal of an RM-mature firm is to merge as much as possible of what were previously solely internal corporate processes (proactively inviting customers to take a role in a corporate process) and individual customer processes (being open to an invitation to take a role in a customer process). This can be achieved by constantly improving the processes and providing resources that help customers to create value in their individual processes (value-in-use; Macdonald et al. 2011). Examples include designing a new product or service, customizing the functional requirements of existing products, changing procedures in logistics or in communication, and also simply making sure customers feel asked/welcomed to co-participate in something that has relevance (Minkiewicz et al. 2016; Svendsen 2011). In consequence, the odds for a successful co-creation are higher the more touch points the company offers its customers and other stakeholders that enable more vivid interaction at different stages of value creation (Grönroos 2011a).

Nonetheless, an increased corporate commitment to co-creation has its limits. The customers have to be able to spend more on individually tailored offers, and the trade-off between the additional co-created value and generated costs should provide a strong argument to support such a decision. This means that the business model of an RM-mature firm that supports value co-creation processes has to be realistic and selective, because not every relationship is able to generate enough value for both sides (Deszczyński 2016a).

The competitive advantage of a company is influenced by the quality of its relationships with its employees and customers, as well as with an array of other stakeholders, including owners/shareholders, competitors, suppliers, distributors and influential institutions (Fonfara 2014). In his concept of 'total relationship marketing', E. Gummesson identifies 30 forms of RM, including the management of nano-relationships (e.g. between marketing and operations management), special relationships (e.g. green relationships and CSR, e-relationships, relationship to a customer's customer, relationship to a dissatisfied customer) and mega-relationships (e.g. personal and social networks; 2017b). The concept of 'total relationship marketing' pinpoints a narrow myopic vantage point of traditional transactional marketing, which extracts the company from its natural environment and struggles to concentrate on the direct short-term market variables only (Gummesson 2012). A mature RM company should, by contrast, clearly reinforce its existential basis, or its RM programme will never develop beyond a technicality (Gummesson 1999). Therefore, in general, RM maturity should be demonstrated in the way business leaders address the moral complexities of RM resulting from diverse stakeholder claims (Lindgreen and Swaen 2010; Jakubów 2016) and balance investments to avoid value asymmetry, which would cause such relationships to deteriorate (Luu et al. 2018; Morgan and Hunt 1994). This is clearly a strategic endeavour, which should be reflected both in declarations of intent and in ongoing business practice.

In their 'CRM strategy framework' A. Payne and P. Frow (2005; 2013) thoroughly discuss the key processes, which they merge into a coherent practice-oriented inductive CRM model. They pay much attention to the strategic importance of RM by incorporating its core characteristics and objectives into the global strategy development process. Such an alignment involves inspiring the mission and vision with the relationship spirit, which goes far beyond making money and cannot be disposed to short-changing (Collins and Porras 2002). In addition, some authors emphasize the necessity to strategically promote business ethics and to position the company in a broader network of relationships including its social partners (Eveland et al. 2018; Hwang and Kandampully 2015; Sheth 2017). This would differentiate an RM-mature company from its transactional competitors, who tend to take the view that business ethics and market competition are contradictory forces (Baumol and Blackman 1991; Teneta-Skwiercz 2008).

All corporate social initiatives beyond legal obligations are generally labelled Corporate Social Responsibility (CSR; Schuler and Cording 2006; Wąsowska and Pawłowski 2011). Nonetheless, a company itself is a social construct, and employees are its strategic public (Grunig 2008). Hence, philanthropy—traditionally linked to CSR—is highly desired and prized (Carroll 1991), but before venturing out to solve larger societal problems, companies should first set their own house in order through practising purpose-driven internal relationship management (Sasidharan Dhanesh 2012). This could act as an instance verifying whether CSR is strategically important or is only a marketing trick (L'Etang 1994). Concerning external relationship management, even without a CSR label a company can act responsibly and attract customers by educating them, discouraging mindless consumption and attaching spiritual value to its brands, which may eventually achieve the status of moral compasses (Peppers and Rogers 2013; Sheth 2017). Such perceptions create relational value and a cognitive and affective basis for customer reciprocal gratitude (Hwang and Kandampully 2015; Lacey et al. 2015). Its behavioural manifestation is consumer preference towards the company, which translates relationship investment into tangible returns on relationship (ROR; de Ruyter et al. 2019).

Among other things, defining key groups of customers (including distribution channel partners) remains a strategically important task (Payne and Frow 2016). A crucial decision to take here is the level of detail of customer insight a company possesses and can effectively utilize, which is reflected in customer segment granularity (Payne and Frow 2005; 2013). The best way to maximize the lifetime value of desirable customer segments, A. Payne and P. Frow propose, is the shift from making, selling and servicing to listening, customizing and co-creating (2013). Therefore, one of the priorities of the top management of a mature RM company should be to specialize in preserving and enhancing its knowledge of the ways its relevant partners create value, and to show a healthy level of flexibility (e.g. customization and individualization) by providing value propositions/resources that fit into its practice constellations (Storbacka et al. 2012).

The selective approach to managing relationships with different customer groups is in line with the Key Account Management/Global Account Management literature (Chari et al. 2016; Guesalaga and Johnston 2010; Marcos-Cuevas et al. 2014; Shi and Gao 2016), Customer Portfolio Management literature (Johnson and Selnes 2004; Thakur and Workman 2016) and SCM literature (Forkmann et al. 2016; Oghazi et al. 2016). The underlying logic of such an approach is again the concept of partner gratitude. Its strategic manifestation is the adoption of preferential treatment policies and tools, which is believed to be one of the most effective ways of strengthening relationships (Huang 2015). Preferential treatment may be translated to a general priority in accessing and integrating firm resources (e.g. reducing waiting time for service) and in demonstrating some extra effort to ensure highly personalized experiences are consistently offered at all times (Ashley et al. 2011; Kumar et al. 2019). However, for an RM-mature firm, granting preferential treatment cannot remain an isolated act. On the contrary, it has to be mirrored by an active participation of engaged customers which, besides resource integration, involves partner knowledge sharing and partner learning, and conditions value co-creation and partner operant resource development (Hollebeek et al. 2019; Ngo and O'Cass 2013). In this context, engaged partners are also an important source of innovative ideas (Dyer and Singh 1998; Prior 2012) and a firm-initiated resource of their own (Alvarez-Milán et al. 2018). Nonetheless, receiving preferential treatment may not always bring positive attitudinal and behavioural consequences, if not based on transparent rules and if the overall quality offered for the wider customer base is not adequate (Xia and Kukar-Kinney 2014).

An open system of value co-creation and multi-layered relational embeddedness challenges all organizations in terms of adaptability and flexibility (Grönroos 2011b). Much of this challenge is about shifting the managerial focus from the firm's to the customers' resources and processes and developing a thorough insight into customers' definitions of quality (Grönroos 2017). As a consequence, a mature RM firm should continuously evaluate all of its processes to the extent that they contribute to customer value creation, much of this in collaboration with its key suppliers (Miocevic and Crnjak-Karanovic 2012). Simultaneously it should control for migrations in its stakeholder portfolio to adjust policies and investment in its human and organizational infrastructure (Keramati et al. 2010). As a consequence, priority must be given to the alignment of synchronized and (if necessary) reengineered processes and varied incentives, encouraging employees to show a proactive attitude towards customer interactions and engagement in delivering the co-creational customer experience (Pozza et al. 2018).

An overarching construct that spans all internal RM activities is corporate culture, which comprises four interrelated components: shared values, norms, artefacts and behaviours (Hogan and Coote 2014; Schein 1990). Exemplary cultural capabilities that have been captured empirically and proven to be effective (at least in terms of creating employee satisfaction) are, for example, collaboration, communication, flexibility and interaction (Conrad et al. 1997; Eisenhardt and Martin 2000; Sriramesh et al. 1996). By contrast, according to customer value-based theory of culture, companies that organize themselves to support customer value delivery processes achieve superior business performance (Slater 1997). However, corporate culture is a source of competitive advantage only when it is deeply internalized and socialized and when it enables the effective execution of the chosen business strategy (Barney 1986; Kim Jean Lee and Yu 2004). In their established model of competing values, R. Quinn and J. Rohrbaugh conceptualized four cognitive culture types characterized by their dominating focus (internal vs. external), organizational structure (flexibility vs. stability), and organizational means and ends (1983). Out of these four, the so-called Human Relations Model, which is widely known as the 'Clan' culture type, is probably the best match for the RM strategy (Slater et al. 2011). Its underlying values—flexibility and internal focus on the well-being and development of employees—create a sense of family belonging and foster good teamwork and employee empowerment (Cameron and Quinn 2011; Denison and Mishra 1995). This is of the highest importance in any internal arrangement where the 'essence' of the firm displaces market-like incentives (Teece et al. 1997). This is exactly the case if decision making is uncertain, long-range planning is difficult and, as seems to be a hallmark of RM and SDL, the degree of work complexity and required outside-the-box thinking makes it infeasible to scrupulously instruct employees and assess their performance (Cameron and Quinn 2011; Yu and Wu 2009).

A complementary approach to cognitive corporate culture research is emotional culture studies. Emotional culture is defined as "shared affective values, norms, artifacts and assumptions that govern which emotions people have and express at work and which ones they are better off suppressing" (Barsade and O'Neill 2016, p. 4). There exists some empirical evidence that by awakening such emotional states as joy, happiness, excitement, and companionate love and warmth, an organization contributes to its employees' psychological need for autonomy, mutual respect, care, competence and relatedness (Ryan and Deci 2017). According to human self-determination theory, this produces trust, satisfaction, mutual control and employee commitment towards such an organization (Barsade and O'Neill 2016; Men and Robinson 2018; Scherer 1997). By contrast, employees in dispirited organizations with a demoting emotional culture of sadness or a tense and anxious culture of fear are less likely to satisfy their psychological needs at work (Creed 2003; Diefendorf et al. 2008; Scherer 1997). In consequence it is expected that most of them will not develop a quality relationship with either the company or its external partners (Barsade and O'Neill 2016).

Corporate culture is, by definition, not a stable phenomenon. Therefore, all cultures incorporate some of the modelled features in different proportions over time. In general, however, an RM-supportive culture ought to serve a purposeful strategy and should be passionate about achieving meaningful objectives (J. Collins and J. Porras, based on their longitudinal observation of corporate high achievers, coined the expression 'Big Hairy Audacious Goals'; 2002). Further on, it should manifest itself in a strong internalization of a long-term customer orientation aligned with less formalized, flexible organizational structure easily facilitating customer knowledge sharing, employee empowerment and behaviour-based evaluation, and work-group socialization (Ling-Yee 2011; Hartline et al. 2000). Finally, it ought to remain adaptable and entrepreneurial (Bratnicki and Brzeziński 2019; Kotter and Heskett 2011). This means it should leave room for experiments allowing the sensing, testing and capture of unanticipated fleeting macro- and micro-market opportunities (Sull and Eisenhardt 2015), so that the organization remains change-friendly and resilient (Kotter and Heskett 2011; Prahalad and Hamel 1994). Figure 3.7 presents a brief summary of the components of the strategic dimension of the RM maturity model integrated with the SDL.

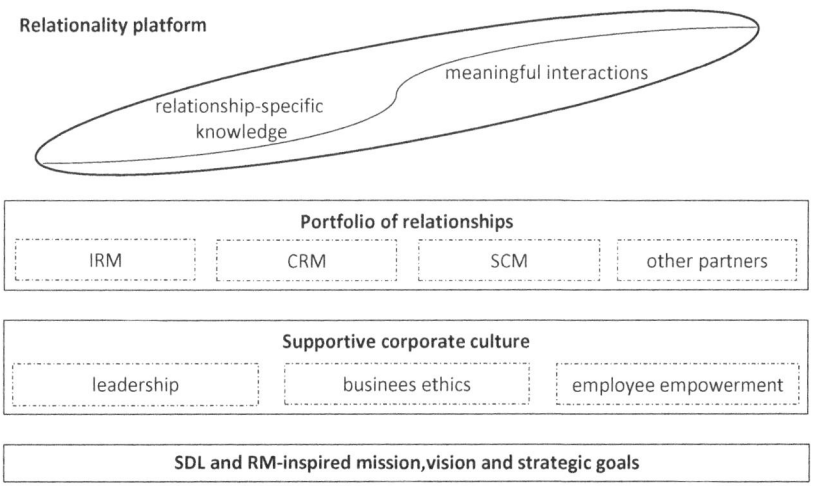

Fig. 3.7 Strategic dimension in preliminary RM maturity model

3.3 THE PROCESSUAL AND ICT DIMENSIONS OF RM MATURITY

The business processes dimension of the RM maturity model mirrors and expands the themes introduced in the previous section. Especially regarding customer-facing processes, the RM literature comes with a variety of ideas and concepts (Cheng and Yang 2013). However, this section starts with employee-focused processes because the alignment between theses two is crucial for successfully implementing the RM business model (Aliyu and Nyadzayo 2018; Pozza et al. 2018).

Sharing the same domain as corporate culture, HRM is a critical process that enhances the individual and collective capabilities of employees (Orr et al. 2011). Process theories of motivation emphasize that apart from extrinsic motivation (e.g. remuneration), there exists also intrinsic motivation derived from the nature of the organization, its management and its culture (do Nascimento et al. 2018). Hence, HRM is affected by corporate culture and at the same time creates this culture as well. As the core element of IRM, HRM directly affects the quality of company–employee relationships (Ryan and Deci 2000), which is an aggregate composed of individual relationships within an organization. Among them, the relationship with the direct supervisor seems to be the most important. Therefore, RM implies lifting the command-and-control management style and requires balancing powers (Herington et al. 2009) as interdependence is crucial to the longevity of any social exchange relationship (Blau 1986; Lambe et al. 2001). The shift from a traditional 'master and slave' management to a 'partnership in a relationship' creates demand for true leaders at all management layers. Their domain is not detailed work distribution and control, but fostering collaboration, strategic planning, leadership and innovation (Hawkins and Little 2011). To better address the needs of their teams, 'transformational leaders' (as they are sometimes called) share power and communicate in an interactive, caring, visionary, passionate and empowering way (Men 2014).

Employee empowerment is an important HRM capability which to a large extent conditions customer value co-creation (Zhang et al. 2018). As these interactions are dialogical, only employees who can act as equal partners of customers and other stakeholders add to a positive encounter (Grönroos 2011b). A typical situation when this is not the case would be a conversation with a customer contact centre employee who behaves as if they had swallowed the service manual and is not allowed to take any decisions. Therefore, it is somewhat impractical to propose a detailed catalogue of isolated high-performing work practices. Autonomy or mutual respect will be differently demonstrated on the manufacturing line, in telemarketing teams, among stock exchange traders, in a police squad, in a philharmonic orchestra or in a monastery. However, there must exist a complementarity among different HRM activities which is effective in a given organizational context (Ichniowski et al. 1997; Colombo et al. 2007).

What can be expected to be important regardless of the organization's specificity is to ensure all team members have a positive perception of their work and their place in the team. In turn, this makes them develop so-called positive psychological contracts with the company, which generally translates to showing reciprocity adequate to formal and informal stimuli received from the company and its representatives (Mangold and Miles 2007). An RM-mature firm will therefore make sure that its HRM policies and activities contribute to a genuine orientation to the internal market (Gounaris 2006). This means that before developing the relationality platform for the external stakeholders, the company has to create conditions for developing an internal one (Grönroos 2016). Such a company makes their employees feel treated fairly, by providing them with satisfactory and time-accurate information on the workflow they are engaged in, by applying transparent work assessment and remuneration criteria, by communicating openly and encouraging open dialogue in the teams, and by being open to innovative ideas (Giannakis et al. 2015; Giannakis et al. 2015; Madhavaram et al. 2014).

The variety of customer-facing processes is wide. However, they all come under the umbrella of the relationship communication process (Payne and Frow 2005), which aims to maximize the value of the relationship during its whole lifetime (initiation, maintenance and termination; Reinartz et al. 2004). As a logical consequence of the RM business model, relational communication is not entirely focused on selling but rather on customer consulting, and is not concentrated on transmitting information but rather on evoking a meaningful dialogue (Balaji et al. 2016; Wagner and Benoit 2015). The reason for this and simultaneously the cornerstone of any successful RM business case is that an RM-mature company should not strive to merely satisfy the customers, but to delight them. Given the range of alternative choices, only completely satisfied customers have a strong reason to stay loyal, as only then is the chance of finding an equivalent offering scarce and the risk of losing a good supplier/vendor high (Jones and Sasser 1995). Setting apart the other factors (e.g. total product satisfaction), delight is mainly driven by interpersonal adaptive behaviour of customer service personnel and directly precedes reciprocal gratitude (Bock et al. 2016). The way to convert relational strategy into relational communication to end up with successful relational selling is not primarily a matter of applying any particular technique (Arli et al. 2018), but is rather an IRM-sponsored product of the internalization of customer orientation (Guenzi et al. 2007), which has been described earlier in this and the previous section. Nonetheless, the literature comes with some tactical ERM processes, which ought to define an RM-mature firm.

In their 'CRM strategy framework' A. Payne and P. Frow organize the general customer communication process by communication channels, which greatly resembles the departmental division of responsibilities (2013). Alternatively, one can study distinct communication processes as they go through departments. The group of such generic interdepartmental processes includes lead management, loyalty management and complaint management (Virtanen et al. 2015; Dorotic et al. 2012; Álvarez et al. 2010).

Lead management is an acquisition process aimed at the systematic registration and timely procession of information about customer interest in company offer (Baran and Galka 2017). The essence of lead management is to provide prospective buyers (both existing and new customers) useful information and solutions in the right place and at the right time. It can take the form of the prompt response to submitted requests or a proactive proposal based on processed customer knowledge.

Companies invest substantial sums in marketing actions generating leads, but most of these are ignored by salespeople (Deszczyński 2016b; Ohiomah et al. 2019). Poor lead follow-up could be the result of competing demands on salespeople's time (Sabnis et al. 2013), but the real cause may be unsatisfactory IRM. Only smooth internal collaboration (e.g. among customer contact units, sales and marketing) enables relational selling and yields a significant improvement in the quality of the lead management process (Smith et al. 2006). In turn, a RM-mature firm should be characterized by a no-waste lead policy.

Loyalty management is commonly associated with loyalty programmes and discounts. However, firms should carefully analyse the potential costs and benefits of such programmes and apply them selectively (Dorotic et al. 2012). Moreover, as loyalty is not a simple mechanism of repeating purchases but a complex behavioural phenomenon, a proper loyalty programme should reach far beyond the surface of frequent purchase promotions and utilize customer knowledge to generate highly appealing proposals. The formula for sustainability of relationships includes customer needs definition, preferential treatment policies preceded by intelligent analytics, integrative communication plans and focus on value co-creation (Galvão et al. 2018; Ma et al. 2018). For an RM-mature firm, loyalty management is also a vital part of its acquisition strategy. Stable relationships produce referrals, which may be a source of sustainable growth (Terho and Jalkala 2017; Van Den Bulte et al. 2018). Such an organic expansion does not proceed at the expense of customer service quality, as the company has time to adjust its infrastructure to increased demand.

A good application of complaint management requires admitting if the company failed to deliver the expected quality and analysing why it happened, learning what the customers expect, providing compensation guidelines and allowing frontline personnel to award an individual redress (if needed; Homburg et al. 2010). The goal is to make customers perceive justice by promptly providing decent solutions to reported problems (Cambra-Fierro et al. 2016). Obviously these problems fall into some foreseeable categories; however, as the individual circumstances may differ, it is not possible to fully automate the process. Thus again, trained, motivated and engaged employees are an indispensable element of positive customer encounters, which in the case of complaint management are not only about settling a problem but also paving the way for relationship recovery and its future development (Álvarez et al. 2010). In this context, for an RM-mature company complaint management is an element that conditions future repurchases and should be treated not as a cost but as a relational investment.

All customer communication processes have to be parameterized to enable their proper management, but also to reflect the discrete relationship economics in more aggregated measures such as RFM (recency – frequency – monetary value), CLV (customer lifetime value) and NPS (Net Promoter Score; de Ruyter et al. 2019; Neslin et al. 2013; Reichheld 2006; Singh and Singh 2016). As a logical consequence of RM business model adoption, these metrics should be followed in a given analytical cross-section by top management with the same attention as financial indicators. In fact, firms that analyse links between non-financial measures and value creation find themselves in a better position to improve the bottom line than those focused on financial indicators only (Mauboussin 2012). Especially an RM-mature company should be aware of the causal links between the variation and trends in length, depth (frequency of contacts including transactions) and breadth (customer wallet share) of relationships across different segments in its portfolio and financial performance (Holm et al. 2012). Measuring the health of relationships also includes following the developments in the employee portfolio (Reichheld 2001).

In addition to the traditional direct ERM processes, Social-CRM (communicating via social media) emerges in many publications as an important CRM process (Hajli et al. 2017; Sheth 2017). However, merely creating a social media presence cannot be viewed as an instance of RM maturity (Heavey et al. 2020). Truly relational Social-CRM activities refer to the way a company interacts with its customers, who are no longer passive information receivers but take the role of active broadcasters whose voices co-create the ultimate online brand–community encounter and influence company operations (Melancon and Dalakas 2018; Zhang et al. 2017). Only these marketer-generated communities, which are primarily centred on meaningful interpersonal interactions, produce social ties that make them resemble consumer-generated offline and online embedded brand communities (Bi 2019; Zaglia 2013). Therefore, going social necessitates tremendous involvement and consistency in following the dialogical principle of 'listening and responding' in order to engage customers in value creating dialogue (Deszczyński 2017; Killian and McManus 2015). Thus, the sustainability of any online brand community depends greatly on the website 'stickiness', which is the ability to stimulate commitment and continued participation in community life (Roy et al. 2014; Wirtz et al. 2013). Social media capability, especially in the B2B sector, also includes proficiency in generating and integrating customer knowledge in the multichannel dialogue process (Trainor et al. 2014). A social online dialogue certainly also has a technological context. The ICT themes will be covered in the coming paragraphs in detail. However, a summary of the themes addressed in the processual dimension of the RM maturity model is presented in Fig. 3.8.

The role of ICT in improving the effectiveness of management had been noted long before CRM systems were introduced (Schwalbe 2008). For example, IT systems are one of the factors influencing business strategy implementation in the McKinsey 7S model (Waterman et al. 1980). Furthermore, collaborative RM processes in medium and large organizations have to be powered by ICT solutions (Payne and Frow 2013). The number of customers, employees, physical and virtual locations, and distribution of interactions over time would otherwise make it virtually

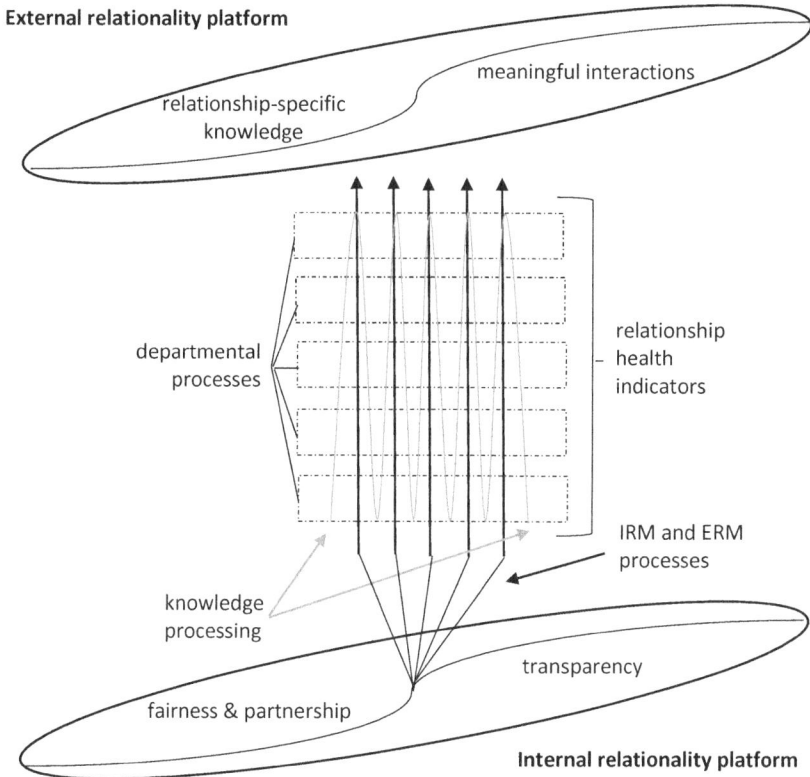

Fig. 3.8 Processual dimension in preliminary RM maturity model

impossible for such companies to offer a seamless and coherent customer service (Ahani et al. 2017; Harris et al. 2011; Jayachandran et al. 2005; Zand et al. 2018). Potential benefits of CRM systems range from time and cost reduction by automating tasks in the sales pipeline and in after-sales programmes and by streamlining administrative duties, to real-time access to insightful customer 360° profiles enabling relational selling (Gentle 2002; Melville et al. 2004; Park et al. 2010). In addition, big data analytics activities, which work on separate systems but utilize the same customer data, improve company competitive advantage. Extracting, processing and providing knowledge for probabilistic algorithms is helpful in accurate targeting of marketing campaigns and enhancing customer profiles with advanced predictive modelling tools (e.g. 'next best action'; Erevelles et al. 2016; Hallikainen et al. 2019).

In an RM-mature company, digitalizing efforts should not only be applied to ERM processes. HRM automation may improve employee hiring, selection and development processes thanks to HR portfolio management, including existing and ex-employees, applicants and trainees (Chang et al. 2013). This is of high importance as, for example, for a newcomer to get fully on board takes from three to twelve months (Stibitz 2015). ICT may also help in decentralizing some standard administrative procedures by introducing employee self-service (Marler and Fisher 2013). This makes it possible to redefine the role of the HR function and to concentrate more on strategic activities such as sparking innovative projects or facilitating KM (Storey 2007).

Converting data into information and information into knowledge facilitated by ICT also includes communication (Lindner and Wald 2011; Teo et al. 2006). Collaborative CRM system functions enable file sharing and editing, online project management, discussions on forums, chat and improvement ideas submissions, and 'know-who' search. In fact, contemporary collaborative CRM systems use Social-CRM technology customized to internal use (Deszczyński 2018). Other social media technology instances include customer social profile data enrichment and sentiment research (Choudhury and Harrigan 2014; Simkin and Dibb 2013).

However, technologies are most effective when combined with other resources and processes (Chang et al. 2010). Moreover, even technology-oriented papers insist that human and organizational resources are more important than the ICT infrastructure itself (Keramati et al. 2010; Nguyen et al. 2007; Zerbino et al. 2018). In fact, poor ICT governance might actually depress relational communication by diverting resources to a botched CRM system implementation and evoking unfavourable sentiments among affected employees (Davis and Golicic 2010). Most commonly the failure lies not exactly within the ICT system, but in the way it was implemented in the organization (Jelinek 2013).

Successful CRM project management starts with top management championship practices. This means that CRM system implementation has to be communicated not solely as an ICT project, but as an integral part of corporate strategy and has to have the ongoing interest of its executive sponsor (Saini et al. 2010). Without such a commitment, which may sometimes involve using top management's authority to resolve disputes on competing interests, CRM system implementation projects are likely to fail (Kotorov 2003). A successful project also needs a project manager who is "… a combination technologist, business expert, drill sergeant, motivational speaker, politician, and psychologist" (Davenport 2000, p. 184). Their responsibility is managing communications and interaction with departments participating in the implementation, ensuring they build their own stake in the project and transfer the knowledge needed for optimal digitalization of business processes (Steel et al. 2013). The active participation of the vanguard of future users may significantly improve the system adoption rate by delivering practice-oriented tools and intuitive functions and by showcasing good system use practices, especially in the first weeks after its launch (Deszczyński 2011; Vella and Caruana 2012). With the ICT dimension, the preliminary RM maturity model is complete as presented in Fig. 3.9.

To conclude, the literature contains diversified vantage points of what RM-oriented companies should do. These varied approaches are now merged into the preliminary RM-maturity concept (refined theory-based RM business model), which can be briefly summed up as balancing focus on the portfolio of internal and external relationships. In particular, IRM is seen as crucial in creating the underlying substance for successful ERM. Both profit from a supportive corporate culture and inspiring mission, vision and corporate strategy, which are lived on a daily basis. ERM is made through some distinct dialogical, usually interdepartmental processes. These processes are knowledge-intensive, selective and measurable. Thus, RM-related sustainable competitive advantage emerges as a function of successful internal and external interactions, which create useful, consistently reapplied knowledge. Both need to be supported by powerful ICT tools, which is only possible if the ICT governance prioritizes human and business requirements over tactical technical goals.

With the literature review completed and the preliminary RM maturity model established, the next chapter will deal fully with the first main goal of this book by empirically testing the notion of RM maturity and verifying whether RM-mature firms possess the ability to achieve sustainable competitive advantage.

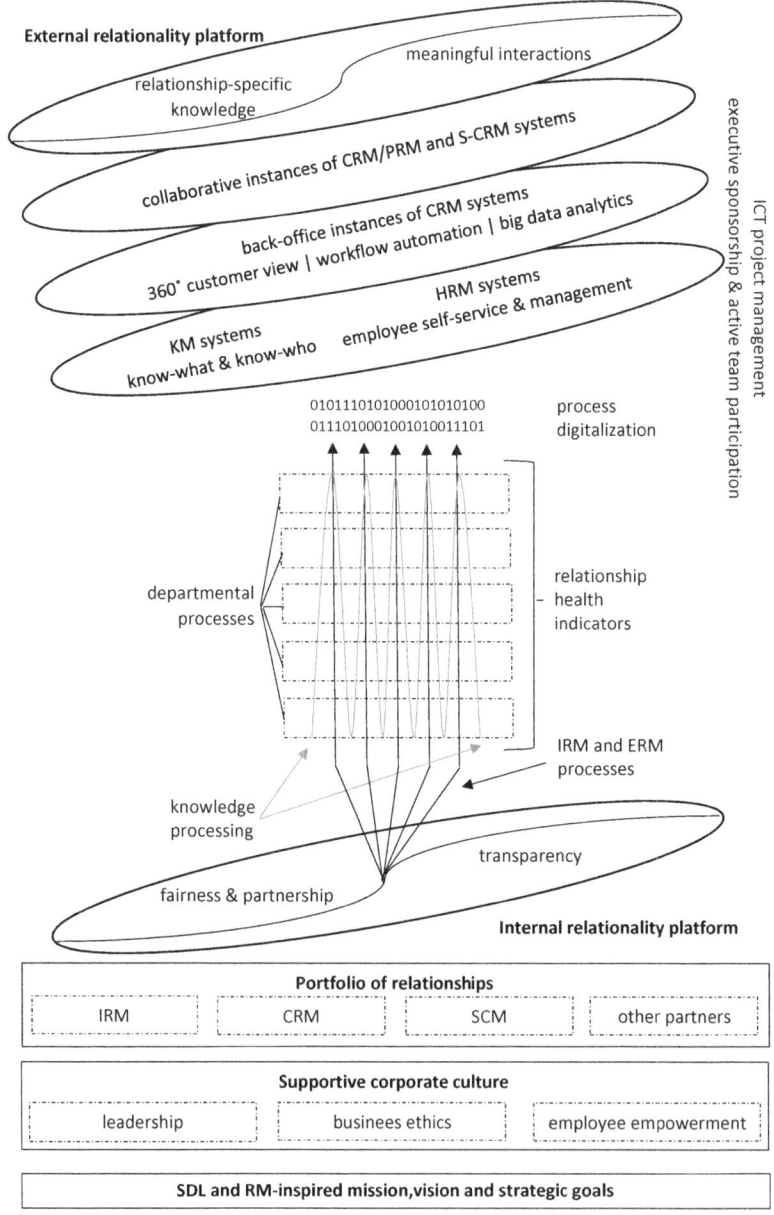

Fig. 3.9 Preliminary RM maturity model

REFERENCES

Abrahamson, Eric. 1991. Managerial Fads and Fashions: The Diffusion and Rejection of Innovations. *Academy of Management Review* 16 (3): 586–612. https://doi.org/10.5465/amr.1991.4279484.

Ahani, Ali, Nor Zairah Ab. Rahim, and Mehrbakhsh Nilashi. 2017. Forecasting Social CRM Adoption in SMEs: A Combined SEM-Neural Network Method. *Computers in Human Behavior* 75: 560–578. https://doi.org/10.1016/j.chb.2017.05.032.

Aliyu, Olayemi Abdullateef, and Munyaradzi Wellington Nyadzayo. 2018. Reducing Employee Turnover Intention: A Customer Relationship Management Perspective. *Journal of Strategic Marketing* 26 (3): 241–257. https://doi.org/10.1080/0965254X.2016.1195864.

Altuntas Vural, Ceren. 2017. Service-Dominant Logic and Supply Chain Management: A Systematic Literature Review. *Journal of Business & Industrial Marketing* 32 (8): 1109–1124. https://doi.org/10.1108/JBIM-06-2015-0121.

Álvarez, Leticia Suárez, Rodolfo Vázquez Casielles, and Ana María Díaz Martín. 2010. Analysis of the Role of Complaint Management in the Context of Relationship Marketing. *Journal of Marketing Management* 27 (1–2): 143–164. https://doi.org/10.1080/02672571003719088.

Alvarez-Milán, Agarzelim, Reto Felix, Philipp A. Rauschnabel, and Christian Hinsch. 2018. Strategic Customer Engagement Marketing: A Decision Making Framework. *Journal of Business Research* 92: 61–70. https://doi.org/10.1016/j.jbusres.2018.07.017.

Arli, Denni, Carlos Bauer, and Robert W. Palmatier. 2018. Relational Selling: Past, Present and Future. *Industrial Marketing Management* 69: 169–184. https://doi.org/10.1016/j.indmarman.2017.07.018.

Ashley, Christy, Stephanie M. Noble, Naveen Donthu, and Katherine N. Lemon. 2011. Why Customers Won't Relate: Obstacles to Relationship Marketing Engagement. *Journal of Business Research* 64 (7): 749–756. https://doi.org/10.1016/j.jbusres.2010.07.006.

Balaji, M.S., Sanjit Kumar Roy, and Khong Kok Wei. 2016. Does Relationship Communication Matter in B2C Service Relationships? *Journal of Services Marketing* 30 (2): 186–200. https://doi.org/10.1108/JSM-08-2014-0290.

Baran, Roger, and Robert Galka. 2017. *Customer Relationship Management: The Foundation of Contemporary Marketing Strategy*. 2nd ed. Abingdon: Routledge Publications.

Barney, Jay B. 1986. Organizational Culture: Can It Be a Source of Sustained Competitive Advantage? *The Academy of Management Review* 11 (3): 656–665. https://doi.org/10.2307/258317.

Barsade, Sigal G., and Olivia A. O'Neill. 2016. 'Manage Your Emotional Culture'. *Harvard Business Review*, January 1. https://hbr.org/2016/01/manage-your-emotional-culture

Baumol, William J., and Sue Anna Bafey Blackman. 1991. *Perfect Markets and Easy Virtue, Business Ethics and the Invisible Hand*. 1st ed. Oxford: Blackwell Publishing Ltd. https://www.abebooks.com/first-edition/Perfect-Markets-Easy-Virtue-Business-Ethics/22861690876/bd.

Bi, Qingqing. 2019. Cultivating Loyal Customers Through Online Customer Communities: A Psychological Contract Perspective. *Journal of Business Research* 103: 34–44. https://doi.org/10.1016/j.jbusres.2019.06.005.

Blau, Peter M. 1986. *Exchange and Power in Social Life*. 2nd ed. New Brunswick: Routledge.

Bock, Dora E., Stephanie M. Mangus, and Judith Anne Garretson Folse. 2016. The Road to Customer Loyalty Paved with Service Customization. *Journal of Business Research* 69 (10): 3923–3932. https://doi.org/10.1016/j.jbusres.2016.06.002.

Bratnicki, Mariusz, and Paweł Brzeziński. 2019. Wykorzystanie myślenia i działania do strategii przedsiębiorczej. *Przegląd Organizacji* 5: 9–15. https://doi.org/10.33141/po.2019.5.2.

Cambra-Fierro, Jesús, Iguácel Melero-Polo, and F. Javier Sese. 2016. Can Complaint-Handling Efforts Promote Customer Engagement? *Service Business* 10 (4): 847–866. https://doi.org/10.1007/s11628-015-0295-9.

Cameron, Kim S., and Robert E. Quinn. 2011. *Diagnosing and Changing Organizational Culture: Based on the Competing Values Framework*. 3rd ed. San Francisco: John Wiley & Sons.

Carroll, Archie B. 1991. The Pyramid of Corporate Social Responsibility: Toward the Moral Management of Organizational Stakeholders. *Business Horizons* 34 (4): 39–49.

Chang, Woojung, Jeong Eun Park, and Seoil Chaiy. 2010. How Does CRM Technology Transform into Organizational Performance? A Mediating Role of Marketing Capability. *Journal of Business Research* 63 (8): 849–855. https://doi.org/10.1016/j.jbusres.2009.07.003.

Chang, Song, Yaping Gong, Sean A. Way, and Liangding Jia. 2013. Flexibility-Oriented HRM Systems, Absorptive Capacity, and Market Responsiveness and Firm Innovativeness. *Journal of Management* 39 (7): 1924–1951. https://doi.org/10.1177/0149206312466145.

Chari, Simos, Anssi Tarkiainen, and Hanna Salojärvi. 2016. Alternative Pathways to Utilizing Customer Knowledge: A Fuzzy-Set Qualitative Comparative Analysis. *Journal of Business Research* 69 (11): 5494–5499. https://doi.org/10.1016/j.jbusres.2016.04.160.

Charmaz, Kathy. 2004. Grounded Theory. In *The SAGE Encyclopedia of Social Science Research Methods*, ed. Michael S. Lewis, Alan Bryman, and Tim Futing

Liao, 441–444. Thousand Oaks: SAGE Publications, Inc. https://doi.org/10.4135/9781412950589.

Chen, Injazz, and Karen Popovich. 2003. Understanding Customer Relationship Management (CRM): People, Process and Technology. *Business Process Management Journal* 9 (5): 672–688. https://doi.org/10.1108/14637150310496758.

Cheng, Lai-Yu, and Chih-Wei Yang. 2013. Conceptual Analysis and Implementation of an Integrated CRM System for Service Providers. *Service Business* 7 (2): 307–328. https://doi.org/10.1007/s11628-012-0160-z.

Cheung, Mee-Shew, Matthew B. Myers, and John T. Mentzer. 2011. The Value of Relational Learning in Global Buyer-Supplier Exchanges: A Dyadic Perspective and Test of the Pie-Sharing Premise. *Strategic Management Journal* 32 (10): 1061–1082. https://doi.org/10.1002/smj.926.

Chomiak-Orsa, I. 2016. Zarządzanie relacjami w organizacjach sieciowych. *Organizacja i Zarządzanie / Politechnika Śląska* 90: 25–44.

Choudhury, Musfiq Mannan, and Paul Harrigan. 2014. CRM to Social CRM: The Integration of New Technologies into Customer Relationship Management. *Journal of Strategic Marketing* 22 (2): 149–176.

Collins, Jim, and Jerry I. Porras. 2002. *Built to Last: Successful Habits of Visionary Companies*. New York: HarperCollins.

Colombo, Massimo G., Marco Delmastro, and Larissa Rabbiosi. 2007. "High Performance" Work Practices, Decentralization, and Profitability: Evidence from Panel Data. *Industrial and Corporate Change* 16 (6): 1037–1067.

Conrad, Craig A., Gene Brown, and Harry A. Harmon. 1997. Customer Satisfaction and Corporate Culture: A Profile Deviation Analysis of a Relationship Marketing Outcome. *Psychology & Marketing* 14 (7): 663–674. https://doi.org/10.1002/(SICI)1520-6793(199710)14:7<663::AID-MAR2>3.0.CO;2-E.

Creed, W.E.Douglas. 2003. Voice Lessons: Tempered Radicalism and the Use of Voice and Silence*. *Journal of Management Studies* 40 (6): 1503–1536. https://doi.org/10.1111/1467-6486.00389.

Czakon, Wojciech. 2011. Paradygmat Sieciowy w Naukach o Zarządzaniu. *Przegląd Organizacji* 11 (5): 3–6.

———. 2015. *Podstawy metodologii badań w naukach o zarządzaniu*. 3rd ed. Ed. Wojciech Czakon. Warszawa: Oficyna a Wolters Kluwer business. https://ruj.uj.edu.pl/xmlui/handle/item/85236

Czakon, Wojciech, Patrycja Klimas, and Arkadiusz Kawa. 2019. Krótkowzroczność strategiczna – metodyczne aspekty systematycznego przeglądu literatury. *Studia Oeconomica Posnaniensia* 7 (2): 27–37. https://doi.org/10.18559/SOEP.2019.2.2.

Davenport, Thomas H. 2000. *Mission Critical: Realizing the Promise of Enterprise Systems*. Boston: Harvard Business Press.

Davis, Donna F., and Susan L. Golicic. 2010. Gaining Comparative Advantage in Supply Chain Relationships: The Mediating Role of Market-Oriented IT

Competence. *Journal of the Academy of Marketing Science* 38 (1): 56–70. https://doi.org/10.1007/s11747-008-0127-8.

Day, George S. 2003. Creating a Superior Customer-Relating Capability. *MIT Sloan Management Review* 44 (3): 77–82.

De Bruin, Tonia, Michael Rosemann, Ronald Freeze, and Uday Kaulkarni. 2005. Understanding the Main Phases of Developing a Maturity Assessment Model. In *Australasian Conference on Information Systems (ACIS)*, ed. D. Bunker, B. Campbell, and J. Underwood, 8–19. Australasian Chapter of the Association for Information Systems. https://eprints.qut.edu.au/25152/.

de Ruyter, Ko, Debbie Isobel Keeling, and David Cox. 2019. Customer-Supplier Relationships in High Technology Markets 3.0. *Industrial Marketing Management* 79: 94–101. https://doi.org/10.1016/j.indmarman.2018.11.011.

Delpechitre, Duleeep, Lisa L. Beeler-Connelly, and Nawar N. Chaker. 2018. Customer Value Co-Creation Behavior: A Dyadic Exploration of the Influence of Salesperson Emotional Intelligence on Customer Participation and Citizenship Behavior. *Journal of Business Research* 92: 9–24. https://doi.org/10.1016/j.jbusres.2018.05.007.

Denison, Daniel R., and Aneil K. Mishra. 1995. Toward a Theory of Organizational Culture and Effectiveness. *Organization Science* 6 (2): 204–223.

Deszczyński, Bartosz. 2011. *CRM. Strategia. System. Zarządzanie zmianą: Jak uniknąć błędów i odnieść sukces wdrożenia*. Warszawa: Wolters Kluwer.

———. 2016a. The Impact of Opportunity Management on the Relationship Business Model (A Study in the Polish Housing Industry). *Journal of Eastern European and Central Asian Research (JEECAR)* 3 (2): 1–10. https://doi.org/10.15549/jeecar.v3i2.137.

———. 2016b. The Maturity of Corporate Relationship Management. *Gospodarka Narodowa* 283 (3): 73–104. https://doi.org/10.33119/GN/100777.

———. 2017. Word-Of-Mouth in Social Media. The Case of Polish Tourist Industry. *International Journal of Management and Economics* 53 (4): 93–114. https://doi.org/10.1515/ijme-2017-0028.

———. 2018. Empowerment pracowników w przedsiębiorstwach branży usług biznesowych. *Studia Oeconomica Posnaniensia* 6, no. nr 4 Funkcjonowanie i rozwój sektora usług biznesowych w Europie Środkowej i Wschodniej-aspekty makro-i mikroekonomiczne: 113–143. https://doi.org/10.18559/SOEP.2018.4.7.

Diefendorf, James M., Erin M. Richard, and Jixia Yang. 2008. Linking Emotion Regulation Strategies to Affective Events and Negative Emotions at Work. *Journal of Vocational Behavior* 73 (3): 498–508. https://doi.org/10.1016/j.jvb.2008.09.006.

do Nascimento, Thaina T., Juliana B. Porto, and Catherine T. Kwantes. 2018. Transformational Leadership and Follower Proactivity in a Volunteer Workforce. *Nonprofit Management and Leadership* 28 (4): 565–576.

Dorotic, Matilda, Tammo H.A. Bijmolt, and Peter C. Verhoef. 2012. Loyalty Programmes: Current Knowledge and Research Directions. *International Journal of Management Reviews* 14 (3): 217–237. https://doi.org/10.1111/j.1468-2370.2011.00314.x.

Doty, D. Harold, and William H. Glick. 1994. Typologies as a Unique Form of Theory Building: Toward Improved Understanding and Modeling. *The Academy of Management Review* 19 (2): 230–251. https://doi.org/10.2307/258704.

Dyer, Jeffrey H., and Harbir Singh. 1998. The Relational View: Cooperative Strategy and Sources of Interorganizational Competitive Advantage. *The Academy of Management Review* 23 (4): 660–679. https://doi.org/10.2307/259056.

Easterby-Smith, Mark, Richard Thorpe, and Paul R. Jackson. 2012. *Management Research*. London: SAGE.

Eisenhardt, Kathleen M., and Jeffrey A. Martin. 2000. Dynamic Capabilities: What Are They? *Strategic Management Journal* 21 (10–11): 1105–1121. https://doi.org/10.1002/1097-0266(200010/11)21:10/11<1105:: AID-SMJ133>3.0.CO;2-E.

Enz, Matias G., and Douglas M. Lambert. 2012. Using Cross-Functional, Cross-Firm Teams to Co-Create Value: The Role of Financial Measures. *Industrial Marketing Management*, IMPASIA 2010, 41 (3): 495–507. https://doi.org/10.1016/j.indmarman.2011.06.041.

Erevelles, Sunil, Nobuyuki Fukawa, and Linda Swayne. 2016. Big Data Consumer Analytics and the Transformation of Marketing. *Journal of Business Research* 69 (2): 897–904. https://doi.org/10.1016/j.jbusres.2015.07.001.

Eveland, Vicki Blakney, Tammy Neal Crutchfield, and Ania Izabela Rynarzewska. 2018. Developing a Consumer Relationship Model of Corporate Social Performance. *Journal of Consumer Marketing* 35 (5): 543–554. https://doi.org/10.1108/JCM-07-2017-2287.

Fink, Arlene. 2010. *Conducting Research Literature Reviews: From the Internet to Paper*. 3rd ed. Los Angeles: SAGE.

FitzPatrick, Mary, Richard J. Varey, Christian Grönroos, and Janet Davey. 2015. Relationality in the Service Logic of Value Creation. *Journal of Services Marketing* 29 (6/7): 463–471. https://doi.org/10.1108/JSM-01-2015-0038.

Fonfara, Krzysztof. 2014. *Marketing Partnerski Na Rynku Przedsiębiorstw*. Warszawa: PWE.

Forkmann, Sebastian, Stephan C. Henneberg, Peter Naudé, and Maciej Mitrega. 2016. Supplier Relationship Management Capability: A Qualification and Extension. *Industrial Marketing Management* 57: 185–200. https://doi.org/10.1016/j.indmarman.2016.02.003.

Galvão, Marcella Brito, Raíssa Corrêa de Carvalho, Lucas Ambrósio Bezerra de Oliveira, and Denise Dumke de Medeiros. 2018. Customer Loyalty Approach Based on CRM for SMEs. *Journal of Business & Industrial Marketing*, June 4. https://doi.org/10.1108/JBIM-07-2017-0166

Gentle, Michael. 2002. *The CRM Project Management Handbook: Building Realistic Expectations and Managing Risk*. London/Sterling. http://search.ebscohost.com/login.aspx?direct=true&db=eoh&AN=0658504&lang=pl&site=ehost-live

Giannakis, Damianos, Michael J. Harker, and Tom Baum. 2015. Human Resource Management, Services and Relationship Marketing: The Potential for Cross-Fertilisation. *Journal of Strategic Marketing* 23 (6): 526–542. https://doi.org/10.1080/0965254X.2014.1001862.

Gough, David, and Michelle Richardson. 2018. Systematic Reviews. In *Advanced Research Methods for Applied Psychology: Design, Analysis and Reporting*, ed. Paula Brough. London: Routledge. https://doi.org/10.4324/9781315517971-8.

Gounaris, Spiros P. 2006. Internal-Market Orientation and Its Measurement. *Journal of Business Research* 59 (4): 432–448.

Grace, Debra, and Joseph Lo Iacono. 2015. Value Creation: An Internal Customers' Perspective. *Journal of Services Marketing* 29 (6/7): 560–570. https://doi.org/10.1108/JSM-09-2014-0311.

Grandey, Alicia A. 2003. When "The Show Must Go On": Surface Acting and Deep Acting as Determinants of Emotional Exhaustion and Peer-Rated Service Delivery. *Academy of Management Journal* 46 (1): 86–96. https://doi.org/10.5465/30040678.

Grönroos, Christian. 2011a. A Service Perspective on Business Relationships: The Value Creation, Interaction and Marketing Interface. *Industrial Marketing Management*, Special issue on Service-Dominant Logic in Business Markets, 40 (2): 240–247. https://doi.org/10.1016/j.indmarman.2010.06.036.

———. 2011b. Value Co-Creation in Service Logic: A Critical Analysis. *Marketing Theory* 11 (3): 279–301. https://doi.org/10.1177/1470593111408177.

———. 2016. *Service Management and Marketing: Managing the Service Profit Logic*. 4th ed. Chichester: Wiley. https://www.wiley.com/en-us/Service+Management+and+Marketing%3A+Managing+the+Service+Profit+Logic%2C+4th+Edition-p-9781118921449.

———. 2017. Relationship Marketing Readiness: Theoretical Background and Measurement Directions. *Journal of Services Marketing* 31 (3): 218–225. https://doi.org/10.1108/JSM-02-2017-0056.

Grunig, James E. 2008. *Excellence in Public Relations and Communication Management*. New York: Routledge.

Guenzi, Paolo, Catherine Pardo, and Laurent Georges. 2007. Relational Selling Strategy and Key Account Managers' Relational Behaviors: An Exploratory Study. *Industrial Marketing Management* 36 (1): 121–133.

Guesalaga, Rodrigo, and Wesley Johnston. 2010. What's Next in Key Account Management Research? Building the Bridge Between the Academic Literature and the Practitioners' Priorities. *Industrial Marketing Management*, Selling and Sales Management, 39 (7): 1063–1068. https://doi.org/10.1016/j.indmarman.2009.12.008.

Gummesson, Evert. 1999. Total Relationship Marketing: Experimenting With a Synthesis of Research Frontiers. *Australasian Marketing Journal (AMJ)* 7 (1): 72–85. https://doi.org/10.1016/S1441-3582(99)70204-1.

———. 2012. *Total Relationship Marketing: Marketing Strategy Moving from the 4Ps–Product, Price, Promotion, Place–of Traditional Marketing Management to the 30Rs–the Thirty Relationships–of a New Marketing Paradigm*. Abingdon: Routledge. https://books.google.pl/books?id=x-iZOqS91eAC.

———. 2017a. From Relationship Marketing to Total Relationship Marketing and Beyond. *Journal of Services Marketing* 31 (1): 16–19. https://doi.org/10.1108/JSM-11-2016-0398.

———. 2017b. *Total Relationship Marketing*. 4th ed. Routledge: Abingdon.

Gummesson, Evert, and Cristina Mele. 2010. Marketing as Value Co-Creation Through Network Interaction and Resource Integration. *Journal of Business Market Management* 4 (4): 181–198. https://doi.org/10.1007/s12087-010-0044-2.

Hajli, Nick, Mohana Shanmugam, Savvas Papagiannidis, Debra Zahay, and Marie-Odile Richard. 2017. Branding Co-Creation with Members of Online Brand Communities. *Journal of Business Research* 70: 136–144. https://doi.org/10.1016/j.jbusres.2016.08.026.

Hallikainen, Heli, Emma Savimäki, and Tommi Laukkanen. 2019. Fostering B2B Sales with Customer Big Data Analytics. *Industrial Marketing Management*, December 24. https://doi.org/10.1016/j.indmarman.2019.12.005.

Harris, Jeanne G., Elizabeth Craig, and David A. Light. 2011. Talent and Analytics: New Approaches, Higher ROI. *Journal of Business Strategy* 32 (6): 4–13. https://doi.org/10.1108/02756661111180087.

Hartline, Michael D., James G. Maxham, and Daryl O. McKee. 2000. Corridors of Influence in the Dissemination of Customer-Oriented Strategy to Customer Contact Service Employees. *Journal of Marketing* 64 (2): 35–50. https://doi.org/10.1509/jmkg.64.2.35.18001.

Hawkins, David, and Bob Little. 2011. Embedding Collaboration through Standards – Part 1. *Industrial & Commercial Training* 43 (2): 106–112.

Heavey, Ciaran, Zeki Simsek, Christina Kyprianou, and Marten Risius. 2020. How Do Strategic Leaders Engage with Social Media? A Theoretical Framework for Research and Practice. *Strategic Management Journal* 41 (8): 1490–1527. https://doi.org/10.1002/smj.3156.

Herington, Carmel, Lester W. Johnson, and Don Scott. 2009. Firm–Employee Relationship StrengthA Conceptual Model. *Journal of Business Research* 62 (11): 1096–1107.
Hogan, Suellen J., and Leonard V. Coote. 2014. Organizational Culture, Innovation, and Performance: A Test of Schein's Model. *Journal of Business Research* 67 (8): 1609–1621. https://doi.org/10.1016/j.jbusres.2013.09.007.
Hollebeek, Linda D., Rajendra K. Srivastava, and Tom Chen. 2019. S-D Logic–Informed Customer Engagement: Integrative Framework, Revised Fundamental Propositions, and Application to CRM. *Journal of the Academy of Marketing Science* 47 (1): 161–185. https://doi.org/10.1007/s11747-016-0494-5.
Holm, Morten, V. Kumar, and Carsten Rohde. 2012. Measuring Customer Profitability in Complex Environments: An Interdisciplinary Contingency Framework. *Journal of the Academy of Marketing Science* 40 (3): 387–401. https://doi.org/10.1007/s11747-011-0263-4.
Homburg, Christian, Andreas Fürst, and Nicole Koschate. 2010. On the Importance of Complaint Handling Design: A Multi-Level Analysis of the Impact in Specific Complaint Situations. *Journal of the Academy of Marketing Science* 38 (3): 265–287. https://doi.org/10.1007/s11747-009-0172-y.
Huang, Min-Hsin. 2015. The Influence of Relationship Marketing Investments on Customer Gratitude in Retailing. *Journal of Business Research* 68 (6): 1318–1323. https://doi.org/10.1016/j.jbusres.2014.12.001.
Hwang, Jiyoung, and Jay Kandampully. 2015. Embracing CSR in Pro-Social Relationship Marketing Program: Understanding Driving Forces of Positive Consumer Responses. *Journal of Services Marketing* 29 (5): 344–353. https://doi.org/10.1108/JSM-04-2014-0118.
Ichniowski, Casey, Kathryn Shaw, and Giovanna Prennushi. 1997. The Effects of Human Resource Management Practices on Productivity: A Study of Steel Finishing Lines. *American Economic Review* 87 (3): 291–313.
Jakubów, Leon. 2016. Ewolucja Planowania Rozwoju Przedsiębiorstwa. Evolution in the Enterprise Development Planning. *Prace Naukowe Uniwersytetu Ekonomicznego we Wrocławiu* 444: 211–221.
Jayachandran, Satish, Kelly Hewett, and Peter Kaufman. 2004. Customer Response Capability in a Sense-and-Respond Era: The Role of Customer Knowledge Process. *Journal of the Academy of Marketing Science* 32 (3): 219–233. https://doi.org/10.1177/0092070304263334.
Jayachandran, Satish, Subhash Sharma, Peter Kaufman, and Pushkala Raman. 2005. The Role of Relational Information Processes and Technology Use in Customer Relationship Management. *Journal of Marketing* 69 (4): 177–192. https://doi.org/10.1509/jmkg.2005.69.4.177.
Jelinek, Ronald. 2013. All Pain, No Gain? Why Adopting Sales Force Automation Tools Is Insufficient for Performance Improvement. *Business Horizons* 56 (5): 635–642. https://doi.org/10.1016/j.bushor.2013.06.002.

Johnson, Michael D., and Fred Selnes. 2004. Customer Portfolio Management: Toward a Dynamic Theory of Exchange Relationships. *Journal of Marketing* 68 (2): 1–17. https://doi.org/10.1509/jmkg.68.2.1.27786.

Jones, Thomas O., and W. Earl Sasser Jr. 1995. Why Satisfied Customers Defect. *Harvard Business Review*, November 1. https://hbr.org/1995/11/why-satisfied-customers-defect

Kaski, Timo, Jarkko Niemi, and Ellen Pullins. 2018. Rapport Building in Authentic B2B Sales Interaction. *Industrial Marketing Management* 69: 235–252. https://doi.org/10.1016/j.indmarman.2017.08.019.

Kazanjian, Robert K., and Robert Drazin. 1989. An Empirical Test of a Stage of Growth Progression Model. *Management Science* 35 (12): 1489–1503. https://doi.org/10.1287/mnsc.35.12.1489.

Keramati, Abbas, Hamed Mehrabi, and Navid Mojir. 2010. A Process-Oriented Perspective on Customer Relationship Management and Organizational Performance: An Empirical Investigation. *Industrial Marketing Management, Selling and Sales Management* 39 (7): 1170–1185. https://doi.org/10.1016/j.indmarman.2010.02.001.

Ketokivi, Mikko, and Saku Mantere. 2010. Two Strategies for Inductive Reasoning in Organizational Research. *Academy of Management Review* 35 (2): 315–333. https://doi.org/10.5465/amr.35.2.zok315.

Killian, Ginger, and Kristy McManus. 2015. A Marketing Communications Approach for the Digital Era: Managerial Guidelines for Social Media Integration. *Business Horizons* 58 (5): 539–549. https://doi.org/10.1016/j.bushor.2015.05.006.

Kim Jean Lee, Siew, and Kelvin Yu. 2004. Corporate Culture and Organizational Performance. *Journal of Managerial Psychology* 19 (4): 340–359. https://doi.org/10.1108/02683940410537927.

Kotorov, Rado. 2003. Customer Relationship Management: Strategic Lessons and Future Directions. *Business Process Management Journal* 9 (5): 566–571. https://doi.org/10.1108/14637150310496686.

Kotter, John P., and James L. Heskett. 2011. *Corporate Culture and Performance*. Reprint edition. New York: Free Press.

Kumar, Vineet, and Werner J. Reinartz. 2006. *Customer Relationship Management: A Databased Approach*. Hoboken: Wiley & Sons.

Kumar, V., Bharath Rajan, Shaphali Gupta, and Ilaria Dalla Pozza. 2019. Customer Engagement in Service. *Journal of the Academy of Marketing Science* 47 (1): 138–160. https://doi.org/10.1007/s11747-017-0565-2.

L'Etang, Jacquie. 1994. Public Relations and Corporate Social Responsibility: Some Issues Arising. *Journal of Business Ethics* 13 (2): 111–123. https://doi.org/10.1007/BF00881580.

Lacey, Russell, Pamela A. Kennett-Hensel, and Chris Manolis. 2015. Is Corporate Social Responsibility a Motivator or Hygiene Factor? Insights into Its Bivalent

Nature. *Journal of the Academy of Marketing Science* 43 (3): 315–332. https://doi.org/10.1007/s11747-014-0390-9.

Lambe, C. Jay, C. Michael Wittmann, and Robert E. Spekman. 2001. Social Exchange Theory and Research on Business-to-Business Relational Exchange. *Journal of Business-to-Business Marketing* 8 (3): 1.

Lambert, Douglas M. 2008. *Supply Chain Management: Processes, Partnerships, Performance*. Sarasota: Supply Chain Management Institute.

———. 2010. Customer Relationship Management as a Business Process. *Journal of Business & Industrial Marketing* 25 (1): 4–17. https://doi.org/10.1108/08858621011009119.

Lichtarski, Jan. 2015. *Praktyczny Wymiar Nauk o Zarządzaniu*. Warszawa: Polskie Wydawnictwo Ekonomiczne.

Lindgreen, Adam, and Valérie Swaen. 2010. Corporate Social Responsibility. *International Journal of Management Reviews* 12 (1): 1–7. https://doi.org/10.1111/j.1468-2370.2009.00277.x.

Lindner, Frank, and Andreas Wald. 2011. Success Factors of Knowledge Management in Temporary Organizations. *International Journal of Project Management*, Complexities in Managing Mega Construction Projects, 29 (7): 877–888. https://doi.org/10.1016/j.ijproman.2010.09.003.

Ling-yee, Li. 2011. 'Marketing Metrics' Usage: Its Predictors and Implications for Customer Relationship Management. *Industrial Marketing Management*, Business-to-Business Marketing in the BRIC Countries, 40 (1): 139–148. https://doi.org/10.1016/j.indmarman.2010.09.002.

Lusch, Robert F., Stephen L. Vargo, and Mohan Tanniru. 2010. Service, Value Networks and Learning. *Journal of the Academy of Marketing Science* 38 (1): 19–31. https://doi.org/10.1007/s11747-008-0131-z.

Luu, Ngoc, Liem Viet Ngo, and Jack Cadeaux. 2018. Value Synergy and Value Asymmetry in Relationship Marketing Programs. *Industrial Marketing Management* 68: 165–176. https://doi.org/10.1016/j.indmarman.2017.10.011.

Ma, Baolong, Xiaofei Li, and Lin Zhang. 2018. The Effects of Loyalty Programs in Services – A Double-Edged Sword? *Journal of Services Marketing* 32 (3): 300–310. https://doi.org/10.1108/JSM-06-2016-0227.

Macdonald, Emma K., Hugh Wilson, Veronica Martinez, and Amir Toossi. 2011. Assessing Value-in-Use: A Conceptual Framework and Exploratory Study. *Industrial Marketing Management*, Service and Solution Innovation, 40 (5): 671–682. https://doi.org/10.1016/j.indmarman.2011.05.006.

Madhavaram, Sreedhar, Elad Granot, and Vishag Badrinarayanan. 2014. Relationship Marketing Strategy: An Operant Resource Perspective. *Journal of Business & Industrial Marketing*, April 1. https://doi.org/10.1108/JBIM-02-2013-0049.

Maher, Patrick. 1996. The Hole in the Ground of Induction. *Australasian Journal of Philosophy* 74 (3): 423–432. https://doi.org/10.1080/00048409612347411.

Mangold, W. Glynn, and Sandra Jeanquart Miles. 2007. The Employee Brand: Is Yours an All-Star? *Business Horizons* 50 (5): 423–433.

Marcos-Cuevas, Javier, Satu Nätti, Teea Palo, and Lynette J. Ryals. 2014. Implementing Key Account Management: Intraorganizational Practices and Associated Dilemmas. *Industrial Marketing Management* 43 (7): 1216–1224. https://doi.org/10.1016/j.indmarman.2014.06.009.

Marler, Janet H., and Sandra L. Fisher. 2013. An Evidence-Based Review of e-HRM and Strategic Human Resource Management. *Human Resource Management Review*, Emerging Issues in Theory and Research on Electronic Human Resource Management (eHRM), 23 (1): 18–36. https://doi.org/10.1016/j.hrmr.2012.06.002.

Martelo, Silvia, Carmen Barroso, and Gabriel Cepeda. 2013. The Use of Organizational Capabilities to Increase Customer Value. *Journal of Business Research*, Strategic Thinking in Marketing, 66 (10): 2042–2050. https://doi.org/10.1016/j.jbusres.2013.02.030.

Mauboussin, Michael J. 2012. The True Measures of Success. *Harvard Business Review*, October 1. https://hbr.org/2012/10/the-true-measures-of-success

Melancon, Joanna Phillips, and Vassilis Dalakas. 2018. Consumer Social Voice in the Age of Social Media: Segmentation Profiles and Relationship Marketing Strategies. *Business Horizons* 61 (1): 157–167. https://doi.org/10.1016/j.bushor.2017.09.015.

Melville, Nigel, Kenneth L. Kraemer, and Vijay Gurbaxani. 2004. Review: Information Technology and Organizational Performance: An Integrative Model of IT Business Value. *MIS Quarterly* 28: 283–322. https://doi.org/10.2307/25148636.

Men, Linjuan Rita. 2014. Strategic Internal Communication: Transformational Leadership, Communication Channels, and Employee Satisfaction. *Management Communication Quarterly* 28 (2): 264–284.

Men, Linjuan Rita, and Katy L. Robinson. 2018. It's About How Employees Feel! Examining the Impact of Emotional Culture on Employee–Organization Relationships. *Corporate Communications: An International Journal* 23 (4): 470–491. https://doi.org/10.1108/CCIJ-05-2018-0065.

Mettler, Tobias. 2011. Maturity Assessment Models: A Design Science Research Approach. *International Journal of Society Systems Science (IJSSS)* 3 (1/2): 81–98.

Minkiewicz, Joanna, Kerrie Bridson, and Jody Evans. 2016. Co-Production of Service Experiences: Insights from the Cultural Sector. *Journal of Services Marketing* 30 (7): 749–761. https://doi.org/10.1108/JSM-04-2015-0156.

Miocevic, Dario, and Biljana Crnjak-Karanovic. 2012. The Mediating Role of Key Supplier Relationship Management Practices on Supply Chain Orientation the Organizational Buying Effectiveness Link. *Industrial Marketing Management* 41 (1): 115–124. https://doi.org/10.1016/j.indmarman.2011.11.015.

Morgan, Robert M., and Shelby D. Hunt. 1994. The Commitment-Trust Theory of Relationship Marketing. *Journal of Marketing* 58 (3): 20–38. https://doi.org/10.1177/002224299405800302.

Neslin, Scott A., Gail Ayala Taylor, Kimberly D. Grantham, and Kimberly R. McNeil. 2013. Overcoming the "Recency Trap" in Customer Relationship Management. *Journal of the Academy of Marketing Science* 41 (3): 320–337. https://doi.org/10.1007/s11747-012-0312-7.

Ngo, Liem Viet, and Aron O'Cass. 2013. Innovation and Business Success: The Mediating Role of Customer Participation. *Journal of Business Research*, Recent Advances in Globalization, Culture and Marketing Strategy, 66 (8): 1134–1142. https://doi.org/10.1016/j.jbusres.2012.03.009.

Nguyen, ThuyUyen H., Joseph S. Sherif, and Michael Newby. 2007. Strategies for Successful CRM Implementation. *Information Management & Computer Security* 15 (2): 102–115. https://doi.org/10.1108/09685220710748001.

Oghazi, Pejvak, Fakhreddin Fakhrai Rad, Ghasem Zaefarian, Hooshang M. Beheshti, and Sina Mortazavi. 2016. Unity Is Strength: A Study of Supplier Relationship Management Integration. *Journal of Business Research* 69 (11): 4804–4810. https://doi.org/10.1016/j.jbusres.2016.04.034.

Ohiomah, Alhassan, Pavel Andreev, Morad Benyoucef, and David Hood. 2019. The Role of Lead Management Systems in Inside Sales Performance. *Journal of Business Research* 102: 163–177.

Orr, Linda M., Victoria D. Bush, and Douglas W. Vorhies. 2011. Leveraging Firm-Level Marketing Capabilities with Marketing Employee Development. *Journal of Business Research* 64 (10): 1074–1081. https://doi.org/10.1016/j.jbusres.2010.11.003.

Park, Jeong Eun, Juyoung Kim, Alan J. Dubinsky, and Hyunju Lee. 2010. How Does Sales Force Automation Influence Relationship Quality and Performance? The Mediating Roles of Learning and Selling Behaviors. *Industrial Marketing Management*, Selling and Sales Management, 39 (7): 1128–1138. https://doi.org/10.1016/j.indmarman.2009.11.003.

Paulk, M.C., B. Curtis, M.B. Chrissis, and C.V. Weber. 1993. Capability Maturity Model, Version 1.1. *IEEE Software* 10 (4): 18–27. https://doi.org/10.1109/52.219617.

Payne, Adrian, and Pennie Frow. 2005. A Strategic Framework for Customer Relationship Management. *Journal of Marketing* 69 (4): 167–176. https://doi.org/10.1509/jmkg.2005.69.4.167.

———. 2013. *Strategic Customer Management: Integrating Relationship Marketing and CRM*. Cambridge University Press.

———. 2016. Customer Relationship Management: Strategy and Implementation. In *The Marketing Book*, ed. Michael J. Baker and Susan Hart, 439–466. London: Routledge. https://doi.org/10.4324/9781315890005-28.

Payne, Adrian, Kaj Storbacka, Pennie Frow, and Simon Knox. 2009. Co-Creating Brands: Diagnosing and Designing the Relationship Experience. *Journal of Business Research*, Advances in Brand Management, 62 (3): 379–389. https://doi.org/10.1016/j.jbusres.2008.05.013.

Peppers, Don, and Martha Rogers. 2013. Extreme Trust: The New Competitive Advantage. *Strategy and Leadership* 41 (6): 31–34. https://doi.org/10.1108/SL-07-2013-0054.

Pöppelbuß, Jens, and Maximilian Röglinger. 2011. What Makes a Useful Maturity Model? A Framework of General Design Principles for Maturity Models and Its Demosntration in Business Process Management. In *ECIS Proceedings*, 28, 13. European Conference on Information Systems (ECIS).

Pozza, Dalla Ilaria, Oliver Goetz, and Jean Michel Sahut. 2018. Implementation Effects in the Relationship Between CRM and Its Performance. *Journal of Business Research* 89: 391–403. https://doi.org/10.1016/j.jbusres.2018.02.004.

Prahalad, C.K., and Gary Hamel. 1994. Strategy as a Field of Study: Why Search for a New Paradigm? *Strategic Management Journal* 15 (S2): 5–16. https://doi.org/10.1002/smj.4250151002.

Preikschas, Michael W., Pablo Cabanelas, Klaus Rüdiger, and Jesús F. Lampón. 2017. Value Co-Creation, Dynamic Capabilities and Customer Retention in Industrial Markets. *Journal of Business & Industrial Marketing* 3. https://doi.org/10.1108/JBIM-10-2014-0215.

Prior, Daniel D. 2012. The Effects of Buyer-supplier Relationships on Buyer Competitiveness. *Journal of Business & Industrial Marketing* 27 (2): 100–114. https://doi.org/10.1108/08858621211196976.

Quinn, Robert E., and John Rohrbaugh. 1983. A Spatial Model of Effectiveness Criteria: Towards a Competing Values Approach to Organizational Analysis. *Management Science* 29 (3): 363–377.

Ramani, Girish, and V. Kumar. 2008. Interaction Orientation and Firm Performance. *Journal of Marketing* 72 (1): 27–45. https://doi.org/10.1509/jmkg.72.1.027.

Reichheld, Frederick. 2001. *Loyalty Rules!: How Today's Leaders Build Lasting Relationships*. Boston: Harvard Business School Press. https://books.google.pl/books?hl=pl&lr=&id=oT3lL0QdWiwC&oi=fnd&pg=PP1&dq=reichheld+2001+loyalty&ots=zD3RjjPbTW&sig=cYD89k0tVodkW2Tc1HhiTuZhacc&redir_esc=y#v=onepage&q=reichheld%202001%20loyalty&f=false.

———. 2006. The Microeconomics of Customer Relationships. *MIT Sloan Management Review* 47 (2): 72–78.

Reinartz, Werner, Manfred Krafft, and Wayne D. Hoyer. 2004. The Customer Relationship Management Process: Its Measurement and Impact on Performance. *Journal of Marketing Research*. https://doi.org/10.1509/jmkr.41.3.293.35991.

Röglinger, Maximilian, Jens Pöppelbuß, and Jörg Becker. 2012. Maturity Models in Business Process Management. *Business Process Management Journal* 18 (2): 328–346. https://doi.org/10.1108/14637151211225225.

Rosemann, Michael. 2006. Potential Pitfalls of Process Modeling: Part A. *Business Process Management Journal* 12 (2): 249–254. https://doi.org/10.1108/14637150610657567.

Rosemann, Michael, and Tonia de Bruin. 2005. Application of a Holistic Model for Determining BPM Maturity. *BP Trends* 2: 1–21.

Roy, Sanjit Kumar, Gul Butaney, Harjit Sekhon, and Bhupin Butaney. 2014. Word-of-Mouth and Viral Marketing Activity of the On-Line Consumer: The Role of Loyalty Chain Stages Theory. *Journal of Strategic Marketing* 22 (6): 494–512.

Russo-Spena, Tiziana, and Cristina Mele. 2012. "Five Co-s" in Innovating: A Practice-based View'. Edited by Evert Gummesson, Cristina Mele, and Francesco Polese. *Journal of Service Management* 23 (4): 527–553. https://doi.org/10.1108/09564231211260404.

Ryan, Richard M., and Edward L. Deci. 2000. Self-determination theory and the facilitation of intrinsic motivation, social development, and well-being. American Psychologist, 55(1), 68–78. https://doi.org/10.1037/0003-066X.55.1.68.

———. 2017. *Self-Determination Theory: Basic Psychological Needs in Motivation, Development, and Wellness*. New York: Guilford Publications.

Sabnis, Gaurav, Sharmila C. Chatterjee, Rajdeep Grewal, and Gary L. Lilien. 2013. The Sales Lead Black Hole: On Sales Reps' Follow-Up of Marketing Leads. *Journal of Marketing* 77 (1): 52–67. https://doi.org/10.1509/jm.10.0047.

Saini, Amit, Rajdeep Grewal, and Jean L. Johnson. 2010. Putting Market-Facing Technology to Work: Organizational Drivers of CRM Performance. *Marketing Letters* 21 (4): 365–383. https://doi.org/10.1007/s11002-009-9096-z.

Sasidharan Dhanesh, Ganga. 2012. The View from Within: Internal Publics and CSR. *Journal of Communication Management* 16 (1): 39–58. https://doi.org/10.1108/13632541211197987.

Schein, Edgar H. 1990. Organizational Culture. *American Psychologist* 45 (2): 109–119. https://doi.org/10.1037/0003-066X.45.2.109.

Scherer, Klaus. 1997. Profiles of Emotion-Antecedent Appraisal: Testing Theoretical Predictions across Cultures. *Cognition and Emotion* 11 (2): 113–150. https://doi.org/10.1080/026999397379962.

Schuler, Douglas A., and Margaret Cording. 2006. A Corporate Social Performance–Corporate Financial Performance Behavioral Model for Consumers. *Academy of Management Review* 31 (3): 540–558. https://doi.org/10.5465/amr.2006.21318916.

Schwalbe, Kathy. 2008. *Information Technology Project Management, Reprint*. 5th ed. Boston: Thomson Course Technology.

Sheth, Jagdish N. 2017. Revitalizing Relationship Marketing. *Journal of Services Marketing* 31 (1): 6–10. https://doi.org/10.1108/JSM-11-2016-0397.

Shi, Linda Hui, and Tao (Tony) Gao. 2016. Performance Effects of Global Account Coordination Mechanisms: An Integrative Study of Boundary Conditions. *Journal of International Marketing*, June 1. https://doi.org/10.1509/jim.15.0103.

Simkin, Lyndon, and Sally Dibb. 2013. Social Media's Impact on Market Segmentation and CRM. *Journal of Strategic Marketing* 21 (5): 391–393.

Singh, Shweta, and Sumit Singh. 2016. Accounting for Risk in the Traditional RFM Approach. *Management Research Review* 39 (2): 215–234.

Slater, Stanley F. 1997. Developing a Customer Value-Based Theory of the Firm. *Journal of the Academy of Marketing Science* 25 (2): 162–167. https://doi.org/10.1007/BF02894352.

Slater, Stanley F., Eric M. Olson, and Carol Finnegan. 2011. Business Strategy, Marketing Organization Culture, and Performance. *Marketing Letters* 22 (3): 227–242. https://doi.org/10.1007/s11002-010-9122-1.

Smith, Timothy M., Srinath Gopalakrishna, and Rabikar Chatterjee. 2006. A Three-Stage Model of Integrated Marketing Communications at the Marketing-Sales Interface. *Journal of Marketing Research* 43 (4): 564–579. https://doi.org/10.1509/jmkr.43.4.564.

Sprenger, Jan. 2011. Hypothetico-Deductive Confirmation. *Philosophy Compass* 6 (7): 497–508. https://doi.org/10.1111/j.1747-9991.2011.00409.x.

Sriramesh, K., James E. Grunig, and David M. Dozier. 1996. Observation and Measurement of Two Dimensions of Organizational Culture and Their Relationship to Public Relations. *Journal of Public Relations Research* 8 (4): 229–261. https://doi.org/10.1207/s1532754xjprr0804_02.

Steel, Marion, Chris Dubelaar, and Michael T. Ewing. 2013. Developing Customised CRM Projects: The Role of Industry Norms, Organisational Context and Customer Expectations on CRM Implementation. *Industrial Marketing Management* 42 (8): 1328–1344. https://doi.org/10.1016/j.indmarman.2012.08.009.

Stibitz, Sara. 2015. How to Get a New Employee Up to Speed. *Harvard Business Review Digital Articles* 22: 2–5.

Storbacka Kaj, Frow Pennie, Nenonen Suvi, and Payne Adrian. 2012. Designing Business Models for Value Co-Creation. Edited by Stephen L. Vargo and Robert F. Lusch. *Special Issue – Toward a Better Understanding of the Role of Value in Markets and Marketing*, Review of Marketing Research, 9: 51–78. https://doi.org/10.1108/S1548-6435(2012)0000009007.

Storey, John. 2007. *Human Resource Management: A Critical Text*. 3rd ed. London: Thomson Learning. http://edu.cengage.co.uk/catalogue/product.aspx?isbn=1844806154.

Strauss, Anselm L., and Juliet M. Corbin. 1998. *Basics of Qualitative Research: Techniques and Procedures for Developing Grounded Theory*. 2nd ed. Thousand Oaks: Sage Publications.

Sull, Donald Norman, and Kathleen M. Eisenhardt. 2015. *Simple Rules: How to Thrive in a Complex World*. Boston: Houghton Mifflin Harcourt.

Svendsen, Freng. 2011. Marketing Strategy and Customer Involvement in Product Development. *European Journal of Marketing* 45 (4): 513–530. https://doi.org/10.1108/03090561111111316.

Tarhan, Ayca, Oktay Turetken, and Hajo A. Reijers. 2016. Business Process Maturity Models: A Systematic Literature Review. *Information and Software Technology* 75: 122–134. https://doi.org/10.1016/j.infsof.2016.01.010.

Teece, David J., Gary Pisano, and Amy Shuen. 1997. Dynamic Capabilities and Strategic Management. *Strategic Management Journal* 18 (7): 509–533. https://doi.org/10.1002/(SICI)1097-0266(199708)18:7<509::AID-SMJ882>3.0.CO;2-Z.

Teneta-Skwiercz, Dorota. 2008. Wymiar Etyczny w Funkcjonowaniu Współczesnego Przedsiębiorstwa. Edited by Jan Lichtarski. *Prace Naukowe Uniwersytetu Ekonomicznego We Wrocławiu* 34: 18–27.

Teo, Thompson S.H., Paul Devadoss, and Shan L. Pan. 2006. Towards a Holistic Perspective of Customer Relationship Management (CRM) Implementation: A Case Study of the Housing and Development Board, Singapore. *Decision Support Systems* 42 (3): 1613–1627. https://doi.org/10.1016/j.dss.2006.01.007.

Terho, Harri, and Anne Jalkala. 2017. Customer Reference Marketing: Conceptualization, Measurement and Link to Selling Performance. *Industrial Marketing Management* 64: 175–186. https://doi.org/10.1016/j.indmarman.2017.01.005.

Thakur, Ramendra, and Letty Workman. 2016. Customer Portfolio Management (CPM) for Improved Customer Relationship Management (CRM): Are Your Customers Platinum, Gold, Silver, or Bronze? *Journal of Business Research* 69 (10): 4095–4102. https://doi.org/10.1016/j.jbusres.2016.03.042.

Trainor, Kevin J., James (Mick) Andzulis, Adam Rapp, and Raj Agnihotri. 2014. Social Media Technology Usage and Customer Relationship Performance: A Capabilities-Based Examination of Social CRM. *Journal of Business Research* 67 (6): 1201–1208. https://doi.org/10.1016/j.jbusres.2013.05.002.

Van Den Bulte, Christophe, Emanuel Bayer, Bernd Skiera, and Philipp Schmitt. 2018. How Customer Referral Programs Turn Social Capital into Economic Capital. *Journal of Marketing Research* 55 (1): 132–146. https://doi.org/10.1509/jmr.14.0653.

Vargo, Stephen L., and Robert F. Lusch. 2004. Evolving to a New Dominant Logic for Marketing. *Journal of Marketing* 68 (1): 1–17.

———. 2008. Service-Dominant Logic: Continuing the Evolution. *Journal of the Academy of Marketing Science* 36 (1): 1–10. https://doi.org/10.1007/s11747-007-0069-6.

———. 2016. Institutions and Axioms: An Extension and Update of Service-Dominant Logic. *Journal of the Academy of Marketing Science* 44 (1): 5–23. https://doi.org/10.1007/s11747-015-0456-3.

Vella, Joseph, and Albert Caruana. 2012. Encouraging CRM Systems Usage: A Study Among Bank Managers. *Management Research Review* 35 (2): 121–133. https://doi.org/10.1108/01409171211195152.

Virtanen, Tatu, Petri Parvinen, and Minna Rollins. 2015. Complexity of Sales Situation and Sales Lead Performance: An Empirical Study in Business-to-Business Company. *Industrial Marketing Management* 45: 49–58. https://doi.org/10.1016/j.indmarman.2015.02.024.

Wagner, Janet, and Sabine Benoit (née Moeller). 2015. Creating Value in Retail Buyer–Vendor Relationships: A Service-Centered Model. *Industrial Marketing Management* 44: 166–179. https://doi.org/10.1016/j.indmarman.2014.10.013.

Wąsowska, Aleksandra, and Marcin Pawłowski. 2011. Metody pomiaru społecznej odpowiedzialności biznesu – przegląd literatury. *Przegląd Organizacji* 11: 14–17. https://doi.org/10.33141/po.2011.11.4.

Waterman, Robert, Thomas J. Peters, and Julien R. Phillips. 1980. Structure Is Not Organization. *Business Horizons* 23 (3): 14–26.

Wendler, Roy. 2012. The Maturity of Maturity Model Research: A Systematic Mapping Study. *Information and Software Technology*, Special Section on Software Reliability and Security, 54 (12): 1317–1339. https://doi.org/10.1016/j.infsof.2012.07.007.

Wirtz, Jochen, and Christopher H. Lovelock. 2016. *Services Marketing: People, Technology, Strategy.* 8th ed. Hackensack: World Scientific Publishing Company.

Wirtz, Jochen, Anouk den Ambtman, Josée Bloemer, Csilla Horváth, B. Ramaseshan, Joris van de Klundert, Zeynep Gurhan Canli, and Jay Kandampully. 2013. Managing Brands and Customer Engagement in Online Brand Communities. Edited by Lerzan Aksoy, Allard van Riel, and Jay Kandampully. *Journal of Service Management* 24 (3): 223–244. https://doi.org/10.1108/09564231311326978.

Xia, Lan, and Monika Kukar-Kinney. 2014. For Our Valued Customers Only: Examining Consumer Responses to Preferential Treatment Practices. *Journal of Business Research* 67 (11): 2368–2375. https://doi.org/10.1016/j.jbusres.2014.02.002.

Yu, Tianyuan, and NengQuan Wu. 2009. A Review of Study on the Competing Values Framework. *International Journal of Business and Management* 4 (7): p37. https://doi.org/10.5539/ijbm.v4n7p37.

Zaglia, Melanie E. 2013. Brand Communities Embedded in Social Networks. *Journal of Business Research*, Thought Leadership in Brand Management II, 66 (2): 216–223. https://doi.org/10.1016/j.jbusres.2012.07.015.

Zand, Jafar Danesh, Abbas Keramati, Farzaneh Shakouri, and Hamid Noori. 2018. Assessing the Impact of Customer Knowledge Management on

Organizational Performance. *Knowledge and Process Management* 25 (4): 268–278. https://doi.org/10.1002/kpm.1585.

Zerbino, Pierluigi, Davide Aloini, Riccardo Dulmin, and Valeria Mininno. 2018. Big Data-Enabled Customer Relationship Management: A Holistic Approach. *Information Processing & Management* 54: 818–846. https://doi.org/10.1016/j.ipm.2017.10.005.

Zhang, Wanrong, and Sujit Banerji. 2017. Challenges of Servitization: A Systematic Literature Review. *Industrial Marketing Management* 65: 217–227. https://doi.org/10.1016/j.indmarman.2017.06.003.

Zhang, Mingli, Lingyun Guo, Mu Hu, and Wenhua Liu. 2017. Influence of Customer Engagement with Company Social Networks on Stickiness: Mediating Effect of Customer Value Creation. *International Journal of Information Management* 37 (3): 229–240. https://doi.org/10.1016/j.ijinfomgt.2016.04.010.

Zhang, Tingting, Can Lu, Edwin Torres, and Po-Ju Chen. 2018. Engaging Customers in Value Co-Creation or Co-Destruction Online. *Journal of Services Marketing* 32 (1): 57–69. https://doi.org/10.1108/JSM-01-2017-0027.

Open Access This chapter is licensed under the terms of the Creative Commons Attribution 4.0 International License (http://creativecommons.org/licenses/by/4.0/), which permits use, sharing, adaptation, distribution and reproduction in any medium or format, as long as you give appropriate credit to the original author(s) and the source, provide a link to the Creative Commons licence and indicate if changes were made.

The images or other third party material in this chapter are included in the chapter's Creative Commons licence, unless indicated otherwise in a credit line to the material. If material is not included in the chapter's Creative Commons licence and your intended use is not permitted by statutory regulation or exceeds the permitted use, you will need to obtain permission directly from the copyright holder.

CHAPTER 4

Validating the Relationship Management Maturity Concept

4.1 THE DESIGN OF A RESEARCH TOOL ON RM MATURITY

The aim of empirical studies in management sciences is to reproduce and elucidate any given business phenomenon without contaminating the research with subjective prejudices concealed in its design or with an authoritative interpretation of the data (Czakon 2015). However, this is not entirely possible as, to a large extent, management sciences involve studying value-laden phenomena, which are not neutral either to the researcher or to the people who are interviewed, observed or tested (Alvesson and Deetz 2000).

In quantitative studies the risk of contaminating the research by the author's preferences is located in the design of the research tool (questionnaire), the choice of analytical tool (statistical methods) and the (mis-)interpretation of extracted data (Ketokivi and Mantere 2010). Moreover, in self-reporting studies, such as the one applied in this book, the results may be biased by the co-occurrence of several behavioural and psychological effects affecting the likelihood that the respondents will be willing or able to inform about the true state of affairs (Donaldson and Grant-Vallone 2002).

Critical positive or negative events may trigger various self-efficacy and defence mechanisms, which change the response lens of the interviewee

(Davidson and MacGregor 1998; Kihlstrom et al. 1999). Acquiescence response style (answering predominately positively especially on questions concerning issues the respondent is not knowledgeable of) or extreme/mid-point response styles (concentrating predominately on a specific scale area regardless of the questioned matter) may bias the results particularly where cross-cultural research is concerned (Clarke 2001; de Jong et al. 2008).

Studies in organizational behaviour in particular are prone to self-reporting bias because the interviewees often believe there is at least a remote possibility that their employer could gain access to their responses (Donaldson and Grant-Vallone 2002). Therefore, leniency or harshness may bias the responses, especially when the questions concern behaviour of the leader/supervisor (Marsh and Roche 2000; Schriesheim 1981). By contrast, so-called managerial sense-making is a product of the combined effects of critical events and individual reality perception, such as self-esteem or cognitive consistency (March and Sutton 1997). These cause managers to report positive aspects of their own capability beyond what is true and stretch to the overall corporate reality perception, especially if the company is performing well (Chandra and Wilkinson 2017; Rong and Wilkinson 2011).

The overall tendency for people to present, regardless of social context, a favourable image of themselves is known as socially desirable responding (Helgeson and Supphellen 2004). Although there are tools effective in uncovering, for example, the tendency towards self-promotion on questionnaires, such as the Crowne-Marlowe Social Desirability Scale (1960), their use is limited, not least because of the feasibility of such tests (this social desirability scale consists of 33 items; van de Mortel 2008). Nonetheless, questionnaires are easy and effective tools to administer in large-scale testing, and are suitable for delivering high-quality results provided a deliberate bias reduction strategy is applied (Krosnick 1999). Such a strategy must minimize the sampling and non-sampling errors by applying various statistical and non-statistical measures. The statistical bias-reducing measures undertaken in this research will be described in Sect. 4.2, 'Analytical strategy'. Still, many of the non-sampling errors, such as specification and measurement errors, come as the effects of these researcher and respondent preferences (Biemer 2010). These problems should be addressed in the questionnaire design by applying appropriate linguistic forms and by using and interpreting measuring scales.

While conducting the literature review for this book, the applied questionnaires were found to quite frequently use terms which are either very general and prone to interpretation or hard to comprehend at all. The examples include such expressions as "We share the same feelings towards things around us", "Communications are accurate", "The supply chain is managed holistically", "We work in close cooperation", "We are good at creating/maintaining relationships with key customers" and "We both try very hard to establish a long-term relationship". The countless possible interpretations of the degree of 'communication accuracy', or of 'being good at something', and the overlaps in perceived meaning of abstract expressions may easily turn the answers to such questions into an incompatible dataset (Palmatier 2008). Therefore, the questionnaire applied in this research, for example, specifies the frequency of particular activities instead of leaving blank expressions such as 'systematically' or 'timely', and requires taking clear positions towards managing concrete processes instead of offering comfortable responses such as 'We attempt to manage process X'.

The other risk is that the accumulation of ambiguous RM characteristics could negatively affect the respondents' concentration and motivation to make meaningful discriminations (Alwin 2007). Such a questionnaire design would instead press them to accommodate in language conventions of positive statements or tautologies rather than to kick back with alternative paths of reasoning, especially if the interview focuses on business performance or effectiveness (Alvesson and Deetz 2000). Uncovering a genuine assessment of the state of affairs also implies avoiding the use of complex systems of judgemental statements, for example:

- A. You are an RM-mature company because you co-create value with customers;
- A.1. Your value co-creation offers make customers satisfied;
- A.2. Loyalty comes as the result of satisfying customers with your value co-creation efforts.

Placed in a fixed leader-follower structure with clearly visible interdependencies, they would cause the respondents to take the implicit researcher view rather to reflect their own. Therefore, staying in line with principle 2 of research design defined in Chap. 3, special effort was taken to ensure that the expressions used in the questionnaire on RM maturity are describing, in a possibly concrete and neutral way, social or business reality rather than individual or shared subjective feelings, impressions, stereotypes, cognitions or perceptions (Alvesson and Sköldberg 2009).

As a result, most of the questions contain complex descriptions, which, at first glance, may leave the impression of asking about many issues without providing the possibility to differentiate the answers. Obviously, applying double-barrelled questions would be a fallacy (Adèr 2008; Rowley 2014). Yet, the proposed descriptions highlight nuances of the same phenomenon and, in fact, only combined describe the postulated state of maturity in a given action or approach. For example, take question D03 listed in Table 4.1, which refers to the maturity in managing customer leads. It would not be enough for a company just to (1) immediately service every customer who is looking for the offer without making sure that (2) these contacts are also registered and processed to salespersons and that (3) the conversion rates are measured. Hence, breaking this process into three separate questions (1, 2, 3) would unnecessarily extend the length of the interviewing procedure and would make it impossible to fully assess the lead management maturity. If a company were to report score '10' for (1) and (3) and score '5' for (2) the mean would fall as much as 8.33. Nonetheless, the logic suggests that if leads are systematically dropped while being processed to the salesperson, (1) is like making an attempt to fill a leaky bucket and (3) is like measuring the fever without actually reading the result.

One could also argue that the applied questions break the other rule of thumb for designing questionnaires, that is, to keep the questions short and simple (Dörnyei and Taguchi 2009; Foddy 1994). However, a question/statement such as "We are good in managing leads", which indeed sounds simple, would likely leave most of the respondents feeling comfortable in giving a 'strongly agree' or reporting a high score in the hypothetical situation presented above. There is no doubt that questions containing complex descriptions require more time to comprehend than short ones. In this study, however, saving time was not a priority, because collecting inconsiderate superficial answers would seriously compromise the application of theory-methodic hypothesis H1tm. Instead, before venturing to collect the bulk of the data, the questionnaire was first tested and corrected in direct interviews and in pilot field research to ensure that all questions could be well explained to and understood by the interviewees (for details see Sect. 4.2, 'Analytical strategy').

The questionnaire displayed in Table 4.1 comprises 40 questions grouped in 3 dimensions, strategy, ICT, and interdepartmental and

Table 4.1 The questionnaire on RM maturity

Code	
	Dimension 1: Strategy
A01	The company has a business plan (business strategy) with a central element which is to nurture long-term relationships with its employees and customers.
A02	Ethical behaviour forms part of the corporate strategy, including fairness towards business partners as well as an active commitment to the well-being of the local community, the natural environment and contribution to people in need.
A03	The company knows the answers to the following questions: Who?: Who are our customers? What?: What kind of needs do they have? When?: When is the next purchase likely to occur?
A04	The company manages relationships with business partners other than customers (suppliers, distributors, etc.) and can, in turn, assess, for example: • the quantitative scale of cooperation: The interdependence between quantitative plans, for example manufacturing or sales plans and particular partners; • the quality of cooperation: The influence of a particular partner on the exact timing of planned operations, manufacturing quality control, customer service and so forth; • cooperation perspectives: The importance of a particular partner for product innovation, sales growth and so forth.
A05	The company knows its best customers and tailors its offer to their individual preferences (products, services, forms of cooperation), and if relationship economics allow this, it provides additional benefits (e.g. servicing priority, personal advisors, earlier access to products, exclusive amenities).
A06	Based on registered information (e.g. offers sent, previous purchases, purchases at competitors), the company differentiates its offer for **every direct customer.**
A07	The company favours and promotes employees who: • have a command of valuable, rare and hard-to-learn capabilities, • have a high level of work engagement.
A08	In the company, there is a knowledge management process supervised by a high-ranking manager (a member of the management board or a manager directly reporting to the board).
Code	**Dimension 2: ICT – CRM systems**
B01	When servicing customers, employees use solely one system (one window), which supports the whole process and integrates all relevant customer data (360° customer view principle).
B02	The CRM system has significantly accelerated the reporting of customer frontline processes (including marketing processes) – There is no need for manual work on weekly or monthly reports.
B03	The company uses a central database (data warehouse), which: • integrates information produced by all customer data processing applications, • enables analytical work (e.g. customer defection prediction).

(*continued*)

Table 4.1 (continued)

B04	The CRM implementation and development project is: • coordinated by a project manager who understands the potential and the limits of information technologies, but originates from a non-IT department, • is actively supported by a member of the management board or a manager directly reporting to the board.
B05	The CRM implementation and development project engaged: • employees with high authority among future system users, • owners of processes to be digitalized.
B06	The company has prepared a detailed CRM business implementation plan (detailed = the report includes measurable benefits, e.g. improvement in marketing conversion).
B07	The company enriches individual customer/partner data stored in the CRM system by their respective social profiles.
Code	**Dimension 2: ICT – Other systems**
B08	The HR department uses a system which enables a search for candidates who have the characteristics and capabilities that match the requirements in current recruitments among: • present and former employees, • trainees and former applicants.
B09	Thanks to access to an internal HR IT system, many everyday matters are dealt with by employees themselves (e.g. taking holidays, settling business trip expenses, participation in training programmes).
B10	Employees are using, on a daily basis, a knowledge management system, which helps in the storage and search of: • know-what knowledge (facts, procedures, processes), • know-who knowledge (knowledgeable employees).
B11	The company uses an IT system which enables informal communication among employees, based on social media-like tools (e.g. chat, forum, blog).
Code	**Dimension 3: Processes – Interdepartmental**
C01	Professional skills, taking care of customers and employees, as well as the ethical behaviour of the company leadership, is the benchmark for all employees.
C02	Customer satisfaction, loyalty and engagement indicators are analysed by the company's top management at least once a month, and if necessary, immediate problem-solving corrections are implemented.
C03	The company actively promotes and appreciates such values and attitudes as: • sincere interest in customer needs, • openness for collaboration within the company and with external partners, • respect for every person, • care for corporate property, • openness to taking on challenges and taking risks, as well as the readiness to learn from mistakes.

(*continued*)

Table 4.1 (continued)

C04	Clear procedures describing the ways important corporate data can be accessed do not cause employees to complain about bureaucratic barriers or a reluctance of fellow-employees, when asked for information sharing or interpretation.
C05	Employees are encouraged to come up with innovative ideas. Every such idea is assessed, and the authors of the best ideas are given a chance to implement them (e.g. they manage the change management project).
C06	The managers at any level devote much more time to motivating and leading their teams than to detailed work division and control.
C07	The employees willingly engage in corporate social responsibility actions of their employer (e.g. working together to help charities, raising money in collections, taking part in educational, health-promoting or environmental protection activities).
C08	A sympathetic and open working ambience creates a corporate environment where professional subordination and belonging to different departments do not harm good communication and cooperation among employees.
C09	Employee mobility is encouraged by offering a chance to participate in interdepartmental projects or teams.
Code	**Dimension 3: Processes – Departmental**
D01	Tailor-made offers for loyal customers are usually more beneficial than offers for new customers.
D02	Sales planning is foremostly based on loyal customer purchases, and efforts are made to systematically take advantage of their referrals.
D03	The company is confident that: • every customer looking for information about an offer is serviced immediately, • these contacts are registered and processed to salespersons, • the sales conversion of these customers is constantly monitored.
D04	Every customer is offered add-ons, such as: • complementary products (e.g. accessories, financial services), • up-sell products. These proposals are based on customer data registered by the company.
D05	Means of direct communication are the main communication tools. The communications select: • meaningful content (tailored to customer needs), • communication channels, • exact time (incorporating the individual product/service use cycle).
D06	The company or its brands have built a continuously engaged online community helpful in: • proliferation and creative transformation of its marketing communication, • inspiring new products and services, • acquiring new customers.

(*continued*)

Table 4.1 (continued)

D07	Customer service does not only address dispute issues, but actively counters defection. Hence this unit has its own budget, which (provided there is a business reason) is used to resolve problems in favour of the customer, even if the factual terms the customer requests are unjustifiable.
D08	Customer feedback (e.g. complaints, requests): • is discussed by the employees concerned and their supervisors within one week after the event occurs, • analysis is included in the employee assessment system.
D09	Employee assessment is based on: • work performance indicators and the supervisor's evaluation, • opinions of fellow-employees, regarding their engagement, knowledge and willingness to cooperate, • self-assessment, • in the case of additional managers on their team's engagement, knowledge and a willingness to cooperate.
D10	The following initiatives are organized: • numerous internal training sessions (conducted by the company's own employees) And • new talent development programmes, supervised by experienced employees where the company's know-how is effectively transferred.
D11	The company, on a regular basis, monitors indicators such as: • RFM – Recency, frequency, monetary value of customer purchases, • NPS – Customer propensity to refer the offer, • CLV – Customer lifetime value (the extrapolated value of customer purchases in the envisaged loyalty cycles).
D12	The company, on a regular basis, monitors customer and employee engagement based on indicators such as: • openness to communication (e.g. participation in surveys), • propensity to refer the company (as a supplier or an employer), • reporting new ideas (e.g. products, services, improvements).
Code	**Company characteristics**
E01	**The company has (a single-choice question):** E1.1 fewer than 100 customers, E1.2 several hundred customers, E1.3 1000 or more customers.
E02	**The company has (a single-choice question):** E2.1 < 10 employees, E2.2 < 50 employees, E2.3 < 250 employees, E2.4 < 999 employees, E2.5 < 4999 employees, E2.6 => 5000 employees.

(continued)

Table 4.1 (continued)

E03	**Market focus (a single-choice question):** E3.1 business-to-customer, E3.2 business-to-business, E3.3 business-to-administration.
E04	**The company's business model is mainly based on (a single-choice question):** E4.1 agriculture, E4.2 production without commerce structures, E4.3 production with commerce structures, E4.4 production with commerce structures and customer service, E4.5 production with commerce structures, customer service and augmented services, E4.6 commerce, E4.7 commerce and customer service, E4.8 commerce, customer service and augmented services, E4.9 services, E4.10 services with commerce structures, E4.11 research and development.
E05	**The company's main industry, according to polish classification of business activities (a single-choice question):** E5.1 agriculture, E5.2 wholesale trade, E5.3 retail, E5.4 construction, E5.5 transport, E5.6 financial services, E5.7 communication and information technologies, E5.8 other services, E5.9 production, E5.10 mining.
E06	**Which description best suits the way your company is managed (a single-choice question):** E6.1 strong leadership and centralization in the hands of the owner/president of the company, E6.2 centralization of decisions in the hands of top management, multiple layers of management, work standardization and formalization, big organizational units, E6.3 decisions in the hands of multiple types of managers and highly qualified specialists, big organizational units, E6.4 high degree of independence of business units (geographically or product related) supervised based on an extensive system of KPIs, E6.5 decisions democratically resulting from the opinions of many employees, small organizational units and matrix structures.

(continued)

Table 4.1 (continued)

E07	During the last two years the company has (multiple choice): E7.1 been steadily expanding in terms of sales or market share, E7.2 been steadily staying ahead of competitors in terms of profits, E7.3 entered a new market, E7.4 been steadily increasing employment, E7.5 taken over (an)other enterprise(s), E7.6 been steadily staying ahead of competitors in terms of customer satisfaction, E7.7 been steadily improving the customer loyalty rate, E7.8 been steadily a sought-after employer.

The items from group A, C, D, which are given in **bold** were incorporated in the final proposal of the RM maturity model.

departmental processes, which mirror the 13 RM themes discussed in the previous chapter. The RM-based service logic is implied in all but the ICT dimensions. Eight questions in the 'strategy' dimension deal with the general approach to baseline RM facets reflected in corporate documents and core capabilities. Eleven questions in the ICT section focus on the functionality and implementation process of CRM-class systems as well as other ICT instances. Two groups of, in total, 21 questions in the processual dimension reflect concrete RM activities that may characterize an RM-mature firm. In addition, in line with principle 3 of research design defined in Chap. 3, seven multiple-choice questions concerning different company characteristics, including its competitive advantage, were placed in section E.

As indicated in Chap. 1, the notion of competitive advantage is a relative phenomenon. Competitive advantage is also not only about generating temporary profits, but about the potential to sustain this ability in the future. Therefore, in this questionnaire the usual short-term financial and market measures of competitive advantage were supplemented with some future-oriented ones, focused on customer and employee value (Feurer and Chaharbaghi 1994; Mauboussin 2012; Zairi 1994). Consequently, the assessment of competitive advantage adopted for this research is based on nine questions divided into two groups of short-term and long-term performance indicators. These questions were not indented for the respondents to require the access and rights to share potentially confidential information based on hard data statements, as this would heavily reduce the number of finished interviews (Vij and Bedi 2016). Instead, the informants were asked to answer closed questions (yes/no), which enabled them to unambiguously position their companies towards the competitors or (when appropriate) dealt with easily observable nominal qualitative or quantitative progress in the last two years. This procedure might have created a potentially diversified group without making any sharp distinction between mediocre and underperforming companies. This was done deliberately, however, without any negative consequences for the research, because the questions on business performance were primarily designed to effectively filter the relatively small group of top-performing companies. The following descriptions were adopted as short-term performance indicators:

- the company has been steadily increasing sales or market share;
- the company has been steadily hiring more employees;
- the company has been steadily outcompeting other firms in terms of revenues;
- the company has taken over some of its competitors.

They describe a temporal success of a company, which may, but does not have to, have sustainable foundations. For example, increase in sales may be the knock-on effect of the accumulation of relationship capital, but may also be a result of extensive promotional programmes. Similarly, high revenues may have fundamental causes, but can also be influenced by some unimaginative direct cost reductions or shifts in how they are accounted and reported (Coyne 1986). The unexpected fall of numerous "Wall Street darlings" is the most striking evidence for this (Sterling 2002). In fact, short-term performance is a necessary but insufficient condition to label a company as having sustainable competitive advantage (Aaker 1989, Davis et al. 2000).

By contrast, the long-term indicators of competitive advantage reflect the positive effects of enduring relationships and strategic planning (Horovitz 1979; Schertzer et al. 2013). Customer-delighting encounters can be produced by accumulating and applying customer-specific knowledge through engaged employees (Sasser et al. 1997). Loyalty, whether of employees or customers, is an even more complex and constantly moving target, which reflects the organizational capability to manage internal and external interactions in a qualitative way time after time (Crosby and Johnson 2004). Thus, in line with models postulating sustainable performance measurement (e.g. Balanced Scorecard, Kaplan and Norton 1992; Performance Prism, Neely et al. 2002; SMART, Cross and Lynch 1988), long-term/sustainable competitive advantage is measured in this research by the following descriptive indicators:

- the company has been steadily outcompeting other firms in terms of customer satisfaction;
- the company has been steadily growing its loyal customer base;
- the company has been a sought-after employer.

Due to the reasons expounded in the Preface to this book and throughout Chap. 3, companies reporting both short-term and long-term competitive advantage characteristics are the central focus of this research. Later in the book, some of these will be described as having 'extremely strong competitive advantage', which translates into their having reported all the long-term and at least three out of four of the short-term competitive advantage descriptions. Three additional cohorts of companies will be presented in the background: companies with 'strong competitive advantage' are those that reported at least two short-term and two long-term descriptions; the label 'uncertain competitive advantage' characterizes companies that reported three descriptions (including no more than one long-term description); finally, the 'no competitive advantage' group consists of companies reporting no more than two short-term advantage descriptions.

According to the discussion on possible differences among companies in their ability to generate relational rents and on the system of RM mid-range theories presented in Chap. 2, the overall impact of RM maturity on competitive advantage should be a stable effect. However, to potentially enrich the RM discourse and in line with research principle 3 defined in Chap. 3, the remaining questions in section E are aimed to additionally characterize the four cohorts of companies from different angles:

- economic sizes measured by the number of customers and the number of employees (the latter based on EU classification; Eurostat 2020a);
- market focus and business model;
- Polish Classification of Business Activities compliant with NACE rev.2 (Eurostat 2020b);
- organizational structure according to H. Mintzberg's typology (1993).

An integral part of a questionnaire is its grading scale. In this study the informants were asked to assess to what extent the descriptions provided matched the realities of their companies on a 0–10 scale. If a score of '10' was chosen, the respondent assessed the given description as completely adequate to the situation in the company. Score '1' meant the opposite, and the other scores were to be applied as shades of intermediary situations. Score '0' could be used if the interviewed person was not knowledgeable in a particular field (McDaniel and Gates 2015).

The ten-point + '0' scale was deliberately chosen for several reasons. First, this scale usually achieves a higher explanatory power and thus a higher nomological validity than fewer-point scales, such as the seven-point Likert scale or even more so the popular five-point Likert scale (Coelho and Esteves 2007a, p. 334). Second, in odd-point scales the midpoint is typically used to reduce the response effort. This results in a fake distribution pattern, which overestimates the true frequency associated with this point (Coelho and Esteves 2007b, p. 549). Third, by having very clearly spread extremes, the ten-point scale seemed to be more capable of differentiating between truly and superficially relationship-oriented firms, which is in line with principle 4 of research design defined in Chap. 3. Moreover, the natural reference of a ten-point scale to the metric system, which is used in Poland, did not demand more effort from the respondents than the Likert odd-point scales. In accordance with E. Cox's guidelines based on information theory and the absolute judgement paradigm of psychophysics, ten response alternatives plus '0' seem to be refined enough to be capable of transmitting most of the information available from informants without unnecessarily encouraging response error (1980).

A related matter was the decision as to what score levels could be qualified as indicating RM maturity. Furthermore, would it be enough to reach the average or mean set at a particular level to qualify for further analysis, or would only descriptions which met a score at the minimum set level in every observation qualify? With reference to the fact that the descriptions used in the questionnaire are generally positive statements and given the articulated acute risk of collecting 'positive illusions' rather than objective facts (Martins and Kambil 1999), and thus the risk of mixing truly relationship-oriented companies with those who are only superficially devoted to RM (what was also reflected in the H1tm theory-methodic hypothesis), it was decided to adopt a stringent qualification mechanism. Therefore, only descriptions rated 9 or 10 in every observation were made eligible as components of the RM maturity model. One can assume that these top answers are significantly less likely to be biased by wishful thinking as they clearly represent the 'positive extreme' associated with easily understandable 90–100% levels. By contrast, scores of 7 and 8 may still provide much comfort for those respondents who nurture their psychological needs by answering in an overly positive way.

This assumption is in line with empirical research, based on Net Promoter Score (NPS) methodology, which is a globally respected measure of customer prospective loyalty (Samson 2006; Schmidt-Subramanian et al. 2019). Its foundations were laid by F. Reichheld and his team at Bain & Company, who managed to link customer declarations of product recommendations with actual referrals and purchasing history. However, this link appeared only to remain true if respondents reported 90–100% certainty. These customers generated 80% of referrals and were two times more likely to repurchase from the same company than customers reporting scores of 7–8 (Reichheld and Markey 2011, pp. 49–52). In other words, the demarcation line between what people merely declare and what really holds lies at score 9, or 90% certainty.

Admittedly, NPS has also been criticized. Some researchers were not able to reproduce the causal link between NPS and revenue growth (Keiningham et al. 2007; Pingitore et al. 2007), albeit not using the same methodology and relying on third-party data (Whitlark and Rhoads 2011). Some have criticized its applicability across different cultures; however, they have failed to provide an adequate empirical refutation (Bendle and Bagga 2016). Others somewhat caustically referred to the title of F. Reichheld's original article in *Harvard Business Review*, "The one number you need to grow" (2003), and the simplicity of NPS, by invoking the limitations he had earlier personally indicated or eliminated (East et al. 2011; Fisher and Kordupleski 2019; Klaus and Maklan 2013; Grisaffe 2007). Some authors have even felt that F. Reichheld's alleged self-critique partly discredits his own work on customer loyalty (Sharp 2008). Nonetheless, NPS has been proved by other researchers to be a valid and stable customer behaviour predictor (Feehan et al. 2009; Samson 2006). Particularly important for the present research is that the same authors who criticize NPS simultaneously agree that the impact of customer satisfaction on the share of customer wallet and firms' revenues is sharply non-linear (Keiningham et al. 2014).

This extensive comment on NPS is not only intended to advocate for the chosen interpretation of empirical results. It will also have an impact on the discussion on RM upper mid-range theory in Chap. 5. In fact, what

F. Reichheld proposes to measure by NPS can be to some extent termed a highly aggregated RM capabilitys indicator. Moreover, some of its limitations can be mapped to the challenges in linking the RM business model and competitive advantage of a firm. However, first let us concentrate on the research methodology and the empirical results.

4.2 Analytical Strategy

The sampling universe consisted of the population of all Polish companies (3,520,272 entities). The sample comprised 608 Polish firms stratified by the main industries according to the Polish Classification of Business Activities compliant with the EU industry standard classification. The stratification also covered company size (in terms of the number of employees). However, the sample deliberately does not truly reflect the population of Polish firms in this respect. According to the Polish Central Statistical Office, more than 96% of registered companies in Poland employ 1–9 employees. As many as 95% of them are run by a single natural person, and in approximately 70% of cases as a form of self-employment (to avoid a tax burden imposed on formal employment). Moreover, 46% of these one-man companies do not survive their first two years, and 69% close within five years of founding (PARP 2011, pp. 17, 49). Since, in this study, the focus is placed on the search of RM patterns of achieving sustainable competitive advantage, such ephemeral companies are not located at the heart of its research interest. Therefore, in terms of size, the sample was divided into almost four equally numerous cohorts (compare in the online appendix attached to this book).

The desired respondents were marketing, sales and HR managers, or in case of the smaller firms, their owners. One-man companies were not contacted at all. There were two pooling methods and three steps in the data collection procedure. To test the questionnaire before the main pooling stage started, the author of this book personally conducted eight direct interviews. The interlocutors were either executive board members or CRM project team members. As a result, some overlapping questions were removed or slightly rephrased to achieve more clarity. The primary data collection method was the Computer Assisted Telephone Interview (CATI), conducted by an external provider. The pooling procedure started with a pilot of 100 net interviews. Before the main group of records was collected, some additional minor amendments in order and wording of the questions were made to reduce the necessity for construing during an interview and the likelihood of misinterpretations of the substance of the asked questions. There were no significant differences between the levels of answers measured in any of the pooling stages. According to the statistics presented in Table 4.2, the response rate for this survey reached 13.1%.

Despite all efforts of survey practitioners (introducing new communication channels, reminders and incentives, optimizing questionnaires) non-response is a persistent and impeding problem (Baruch 1999; Baruch and Holtom 2008; Hansen and Hurwitz 1946). However, a high nominal response rate should not be an end in itself. A survey that yields a low response rate can still do a fairly good job, if the effectively interviewed population is similar to the whole population from which it was originally drawn (Dillman 1991). The errors in survey coverage due to unit non-response can be compensated by applying weighting procedures (Dey 1997). Among various weighting methods, in this research, auxiliary information for the intended respondents was applied (Holt and Elliot 1991). Therefore, the sample design included the application of replacement samples to mimic the target population distribution in terms of industrial sectors and company size. To complete 600 telephone interviews, 9 replacement samples were needed. The whole process took only a few weeks; hence the time factor did not have an impact on the variance of results. In addition, the responses of the two halves of the dataset were compared. No significant differences between the variables were identified, which suggests that unit non-response bias is unlikely.

Item non-response mainly affected group B questions regarding ICT (e.g. CRM systems) and, to some extent, group D questions regarding departmental processes (e.g. nurturing online brand community). This is due to the number of companies that did not use any class of the surveyed ICT systems or did not manage the processes they were asked for. Usually data imputation is applied to prevent the reduction of sample size by

Table 4.2 Response statistics in CATI survey

Status	Quantity
No phone connection	721
Refusal	2726
Postponed and not completed	535
Completed	600
Total	4582

Source: CATI research agency Biostat

discarding incomplete records from the analysis. However, data imputation works on an assumption of a random item non-response, which may produce another class of error (Gilley and Leone 1991). Also, in the case of this research the risk of heavily distorting the data patterns by the application of distance functions was too high. For example, illogical random similarities to CSR or HR might have been used to impute ICT governance. Post-stratification was also not applied, although this procedure is commonly used to adjust the sampling weights so that the estimated population sizes remain as they were in the stratified sample (Lumley 2011). In the subject dataset, however, none of the descriptive items affected by a relatively high non-response could potentially influence the final proposal of the RM maturity model, as they all scored too low to be qualified for further analysis. The distribution of missing data for all the questions is reported as '0' in the online appendix attached to this book.

The dominant method in quantitative empirical research on marketing and strategic management is the use of structural equation models (SEM; Chin et al. 2008; Shook et al. 2004). These are often built on a set of several questions of different granularity, which deal with more or less important business practices that are arbitrarily combined in several constructs directly or indirectly influencing the business results (Hair et al. 2012). The discussion or conclusions tend to comment on the statistical importance of the aggregated measure, while the outstanding activities are often listed only in the appendixes (if provided). In particular, although SEM can be used to systematically highlight the estimated strength of the relationships among assumed variables, the nature of these relationships and the actual ordering of the variables is always a matter of adopted convention (Bacharach 1989). Meanwhile, causal links between the variables may coexist with reciprocal ones, or some variables may only randomly correlate with important constructs (Scott 2002). Nonetheless, if the theory 'fits the data', the alternative explanations will typically not be analysed (Carter and Hodgson 2006). Meanwhile, approximately 75% of SEM-based papers are reported to have at least one radically different equivalent model (Rong and Wilkinson 2011, p. 137). It is not surprising that quantitative research has been criticized as an impressive way of diminishing reality by providing 'exactly approximate' variables, averages and distributions (Gummesson 2017).

Given all the challenges in studying the RM maturity and owing to the fact that the H-D theory confirmation method does not provide selection criteria for choosing among analytically valid explanations of empirically captured phenomena (Ketokivi and Mantere 2010), instead of SEM-based inference this research applies machine learning techniques in the form of basket analysis/association rules mining. By harnessing sophisticated mathematical algorithms, these techniques offer simplicity and parsimony in data presentation without sacrificing the virtue of empirical adequacy (Hruschka 2019). The basic idea behind basket analysis/association rules mining can be best related to the dilemma of a retailer. If a customer buys product α and product β, how likely is it that they will be interested in buying product γ? Provided there is evidence in the data for some kind of rule linking α, β, γ and more complicated variables containing sets of products, a retailer might find a key to successfully promote a basket of products that the given customer is likely to purchase as a bundled offer. The method is also suitable for the analysis of complex phenomena such as multilevel processes involving micro (e.g. organizational behaviour) and macro (organizational strategy) variables (Aguinis et al. 2013). The same applies to rules linking RM activities and the approaches of highly successful companies.

Let $I = \{i1, i2, ..., ik\}$ be a set of k binary attributes called items, where k denotes the number of attributes.

In a set of transactions (answers to questions), each transaction contains a subset of I, marked by an individual respondent's identifier.

Let $Tj = \{t1, t2, ..., tn\}$, where $Tj \in = I$ is a set of transactions, where n denotes the number of respondents.

Basket analysis focuses on finding non-trivial patterns within the answers of respondents, which are defined as:

$$A \Rightarrow B$$

where A, B $\in I$ and A $\cap$ B = $\emptyset$. The subset of items A is called antecedent (left-hand side—LHS) and the subset of items B is called consequent (right-hand side—RHS). The symbol $\Rightarrow$ indicates the rule linking the item sets.

Unlike in the case of SEM, where it would be necessary to build an ex ante model assuming the existence of relationships between items aggregated to a limited number of variables and constructs, the adopted method made it possible to avoid biasing the results of statistical inference with a predefined vision of what the final RM maturity model should look like. Certainly, the applied questionnaire does also entail a vision of what activities and approaches may characterize an RM-mature company. However, it is proposed as the preliminary model, a wide palette of options, which could be only partly relevant and relatively freely intertwined without any harm to the final model. In this sense this research has an exploratory character.

Another advantage is the freedom in defining target variables (different levels of competitive advantage) as combinations of questions self-reported by the respondents, without having to assume any latent variable(s) that might be measured by their answers. Instead, the focus was placed on uncovering hidden complex relationships between the descriptive variables in an intuitive way that can be easily communicated to wider audiences (Aguinis et al. 2010). Moreover, the multiple-choice questions concerning different company characteristics (including the question on competitive advantage) are based on a nominal measuring scale, and the 40 descriptive questions incorporate a ten-point interval scale supplemented by an additional '0' answer. This limits the applicability of classic SEM inference, which requires at least the use of ordinal scales. Basket analysis/association rules work well even with weak scales and allow item non-response without having to take the risk of data imputation (Aguinis et al. 2013; Aumann and Lindell 2003).

Finally, the computed rules can be easily quality controlled by the use of several notations. This is of particular importance in large databases, as in a dataset consisting of k items, the square of k combinations is possible. Therefore, following Hornik et al. and Hahsler (2005; 2011), three notations were introduced: support, confidence and lift.

Support is the frequency of transactions containing all the items in both item subsets A and B. In other words, support denotes the probability of simultaneously observing A and B in the dataset.

$$A \Rightarrow B = P(A \cap B) = \frac{n(A \cap B)}{N.}$$

where N is the total number of all transactions and $n(x)$ is the number of transactions containing x.

In this research the minimum support was set to 0.5, which means that any of the presented rules will appear in at least 50% of transactions.

Confidence indicates how often a particular rule has been found to be true. In other words, confidence denotes the conditional probability of observing the RHS of the rule in transactions that also include the LHS selected in the first place. This can be assessed through the proportion of supports:

$$A \Rightarrow B = P(B|A) = \frac{n(A \cap B)}{n(A)}$$

where $n(x)$ is the number of transactions containing x.

In this research the minimum confidence was set to 0.9, which means that any of the rules will appear true in at least 90% of instances they apply to.

Lift represents the ratio of the observed support to that to be expected if A and B were independent. If the antecedent and the consequent that build a rule are dependent on one another, lift should be greater than 1. In other words, lift indicates the probability of selecting B if A was selected.

$$A \Rightarrow B = \frac{(confidence)}{P(B)} = \frac{P(B|A)}{P(B)}$$

In this research the minimum lift was set to 1.25, which means that any of the rules will imply the increase in probability of co-occurrence of its antecedent and consequent by at least 25%.

With reference to the discussed theoretical assumptions and the adopted bias reduction strategy, the association rules mining procedure concentrates entirely on the companies reporting 9- or 10-rated relational activities and approaches, and thus mainly on the 'extremely strong competitive advantage' group. Therefore, before the actual statistical analysis started, each of the 40 descriptive questions incorporated in the preliminary RM maturity model were coded according to the following rule:

$$ik = \begin{cases} 1 \text{ if } Qk \in \{9,10\} \\ 0 \text{ otherwise} \end{cases}$$

where Qk designates the original answers from the respondents to question k and notes that possible values were $Qk \in \{1, ..., 10\}$. Only variables denoted by ik were further analysed within the group of companies with 'extremely strong competitive advantage'. This allowed the analysis to be narrowed down to items that may have the highest impact on RM maturity.

4.3 The Empirical Results on RM Maturity and Competitive Advantage

The statistical analysis of the empirical material was powered by the 'R' system enhanced by the packages 'arules' and 'arulesViz', which facilitate mining and visualization of association rules and frequent item sets. Table 4.3 shows the share and number of companies in the dataset characterized by different levels of competitive advantage.

Before presenting the actual rules, some introductory descriptive statistics will be analysed. Figure 4.1 shows a regular ascending tendency across all RM maturity characteristics (small grey dots), in the overall means (big grey dots in the boxes), quartiles 1 and 3 (the bottom/upper parts of the boxes), and medians (the black lines in the boxes) in relation to the competitive advantage achieved. In addition, Fig. 4.2 depicts the differences between the companies having 'extremely high competitive advantage' and the 'no competitive advantage' group in each and every factor. Both figures indicate that the companies with 'extremely high competitive advantage' had higher mean scores for almost every item. The only notable exceptions are a few items from group B (ICT systems). Nonetheless, these differences are small (no more than 3.7%), and the overall average score level of all group B items is the lowest in the pool. Therefore, they must be playing only a background role in achieving competitive advantage.

These findings are of particular importance with regard to the relatively small number of companies with 'extremely high competitive advantage' in the analysed sample. For obvious reasons, top-performing companies are always scarce in the population of business entities, whenever competitive advantage or (as it seems based on this data) RM maturity is concerned. Therefore, it is important that the concept of RM maturity based on association rules computed in this small group is also indirectly justified by the trends observed in the whole dataset.

Table 4.3 Companies of different competitive advantage in the dataset

Competitive advantage	*Share of companies (%)*	*Number of companies*
Extremely strong	4	24
Strong	15	92
Uncertain	13	76
None	68	416

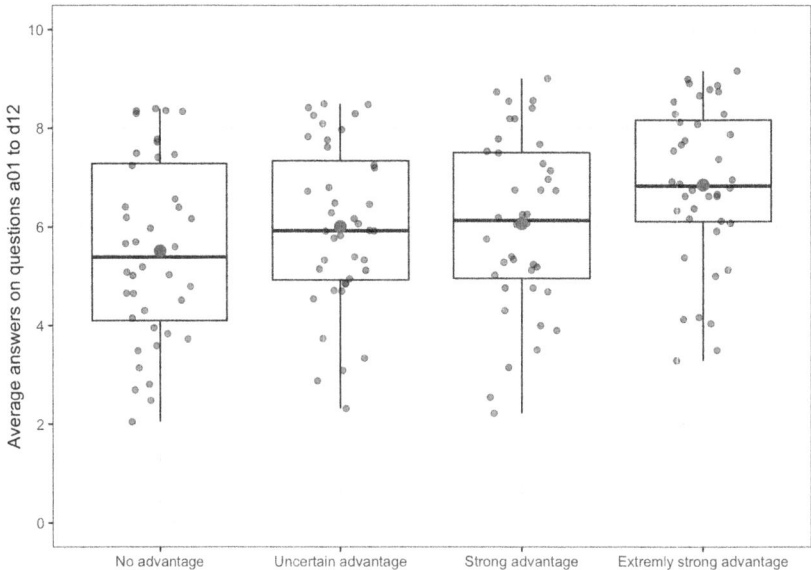

Fig. 4.1 Mean results for every item in the dataset broken down by competitive advantage groups

The legitimacy of the elaborated results based only on the 'extremely high competitive advantage' group of firms could also be potentially questioned, if this group were to reveal some important characteristics other than proficiency in distinct RM activities and approaches and the highest level of competitive advantage. Figure 4.3 condenses the information on the four clusters of companies based on their questionnaires' section E characteristics. The first impression is that the companies with at least some elements of the competitive advantage compound are in many aspects much more comparable than the 'no competitive advantage' group of companies. They tend to be larger and more likely to have numerous clients and employees. By contrast, the most significant peculiarity of the 'extremely strong competitive advantage' group of companies is its dominant B2B focus. This, however, does not come as a surprise as RM originates in industrial marketing (Payne and Frow 2017), and CRM is technically easier to facilitate in contractual markets (Deszczyński 2008).

Concerning the declared business model and the main industry, the top-performing companies report activities in all three major business

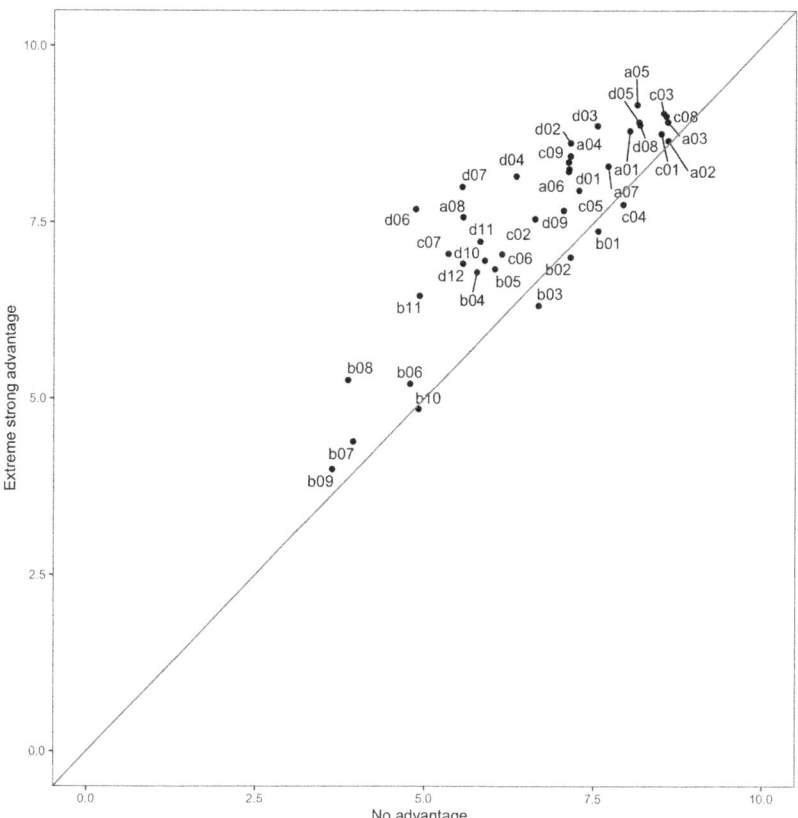

Fig. 4.2 Comparison of differences in the mean results between the 'extremely high competitive advantage' and 'no competitive advantage' groups of companies

domains, production, commerce and services, which confirms the findings of Reinartz et al. (2004), who insist that CRM benefits do not vary significantly across industries. Notably, and in line with the SDL, the greatest share among these companies were those who declared organizing a complex chain of value creation (services or production and commerce structures, customer service, and augmented services). Interestingly, all groups of companies are relatively comparable in terms of organizational structure according to H. Mintzberg's typology (1993). Although by having a stronger profile of small entities, the 'no competitive advantage group' of

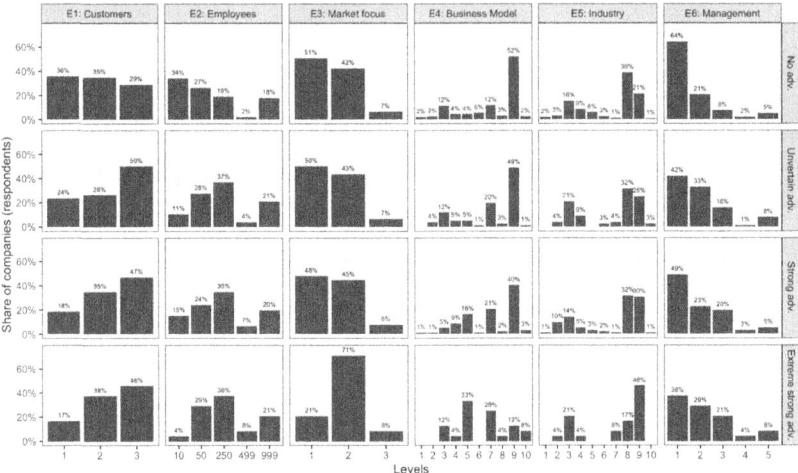

Fig. 4.3 Companies' characteristics across groups of achieved competitive advantage. Note: For decoding the results on the X axis, please refer to section E of the questionnaire

companies stands out with its proportion of 'strong leadership and centralization' type. Nonetheless, given other similarities, the organizational structure seems not to have a decisive impact on the likelihood of achieving sustainable competitive advantage. To sum up, the 'extremely high competitive advantage' group of companies remains diversified and relatively similar to other groups of companies, with only a few notable but logical differences. This is in line with the conclusions of other researchers who did not find any significant differences in industry type and commoditization among companies achieving relationally based competitive advantage (Coviello et al. 2002; Sharma and Iyer 2007; Reimann et al. 2010). Therefore, what these companies achieve in terms of RM maturity is valid and potentially transferable to all entities, and thus these results are generalizable. Hence, the identified set of association rules computed for the group of companies with 'extremely strong competitive advantage' can be viewed as representing a bundle of capabilities that forms a critical mass of proficiency in RM and foretells a sustainable competitive advantage.

Table 4.4 contains a list of rules, with the level of notations and the number of companies with these rules identified. Figure 4.4 visualizes the

Table 4.4 Association rules computed for the 'extremely strong competitive advantage' group of companies

Rule	LHS		RHS	Count	Support	Confidence	Lift
1	A06	⇒	A05	12	0.52	1.00	1.25
2	C01	⇒	C03	12	0.52	1.00	1.53
3	C01	⇒	C08	12	0.52	1.00	1.53
4	A02	⇒	D05	12	0.52	0.92	1.42
5	A02	⇒	C03	12	0.52	0.92	1.42
6	A04	⇒	C08	12	0.52	0.92	1.42
7	C03	⇒	C08	12	0.61	0.93	1.43
8	C08	⇒	C03	12	0.61	0.93	1.43
9	C01, C03	⇒	C08	12	0.52	1.00	1.53
10	C01, C08	⇒	C03	12	0.52	1.00	1.53
11	C03, D03	⇒	C08	12	0.52	1.00	1.53
12	C08, D03	⇒	C03	12	0.52	1.00	1.53
13	C03, D05	⇒	C08	12	0.52	0.92	1.42
14	C08, D05	⇒	C03	12	0.52	1.00	1.53
15	C03, D08	⇒	C08	12	0.52	1.00	1.53
16	C08, D08	⇒	C03	12	0.52	0.92	1.42

Note: For decoding the LHS and RHS, please refer to sections A, C and D of the questionnaire provided in Table 4.1. Count represents the number of companies for which the particular rule was reported. By coincidence, for every rule it equals 12, but the set of companies reporting the rules differs in every case.

same results in a network structure highlighting multifaceted associations between the items. Thus, the task of verifying the elements that constitute the final proposal of the RM maturity model (empirically validated successful RM business model) is completed.

What is worth noting is that the association rules based on 9/10 scores could only be computed among the top-performing companies, whereas the differences between the means of the top-performing and underperforming companies on average reached no more than 30%, and in most cases around 10%. The only exception was a single rule identified in the group of companies with 'strong competitive advantage' linking items C01 and C03. However, the same rule (R2) was also reported for the companies with 'extremely strong competitive advantage'. This observation not only directly validates the R2 rule, but also matches the reported correlation of ascending levels of competitive advantage and RM maturity. Hence, the discovered rules do not appear to be an accidentally isolated effect but rather indicate a non-linear regularity.

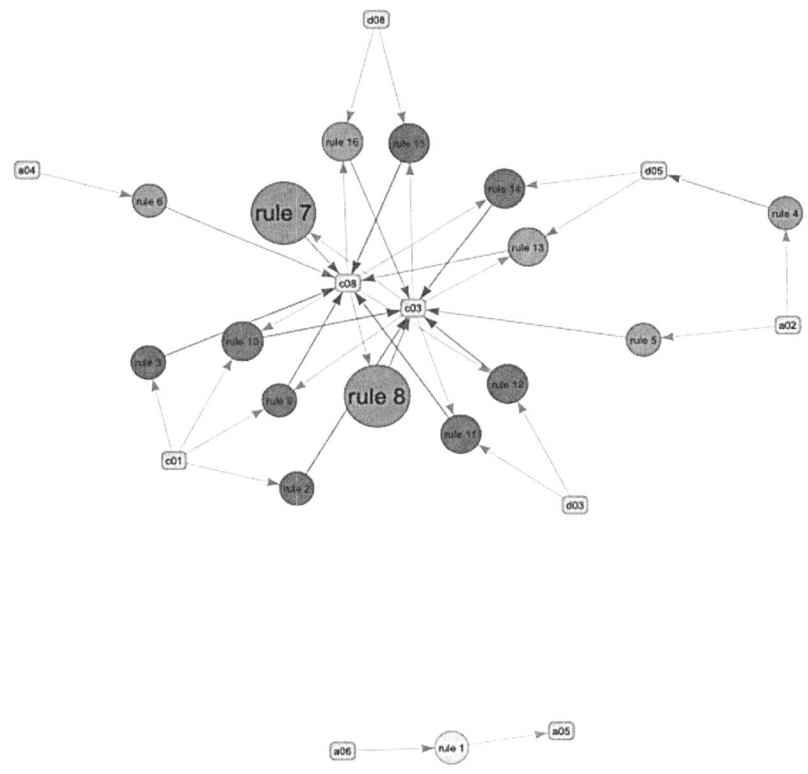

Fig. 4.4 The network of association rules. Note: For decoding the item subsets composing the rules, please refer to sections A, C and D of the questionnaire

The first impression after analysing the basket containing the RM activities and approaches marked by the association rules is that both RM maturity and sustainable competitive advantage correlate with ethics. Thirteen out of sixteen rules linking distinctive RM characteristics, reported by market leaders, include items which directly deal with collaboration, fairness, openness and respect. The strongest rules supplied in the analysis (R7 and R8) include two reciprocally correlated items (C03 and C08): the promotion of positive values and attitudes of the company creates a working ambience, which supports communication and cooperation, and in turn, good communication and cooperation (regardless of structure and hierarchy) contribute to the perception of corporate efforts to instil positive values and attitudes as meaningful and sincere. At the same time, an ethical company does not seem to be necessarily concentrating on its external stakeholders, but rather it starts by taking care of the well-being of its own employees (note that item C07 concerning CSR-labelled engagement did not qualify for any of the top rules).

A good working ambience coincidences with a positive perception of company leadership, and in an even stronger way it emphasizes the internal nature of RM maturity. Rules R2 and R3, as well as rules R9 and R10, which incorporate items C01, C03 and C08, reinforce this view by emphasizing the importance of authentic leadership based on professionalism, a sense of responsibility (subsidiarity to employees) and an admirable moral stance. It seems that, regardless of times and social context, people need leaders, and they adjust their attitudes towards leader-sponsored ventures according to the trust and engagement they cultivate. In this context leadership and management skills, including the ability to balance the ever-present pressure for short-term profits with the investment of time and money in an employee-friendly working environment, advance to a central point in the top management's agenda (Chmielecki and Sułkowski 2018). It seems also that a basic tool of leadership (aside from someone being a living example of right behaviour) is open communication (the willingness and ability to listen to and discuss peoples' ideas, expectations and problems).

Rules R4 and R5 include the third ethical item (A02), which presents an official rooting of ethical behaviour in a corporate strategy. The link between this declaration and the actual behaviour in R5 is clear. By contrast, R4 requires a deeper reflection, as it links the composite of ethics with the dominant role of direct communication with customers. However, it seems that the ethical approach to business creates an environment for communication which is both meaningful for customers and beneficial for the company (e.g. in terms of marketing conversions). Known as extreme customer-centricity or customer value-based organizational culture, this means, rather than spamming customers with remote offers, educating them about the impact of their choices on community and society and making sure no customer makes a mistake or overlooks some benefit (Peppers and Rogers 2013; Sheth 2017). In other words, being ethical also means that the companies have something relevant to say to their individual customers/business partners that can be most effectively communicated in a one-to-one interaction. The ethical issues, partnership cooperation and good communication go hand-in-hand in the pairs of rules R11 and R12, R13 and R14, and R15 and R16, where they change positions as LHS and RHS, accompanied by processual D-type items: D03, D08 and D05. In terms of D05, again the link between fairness and a good working climate and the ability to communicate relevantly is reinforced. The other items also deal with communication, but in a more specific context of lead management (D03) and customer feedback analysis (D08).

Regrettably, lead management is quite a rare subject of scientific examination. However, in the author's own research conducted across several industries in Poland, a catastrophic underperformance in managing leads was reported, marked by an average 30% loss of prospective buyers only because companies failed to give any answer to customers' enquiries (Deszczyński 2016; Deszczyński and Mielcarek 2014). Although many tactical answers could partly explain such poor performance, the roots of this problem most likely lie in the hands of top management, who created a working environment of disengagement (Bonner et al. 2016; Kelleher 2011). To make matters worse, if companies are not able to partner in a dialogue with their customers at a point so close to sales, an even poorer performance can be expected elsewhere, particularly when customers report dissatisfaction. Hence, according to rules R11, R12, R15 and R16, lead management and customer feedback analysis can act as a relatively easy way to capture indicators reflecting the degree of a company's RM maturity.

The ability of a company to manage relationships with non-customer external stakeholders is reflected in rule R6. It directly links items A04 and C08, which means that the ability to holistically assess, for example, the role of a supplier in a total-cost-of-ownership perspective indicates a good internal working culture. In a business practice, this can mean that, for example, a purchasing department's focus is not only placed on traditional short-term savings, but it also takes into account the quality or logistical issues important for other departments (Kahkonen and Lintukangas 2018).

Finally, rule R1 links the ability to purposefully manage relationships with all direct customers of a company (A06) to the ability to do this selectively towards the very best of them (A05). It looks like a remote phenomenon detached from the network of the other 15 rules (compare Fig. 4.4). However, assessed from the perspective of the ability to effectively communicate, represented by the focal C03 and C08 items, it perfectly complements the whole picture of mature RM orientation. In addition, among all the others, item A06 reached the highest mean score (9.17) and quartile 1 score (8.75), which positions the selective individualization of relationship management (distinct from ICT-powered mass customization efforts) as a central characteristic of a mature relationship-oriented company.

Although the fact that not all of the RM dimensions contribute equally to business performance was evidenced in the literature (Pozza et al. 2018), what comes as something of a surprise is the total absence of technological issues in the final proposal of the RM maturity model. Moreover, top-performing companies scored slightly worse on some of the ICT-related items, with B03 (referring to a central customer data warehouse) as the most striking example (the average of top-performing companies was 3.7% below the average of poor performers). This does not mean companies can do away with ICT tools. The global COVID-19 crisis has shown that modern communication technology is a vital aspect for every business, whether internal or external communication is concerned. However, it seems that ICT plays a secondary, supporting role, facilitating the way to success for companies that have already mastered RM as a predominately human-to-human concept. Owing to the fact that this research was conducted before the outbreak of the COVID-19 crisis, some additional comments concerning ICT issues are offered in the Final Note.

Although not included in the list of the strongest rules, the position of items A08, D06 and D07 is also worth noting. On average, all of them scored no more than 8.0 and no more than half of the scores were 9 s or 10s, but they exhibit the largest (more than 2 points on average) distance between the companies with 'extremely strong competitive advantage' and the 'no competitive advantage' group. This may mean that they are particularly challenging, also for the best companies, even if from a benchmarking point of view they do a good job. However, for whatever reason the current level of competition does not necessitate more performance in these respective areas, so they can be seen as additional key factors of RM competence in the future. Moreover, describing a part of the customer interface, items D06 and D07 may potentially complement items D03 and D08 as relatively easy to capture and test indicators of RM maturity. All of them seem to be putting the coordination of CRM activities to a real test.

Although the empirical research validates and refines the RM maturity model and provides substance to formulate reasonable guidelines for its successful implementation, the very concept, like any H-D framework, only explains the selected realm of business reality. While company characteristics provided in group E of the questionnaire generally showed that the RM maturity model is not discriminatory towards any particular industry, company size or even management style, some unidentified internal or external factors may have influenced the ability of some companies to capitalize on their relationship portfolio. Hence, there are questions that need to be further discussed. In particular, why is achieving RM-based sustainable competitive advantage largely a game of all or nothing? In the end, 70% or 80% performance is still a fairly good result. And how is it possible that RM-immature firms could ever survive facing the competition of their truly RM-oriented rivals? These and other issues cannot be addressed by the RM maturity model alone, but need a wider perspective offered by the discussion on the RM upper mid-range theory conducted in the next and final chapter.

References

Aaker, David A. 1989. Managing Assets and Skills: The Key to a Sustainable Competitive Advantage. *California Management Review* 31 (2): 91–106. https://doi.org/10.2307/41166561.

Adèr, Hermanus Johannes. 2008. *Advising on Research Methods: A Consultant's Companion*. Huizen: Johannes van Kessel Publishing.

Aguinis, Herman, Steve Werner, JéAnna Lanza Abbott, Cory Angert, Joon Hyung Park, and Donna Kohlhausen. 2010. Customer-Centric Science: Reporting Significant Research Results With Rigor, Relevance, and Practical Impact in Mind. *Organizational Research Methods* 13 (3): 515–539. https://doi.org/10.1177/1094428109333339.

Aguinis, Herman, Lura E. Forcum, and Harry Joo. 2013. Using Market Basket Analysis in Management Research. *Journal of Management* 39 (7): 1799–1824. https://doi.org/10.1177/0149206312466147.

Alvesson, Mats, and Stanley Deetz. 2000. *Doing Critical Management Research*. London: SAGE.

Alvesson, Mats, and Kaj Sköldberg. 2009. *Reflexive Methodology: New Vistas for Qualitative Research*. London: SAGE.

Alwin, Duane F. 2007. *Margins of Error: A Study of Reliability in Survey Measurement*. Hoboken: John Wiley & Sons.

Aumann, Yonatan, and Yehuda Lindell. 2003. A Statistical Theory for Quantitative Association Rules. *Journal of Intelligent Information Systems* 20 (3): 255–283. https://doi.org/10.1023/A:1022812808206.

Bacharach, Samuel B. 1989. Organizational Theories: Some Criteria for Evaluation. *The Academy of Management Review* 14 (4): 496–515. https://doi.org/10.2307/258555.

Baruch, Yehuda. 1999. Response Rate in Academic Studies-A Comparative Analysis. *Human Relations* 52 (4): 421–438. https://doi.org/10.1177/001872679905200401.

Baruch, Yehuda, and Brooks C. Holtom. 2008. Survey Response Rate Levels and Trends in Organizational Research. *Human Relations.* https://doi.org/10.1177/0018726708094863.

Bendle, Neil T., and Charan K. Bagga. 2016. The Metrics That Marketers Muddle. *MIT Sloan Management Review* 57 (3): 73–82.

Biemer, Paul P. 2010. Total Survey Error: Design, Implementation, and Evaluation. *Public Opinion Quarterly* 74 (5): 817–848. https://doi.org/10.1093/poq/nfq058.

Bonner, Julena M., Rebecca L. Greenbaum, and David M. Mayer. 2016. My Boss Is Morally Disengaged: The Role of Ethical Leadership in Explaining the Interactive Effect of Supervisor and Employee Moral Disengagement on Employee Behaviors. *Journal of Business Ethics* 137 (4): 731–742. https://doi.org/10.1007/s10551-014-2366-6.

Carter, Richard, and Geoffrey M. Hodgson. 2006. The Impact of Empirical Tests of Transaction Cost Economics on the Debate on the Nature of the Firm. *Strategic Management Journal* 27 (5): 461–476. https://doi.org/10.1002/smj.531.

Chandra, Yanto, and Ian F. Wilkinson. 2017. Firm Internationalization from a Network-Centric Complex-Systems Perspective. *Journal of World Business* 52 (5): 691–701. https://doi.org/10.1016/j.jwb.2017.06.001.

Chin, Wynne W., Robert A. Peterson, and Steven P. Brown. 2008. Structural Equation Modeling in Marketing: Some Practical Reminders. *Journal of Marketing Theory and Practice* 16 (4): 287–298. https://doi.org/10.2753/MTP1069-6679160402.

Chmielecki, Michał, and Łukasz Sułkowski. 2018. Cultural Factors of Trust in a Public Organization as a Workplace. In *Managing Public Trust*, ed. Barbara Kočuch, Sławomir J. Magala, and Joanna Paliszkiewicz, 99–114. Cham: Springer International Publishing. https://doi.org/10.1007/978-3-319-70485-2_7.

Clarke, Irvine. 2001. Extreme Response Style in Cross-cultural Research. *International Marketing Review* 18 (3): 301–324. https://doi.org/10.1108/02651330110396488.

Coelho, Pedro S., and Susana P. Esteves. 2007a. The Choice between a Fivepoint and a Ten-Point Scale in the Framework of Customer Satisfaction Measurement. *International Journal of Market Research* 49 (3): 313–39. https://doi.org/10.1177/147078530704900305.

Coelho, Pedro S., and Susana P. Esteves. 2007b. Correspondence Regarding "The Choice between a Five-Point and a Ten-Point Scale in the Framework of Customer Satisfaction Research", by Pedro S. Coelho and Susana P. Esteves. *International Journal of Market Research* 49 (5): 547–49.

Coviello, Nicole E., Roderick J. Brodie, Peter J. Danaher, and Wesley J. Johnston. 2002. How Firms Relate to Their Markets: An Empirical Examination of Contemporary Marketing Practices. *Journal of Marketing* 66 (3): 33–46. https://doi.org/10.1509/jmkg.66.3.33.18500.

Cox, Eli P. 1980. The Optimal Number of Response Alternatives for a Scale: A Review. *Journal of Marketing Research* 17 (4): 407–422. https://doi.org/10.1177/002224378001700401.

Coyne, Kevin P. 1986. Sustainable Competitive Advantage-What It Is, What It Isn't. *Business Horizons* 29 (1): 54.

Crosby, Lawrence A., and Sheree L. Johnson. 2004. The Three Ms of Customer Loyalty. *Marketing Management* 13 (4): 12–13.

Cross, Kelvin, and Richard Lynch. 1988. The "SMART" Way to Define and Sustain Success. *National Productivity Review* 8 (1): 23–33.

Crowne, Douglas P., and David Marlowe. 1960. A New Scale of Social Desirability Independent of Psychopathology. *Journal of Consulting Psychology* 24 (4): 349–354. https://doi.org/10.1037/h0047358.

Czakon, Wojciech. 2015. *Podstawy metodologii badań w naukach o zarządzaniu*. 3rd ed. Ed. Wojciech Czakon. Warszawa: Oficyna a Wolters Kluwer business. https://ruj.uj.edu.pl/xmlui/handle/item/85236

Davidson, Karina, and Michael William MacGregor. 1998. A Critical Appraisal of Self-Report Defense Mechanism Measures. *Journal of Personality* 66 (6): 965–992. https://doi.org/10.1111/1467-6494.00039.

Davis, James H., F. David Schoorman, Roger C. Mayer, and Hwee Hoon Tan. 2000. The Trusted General Manager and Business Unit Performance: Empirical Evidence of a Competitive Advantage. *Strategic Management Journal* 21 (5): 563–576. https://doi.org/10.1002/(SICI)1097-0266(200005)21:5<563::AID-SMJ99>3.0.CO;2-0.

De Jong, Martijn G., Jan-Benedict E.M. Steenkamp, Jean-Paul Fox, and Hans Baumgartner. 2008. Using Item Response Theory to Measure Extreme Response Style in Marketing Research: A Global Investigation. *Journal of Marketing Research* 45 (1): 104–115. https://doi.org/10.1509/jmkr.45.1.104.

Deszczyński, Bartosz. 2008. Zewnętrzne Bariery Wdraèania Strategii CRM w Integrującej Się Europie. In *Polityka Unijnej Integracji: Wybrane Relacje Zewnętrzne i Wewnętrzne*, 361–376. Zielona Góra: Uniwersytet Zielonogórski.

———. 2016. The Maturity of Corporate Relationship Management. *Gospodarka Narodowa* 283 (3): 73–104. https://doi.org/10.33119/GN/100777.

Deszczyński, Bartosz, and Paweł Mielcarek. 2014. The Online/Offline Gap in Lead Management Process. *Przegląd Organizacji* 8: 42–49. https://doi.org/10.33141po.2014.08.07

Dey, Eric L. 1997. Working with Low Survey Response Rates: The Efficacy of Weighting Adjustments. *Research in Higher Education* 38 (2): 215–227. https://doi.org/10.1023/A:1024985704202.

Dillman, Don A. 1991. The Design and Administration of Mail Surveys. *Annual Review of Sociology* 17 (1): 225–249. https://doi.org/10.1146/annurev.so.17.080191.001301.

Donaldson, Stewart I., and Elisa J. Grant-Vallone. 2002. Understanding Self-Report Bias in Organizational Behavior Research. *Journal of Business and Psychology* 17 (2): 245–260. https://doi.org/10.1023/A:1019637632584.

Dörnyei, Zoltán, and Tatsuya Taguchi. 2009. *Questionnaires in Second Language Research: Construction, Administration, and Processing*. Routledge. https://doi.org/10.4324/9780203864739.

East, Robert, Jenni Romaniuk, and Wendy Lomax. 2011. The NPS and the ACSI: A Critique and An Alternative Metric. *International Journal of Market Research* 53 (3): 327–346. https://doi.org/10.2501/IJMR-53-3-327-346.

Eurostat. 2020a. Small and Medium-Sized Enterprises (SMEs) – Eurostat. https://ec.europa.eu/eurostat/web/structural-business-statistics/structural-business-statistics/sme

———. 2020b. Europa – RAMON – Classification Detail List. https://ec.europa.eu/eurostat/ramon/nomenclatures/index.cfm?TargetUrl=LST_NOM_DTL&StrNom=NACE_REV2&StrLanguageCode=PL&IntPcKey=&StrLayoutCode=HIERARCHIC

Feehan, Michael, Cristina Ilangakoon, and Penny Mesure. 2009. Keeping Score. *Marketing Research* 21 (4): 6–10.

Feurer, Rainer, and Kazem Chaharbaghi. 1994. Defining Competitiveness: A Holistic Approach. *Management Decision* 32 (2): 49–58. https://doi.org/10.1108/00251749410054819.

Fisher, Nicholas I., and Raymond E. Kordupleski. 2019. Good and Bad Market Research: A Critical Review of Net Promoter Score. *Applied Stochastic Models in Business and Industry* 35 (1): 138–151. https://doi.org/10.1002/asmb.2417.

Foddy, William H. 1994. *Constructing Questions for Interviews and Questionnaires: Theory and Practice in Social Research*. Cambridge: Cambridge University Press.

Gilley, Otis W., and Robert P. Leone. 1991. A Two-Stage Imputation Procedure for Item Nonresponse in Surveys. *Journal of Business Research* 22 (4): 281–291. https://doi.org/10.1016/0148-2963(91)90035-V.

Grisaffe, Douglas B. 2007. Questions About the Ultimate Question: Conceptual Considerations in Evaluating Reichheld's Net Promoter Score (NPS). *Journal of Consumer Satisfaction, Dissatisfaction and Complaining Behavior* 20: 36–53.

Gummesson, Evert. 2017. From Relationship Marketing to Total Relationship Marketing and Beyond. *Journal of Services Marketing* 31 (1): 16–19. https://doi.org/10.1108/JSM-11-2016-0398.

Hahsler, Michael, Sudheer Chelluboina, Kurt Hornik, and Christian Buchta. 2011. The Arules R-Package Ecosystem: Analyzing Interesting Patterns from Large Transaction Data Sets. *Journal of Machine Learning Research* 12 (June): 2021–2025.

Hair, Joseph F., Marko Sarstedt, Torsten M. Pieper, and Christian M. Ringle. 2012. The Use of Partial Least Squares Structural Equation Modeling in Strategic Management Research: A Review of Past Practices and Recommendations for Future Applications. *Long Range Planning*, Analytical Approaches to Strategic Management: Partial Least Squares Modeling in Strategy Research, 45 (5): 320–340. https://doi.org/10.1016/j.lrp.2012.09.008.

Hansen, Morris H., and William N. Hurwitz. 1946. The Problem of Non-Response in Sample Surveys. *Journal of the American Statistical Association* 41 (236): 517–529. https://doi.org/10.1080/01621459.1946.10501894.

Helgeson, James G., and Magne Supphellen. 2004. A Conceptual and Measurement Comparison of Self-Congruity and Brand Personality: The Impact of Socially Desirable Responding. *International Journal of Market Research* 46 (2): 205–233. https://doi.org/10.1177/147078530404600201.

Holt, D., and D. Elliot. 1991. Methods of Weighting for Unit Non-Response. *Journal of the Royal Statistical Society: Series D (The Statistician)* 40 (3): 333–342. https://doi.org/10.2307/2348286.

Hornik, Kurt, Bettina Grün, and Michael Hahsler. 2005. Arules – A Computational Environment for Mining Association Rules and Frequent Item Sets. *Journal of Statistical Software* 14: 1–25.

Horovitz, J. 1979. Strategic Control: A New Task for Top Management. *Long Range Planning* 12 (3): 2–7. https://doi.org/10.1016/S0024-6301(79)80001-1.

Hruschka, Harald. 2019. Comparing Unsupervised Probabilistic Machine Learning Methods for Market Basket Analysis. *Review of Managerial Science*, August 23. https://doi.org/10.1007/s11846-019-00349-0.

Kähkönen, Anni-Kaisa, and Katrina Lintukangas. 2018. Sustainable Supply Management Practices: Making a Difference in a Firm's Sustainability Performance. *Supply Chain Management: An International Journal* 23 (6): 518–530. https://doi.org/10.1108/SCM-01-2018-0036.

Kaplan, Robert, and David Norton. 1992. The Balanced Scorecard – Measures That Drive Performance. *Harvard Business Review* January–February: 71–79.

Keiningham, Timothy L., Bruce Cooil, Tor Wallin Andreassen, and Lerzan Aksoy. 2007. A Longitudinal Examination of Net Promoter and Firm Revenue Growth. *Journal of Marketing* 71 (3): 39–51. https://doi.org/10.1509/jmkg.71.3.039.

Keiningham, Timothy L., Lerzan Aksoy, Edward C. Malthouse, Bart Lariviere, and Alexander Buoye. 2014. The Cumulative Effect of Satisfaction with Discrete Transactions on Share of Wallet. *Journal of Service Management* 25 (3): 310–333. https://doi.org/10.1108/JOSM-08-2012-0163.

Kelleher, Bob. 2011. Engaged Employees Equals High-Performing Organizations (Achieving Successful Employee Engagement). *Human Resource Management International Digest* 19 (6). https://doi.org/10.1108/hrmid.2011.04419faa.011.

Ketokivi, Mikko, and Saku Mantere. 2010. Two Strategies for Inductive Reasoning in Organizational Research. *Academy of Management Review* 35 (2): 315–333. https://doi.org/10.5465/amr.35.2.zok315.

Kihlstrom, John F., Eric Eich, Deborah Sandbrand, and Betsy A. Tobias. 1999. Emotion and Memory: Implications for Self-Report. In *The Science of Self-Report*, ed. Arthur Stone, Christine Bachrach, Jared Jobe, Howard Kurtzman, and Virginia Cain, 93–112. Psychology Press. https://doi.org/10.4324/9781410601261-12.

Klaus, Philipp 'Phil', and Stan Maklan. 2013. Towards a Better Measure of Customer Experience. *International Journal of Market Research* 55 (2): 227–246. https://doi.org/10.2501/IJMR-2013-021.

Krosnick, Jon A. 1999. Survey Research. *Annual Review of Psychology* 50: 537–567.

Lumley, Thomas. 2011. *Complex Surveys: A Guide to Analysis Using R*. Hoboken: John Wiley & Sons.

March, James G., and Robert I. Sutton. 1997. Crossroads – Organizational Performance as a Dependent Variable. *Organization Science* 8 (6): 698–706.

Marsh, Herbert W., and Lawrence A. Roche. 2000. Effects of Grading Leniency and Low Workload on Students' Evaluations of Teaching: Popular Myth, Bias, Validity, or Innocent Bystanders? *Journal of Educational Psychology* 92 (1): 202–228. https://doi.org/10.1037/0022-0663.92.1.202.

Martins, Luis L., and Ajit Kambil. 1999. Research Notes: Looking Back and Thinking Ahead: Effects of Prior Success on Managers' Interpretations of New Information Technologies. *Academy of Management Journal* 42 (6): 652–661. https://doi.org/10.5465/256986.

Mauboussin, Michael J. 2012. The True Measures of Success. *Harvard Business Review*, October 1. https://hbr.org/2012/10/the-true-measures-of-success

McDaniel, Carl, Jr., and Roger Gates. 2015. *Marketing Research*. Hoboken: John Wiley & Sons.

Mintzberg, Henry. 1993. *Structure in Fives: Designing Effective Organizations*, Structure in Fives: Designing Effective Organizations. Englewood Cliffs: Prentice-Hall.

Neely, Andy, Chris Adams, and Mike Kennerley. 2002. *The Performance Prism: The Scorecard for Measuring and Managing Business Success*. London: Pearson Education.

Palmatier, Robert W. 2008. Interfirm Relational Drivers of Customer Value. *Journal of Marketing* 72 (4): 76–89. https://doi.org/10.1509/jmkg.72.4.076.

PARP. 2011. *Raport o stanie sektora małych i średnich przedsiębiorstw w Polsce.* Ed. Anna Brussa and Anna Tarnawa. Warszawa: Polska Agencja Rozwoju Przedsiębiorczości.

Payne, Adrian, and Pennie Frow. 2017. Relationship Marketing: Looking Backwards towards the Future. *Journal of Services Marketing* 31 (1): 11–15. https://doi.org/10.1108/JSM-11-2016-0380.

Peppers, Don, and Martha Rogers. 2013. Extreme Trust: The New Competitive Advantage. *Strategy and Leadership* 41 (6): 31–34. https://doi.org/10.1108/SL-07-2013-0054.

Pingitore, Gina, Neil A. Morgan, Lopo L. Rego, Adriana Gigliotti, and Jay Meyers. 2007. The Single-Question Trap. *Marketing Research* 19 (2): 9–13.

Pozza, Dalla Ilaria, Oliver Goetz, and Jean Michel Sahut. 2018. Implementation Effects in the Relationship Between CRM and Its Performance. *Journal of Business Research* 89: 391–403. https://doi.org/10.1016/j.jbusres.2018.02.004.

Reichheld, Frederick. 2003. The One Number You Need to Grow. *Harvard Business Review*, December: 1–11.

Reichheld, Frederick, and Rob Markey. 2011. *The Ultimate Question 2.0: How Net Promoter Companies Thrive in a Customer.* Boston: Harvard Business Publishing. https://books.google.pl/books?hl=pl&lr=&id=e8jhiYjQrU0C&oi=fnd&pg=PR7&dq=reichheld+markey&ots=CC1eQacr8I&sig=iSgh_lWq6TPhrVgOpVEfeP3Hnzw&redir_esc=y#v=onepage&q=reichheld%20markey&f=false.

Reimann, Martin, Oliver Schilke, and Jacquelyn S. Thomas. 2010. Customer Relationship Management and Firm Performance: The Mediating Role of Business Strategy. *Journal of the Academy of Marketing Science* 38 (3): 326–346. https://doi.org/10.1007/s11747-009-0164-y.

Reinartz, Werner, Manfred Krafft, and Wayne D. Hoyer. 2004. The Customer Relationship Management Process: Its Measurement and Impact on Performance. *Journal of Marketing Research.* https://doi.org/10.1509/jmkr.41.3.293.35991.

Rong, Baiding, and Ian Wilkinson. 2011. What Do Managers' Survey Responses Mean and What Affects Them? The Case of Market Orientation and Firm Performance. https://doi.org/10.1016/j.ausmj.2011.04.001.

Rowley, Jenny. 2014. Designing and Using Research Questionnaires. *Management Research Review* 37 (3): 308–330. https://doi.org/10.1108/MRR-02-2013-0027.

Samson, Alain. 2006. Understanding the Buzz That Matters: Negative Vs Positive Word of Mouth. *International Journal of Market Research* 48 (6): 647–657. https://doi.org/10.1177/147078530604800603.

Sasser, W. Earl, Leonard A. Schlesinger, and James L. Heskett. 1997. *Service Profit Chain*. New York: Simon and Schuster.

Schertzer, Susan M.B., Clinton B. Schertzer, and F. Robert Dwyer. 2013. Value in Professional Service Relationships. *Journal of Business & Industrial Marketing* 28 (8): 607–619.

Schmidt-Subramanian, Maxi, Harley Manning, Sam Karpinsky, and Shayna Neuburg. 2019. The Top 10 NPS Questions Answered What CX Professionals Should Know About Net Promoter Score. *Forrester*, November 7. https://www.forrester.com/report/Executive+QA+Top+10+NPS+Questions+Answered+For+CX+Professionals/-/E-RES60925.

Schriesheim, Chester A. 1981. The Effect of Grouping or Randomizing Items on Leniency Response Bias. *Educational and Psychological Measurement* 41 (2): 401–411. https://doi.org/10.1177/001316448104100219.

Scott, W. Richard. 2002. *Organizations: Rational, Natural, and Open Systems*. 5th ed. Upper Saddle River: Prentice Hall.

Sharma, Aran, and Gopalkrishnan R. Iyer. 2007. Country Effects on CRM Success. *Journal of Relationship Marketing* 5 (4): 63–78. https://doi.org/10.1300/J366v05n04_05.

Sharp, Byron. 2008. Net Promoter Score Fails the Test. *Marketing Research* 20 (4): 28–30.

Sheth, Jagdish N. 2017. Revitalizing Relationship Marketing. *Journal of Services Marketing* 31 (1): 6–10. https://doi.org/10.1108/JSM-11-2016-0397.

Shook, Christopher L., David J. Ketchen, G. Tomas M. Hult, and K. Michele Kacmar. 2004. An Assessment of the Use of Structural Equation Modeling in Strategic Management Research. *Strategic Management Journal* 25 (4): 397–404. https://doi.org/10.1002/smj.385.

Sterling, Theodore F. 2002. *The Enron Scandal*. New York: Nova Publishers.

van de Mortel, Thea F. 2008. Faking It: Social Desirability Response Bias in Self-Report Research. *The Australian Journal of Advanced Nursing* 25 (4): 40.

Vij, Sandeep, and Harpreet Singh Bedi. 2016. Are Subjective Business Performance Measures Justified? *International Journal of Productivity and Performance Management*, June 13. https://doi.org/10.1108/IJPPM-12-2014-0196.

Whitlark, David B., and Gary K. Rhoads. 2011. Scoring Success. *Marketing Research* 23 (1): 8–13.

Zairi, Mohamed. 1994. Benchmarking: The Best Tool for Measuring Competitiveness. *Benchmarking for Quality Management & Technology* 1 (1): 11–24. https://doi.org/10.1108/14635779410056859.

Open Access This chapter is licensed under the terms of the Creative Commons Attribution 4.0 International License (http://creativecommons.org/licenses/by/4.0/), which permits use, sharing, adaptation, distribution and reproduction in any medium or format, as long as you give appropriate credit to the original author(s) and the source, provide a link to the Creative Commons licence and indicate if changes were made.

The images or other third party material in this chapter are included in the chapter's Creative Commons licence, unless indicated otherwise in a credit line to the material. If material is not included in the chapter's Creative Commons licence and your intended use is not permitted by statutory regulation or exceeds the permitted use, you will need to obtain permission directly from the copyright holder.

CHAPTER 5

Developing the Relationship Management Upper Mid-Range Theory

Placing the envisioned RM mid-range theory under the umbrella of Resource-Advantage Theory of Competition (R-A theory) requires incorporating some of its basic micro-economical premises, which constitute the general boundaries of RM-based competitive advantage programmatic research. These have been discussed throughout this book; however, at this juncture, bringing them together will help to clearly mark the area where R-A theory ends and the RM upper mid-range theory should begin.

A theory of competitive advantage at the microeconomic level should foremostly explain the diversity of firms and the differences in their performance. R-A theory does this by articulating the heterogeneity and instability of markets, which implies the possibility for firms in the same industry to supply them differently (Hunt and Morgan 1996). This dual specificity of individual and institutional clients' needs, preferences and tastes even within a generic offer class, and of the varied ways companies cater to these needs, preferences and tastes, implies that there can be better and worse matches of what clients expect and of what is delivered.

In terms of clients' needs, R-A theory emphasizes imperfect information about the offerings available in the market and that the information search involves costs (at least the cost of time). In addition, R-A theory opposes the 'homo economicus' view of human choices (as consumers, employees and managers) as these choices are not only motivated by self-interest (that can be reduced to pleasure), but also by moral choices (doing not only what is allowed by what is right, ethical; Hunt and Morgan 1995).

Based on the premise that companies are expected to generate profits and that worse matches between customer expectations and firms' offerings generate reduced or zero profits, R-A theory insists that worse performing companies are also worse equipped with the resources needed to achieve better matches. Given the endless diversity of possible resource bundles, the main task of management is to decide on resource configurations that will bring the company a competitive advantage now and in the future. Hence, firms also differ in their strategy choices, which are influenced but not caused by the external environment (Hunt and Morgan 2005).

Following RBV, R-A theory distinguishes between tangible and intangible resources, including relational capital. Further on, it acknowledges that relationships are not owned, but only temporarily co-shared by firms. Lastly, R-A theory emphasizes that, given the importance of relationships but also their varying quality, companies should develop and manage a relationship portfolio (Hunt 1997). However, it does not give instructions as to how to do this. This is exactly the point where the RM upper mid-range theory takes the baton.

The central challenge for the RM upper mid-range theory is to propose a relational response to the question that lies at the heart of the strategic management research agenda (Rumelt et al. 1995): how companies achieve and sustain competitive advantage. Obviously, the final proposal of the RM maturity model will be very helpful in providing this answer. However, the epistemological potential of the RM mid-range theory would not be fully exploited if it remained silent about other important related questions. These include:

- Why is achieving RM-based sustainable competitive advantage essentially limited to RM-mature firms only?
- If RM-maturity heavily impacts the ability to achieve sustainable competitive advantage, why have RM-mature firms not seized the whole market?
- What determines the scale and scope of RM-mature firms?
- Are there markets/industries/segments/customer groups that favour RM-mature firms and simultaneously those which do not?

All these questions will be addressed in the following two sections.

5.1 The Final Proposal of the RM Maturity Model and Its Practical Interpretation

From the theoretical point of view, the overall message of this research is that if RBV (extended by the dynamic capabilities concept), SDL and RM are analysed as intertwined theories, employees emerge as the key internal resource, the mother of all intangible resources. Consequently, an ethical IRM capability emerges as a fundamental driver of sustainable competitive advantage, preceding customer (and other external stakeholders') relationship management capability.

On the basis of the final proposal for the RM maturity model, nothing seems to be more important than excellent internal vertical and horizontal communication. Its existence would reveal itself in showing full respect to every person, sincere and sympathetic interest in each other's well-being, being absolutely transparent about individual and group challenges, and demonstrating the willingness to learn and adapt. Whilst this applies to all employees, it is more of a personal challenge for the management. True leadership, in this context, does not end with managers' factual knowledge, but extends to the very core of their humanity, which is a fundamental guiding reference for the team to follow. In turn, this attitude is transferred further into external relationships and consumed as a service (be it a consumer or business partner experience).

RM maturity exhibited in such a way should have a positive impact on both the cost and revenue sides of a business. In the case of management costs, savings may be a result of largely replacing the supervisor–subordinate mode of control by the much more effective mechanism of individual and group self-control (cutting red tape and reducing the corporate "game of deception" in favour of employee empowerment and engagement; Kegan et al. 2014). However, there is more. Sales, marketing, distribution and administration expenses are usually supervariable (they rise faster than sales volume), provided a company expands by traditional means of mass marketing and price promotions (Kaplan and Cooper 1998). If growth is more organic, largely by taking advantage of positive word-of-mouth and customer referrals, the customer acquisition costs are minimized, and the investment in infrastructure (people, processes, physical) keeps up with rising demand. On the revenue side, the use of customer-specific knowledge is likely to create positive sales and after-sales experiences (including co-creation experiences), which enhance the customer propensity to buy more, and more frequently (Reichheld and Teal 2001).

Hence, the existence of an RM-mature company is determined by its ability to co-create and share value with all its stakeholders, according to their merits and position in the value creating chain. Although a part of this value will have a transactional character, for example the basic utility value of a product or service against the price paid or salary against labour, the real difference is made by the value of relationships, for example manifested in the comfort of having a trusted partner/advisor, or a friendly work ambience. What may sound like a pipe dream is measurable on the bottom line, and this book is not the only one to say this. A notable example is the concept of the Service-Profit Chain (Heskett et al. 2008a). This linkage model shows the relationships between organizational performance and customer and employee satisfaction and loyalty (Sasser et al. 1997). Although there are very few companies who have continuously tried to explore all its linkages, its underlying ideas seem to clearly reflect the practices of leading global service organizations (Payne and Frow 2013). Moreover, even if the original model was publicized as an attractive managerial concept (Heskett et al. 2008b) and not as a theory-based contribution, it corresponds well with the notion of RM maturity. In contrast, the Gallup Institute claims customer and employee engagement potentiate one another and improve overall financial performance by up to 240% (according to the Gallup Q12 survey instrument, if both metrics score above 50% in comparison to companies that stay below this level (Robinson 2008)). And in the meta-analysis of 339 independent research studies, Krekel et al. (2019, p. 2) found a significant, strong, positive correlation between employees' wellbeing, productivity and customer loyalty, which were ultimately positively correlated with business-unit profitability levels.

Figure 5.1 depicts the final proposal of the RM maturity model, which highlights the key elements of its preliminary version verified in the empirical research. It is evident that almost half of these elements are oriented to managing internal relationships (IRM). Hence, the final proposal of the RM maturity model strongly resembles the strategic dimension of the preliminary version. The main difference between Fig. 3.7 'Strategic dimension in preliminary RM maturity model' and Fig. 5.1 are three key ERM processes labelled as a quick RM-maturity test. All three processes have empirically proven legitimacy directly embedded in research items D03, D05 and D08 linked by the association rules R4 and R11–R16 in congruence with items A05 and A06 linked by the association rule R1. These three processes may function as a compact basic guiding reference for

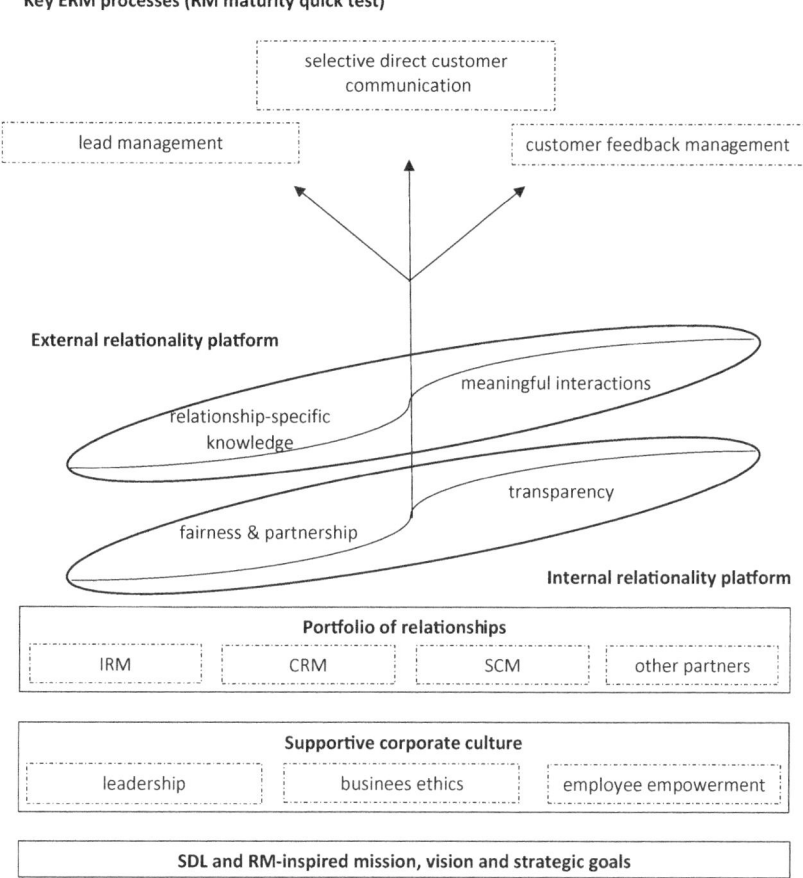

Fig. 5.1 Final proposal of the RM maturity model

managers looking to achieve an RM-based sustainable competitive advantage.

In the case of the lead management process (D03), achieving RM maturity means adopting a non-waste lead policy. This translates into systemic utilization of every organically acquired or marketing campaign-generated customer contact across the whole communication process, starting with the first interaction and closing with the 'deal won' or 'deal lost' status. As a result, the investment in both individual relationship development and in marketing campaigns is optimally converted into sales. To ensure the lead management process runs properly, the interested manager should demand transparent reporting on conversion rates at all major stages in the sales funnel. This puts interdepartmental coordination and the quality of internal and external communication to the test (Deszczyński 2016a). For example, the marketing department may launch a campaign, which initially generates much resonance and leads, but the excessive promises used to lure potential customers, which are not supported by the factual attractiveness of the offer, clog the sales funnel with disappointed prospect buyers having no real propensity to buy. The result should be visible in heavy losses in lead conversion in the initial steps, extended waiting time for leads to be processed, and high lead drop-off ratio after passing them on to sales. The same can happen if, for example, the customer contact teams' or sales organization's work is in excess of their capabilities, fulfilling massive bureaucratic tasks or simply being too scarce.

The second area where an interested manager can quickly test the RM maturity of a company is by examining its means of communication (D05). An RM-mature organization should mainly use direct communication channels, because only then is there a possibility for a customer-specific dialogue based on customer-generated knowledge. It is also the prerequisite to co-creating value with customers in an RM sense. However, as indicated by the low scores in the empirical tests of the technological RM dimension, merely having a customer database is not enough. Therefore, a manager should ask whether the company has good answers to the basic yet fundamental questions: "Who are our customers?" "What do they expect from us?" and "When is the best time to tap into their demand?" (Deszczyński 2016b; Lusch and Vargo 2014). In particular, these questions should be addressed with a view to identifying the relatively small group of the most valuable customer relationships which, according to the Pareto principle, largely decide a company's prosperous development (Buttle and Maklan 2019). The capacity to maintain selective, adaptable, largely autonomous interactions with these key customers should be the hallmark of an RM-mature company. This puts the motivation and engagement of the front-line personnel to the test. Much of the content of these highly satisfying interactions cannot be centrally set or controlled. Truly meaningful one-to-one interactions are only possible when both the customer and the employee are empowered to flexibly integrate the resources the company provides (Lusch et al. 2007). However, this means that the company partially loses control over the way its resources are allocated, which poses some problems to organizations not having developed a partnership with their staff (Mayer et al. 2010). First, the employees may not be ready to take on such a responsibility (Ahearne et al. 2005; Barner 1994). Second, they may use such an opportunity to commit fraud or for indirect personal benefit at the expense of a company (e.g., buying customer silence to spare excessive work or to cover up errors committed; Comer 1998; Hooks et al. 1994). If there is a high risk that one or both of these problems may occur, relational communication and relational selling will not be possible, and thus the company will not be capable of achieving sustainable RM-related competitive advantage.

Finally, the integration of customer feedback into a firm's continuous improvement efforts (D08) has to be examined. For an RM-mature company, the willingness of customers to participate in a dialogue is a chance for further developing the relationship. There are, of course, varied reasons customers may wish to interact with the company. In fact, both lead management and selective direct customer communication are also processes built on interaction: the first mainly of a transactional type, the second of transactional and non-transactional types. However, an organization can only actively shape its future by seeing beyond the current customer loyalty cycle. Therefore, an interested manager should make sure that, as with leads, no customer request or complaint passes without analysis and response. The annual aggregated complaint statistics may expose some trends, for example in the general quality of customer encounters, but only short loop analysis by the responsible team gives the company a chance not only to restore the individual customer's trust, but to mitigate the risk of committing the same mistakes again soon (Wirtz and Tomlin 2000). A strong indicator for making the management of customer feedback a priority among other business goals is its incorporation in the employee assessment system (Pollack and Pollack 1996). If a company recognizes and rewards only immediate sales increase or cost reduction, this sends a clear 'it's all about the money' message to its employees. Such a tactic reduces their perspectives to the forthcoming bonus cycle and is an example of paraded RM (Lusch and Vargo 2014). Similarly, care for the quality of customer encounters may also take the paraded form if employees are only penalized for reported problems instead of treating this as an opportunity to learn from mistakes (Wirtz et al. 2010).

What might an interested manager do if facing such problems? Of course, they may try to tackle them at the operational level, but what this research suggests is that such problems are unlikely to occur without any fundamental reasons caused by lame IRM. A company that deprives salespeople of the willingness to cultivate long-term profitable relations or that is pretending to be satisfied by an tentative and undifferentiated 'omnivorous' sales approach is also most likely having problems with employee turnover, morale and widespread mediocrity caused by toxic corporate culture, devoid of inspiring goals and leadership. Probably the most concise answer to the question of what companies should do to achieve and sustain RM-related competitive advantage is the 'Employees first, customers second' transformation started by Indian IT-services giant HCL, which was publicized by the company's former CEO V. Nayar in his similarly titled book (2010). By acknowledging that it is the employee/customer interface where the most value is created, companies like HCL find motivation to turn conventional management upside down and become a company of 'ideapreneurs'—self-run, self-governing and highly profitable (HCL 2020).

Why corporate success may have IRM-based roots is also presented in two of the illustrative examples of RM practice provided in Sect. 5.3. The first (Illustration 1) shows the volatility of corporate culture in the example of 'Medium-sized home décor online retailer', where a single person undermined the very core of the firm's identity in the shortest time. The second (Illustration 2) presents the redefinition of the roles of managers and employees in a 'Large manufacturing company operating in the FMCG market'.

5.2 Relational Niche

Defining the RM recipe for achieving sustainable competitive advantage begs the question: Why is it a relatively exclusive strategy? After all, even bringing together the 'extremely strong competitive advantage' group of companies with the 'strong competitive advantage' group (which includes companies having reported some of the long-term competitive advantage indicators while being able to report only one out of 16 rules characterizing RM maturity based on the 9/10-score level) only accounts for roughly 19% of the whole examined company population. Probably the best explanation of this phenomenon can be deduced from the nature of loyalty. Although the notion of loyalty has been addressed several times in this book, at this juncture a short recap is needed.

The state of being loyal to anybody or anything has to have strong reasons, because patronizing one object of some kind automatically implies refraining from others, thus narrowing one's choice (Varelius 2009). In many product/service categories, the differences in utility (based on similar technologies) and in brand perception (following the homogeneity in marketing messages and loyalty programmes) are very small (Uncles et al. 2003). As all alternatives are likely to be satisfactory, there is little opportunity for anything more than superficial habitual loyalty (Wood and Neal 2009). This is because the perception of the purchase as a transaction that fully accommodates the exchange (based on the pure market-pricing mechanism; Fiske 1992) leaves no room for the important loyalty-driving equality-matching mechanism of reciprocal gratitude (Fiske 1992; Henderson et al. 2011;). Its occurrence is more likely when the customer has developed loyalty ties to (an) individual employee(s) (Palmatier et al. 2007). They, in turn, are related to a history of successful interactions incorporating value co-creation and partnership that appears to be benevolently motivated and offered just as the customer needs assistance (Palmatier et al. 2009). However, a randomized quality of encounters cannot evoke customer attitudinal loyalty, just as a friend who is only occasionally willing to help is not a real friend. Offering a 'merely' good level of service is only enough to become an acquaintance, alongside many others. Thus, the external manifestation of RM maturity that can be assessed by customers is either continuous, highly personalized, 'intimate' customer encounters or top-notch quality of individualized solutions based on a deep understanding of customers' needs and purchase motivations, or, preferably, both (Payne and Frow 2013).

The issue of individual relationships between customers and employees is discussed in two further RM illustrations. Illustration 3 discusses the impact of informal relations on business relations and its changing characteristics over the last 30 years upon the experiences of Pamapol, a large ready meals manufacturing company. Illustration 4 shows the role of personal relationships between high-ranked managers in the example of 'Medium production company representing chemical industry'.

The sketched dichotomy between delighting customers to develop relationships that last and 'only' fulfilling the expected standards and luring random customers to conclude a single transaction is clearly reflected in the Net Promoter Score (NPS) concept and methodology (Reichheld 2003). Labelled as a 'highly aggregated RM capability indicator' in the previous chapter, NPS precisely measures the ability of a company to deliver the high-end performance reflected in total customer satisfaction and in the willingness to repurchase and make referrals to other customers. The design of NPS with only 9/10 scores linked to customer loyalty reproduced in the RM maturity research methodology indicates that, unlike a typical maturity model, there is nothing like an RM maturation path (De Bruin et al. 2005), at least in the sense of establishing a linear relationship between subsequent levels of quality in customer encounter, customer loyalty and the company's bottom line. Instead, the sharply curvilinear correlation (Reichheld and Markey 2011) supports the totality of the RM maturity model exposed in the empirical hypothesis H1e. However, this does not provide an answer to the next question: How is it possible that RM-mature firms did not outcompete the transaction-oriented ones and what limits their scale and scope? For example, in Forrester's 'Net Promoter Benchmarks, 2019 (US)', the overall NPS scores ranged from +59 to -47[1] (Schmidt-Subramanian 2019); this means that the companies that achieved an almost 60% net predictive loyalty rate coexisted with those whose customer base predominately included detractors. Moreover, 25% of the interviewed companies in the research presented in this book reported growing sales, expansion to new markets or sometimes even scoring above-average profits without achieving RM maturity.

The coexistence of companies applying different business models and strategies, having diverse corporate cultures and structures, servicing different industries and market segments, and achieving varied business results has been the reality noted by many researchers (Romanowska 2014). One of the most fruitful research traditions in this respect is configuration theory, which posits that, for companies to be successful, they have to match their organizational characteristics with the adopted business strategy (Slater et al. 2011). Prominent representatives of this tradition, O. Walker and R. Ruekert, in their award-winning article (1987) defined companies in terms of two dimensions:

- the intended major method of competing (cost leadership and differentiation), which they adopted from M. Porter's strategy framework (1979);
- the desired rate of new product–market change (aggressive position in a broadly defined market—Prospectors, and conservative position in a narrower market segment—Low-cost or Differentiated Defenders), which they adopted from R. Miles et al.'s strategy–structure–process typology (1978).

Their findings based on theoretical and empirical evidence were that the strategic fit between the adopted generic marketing strategy and its internal characteristics (structures, policies, programmes, procedures) heavily impacts business performance regardless of how the adopted strategy fits the changing external environment (1987). Interestingly, the detailed characteristic of Differentiated Defenders strongly resembles the RM-mature company (Olson et al. 2018; Slater and Olson 2001):

- relatively high quality of well positioned products and services;
- relatively high prices and sales force expenditures;
- relatively greater forward integration;
- customer relationships as most valuable assets;
- customer service and product/service innovation as core competences.

What is also particularly noteworthy is that in O. Walker and R. Ruekert's empirical research and the work of researchers that followed them, among three identified types of companies, the Differentiated Defenders scored best in terms of return on investment (ROI), while being less successful with market share and new products; the Prospectors were quite the opposite; whereas the Low-cost Defenders were fairly successful when it came to ROI, but very poor in new product development (1987, p. 20).

Also, diversification theory explains the coexistence of differently performing firms. Its foundational premise links expansion with excess capacity of productive factors and stipulates that the wider a company diversifies, the lower will be its average margins (Teece 1982). Further on, diversification theory links the average margins with the specificity of these factors. The more specific the factors (in RBV terminology, the more these factors resemble VRIO resources and dynamic capabilities), the higher average margins can be generated in new markets, provided the new market entry opportunities are located 'nearby'—that is, the new application of company resources and capabilities does not require them to be modified extensively (Chatterjee and Wernerfelt 1991). Therefore, companies with specific, idiosyncratic resources and capabilities will generate high average margins when diversifying narrowly or not diversifying at all, while companies with less specific resources and capabilities will generate medium average margins when diversifying narrowly and low average margins when diversifying widely to 'distant' new market opportunities (Montgomery and Wernerfelt 1988).

By combining what configuration theory and diversification theory have to say about resource specificity, market focus, and business performance and by relating it to RM-mature firms, one can assume that these entities are likely to adopt a niche strategy. Traditionally, niche marketing strategies were associated with small innovative firms concentrating on product innovation matching new technology with unmet customer needs (Pavitt 1990). However, the definition of a niche market does not explicitly imply that its borderlines are of a technological nature (Stankiewicz 2000). It is enough that a niche is sufficient in size and shows the potential for profitable growth based on the goodwill of customers who expect special treatment and who have been, up to now, ignored by companies supplying the broad volume market (Dalgic 1998).

How about a relational niche? A subdivision of a market with only one company focused on a niche of customers, which has built an ecosystem of mature relationships stabilizing and growing its business through an RBV-style mechanism of isolation that prevents imitation (Galvão et al. 2018; Lepak et al. 2007)? Such a company could largely coexist undisturbed with neighbouring major players fighting for market dominance in a pursuit of a monopolistic rent (Teece 1984), while building its own sustained competitive advantage on a relationship rent (Dyer and Singh 1998). Consequently, instead of wasting resources on analysing and counteracting rivals' activities (strategizing), it could concentrate on co-creating superior value (economizing; Williamson 1991) and generating excess surpluses, which could be shared with its partners.

It seems that virtually every industry offers a room for a relational niche even in, to date anonymous, B2C markets. Let's take the breakfast cereals segment as an example. End-customers have traditionally purchased this product via extensive FMCG (fast-moving consumer goods) retailing distribution networks. Yet, some of them are now ordering breakfast cereals online from specialized providers, who offer a number of product variations which no shop shelf would ever accommodate plus individualized nutrition advice, recipes, and customer care powered by online behaviour tracking. In contrast, let's examine the roots of success of a small grocery shop. For a number of clients, the proven freshness of food and its traceable origins, the convenience of individualized orders, and the comfort of personal chat with the shop assistant could be the arguments prevailing over the competitive price and the wide availability of merchandise offered by retailing giants. Both entities may successfully operate in niches separated from the surrounding volume markets, through major distinguishing characteristic of high quality-oriented customers.

The two examples provided may leave the impression that relational niches are, by definition, very modest in size. However, a company servicing a relational niche does not have to remain nominally small provided the demand for personalized customer encounter and/or highly individualized quality offerings is sufficient high, or its relationships can be extended or used in other market segments. The example of Konimpex-Invest (Illustration 5), a medium-sized real estate development company, demonstrates that a company can even place the bulk of its operations in the volume single transaction market, while proactively catering to the needs of these customers, whose special preferences create room for separating a profitable relational niche.

Figures 5.2 and 5.3 will be helpful in further discussing the coexistence of RM-mature and RM-immature firms. They depict two market situations. The initial one is a model of a market with two transaction-oriented rival companies T1 and T2.[2] These companies devote a great deal of resource to acquiring new customers; however, as they conclude a transaction, their interest in customers sharply disappears. In turn, most of their

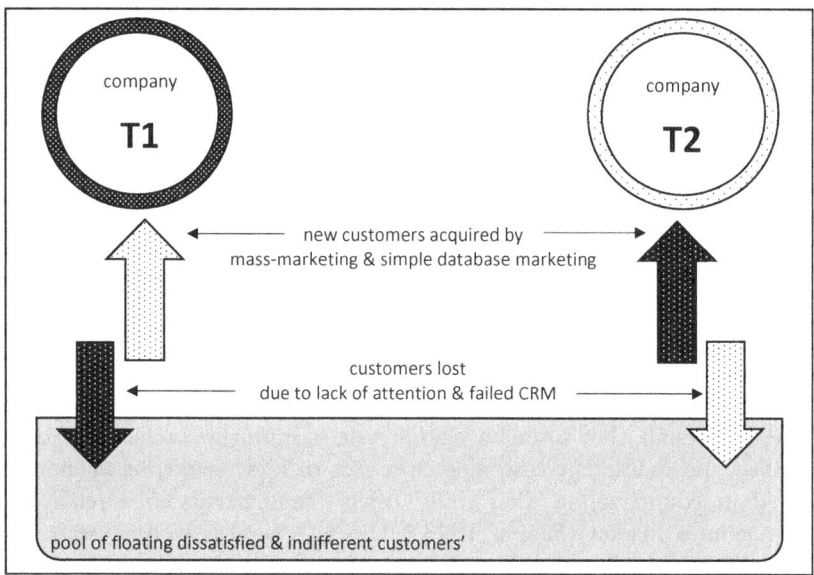

Fig. 5.2 Model of transactional rivalry. Note: The picture has an indicative character and does not show oligopoly. The actual number of companies does not matter as long as customers have a choice of comparable alternatives

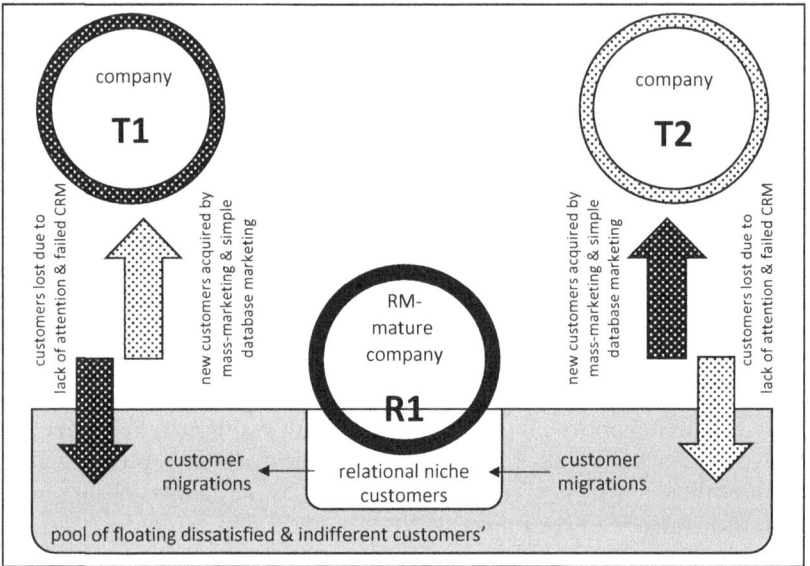

Fig. 5.3 The coexistence of RM-mature and transaction-oriented companies. Note: The picture has an indicative character. There could me more RM-mature companies in the market, which would isolate their relational niches. There could be cross-sections of these niches; however, the modus operandi of RM-mature companies would remain the same

newly acquired customers are dissatisfied or find no strong reasons to stay loyal and migrate to the 'floating customers' pool.

Therefore, to sustain their business, companies T1 and T2 have to concentrate even more on acquiring new customers whom they, by definition, do not know well. In consequence they often communicate by using very simple and unspecific arguments (e.g. price promotions) via mass marketing channels trying to appeal to an 'average customer'. By continuing this modus operandi, they sustain a vicious cycle of mutually 'exchanging' dissatisfied and indifferent customers at a cost of high marketing spending aimed in counteracting their rivals' offers (strategizing) in a relatively homogenous market (Peteraf 1993). This is a familiar picture perfectly depicted in M. Porter's Five Forces Model (1979). The notion of RM-maturity implies that this model of competition will not substantially change even if rival companies were to temporarily gain a partial competitive advantage based on low-scaled RM-resources (e.g. a single highly-engaged sales team or an individual employee). One can expect that within a short time, any major customer-centric initiatives in such companies are likely to be dragged down by the dominance of their volume-oriented focus, which implies the need to compensate excessive marketing costs by cutting expenses on customer care. In the end neither these companies nor their customers (and presumably most of their employees) create optimal value.

Alternatively, it is also possible that due to some market or macroeconomic policy failure these companies will refrain from competing and will instead fix prices, limit or control production, markets, technical development, or investment. Oddly enough, such collusions are also the outcomes of corrupted RM aimed at satisfying the interests of corporate elites only. Such RM-based collusive practices are illustrated by the example of the bidding process for water rescue services for Termy Maltańskie, the biggest waterpark in Poland (Illustration 6).

Figure 5.3 shows the same market occupied by transaction-oriented rivals T1 and T2. In addition, a third player, the RM-mature company (R1), enters the market. However, although R1 offers superior quality of customer encounter, it does not seize the whole market. Instead, it isolates a part of the market populated by the most demanding quality-oriented customers, who can afford to pay a premium on an offer that optimally caters to their needs (relational niche-customers). To differentiate by effective offer personalization, company R1 is virtually immersed in the niche its serves by receiving even faint signals sent by its customer base. Occasionally some customers leave and some enter its relational niche, but it remains stable as long as the company cultivates its relationships and no major external shock occurs (e.g. radical technological change which the company was not participating in). Company R1 does not expand more than its relationship resources and the demand of relational niche-customers allow. Thus, companies T1 and T2 may continue their competing strategies, barely noticing that the market they operate in is now somewhat smaller. They may also try to attack the position of company R1, but as they fundamentally lack the RM competitive factors these attacks can only appeal to the peripherals of the relational niche, where relatively more price-sensitive customers reside.

The idea of the relational niche equally explains the coexistence of transaction-oriented (RM-immature) and RM-mature companies as well as the somewhat limited scale and scope of the latter. As the relational rent resembles a Ricardian type of rent, it is generated at maximum output. Thus, the growth of an RM mature company is limited by the uniqueness and scarce supply of its relationship capital (Peteraf 1993). The rapid elastic growth is, therefore, impossible unless the company decides to finance expansion at the expense of relationship capital. This may yield additional volume and short-term financial benefits; however, as the isolating mechanisms of the firm's niche are the relationships it maintains, these barriers will disappear once those relationships weaken. In this context, the most likely threat to the comfortable position of an RM-mature company is the company itself. After all, it does not take long to destroy what was previously an unconquered fortress from the inside, for example, by hiring some new managers who pull their weight, instead of motivating their teams (this risk is showed in Illustration 1) or by doubling the number of customers served per employee. This is probably also one of the reasons for the ambiguity of links between RM and company performance highlighted in the introduction, in the theory-methodic hypothesis H1tm, and generally throughout this book. When a company has abandoned its relational niche some time ago (e.g. for the sake of realizing ambitious volume expansion plans) and it faces unstable or price sensitive demand, but still classifies itself as RM-oriented, this can be misinterpreted as evidence for RM-strategy failure.

What still remains unaddressed is the size of the relational niche. Admittedly, there will be markets where the process of cultivating a relational niche will be easier and others where the potential niche will be 'by nature' very small. This seems to be a boundary issue between the RM upper mid-range theory and the RM mid-range theories of particular market types (compare Chap. 2 Fig. 2.4). The latter may address more specific, e.g., industry-based factors affecting the characteristics of the relational niche, while the RM upper mid-range theory may discuss the universal ones.

An analysis of the universal external factors having an impact on the size of a relational niche should begin by examining whether a company may have direct access to the customers. Based on social network research, such as M. Granovetter's work on the "strength of weak ties" (1977), one can assume that the better this is, the more likely a significant relational niche could be developed. More precisely, in line with the media multiplexity theory (Haythornthwaite 2000), the level of interdependence between the actors in a relationship is positively associated with the number of media used in that relationship (Haythornthwaite 2005; Ledbetter 2010). If a given market is anonymous, companies can only observe general trends in demand and may eventually try to establish a brand preference through diverse marketing activities. This situation applies to the aforementioned FMCG market as well as to all industries where the suppliers (mainly manufacturers) sell their offers through independent intermediaries (Payne and Frow 2013). Even if they may occasionally connect to their end-clients by organizing prize competitions or surveys, these companies were traditionally not in a position to maintain a dialogical communication. However, some of them may break the impotence of mass communication by virtualizing their operations, just as indicated in the example of specialized breakfast cereals suppliers. Still, the additional logistics costs and the inability to purchase all the complementary products (e.g. milk, to stay with the cereals example) or the unavailability of the broad merchandise that is conveniently offered together (e.g. food in the supermarket, which is situated in the shopping mall that accommodates other types of shops) should normally significantly reduce the potential size of the relational niche such companies can tap into. In other words, there will be fewer customers potentially interested in developing relationships with a specialized supplier/provider, the more inconveniences such relationships demand.

Four issues are worth commenting on at this point. The first is the role of online shopping platforms such as Allegro and Amazon. Their intermediation removes the inconvenience of separate shopping for different types of products. Some product categories may be even better represented, compared to traditional distribution channels (while others, such as fresh food, are worse). However, these platforms do not provide tools for developing end-customers' loyalty towards their merchants, as this would undermine their position as intermediaries. Therefore, they help in achieving volume goals rather than in cultivating relationships (Dolata 2017).

The second issue is the role of social media technologies. Although useful in creating online brand communities, these tools do not have (at least currently) the potential to effectively integrate and manage all points of customer contact, including transactional contacts. Nonetheless, in the case of fully virtual communication modes, the integration of social media with other online tools, such as e-commerce platforms and CRM systems, may open the gate wider to connecting to niche customers and nurturing relationships with them (Chatterjee et al. 2019).

The third issue is that every company can try to develop relationships with its direct business customers, who may well have very specific needs that can be best met by a specialized partner. The inexistence of fundamental barriers in locating and communicating to B2B customers makes the relational niche an even more likely phenomenon than in the B2C market setting, where the large number of customers necessitates, for example, the investment in CRM systems implementation to effectively manage all the interactions (Buttle and Maklan 2019).

Finally, the fourth issue is that even relatively easy access to customers does not automatically imply the existence of a relational niche. Take telecommunications and cable television providers. As these services are predominately offered on a contractual basis, their providers are in a superior situation compared to, for example, durable goods manufacturers. Still, this industry has traditionally suffered from one of the highest churn rates, even if the average loyalty cycles sanctioned by these contracts are relatively long (Ahn et al. 2006; Kotler and Keller 2009). However, as the main focus of these firms is placed on attracting new customers, the relatively frequent direct contacts they maintain with their customers (based on monthly billing) do not necessarily create customer satisfaction. The most evident proof for the illusion of fake contractual loyalty was the mass defection movement as soon as governments across the globe introduced wireless number portability laws (Eshghi et al. 2007).

Two companies from contractual industries showcased in the RM-Illustrations are currently coping with the challenge of maintaining a true focus on their relationships. Sugar-refining group (Illustration 7) discovered how undeveloped its business relationships were as soon as the sugar market was deregulated in the European Union. By contrast, Aquanet (Illustration 8), a water and sewage processing municipality-owned company, decided to improve its relationships with individual and corporate clients by starting first to improve its relationship with its employees.

Another universal factor that should have an influence on the potential size of an RM-niche is the relative importance of the given offer category for the customer's overall value creation chain. It should be significant and enduring enough so that interested firms could develop a performance gap reflected in the relationally-affected key buying attributes of their offer that make true difference to their targeted customers (Bharadwaj et al. 1993). In the case of B2C markets, it will be the extent to which the offer impacts the lives of individuals based on the personal psychographic and behavioural context (Zhang et al. 2017). In the case of B2B markets, it will be the share that the offering may have in the corporate value adding process (Hakanen and Jaakkola 2012). Although price may be regarded as only a simplified measure of that influence, one can assume that the higher the monetary value of single transactions or alternatively the cumulated value of frequent transactions that are typically concluded in a given market segment, the more important the offer category and the more likely a relational niche can be developed. On the one hand, a nominally high price implies that customer offer evaluation is likely to be complicated and involve a time-consuming learning process necessary to acquire enough knowledge and skills to effectively assess the offer and integrate resources to facilitate value-creation (Hibbert et al. 2012). For example, while consumers tend to choose casual garments on impulse, tailored clothing necessitates some search for the craftsman, advice taking, and active cooperation as measurements is taken and the suit is sewn. Similarly, the procurement department can autonomously acquire standard machining blades replacement, but if a new manufacturing line is being designed it will be the whole team of specialists that work together with the vendor to search for new ways of reducing time and waste, and increasing the reliability of the new solution. In both advanced situations the intensity of interactions and the individualized value they produce open the way for capable companies to create their own relational niches. Simultaneously, high price creates room for high premiums, which can be partly reinvested in the relationship (e.g. customized technical solutions or process design, preferential treatment policies, and individualized communication). Such special commitments further stabilize the relationships and make creating and sustaining the relational niche even more probable (Pervan et al. 2009).

An additional factor that can indicate the relatively high importance of the given product category, especially in B2C markets, is its potential to emotionalize communication. If consumers become somehow bonded to the brand or can admit that they feel something akin to love or friendship for the brand, they substantially increase usage and purchase of the brand (whether product or service; Morrison and Crane 2007; Rossiter and Bellman 2012). Obviously, not every brand in a category will manage to advance beyond rational perception. For example, some cars are bought mainly for mobility reasons, while others are a symbol of success and prestige as well. Nonetheless, thanks to a relatively strong person-product relationship, car manufacturers have a generally much better starting position for emotional communication than, for example, photo camera producers (Mugge et al. 2005). They, in turn, may generally count on more customer emotional attachment than manufacturers of cosmetics, and so on. Therefore, for consumer markets, where emotional attachment for products may exist for a significant group of customers, a relational niche may well also exist, provided these customers may be effectively directly contacted by the company.

Through the discussion so far on the universal external factors that impact the existence of a relational niche, the issue of services has been left unaddressed, except to place it in the context of the other factors. Owing to the classification of RM-mature companies as being basically similar to Differentiated Defenders and the extensive explanation of the overlaps between RM and SDL provided in Chap. 3, one can stipulate that the likeliness and the size of a relational niche will be also dependent upon the degree of 'servicization' that can be applied in the given market segment.

There are four basic categories of services, which are directed at (Lovelock 1983):

- peoples' bodies;
- physical possessions;
- peoples' minds (mental stimulus processing);
- intangible assets (information processing).

While the first two categories are tangible actions whose effects are visibly projected in, for example, a new haircut or shipping a parcel, the other two are intangible actions. Apart from being standalone service categories (e.g. education and banking), they may be an ingredient of every offer (Wirtz and Lovelock 2016). For example, 17 out of 22 questions employed in SERVQUAL—one of the widest applied instruments for evaluating service quality—have an intangible and usually employee-related focus (e.g. "Excellent [companies] will give customers individual attention", "Employees of excellent [companies] will always be willing to help customers"; Parasurman et al. 1988; 1991).

While tangible characteristics of the offer can be relatively easily researched and compared before purchase (e.g. price, location, technical equipment, ingredients), the intangible ones constitute the most variable and flexible part of the offer that is rich in experiences and credence-based (Parasuraman et al. 1985). Therefore, they usually dominate value creation and its overall perception because they incorporate such attributes, which are difficult to evaluate even after consumption. Their evaluation process necessitates adopting some kind of a proxy, which is commonly a matter of having belief in the benevolence and skills of the offer provider (Lovelock et al. 2014; Schumann et al. 2010). For example, the hairdresser has to master their craft which, in fact, most hairdressers do.

However, whether the client feels comfortable, is amused, and appreciates the work done largely depends on the small-talk concerning client-relevant topics and the personal aura given off by the hairdresser. This suggests that value perception is phenomenologically determined by the temporal, spatial, and social context (Vargo et al. 2020). This, in turn, implies the need for ongoing micro-adaptations, which can be best applied at the employee-customer level. Figure 5.4 lists all the discussed external factors having an impact on the likelihood of the existence of a relational niche.

At this juncture, however, an important remark has to be added. The intangibility of service elements should not be artificially applied just for their own sake. For example, banking (especially internet banking) is probably one of the most intangible types of service (Shostack 1982), and yet financial institutions are believed to suffer from exceptionally high annual churn rates ranging from 20% to 27% (du Toit and Burns 2014; Kotler and Keller 2009). However, if the two intangible service categories

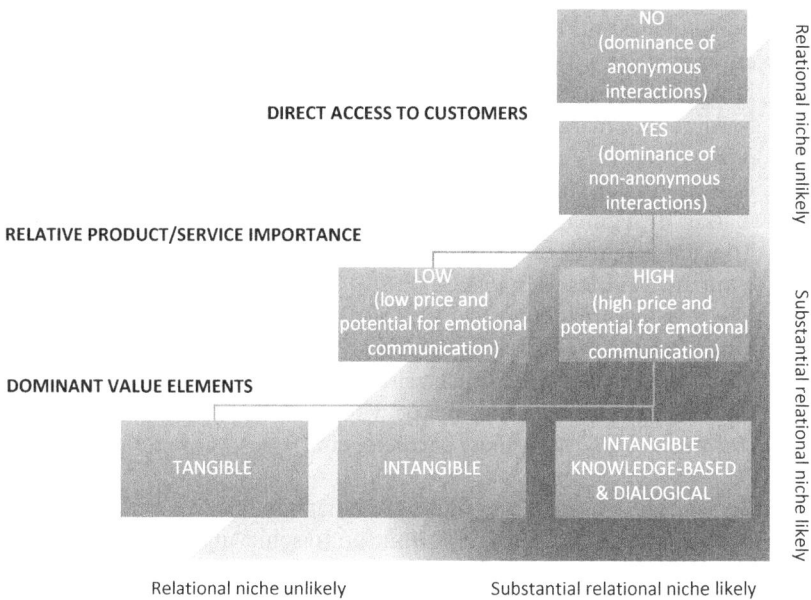

Fig. 5.4 Factors influencing the size of relational niche. Note: The more intense gradient in the triangle, the more likely a substantial relational niche can be built

can be balanced and effectively designed in the overall offer, the chance for cultivating a relational niche by capable companies should be higher. This is because the intangible elements of service are simultaneously the essence of CRM (Grönroos 2017), which in its highest form is both knowledge-based and dialogical (Payne and Frow 2013), and ultimately co-creative (FitzPatrick et al. 2015). Hence, although the emergence of a relational niche is influenced by the discussed universal external market factors, its development is, in the end, a function of a company's ability to effectively differentiate on the basis of customer-perceived individualization. In other words, it is primarily the maturity of company's relationship management activities and approaches that creates a relational niche.

Further discussion on the characteristics of a relational niche leaves the area reserved for the RM upper mid-range theory and enters the realms of the RM mid-range theories of particular market type. These should, inter alia, address the following issues:

- What are the detailed premises which favour the existence of relational niches and RM-mature firms in different markets and in different industries, segments, and customer groups?
- How can new technologies or business practices help in crossing the borders into markets where RM-mature firms were traditionally not represented?
- Can a company partially adopt an RM business model in a given market or segment, while remaining transaction-oriented in others?
- To what extent does the phenomenon of RM-maturity influence the company business network?
- Do RM-mature networks exist, and do they successfully compete in markets?
- What are the barriers for successful RM business model implementations in a given organization type with regard to their size, structure, commercial goals, business partners, etc.?

To address these issues, a series of programmatic industry-specific research is needed. In this book, a small contribution to achieving these broadly-set research goals are the following illustrations which complement this chapter.

5.3 Illustrative Examples of RM Practice

In course of the RM-maturity research project the author of this book visited several firms in search for stories of RM 'in motion', which could deliver first-hand observations illustrating some of RM-facets and challenges companies face in implementing RM business model. Although they do not have a theory-building or theory-confirmative role, they may help the reader to comprehend and interpret the theoretical material and the qualitative empirical evidence provided in Chaps. 2, 3, 4, and 5. This book contains eight such RM-Illustrations, which were briefly announced in this chapter. They were chosen upon the criteria of their horizontal compatibility and the quality of presented examples dealing with a particular RM-area.

The material was collected in course of direct face-to-face and/or telephony interviews with up to four employees currently employed by the company. Their positions and work experience as well as other details concerning the companies are provided within every illustration. Every interview lasted between 60 and 90 minutes. The interview was semi-structured upon the RM-maturity questionnaire, which was sent to the interviewees in advance. Nonetheless, by evoking subsequent elements of the preliminary RM maturity model reflected in the questionnaire the author aimed in involving the interlocutors in a deeper analysis of one or two most important features of their corporate reality with a clear RM context. As mentioned in Chap. 4, the interviews had also helped to test the questionnaire before the field research started.

The filled-in questionnaires and the author notes were used to compose the texts that were all sent back for review and (where needed) to be supplemented. In several cases this involved consultations with other than the originally interviewed persons. For internal firm policy reasons, some of the illustrations had to be anonymized what, however, made it possible to leave the material classified as sensitive intact. Although RM-Illustrations are generally separate contributions, some of them include comments, which repeatedly link the observed phenomena.

Illustration 1. International medium-sized home décor online retailer (Home décor retailer)*

Interviewees
1. Interim manager (sales, marketing, finance), employment history: 4 years.
2. Finance manager, employment history: more than 5 years.
3. Production manager, employment history: more than 5 years.
4. Marketing department employee, employment history: 3 years.
5. Marketing department employee, employment history: more than 5 years.
6. Sales department employee, employment history: more than 5 years.

General Corporate Profile
The company was founded in 2003 in Cracow by a Dutchman, who spotted the chance to take part in the dynamic growth of the Polish e-commerce market. He chose a niche segment (at that time) of high-quality individualized home décor products.

Currently Home décor retailer is present in 17 international markets, including the US-market, where it uses Amazon and eBay online platforms. Despite the fact that the company maintains a zero stock policy, the full order-production-delivery cycle for the American market takes only five working days. Approximately 70% of the 50,000 monthly processed orders are delivered via the intermediation of big e-commerce portals. In addition, Home décor retailer cooperates with a few hundred small e-shops. In both distribution channels the dropshipping model is applied: the order is processed via the webpage of an e-shop or e-platform, and production and delivery is handled directly by Home décor retailer. The third distribution channel are own e-commerce shops, which use own company brand or one of the brands from the company's portfolio.

The company employs more than 250 people, mainly in production, sales, marketing, customer care, and IT. These are simultaneously the business areas which, apart from product quality and reliable logistic processes, play a crucial role in shaping the company's success. The company is highly dependent on customer satisfaction indexes, which constitute its daily performance review. They directly impact the choices of subsequent buyers and influence or sometimes even condition the possibility to sell via reputable e-commerce portals. The overview of the company's characteristics is given in Table 5.1.

Table 5.1 Overview: Home décor retailer

Number of direct customers	Thousands of customers
Number of employees	Between 250 and 999
Main market served	B2C/B2B
Main business focus	Production with commerce structures and customer service
Polish classification of business activities	Production/commerce
Dominant management style	Centralization of decisions in the hands of top management, multiple layers of management, work standardization and formalization, big organizational units
Main perceived success factors	The owner/president of the company Highly qualified and engaged team
Competitive advantage indicators (in the last two years)	Steady expansion in terms of sales or market share Steadily ahead of competitors in terms of profits Entered a new market Steady increase of employment Steadily ahead of competitors in terms of customer satisfaction Steadily improving the customer loyalty rate

* Descriptive company name—the company representatives agreed to share information only under the condition its name will not be revealed. Some of the company's characteristics, which could lead to its identification, were changed. They, however, do not influence the core substance of this illustration.

Main Focus of Illustration
Corporate Culture

Description
Although revenues are always of crucial importance, for the top management of Home décor retailer, a good working ambience is even more important. The company's management defines this as smooth communication, the enthusiasm to learn from each other, and the acceptance that people sometimes make mistakes. In this company every manager knows much about their employees and is interested in their talents, problems, and life in general. The company promotes the 'attitude of wealth' among its managers (inspired by Charles Richards' book—*Psychology of Wealth*). According to this approach, the value of a manager is reflected not only in their personal achievements but also in what their employees achieve. It increases the willingness to share knowledge and experience from fields other than the company's own business. An example can be lectures organized in the company, which touch topics other than e-commerce with the aim of stimulating 'out-of-the-box' thinking, such as "How to make a

company bankrupt in half a year" or "Unknown masters: how middle-sized German family businesses became leaders in their niche segments". Mutual openness and the feeling of belonging to a valued team of people make employees who made a mistake feel personally affected and disappointed. Therefore, instead of additionally penalizing them, the company concentrates on drawing conclusions which will be helpful to avoid committing the same mistake again. Penalties are perceived as a tool that does not motivate to better performance, but leads to hiding mistakes.

The great commitment of the company's leadership to a positive work ambience is reflected in some recent incidents. Home décor retailer employed an experienced British e-commerce consultant. This person was looking down on others and acted as if he had a monopoly on good ideas. Having extensive plenipotencies, the consultant wanted to introduce a lot of changes without explaining their scope and the expected outcome. This quickly caused many employees from different departments to complain about this situation directly to the firm's owner. This conflict came to a head within a couple of months. Despite the fact that it was very costly, the company's owner decided to terminate the contract with the said consultant as requested by the whole team, as otherwise the company would face the resignation of many crucial employees. A similar situation, although of a lesser scale, happened again with the employment of the new IT manager. With respect to the company's development, he recruited several new employees who had been working for his former employer. One of them behaved just like the British consultant. His knowledge was indisputable, but his interpersonal skills were very poor. For example, he made it clear to the team he managed that the actual hierarchical position in the company structure reflects personal skills and abilities. As a result, this employee was offered another position, where his individual skills were much more important than cooperating in the team, and ultimately he was laid off.

The inability to work in a group is not only a managerial issue. Not every boss that has an unfavourable opinion about their employees is the cause of the problem. As the new production manager started his role, he had to objectively improve poor departmental quality performance indicators. At the time of carrying out the interview it was not possible to trace back what were the actual origins of the situation: for example, poor managerial skills of the former boss or poor recruitment policies. With high certainty these and other issues had had a mutually reinforcing effect on the team performance. Only after changing 75% of the staff and after precisely articulating goals and making available appropriate organizational tools, the wave of indolence, lack of engagement, and mistakes was stopped. The production team was re-born, and currently these employees enjoy much freedom and rarely make mistakes.

Also among office line employees there were some individuals whose behaviour was negatively influencing the team spirit. One of them was a particular employee who despite committing a lot of mistakes was given another chance and prolonged employment contract by their supervisor. However, this employee soon accused their boss of having committed bullying towards her and began to snoop on team members looking for their mistakes. All this resulted in the atmosphere in the team being so tense that most of employees announced they would collectively quit if this person stayed any longer.

The corporate culture of Home décor retailer, as is the case of every organization, is an ephemeral phenomenon. The extent to which it effectively facilitates the coexistence of a group of people in pursuing team and individual goals changes continuously. This dynamism is shaped by ongoing experiences, interactions, and the determination of the management and the team to interpret the formally and informally adopted values in a genuine way. The example of Home décor retailer simultaneously shows the strengths and the weaknesses of the relational business model. The ability to create working conditions that foster self-control and self-motivation and make people engaged is arguably one of the core corporate success factors reflecting the RBV concepts of VRIO resources and dynamic capabilities. The difficulty in preserving this ability and in developing human resources poses a major challenge for a company that is temporarily enjoying its effects. The example of Home décor retailer shows that even single personnel decisions may heavily impact this ability and disperse human resources, which have up to now been providing its strength. It is exactly this ephemeral quality of internal relationships which makes it hard to empirically validate the leverage power of RBV, especially in quantitative research. The intermittent nature of this phenomenon often makes the position of yesterday's leaders quickly erode. Sometimes much quicker than the publishing cycle of scientific papers.

Illustration 2. Large manufacturing company operating in the FMCG market*

Interviewees
1. Sales manager—traditional distribution channels, employment history: more than 5 years.
2. Sales manager—new distribution channels, employment history: more than 5 years.
3. Key account field manager, employment history: more than 5 years.

General Corporate Profile
"Large manufacturing company operating in the Fast Moving Consumer Goods market" (Large FMCG manufacturer) supplies numerous international markets with various cosmetic and food brands. In its sustainable development strategy the company emphasizes achieving a balance between economic outcomes and the ability to influence everyday human lives (consumers, employees, small suppliers) in a positive way as well as reducing its negative impact on the natural environment. The overview of the company's characteristics is given in Table 5.2.

Main Focus of Illustration
Managerial Tasks

Description
FMCG companies have been traditionally the largest advertisers using electronic media. The FMCG markets are characterized by immanent anonymity, which means that these companies need intermediaries to reach their end consumers. One opportunity for a direct dialog with their clients for such companies is social media. However, even if a great interactive platform, social media are not without disadvantages. For example, they are mainly a source of information about customer buying intentions but not actual buying behaviour. Such data is only available in teller systems and systems servicing loyalty programmes owned by retail chains.

Until recently, the cooperation with retailers has been carried out in line with the schema described in Illustration 3 (Pamapol). The FMCG-companies have been trying to combine a marketing pull strategy (e.g., ongoing advertising) with a push strategy (e.g., sales representatives frequently visiting diverse types of intermediaries to mobilize them to participate in simple consumer and trade promotions). Nowadays the job of a

Table 5.2 Overview: Large FMCG manufacturer

Number of direct customers	Thousands and more
Number of employees	Between 999 and 4999
Main market served	B2C
Main business focus	Production with commerce structures, customer service and augmented services
Polish classification of business activities	Wholesale trade
Dominant management style	
• strategic company level	Centralization of decisions in the hands of top management, multiple layers of management, work standardization and formalization, big organizational units
• operating company level	Decisions in the hands of multiple types of managers and highly qualified specialists, big organizational units
Main perceived success factors	Highly qualified and engaged team, excellent corporate reputation/very strong brand
Competitive advantage indicators (in the last two years)	Steady expansion in terms of sales or market share Steadily ahead of competitors in terms of profits Entered a new market Steadily a sought-after employer

* Descriptive company name—the company representatives agreed to share information only on condition its name will not be revealed. For the same reason, the general corporate profile does not provide any particular facts and data. The illustration represents the opinions of white collar employees.

sales representative resembles more consulting services than short-term project management. In the case of big retail chains, such cooperation involves joint volume analysis and customer buying behaviour analysis that enables the launch of dedicated products or the introduction of advanced Supply Chain Management solutions (from sales prediction through to Just-in-Time supply).

Such a work environment demands adaptable decision making and handling based more on data analysis, intuition, and on-the-job experience than on reproducing learnt schematic procedures. This is a great challenge not only for the sales representatives, but even more for their supervisors. For more than a year, Large FMCG manufacturer has been implementing changes aimed at helping its managers move their focus from plain sales reports, controlling, and providing simple instructions to managing by observation, listening, and coaching. This change has been marked in a symbolic way by the transition from MS Excel sheets to the MS Word text processing editor in preparing employee assessment reports.

The latter became more descriptive and oriented to soft skills as an alternative to 'hardline' KPIs.

Large FMCG manufacturer's managers of all layers make use of the help of external coaches, whose role is to develop their ability to listen and to understand people and their emotions (also based on psychological knowledge), to build trust and to adequately react to varied situations. The company acknowledges the role of the human psyche on their functioning in any social context and that one of the major sources of stress or irritation can be the direct supervisor. This is more than mere declarations: if required, the company offers its employees free-of-charge consultations with a psychologist.

In the course of said change management, a 70/20/10 work time breakdown of a manager has been proposed. According to this model, managers should devote most of their time to the individual development of their employees, 20% to issues concerning the whole team, and only the remaining 10% to directly discussing ongoing business tasks. Hence, at Large FMCG manufacturer, all meetings begin by discussing human-related issues, like their well-being, and barriers, problems, and challenges they face. Only afterwards comes the time to review the ongoing work, because the company assumes that the employees know what to do, and if they have problems they simply report them and are not afraid to ask for advice. By introducing the 70/20/10 rule, the company hoped to change the perception of a manager primarily as a principal and controller towards the image of a leader and coach. Therefore, the main goal of a manager in Large FMG manufacturer is to make sure that their employees have motivation to work—not in an oppressive manner, but so that they bring out the best in themselves. Thanks to the development of their emotional intelligence and interpersonal skills, the managers are closer to their employees. They should reduce the dialogue-blocking distance and present a receptive and engaged attitude towards the people that have been entrusted to them. By fostering team spirit and positive one-to-one relationships, the employees should gain a broadly understood psychological comfort, starting with personal security and dignity and ending with the perception that they are not stuck in the company but that they keep on learning new things and finding challenges worth their endeavour. This, in the end, will advance them to the position of a valuable partner in customer relationships.

Illustration 3. Pamapol S.A.

Interviewees
1. Marketing director, employee history: more than 19 years.
2. Sales director, employee history more than 20 years.

General Corporate Profile
Pamapol is #2 in the Polish convenience food market. The product range the company offers also includes tinned food, pâtés, ready-to-cook soups, and preserved vegetables. Pamapol distributes products in traditional channels via wholesalers as well as directly supplying large retailer chains. The company builds up its position both by developing its own brands and by acquiring entities having a strong position in complementary market segments. Pamapol is also one of the biggest private brand convenience food supplier to leading retail organizations. The overview of the company's characteristics is given in Table 5.3.

Main Focus of Illustration
The impact of personal/informal relationships on business relations

Table 5.3 Overview: Pamapol S.A.

Number of direct customers	Several hundred
Number of employees	Between 250 and 999
Main market served	B2B
Main business focus	Production with commerce structures and customer service
Polish classification of business activities	Manufacturing
Dominant management style	Centralization of decisions in the hands of top management, multiple layers of management, work standardization and formalization, large organizational units
Main perceived success factors	Highly qualified and engaged team Technical excellence
Competitive advantage indicators (in the last two years)	Steady expansion in terms of sales or market share Steadily ahead of competitors in terms of profits Entered a new market Steady increase of employment

Description
With its own and associated brands, Pamapol has been an active player in the convenience food market for several years (although the history of the oldest brand owned by the company—Kwidzyń—dates from the year 1934). After the year 1989, the Polish FMCG retailing market underwent a general change. The dominant roles were seized by a large-scale retail chain and some of the biggest chains of the wholesale and semi-wholesale trade, which diminished the position of small local stores and wholesalers. The intensification of competition also forced smaller players to increased professionalization. The longitudinal presence of Pamapol's sales force has made it possible to make interesting observations showcasing the evolution that this market has undergone, also with regard to personal and business relations.

The specifics of sales representatives' work are that they maintain ongoing contacts, including face-to-face contact, with their clients. As a natural consequence, some intimacy and trust is built. In turn, the customer is more open for a dialogue and ready to take account of their suggestions, proposals, or even requests. However, according to Pamapol's observations, this personal influence seems to get weaker the more professional the client organization becomes. During the pioneering times when the contemporary retail market organization was only beginning to crystalize, a store or wholesale company owner was willing to place an order without conducting any market analysis—purely after an informal recommendation of the sales representative (e.g., "Take 10 palettes of product X, people will buy it for sure"). In over-the-counter selling shops, it was even profitable to maintain relations with particular personnel members. As these shop assistants were not anonymous to the end-consumers, they were willing to make recommendations in exchange for low-value gadgets, and thus they were contributing to meeting the sales targets. Nowadays, however, at least in the case of ready-made meals, having a good relationship with the decision-maker only enables them to be easily reached and to count on their attention, but it has no major influence on their decisions. In other words, if the market analysis based on statistically processed data does not indicate a chance of making good business, the only courtesy that the decision-makers will offer to the befriended sales representative is to give detailed feedback on why the offer is declined. Their position will not be significantly different than any other sales representative offering an unattractive proposal.

Nonetheless, Pamapol managers still maintain that, in particular situations, personal, informal relationships may make a big difference. They link them, however, with more significant transactions. A good example is the history of contacts with a particular facility manager, whom the representatives of Pamapol have been meeting at industrial fairs, at informal dinners and at 'in-the-corridors talks'. Six years of such informal dialogue has finally brought a major transaction. Still, it should be assumed that this business was basically beneficial to both parties, and the long time that had passed before the customer decided to conclude it indicates that it was well though-out, not an emotional decision.

What links the behaviour of both smaller and larger companies' business partners is the professional procurement process. In contrast to the early times of Polish capitalism in the late twentieth century, the contemporary electronic analytical systems and the multi-criteria formal decision-making procedures in the B2B sector seem not to leave much room for personal relationships. This is, however, only an apparent change. Although the recommendations of Pamapol's sales representatives for novice shop owners were informal and intuitive, they must, however, have been generally beneficial to them. Otherwise their businesses would have deteriorated, which in the end would also have hit Pamapol. These relationships had always to be mutually beneficial, though the ways or tools to succeed in those times were simpler. Similarly, nowadays a personal relationship cannot make up for lacking business perspectives. Being aware of this, Pamapol started its own R&D activities. Thanks to this it can offer products tailored to customer needs. A good example is meatballs in dill cream sauce, which Pamapol delivers to the biggest retail chain in Poland, 'Biedronka', whereas the standard product is offered in tomato sauce. A lack of willingness or possibility to change the product recipe would arguably have caused Pamapol to lose its important client despite good personal relations. By contrast, however, very good relationships among buyer and supplier representatives help to make the client aware of the firm's competences, to present product arguments, to learn about the motives, needs and client business specificity and, occasionally, to benefit from personal preference, provided the alternatives offered by the competitors are comparable.

To sum up one can say that, from Pamapol's managers' perspective, the most important issue in B2B relations is the ability of the supplier to jointly co-create attractive value with its clients. Lacking good personal relationships may, however, delay or even disallow the development of tighter cooperation, because the customer will not recognize its potential. In contrast, in the case of temporarily lacking the ability to propose attractive cooperation, the openness for communication will help the supplier in precisely identifying its own weaknesses. The relationship capabilities are, therefore, one of the core corporate competences.

Illustration 4. Medium manufacturing company representing chemical industry*

Interviewees
1. Member of the executive board, employment history: 15 years; simultaneously acting executive board member in other enterprises and industrial associations, and executive boards' advisor.

General Corporate Profile
Several decades have passed since the foundation of 'Medium manufacturing company representing chemical industry' (Chemicals' manufacturer). During that time the company has become the industry leader, distributing its products to numerous international markets. The company is active mainly in the automotive and building sectors. It has its own brands dedicated to various market segments and develops its own technologies. The overview of the company's characteristics is given in Table 5.4.

Main Focus of Illustration
Personal relations between high-ranked executives in the B2B markets

Description
Manufacturing companies generally believe that the success of a company is mainly shaped by the ability to deliver a good product in a good price. Nowadays, in many industries, this still remains the basic though not sufficient requirement. The differences among basic product/price characteristics are so narrow that the development of a company and acquiring new customers are (according to the quoted interlocutor) only enabled by personal relations. However, this is not about shallow ad hoc contacts, but a long-term, sincere relationship. From the business point of view, the actual content of such relationships is the ability to get access to undisclosed information. In the end, it all comes down to customer needs definition—needs that could be satisfied by many potential suppliers, if they knew the broader context of customer decision-making. Without such

Table 5.4 Overview: Chemicals' manufacturer

Number of direct customers	Several hundred
Number of employees	Between 50 and 250
Main market served	B2B
Main business focus	Production with commerce structures, customer service and augmented services
Polish classification of business activities	Manufacturing
Dominant management style	Centralization of decisions in the hands of top management, multiple layers of management, work standardization and formalization, large organizational units
Main perceived success factors	Highly qualified and engaged team
Competitive advantage indicators (in the last two years)	Steady expansion in terms of sales or market share Entered a new market

* Descriptive company name—the company representatives agreed to share information only under the condition its name will not be revealed. For the same reason the general corporate profile does not provide any particular facts and data.

intelligence they can only compete on quality and price of the standard offer, and on some additional blindly chosen supplementary arguments, which sharply reduces their chances of success.

Meanwhile, in order to co-create substantial value with the customer, their openness and attention is needed. In this context, the attitude of the leaders on both sides is very important including their mutual attitudes, interpersonal skills, and value systems. If they can communicate sincerely and place their trust in each other, their talks will be effective and they can quickly move joint ventures forward. An example of such transparency could be the supplier quickly reporting that the requested technical or financial boundary conditions cannot be met because of concrete, factual reasons that the final combined product recipient (the client of the client) might have not been aware of. An alternative could be an attempt to formally meet these requirements, but at the cost of some compromise (e.g. with regard to quality) that the final product recipient did not foresee or such that would not have been possible to verify.

Certainly, not every business opportunity leads to direct contacts of top executives. In general, the greater the disproportion between the companies, the harder it is to establish such a connection. Larger organizations are also usually less flexible because of the structural and processual costs of servicing (what they assess as) niche markets, needs, and processes. This gap is bridged by specialized middlemen. These very well connected individuals can be labelled 'relationship brokers'. They are usually experienced managers, who retired after a long service in multinational companies and influential industrial bodies and who still observe the market from close up. Owing to this, they analyse industrial trends, planned investment and the motives of decision makers to effectively connect people, firms and projects. Being 'relational know-how masters', they offer their knowledge and advice to firms whose relationship capital is insufficient to become a recognized business network member on their own.

To conclude, one can say that the business practice of Chemicals' manufacturer contradicts the view that the transparency of the institutional markets precludes the possibility to effectively use personal relations for business purposes. First, only products based on some industry standards are fully transparent, but not dedicated solutions that have to be co-developed with the customer. Second, personal relationships seem to be equally important in B2B and B2C markets provided the relationship is established between individuals, who treat themselves as partners and possess the authority to take binding decisions in the given business case. Even if the decision-making process in the B2B setting is more complicated and more professional, the decisions are taken in bounded rationality, which causes risks that can be intuitively mitigated by trusted partners.

Illustration 5. Konimpex-Invest Sp. z o.o

Interviewees
1. General director, employment history: more than 5 years.
2. Manager of customer service office, employment history: more than 5 years.

General Corporate Profile
Konimpex-Invest is a medium real estate developing company that has been operating in Poznań and Konin areas for 15 years. The company coordinates the building activities of several real estate investments, mainly targeted at individual clients. This implies that the company does not manage its own building teams, but focuses on searching and purchasing attractive construction land, giving guidelines and placing orders for architectural plans that should cater to contemporary customer needs, and supervising construction works. In addition, Konimpex-Invest offers administration services in own-built estates via its associated company.

Table 5.5 Overview: Konimpex-Invest Sp. z o.o.

Number of direct customers	Several hundred
Number of employees	Between 10 and 50
Main market served	B2C
Main business focus	Commerce, customer service and augmented services
Polish classification of business activities	Construction
Dominant management style	Decisions in the hands of multiple types of managers and highly qualified specialists, large organizational units
Main perceived success factors	Highly qualified and engaged team Excellent corporate reputation/very strong brand
Competitive advantage indicators (in the last two years)	Steady expansion in terms of sales or market share Steadily ahead of competitors in terms of profits Steady increase of employment Steadily improving customer loyalty rate

The company is part of Konimpex capital group, which operates in diversified industries. The parent company has been specializing in the trade of raw materials and industrial and chemical components for 30 years. In addition, the group consists of Konimpex-Plus (outdoor clothing and equipment distributor), Konimpex Trading (facilitating trade between Poland and Uzbekistan), and publishing house "Przegląd Koniński"—a publisher of three regional magazines. The overview of the company's characteristics is given in Table 5.5.

Main Focus of Illustration
Barriers to developing relationships with customers and suppliers

Description
Theoretically, companies in the real estate development industry have a superior starting position for customer relationship management. Direct access to customers, very high value of transactions and their emotional importance make them open to non-anonymous contacts via varied communication channels. What is, however, somewhat problematic, is the repeatability of transactions. According to varied sources, an average Pole changes accommodation 2–5 times in a lifetime (however, no research is available that would differentiate between changing to a new or pre-owned flat (Badowski 2017; Polskie Radio 2014)). Buying an apartment from the same developer again is therefore unlikely. This places contacts

with companies such as Konimpex-Invest more in a transactional than a relational context. Naturally, a real estate company cannot afford to deliver a poor quality apartment or to break given promises (e.g. failing to build a playground once the building is ready). Nonetheless, in the case of most customers, carrying out the proactive elements of CRM strategy does not apply in the after-sales period when, owing to a very distant prospect of buying an apartment again, customer interest in maintaining contact with the company falls dramatically. Also, possible referrals will be based rather on the material elements of the offer (apartment) than on after-sales contacts with the company.

Nonetheless, Konimpex-Invest found a way to widen the spectrum of relational cooperation with its customers. Being aware of the fact that the actual possibility to engage the customer in a relationship cumulates in the period before the apartment is handed over, the company proposes a programme called 'Reciprocal package'. It is aimed at motivating customers towards activities benefiting the company in exchange for financial allowance in the form of free of charge transfer of the apartment ownership rights. 'Reciprocal package' is based on a points system. Half of these points are granted for using the add-on services Konimpex-Invest provides (e.g. mortgage and finishing works intermediation). The other half is linked with activities on social media: leaving positive comments on the company's Facebook fan page and providing a recommendation on Facebook or Google maps.

The said programme does not impact long-term relationship management. However, the second initiative of Konimpex-Invest does. Most clients are looking for a new flat for themselves. However, there is a tiny group of people who buy new apartments with the intention to rent them. Many of these individual investors have built private real estate portfolios, which creates the potential for mutual long-term cooperation. Even if the main substance of the transaction is the apartment, the emphasis is placed on after-sales services. With regard to service logic, the duration and profitability of the relationship is mainly shaped by the extent that the company enables its customers to unfold their real estate investment strategy without having to be personally involved in the renting activities. Hence Konimpex-Invest, via its partner company, offers convenient services ranging from financial bookkeeping to full legal, technical, and maintenance-administrative services.

Overcoming the barriers of the transactional business model with the help of a selective relational strategy and the servicization of the offer indicates an advanced approach to RM. Nonetheless, the transactional logic dominates not only in the case of the bulk of the individual clients, but also towards the company's suppliers. Konimpex-Invest purposefully does not develop strategic relationships with any of the construction companies because it assesses that exploiting the full potential of a given construction project is much more probable if it is separately negotiated each time. Such an approach is exemplified in periodical change of analysts assessing the offers and of frontline personnel directly contacting the construction companies. Konimpex-Invest does this to avoid personal acquaintance impacting the professionalism of the tender assessing process.

Moreover, it is a rule of thumb to cooperate with multiple construction companies even if the finished investment projects are highly satisfactory. Such a policy is dictated by the logic of tender offer procedure. Although, as a private investor, Konimpex-Invest does not have to select based on the lowest price, the company expects to receive competitive offers. However, owing to the fact that preparing such an offer is very time-consuming and costly, the construction companies carefully analyse the likelihood of gaining the contract before they decide to begin to tender. If one company kept winning all tenders organized by Konimpex-Invest, it would soon only be this offerer that would stand for the next tender, which could heavily impact its pricing policy.

The same logic is reproduced in the sugar market (compare Illustration 7), where the main buyers purposefully divide their orders so that no supplier gains the upper hand and in the case of Termy Maltańskie (Illustration 6), although this time the market is being intentionally divided not by the buyer, but by the supplying companies. The example of Konimpex-Invest and these firms indicates that relational-based competitive advantage mainly emerges when there exists room for joint individualized value co-creation. In such a case one can assume that the market is best coordinated by managing relationships. However, if the potential for co-creating individualized value in a long-term relationship is unlikely or it mainly depends on the buyer (so that the buyer could achieve a comparable effect with any partner), relational cooperation loses ground as the most effective market coordination method. This may be one of the reasons for the difficulties hitherto in proving the positive assumptions of RBV. Corporate resources may be relatively valuable, rare, inimitable, and organized so that the company holds a strong position among the limited number of market leaders and simultaneously still too generic to achieve absolute dominance.

Illustration 6. Termy Maltańskie Sp. z o.o

Interviewees
1. President of the executive board, employment history: more than 5 years.
2. Executive board member, employment history: more than 5 years.

General Corporate Profile
Termy Maltańskie is the biggest waterpark in Poland and the third biggest in Europe. The company is fully owned by the municipality of Poznań. The facility was put into service in 2011 and its development was listed as one of the key investments coordinated with the European Football Championships UEFA EURO 2012, for which Poznań was one of the hosting cities. The facility contains recreational and sports swimming pools and a sauna zone, which are visited by 1.2 million guests annually (based on data from 2019; COVID-19 crises brought sever losses in guest numbers in 2020). The complex holds several cooperating companies including swimming school, fitness, dance school, and restaurant. The overview of the company's characteristics is given in Table 5.6.

Main Focus of Illustration
Supplier–buyers Relationships

Table 5.6 Overview: Termy Maltańskie Sp. z o.o.

Number of direct customers	Thousands and more
Number of employees	Between 50 and 250
Main market served	B2C
Main business focus	Services with commerce structures
Polish classification of business activities	Other services
Dominant management style	Democratic decisions resulting from the opinions of many employees, small organizational units and matrix structures.
Main perceived success factors	Highly qualified and engaged team Convenient localization
Competitive advantage indicators	Steady expansion in terms of sales or market share Steadily ahead of competitors in terms of profits Steadily improving customer loyalty rate

Description
One of the priorities for a company offering leisure time spending in water is safety. Among many facets of this problem, which include such issues as the technical reliability of facilities and their proper maintenance and cleanliness, the number of lifeguards and their training seems to play the most important role. Despite the fact that the said service is rather uncomplicated (many young people earn a lifeguard licence after attending an one-week course and passing the exam), in a business context it bears high risk, which has to be reduced, especially by a publicly-owned company. For its management, every case of drowning, even if all official rules were followed, would be highly likely to end in having an argument with the public on potential additional safety measures that might have saved a human life.

Owing to this, whatever investment in security the company would allocate (e.g. hiring additional lifeguards) could be seen as insufficient. Therefore, a more effective way of elevating the level of security is to share this risk with a specialized partner. A lifeguarding company is responsible for the recruitment, required licences, training level, and the general work attitude of its employees. It has to guarantee that enough personnel will be available even in the summertime, when the demand for lifeguarding increases sharply. The additional specificity of Termy Maltańskie is that, as a publicly-owned company, it is obliged to follow the rules of Public Procurement Law, if the annual worth of products or services of the same kind exceeds 30,000 EUR. Following this, Termy Maltańskie has to carry out complex tendering procedures, inter alia, for lifeguarding services.

Theoretically, the party that purchases products or services has an advantage over the supplier, at least until the transaction is concluded. The buyer can exert pressure on the supplier, and if the offered conditions are not satisfactory, they may well choose another one. This is a classical imbalance of contracting parties, which heightens the more competitive the market and the more generic the offer at stake. A public tender is a tool that mostly takes into account the price, and therefore it follows the transactional logic of doing business. On the other hand, lifeguarding service providers are aware of their critical importance for big waterparks, and they have become experts in public tendering. This has allowed the relationships among the big lifeguarding firms to flourish.

The tendering process is expected to create transparency and optimize public funds disbursement. However, according to the practice of Termy Maltańskie and other similar firms, these objectives are, at least partly, not met. In order to meet the strict safety regulations, waterparks have to set rigorous requirements, which allow them to formally accept an offer for further detailed examination. However, this reduces the number of potential service providers to only a few of the largest ones in Poland. As this situation has repeated again and again, a quasi-monopoly in the niche of lifeguarding services for large facilities has emerged.

A closer look at the pattern of behaviour of large lifeguarding companies brings similar observations. One of them places a dumping offer, another an expensive one and the third one the offer with a targeted price level. Initially, the lowest-price logic favours the first offer, which is, however, placed only in case an unexpected competitor emerges. As soon as the list of offers is closed and there is no such danger, the lowest offer is withdrawn, and the tendering is won by the 'third' company. The offer with the highest price acts as the background for the whole tendering process, so that it cannot be annulled. This schema is being reproduced elsewhere across the country. The only difference is the changing roles of the companies.

The collusive behaviour of the three companies is most evident. It is simultaneously proof of managing relationships—even if not, as usual, with customers, but with competitors. So it seems, a company does not necessarily have to adopt a total RM strategy. This means that the relationship management capability with some actors does not exclude adopting a transactional strategy towards others. RM is, therefore, not a 'natural strategy', which will prevail once the external and internal barriers of its implementation are overcome. A healthy business relationship is only possible when the partners of the relationship have a free choice and maintain comparable positions, and the more likely this is, the higher the chance for synergistic added value generation.

Interestingly, by imposing the transactional logic of tendering to prevent the relationships between the representatives of buyer and seller going against the interest of the tax payer, the legal regulations have, in fact, undermined the position of the publicly-owned company. However, arguably, in the given circumstances, also the classical 'invisible hand of the market' would probably also not guarantee a better outcome, because the rent resulting from the collusive relationship seems to be higher than the theoretical rent resulting from unforced customer loyalty-making. Paradoxically, the intervention of the state would be most welcome—not in the form of tendering but in effective anti-cartel regulations.

Simultaneously, although RBV clearly describes the intra-company mechanism for generating sustained competitive advantage based on VRIO resources and dynamic capabilities, the example of Termy Maltańskie indicates that business performance may be strongly affected by the external market forces described by M. Porter (1979). In the case of the lifeguarding services' market, the bargaining power of suppliers and buyers is balanced, as there are few of them on either side. The substitute for outsourcing of lifeguarding services is organizing these services by the waterparks themselves, which, owing to the highlighted risks is not a comfortable option. The industry rivalry is not intense, because of mutual relationships and shared market servicing strategy, which is directed to minimize the threat of new entrants (by applying the mechanism of the dumping offer). Hence, even if lifeguarding is a generic service, the threat of new entrants is also not acute, which, in the end, stabilizes the market structure.

Illustration 7. Sugar-refining group*

Interviewees
1. Finance Manager, employment history: more than 5 years.
2. Sales Manager, employment history: more than 5 years.

General Profile
Sugar-refining group is a European sugar manufacturer present in 18 countries. The company (the first sugar refinery) was found in nineteenth century by several small investors in Germany. The company generates 60% of its turnover in the market of big consignees, such as manufacturers of sweets and soft drinks. In addition, it owns sugar consumer brands. Sugar-refining group holds the strongest position in northern Europe. In Poland it belongs to the group of the three biggest sugar manufacturers. The overview of the company's characteristics is given in Table 5.7.

Main Focus of Illustration
The influence of competition and unfavourable market conditions on the importance of customer relationship management.

Description
Not long ago the sugar market on the territory of the European Union was fully regulated. In 2012 the price regulation was lifted, and in 2017 the production limits were also lifted. The result was sharp price

Table 5.7 Overview: Sugar-refining group

Number of direct customers	Several hundred
Number of employees	Between 999 and 4999
Main market served	B2B
Main business focus	Production with commerce structures, customer service and augmented services
Polish classification of business activities	Manufacturing
Dominant management style	Centralization of decisions in the hands of top management, multiple layers of management, work standardization and formalization, big organizational units
Main perceived success factors	Highly qualified and engaged team Excellent corporate reputation/very strong brand
Competitive advantage indicators (in the last two years)	Steadily ahead of competitors in terms of profits

* Descriptive company name—the company representatives agreed to share information only on condition its name will not be revealed.

fluctuations from a record high of approximately 600 EUR/tonne to very low 250 EUR/tonne—as the interview was being held. This situation was influenced by the expansion of sugar production area across EU-countries and very good sugar beet crops in the European Union and sugarcane harvests in Brazil. This heavily affected the financial outcomes of sugar manufacturers, because they usually rely entirely on selling sugar and its low-processed products (e.g. special sugars like sugar with cocoa and powdered sugar). The knock-on effect was fierce competition that was reflected by the willingness to ship sugar over large distances. Up to this point a relatively stable market allocation was cultivated, which was sanctioned by the long tradition and the high costs of shipping sugar in relation to the shipment value.

Sugar-refining group identifies three main client groups:

- food manufacturers,
- retail sugar distributors in the markets, where the company maintains geographically-based competitive advantage,
- sugar distributors in export markets.

The portfolio of the key clients from the first group has been stabile for years. This is not due to long-term contracts (these are usually signed annually), but because of:

- market price transparency (sugar is traded on commodity exchanges, therefore the buyers may easily negotiate a satisfactory price without having to change supplier);
- the policy of the key buyers, who divide their orders across two or three suppliers (so that none of them would get a dominating position).

It seems that the policy of balancing the market is very important for the major sugar buyers. A good example of how this policy is being implemented can be seen in the situation of a particular food manufacturing facility, which is situated a couple of miles from the sugar refinery and yet it purchases only a part of the required sugar quantity there. The rest is supplied by refineries owned by the other sugar corporations, even if the shipping costs are much higher.

Being an established market player, Sugar-refining group has always relied on the principle of maintaining long-term customer relationships. However, the sugar oversupply crisis has made it clear to the company's management that even if cooperation with the food manufacturers is of mutually strategic importance, Sugar-refining group's impact on the value creation processes of its clients is marginal. It is entirely based on one homogenous product and, as purchasing managers from food industry say: "sugar remains sugar". Therefore, the relations Sugar-refining group holds with these clients can be characterized in the following way:

- it is important with regard to transactional volume, but of low intensity and generally maintained by necessity;
- it is heavily shaped by exogenous factors;
- it is marked by the advantageous position of the buyers, who make use of sugar price transparency and 'regulate' the market, only expecting that the supplier react to the required demand.

In the case of the second group of clients—the retail sugar distributors located in the markets where Sugar-refining group maintains a geographically-based competitive advantage, the oversupply of sugar has also impacted the margins of the company, even if the costs of shipping sugar from Western or Central Europe via the Baltic See or Danish Straits moderately stabilized the price reduction. On the other hand, the crisis has made it evident that also in the case of these clients, the stability of business relationship is generally exogenically-based, and the only tangible effect of the strategic partnership with the retailing distributors are the 'innovative' special sugars, which remain low-processed products. That is why in countries such as Poland, where there are several major sugar suppliers, the retailing distributors do not develop strong exclusive ties with any of them, especially owing to the fact that they usually sell sugar under their private labels. Probably the only way of taking advantage of relationship rent by sugar manufacturers remains on the basis of individual relationships between the employees of the buyer and supplier. However, this mainly translates into an information advantage, but not to ultimate buying preference. Moreover, many retailing distributors keep on changing the areas of responsibilities of their purchasing staff to minimize what they perceive as the risk of bribery.

To sum up, one can state that longitudinal relationships in a market of limited competition where a low-processed, homogeneous, non-innovative product is traded is not a proof of relationship maturity. In the case of Sugar-refining group and similar companies, the longstanding relative market stability have clouded their capability to further develop relationships and left their clients in a state of (probably) partly unmet or unconscious needs.

The supply shock has made Sugar-refining group start concept work on ways to develop its competitive position in the new market conditions. One of these ways is to further expand by taking over sugar refineries from areas where the company currently does not hold a dominant position. Another relies on looking for innovative products based on the special sugars developed for the northern markets. The goal of the third one is to increase the share of services in its portfolio so that Sugar-refining group can advance to a more strategic position in the value creation process of its main clients. Currently the potential for improving the level of services already offered is being evaluated as well as new services being conceptualized. A good example of such a new service may be the improvement in flexibility of sugar supply, so that the order is delivered within 24 hours from ordering. Also important is making both their own sales representatives and the clients aware that even today the company is offering some add-on services which allow them to positively differentiate their offer against competitors (e.g. free of surcharge weekend sugar deliveries).

As the example of Sugar-refining group and some of the previous illustrations show, despite declaring overly positive relationship values like responsibility and engagement, the relational model of company development is not more natural or probable than strategizing in the manner of M. Porter's five forces model, at least when it comes to generic products. Moreover, if possible, these markets will rather motivate the suppliers to strive for achieving some state of monopoly by showing all the external signs of willingness for partnership, however being reduced to the mere desire to have a stable buyer. On the other hand, the buyers will try to maintain as much flexibility and freedom of decisions as possible, which is, in fact, likely to leave mutual relations on the transactional level.

Illustration 8. Aquanet S.A.

Interviewees
1. Senior customer care specialist, employment history: more than 5 years.
2. Manager of customer care department, employment history: more than 5 years.

General Corporate Profile
The company offers water and wastewater services for the Poznań area and for neighbouring municipalities populated by approximately 900,000 customers. More than 70% of the company's shares are owned by the city of Poznań, the rest by other municipal authorities. The Aquanet capital group includes several entities that are subcontractors to parent company. Examples of their services include: design and construction of new water and wastewater network, maintenance and breakdown removal, and water quality surveillance. The overview of the company's characteristics is given in Table 5.8.

Main Focus of Illustration
Formulation of relational targets under the conditions of a natural monopoly

Description
The idea of the complex implementation of a relationship approach is relatively new to Aquanet. For decades the company has been concentrating mainly on technical, engineering operations. The changes in the

Table 5.8 Overview: Aquanet S.A.

Number of direct customers	Thousands and more
Number of employees	Between 250 and 999
Main market served	B2C
Main business focus	Services
Polish classification of business activities	Other services
Dominant management style	Centralization of decisions in the hands of top management, multiple layers of management, work standardization and formalization, large organizational units
Main perceived success factors	Excellent corporate reputation/very strong brand Weak, dispersed or non-existent competition
Competitive advantage indicators (in the last two years)	Steady expansion in terms of sales or market share Entered a new market

company's environment (e.g. the coordination of activities of municipal companies to serve the overall policy of the city of Poznań) and the professionalization of general corporate management has brought numerous initiatives, whose general aim was to increase the maturity of relationship management with Aquanet's stakeholders. The situation of the company is, however, specific. Owing to its public service mission and municipal ownership, the company was in position to set the goal of elevating customer satisfaction, however without linking it with improved financial results. Aquanet cannot actively follow a sales increase objective (except for the extensive expansion of water and wastewater network). On the contrary, the company should get its clients to save water. A revenue increase might be achieved by cross-selling add-on services; however the primary goal would have to remain entirely focused on facilitating customer activities when connecting to the network or operating connecting pipes, not on generating additional income. Hence, the RM business case cannot be based on revenue increase. In contrast, the motivation to increase customer satisfaction is somewhat dimmed by their indifference. The majority of the company's customers only expect that their taps provide water, without needing closer relationships with the supplier. Therefore, most of Aquanet's proactive consumer activities take a form bordering on public relations and corporate social responsibility.

The aim of these activities is broadly defined as education and fun. Some of the events organized by Aquanet are relatively loosely linked with company's core business area. The company acts here as a sponsor supporting activities financed and organized by the city of Poznań. The examples of such initiatives include, for example, patronage over theatre performances organized in the City Hall courtyard and partnering non-governmental organizations. Activities directly linked to water are, of course, present including ecological education and influencing consumer attitudes towards water saving and reducing water waste.

Arguably, the highest potential for improving both customer satisfaction based on direct contacts with the company as well as its financial results can be linked with the activities focused on Aquanet's employees. These activities can be divided into two groups: general culture formation and internal process optimization. The company impresses with a persistent determination in the evolutionary transformation from a 'divide and rule' corporate culture into an effective relational culture. This is confirmed, inter alia, by the fact that the aforementioned CSR activities are implemented with reference to the sustainable development and responsible business strategy for 2017–2022, which was prepared with the active involvement of Aquanet's employees. This was a logical step, which followed the earlier development of a system of corporate values aimed to govern the activities of every employee, irrespective of work history and position, and the Book of Customer Servicing Standards, which regulates the approach to external relations.

The implementation of the new values and standards was backed by a training programme aimed in making employees familiar with the content and meaning of these changes. New training proposals, such as stress management and team management, were also introduced. The selected employees got feedback on their strengths, weaknesses, and possible self-development during special sessions. In addition, managers participated in training on employee-development interviewing. Later, a Code of Ethics was prepared to promote cultivating the adopted corporate values among both employees and Aquanet's business partners. Compliance with the Code of Ethics is supervised by the Ethics Committee. All these initiatives do not exhaust the necessity for further work. At the point when this illustration was prepared, Aquanet finds itself in the transition phase from transactional to relational management.

Low employee turnover and the longstanding employment history of most employees (which is generally positive) suggest that the corporate memory stores the behaviours and attitudes embedded in earlier times. If these characterize the majority of employees of a particular organizational unit and, above all, its boss, they may be reproduced and adopted by newcomers. Such a silent, not entirely intentional resistance to change may persist and negatively influence the corporate culture for a long time. In turn, any culture change remains superficial and requires ongoing external engagement, because the intra-departmentally projected mode of behaviour will be still different than expected.

What also challenges the company's change management programme is ineffective internal organizational processes preserved by a complex IT infrastructure. Hence, a durable and fundamental advancement toward RM maturity will only be possible once all the processes are mapped (what has already taken place), optimized, and digitalized by new integrative IT tools. The company's transformation will be completed once the processual and technical change enables it to confer responsibility, knowledge, and authority to line employees.

The processual change has also opened the door to achieving work effectiveness-based financial benefits. Simplification of procedures reflected in their reduced labour-intensity and time-consumption, as well as the improvement in internal communication, will not only positively influence internal and external customer satisfaction but will also pay off in reduced costs. Cutting red tape by simultaneously ensuring the transparency of the outputs of business processes should enable the company to fully unlock the potential hidden in individual employees and in whole teams. This, in turn, enables fully meeting the implicit customer service standards (not possible for detailed regulation and controlling) and evoking entrepreneurial (innovative) attitudes among employees.

To sum up, the example of Aquanet shows a particularly important pattern. The benefits linked to RM maturity can be realized even by organizations which, due to multiple barriers in their environment, cannot directly benefit from relationship rent obtained with their external partners. However, the quality of internal relationships is not always reflected in low employee turnover (as an equivalent for customer loyalty), because they may be based by stagnation and reduced expectations. Simultaneously, even if the company remains in an advantageous position towards its partners (in the case of Aquanet, towards customers), a change aimed at improvement in their satisfaction (reflected at least in reduced time to generate the expected servicing outcome) may positively impact corporate effectiveness. In the end, the foundations for cost reduction-based competitive advantage are laid, and simultaneously the ability to react to new external stimuli is improved. Such a resilience mechanism may be activated, for example, in the case of market deregulation or new market entry (the relationship capital stabilizes customer outflow) or when new market opportunities emerge (the ability to react quickly thanks to resource potentiation). Another type of argument for developing a relationship approach to business may also be the golden rule prevalent in almost all the world's religions and cultures: "treat others as you would like to be treated" (Reichheld and Markey 2011, p. 13). Creating a better company does not cost more than a worse one. Simultaneously, a better company positively impacts the environment and the lives of many people and makes the world a better place to live.

Notes

1. NPS is calculated by subtracting the percentage of Detractors (customers who answered the question 'How likely is it that you would recommend [brand] to a friend or colleague?' by giving scores 0–6) from the percentage of Promoters (customers who answered the same question by giving scores 9–10). Customers who answered the same question by giving 7–8 scores are treated as Passives and their scores are not calculated. NPS can range from −100 (if every customer is a detractor) to a +100 (if every customer is a promoter).
2. The label 'transaction-oriented company' is given to separate the rest of the companies from the RM-mature ones in the upcoming models of market competition. As already indicated in Chap. 2, these companies do not have to represent a homogenous group and they may even define themselves as RM-oriented. However, given the totality of the RM-maturity model, by all possible diversity of actions and approaches, they have one thing in common: they do not generate a relational rent.

References

Ahearne, Michael, John Mathieu, and Adam Rapp. 2005. To Empower or Not to Empower Your Sales Force? An Empirical Examination of the Influence of Leadership Empowerment Behavior on Customer Satisfaction and Performance. *Journal of Applied Psychology* 90 (5): 945–955. https://doi.org/10.1037/0021-9010.90.5.945.

Ahn, Jae-Hyeon, Sang-Pil Han, and Yung-Seop Lee. 2006. Customer Churn Analysis: Churn Determinants and Mediation Effects of Partial Defection in the Korean Mobile Telecommunications Service Industry. *Telecommunications Policy* 30 (10): 552–568. https://doi.org/10.1016/j.telpol.2006.09.006.

Badowski, Artur. 2017. Dlaczego i Jak Często Się Przeprowadzamy? *Strefa Biznesu*. https://strefabiznesu.pl/dlaczego-i-jak-czesto-sie-przeprowadzamy/ar/c3-11719258

Barner, Robert. 1994. Enablement: The Key to Empowerment. *Training & Development* 48 (6): 33–37.

Bharadwaj, Sundar G., P. Rajan Varadarajan, and John Fahy. 1993. Sustainable Competitive Advantage in Service Industries: A Conceptual Model and Research Propositions. *Journal of Marketing* 57 (4): 83–99. https://doi.org/10.2307/1252221.

Buttle, Francis, and Stan Maklan. 2019. *Customer Relationship Management: Concepts and Technologies*. London: Routledge.

Chatterjee, Sayan, and Birger Wernerfelt. 1991. The Link Between Resources and Type of Diversification: Theory and Evidence. *Strategic Management Journal* 12 (1): 33–48. https://doi.org/10.1002/smj.4250120104.

Chatterjee, Sheshadri, Soumya Kanti Ghosh, Ranjan Chaudhuri, and Bang Nguyen. 2019. Are CRM Systems Ready for AI Integration? A Conceptual Framework of Organizational Readiness for Effective AI-CRM Integration. *The Bottom Line* 32 (2): 144–157. https://doi.org/10.1108/BL-02-2019-0069.

Comer, Michael J. 1998. *Corporate Fraud*. 3rd ed. Burlington: Gower Publishing, Ltd.

Dalgic, Tevfik. 1998. Niche Marketing Principles: Guerrillas versus Gorillas. *Journal of Segmentation in Marketing* 2 (1): 5–18. https://doi.org/10.1300/J142v02n01_02.

De Bruin, Tonia, Michael Rosemann, Ronald Freeze, and Uday Kaulkarni. 2005. Understanding the Main Phases of Developing a Maturity Assessment Model. In *Australasian Conference on Information Systems (ACIS)*, ed. D. Bunker, B. Campbell, and J. Underwood, 8–19. Australasian Chapter of the Association for Information Systems. https://eprints.qut.edu.au/25152/.

Deszczyński, Bartosz. 2016a. The Impact of Opportunity Management on the Relationship Business Model (A Study in the Polish Housing Industry). *Journal of Eastern European and Central Asian Research (JEECAR)* 3 (2): 1–10. https://doi.org/10.15549/jeecar.v3i2.137.

———. 2016b. The Maturity of Corporate Relationship Management. *Gospodarka Narodowa* 283 (3): 73–104. https://doi.org/10.33119/GN/100777.

Dolata, Ulrich. 2017. *Apple, Amazon, Google, Facebook, Microsoft: Market Concentration – Competition – Innovation Strategies*, Working Paper. SOI Discussion Paper. https://www.econstor.eu/handle/10419/152249

du Toit, Gerard, and Maureen Burns. 2014. How Banks Can Turn the Tide of Customer Defection. *American Banker*, December 24. https://www.americanbanker.com/opinion/how-banks-can-turn-the-tide-of-customer-defection

Dyer, Jeffrey H., and Harbir Singh. 1998. The Relational View: Cooperative Strategy and Sources of Interorganizational Competitive Advantage. *The Academy of Management Review* 23 (4): 660–679. https://doi.org/10.2307/259056.

Eshghi, Abdolreza, Dominique Haughton, and Heikki Topi. 2007. Determinants of Customer Loyalty in the Wireless Telecommunications Industry. *Telecommunications Policy* 31 (2): 93–106. https://doi.org/10.1016/j.telpol.2006.12.005.

Fiske, Alan Page. 1992. The Four Elementary Forms of Sociality: Framework for a Unified Theory of Social Relations. *Psychological Review* 99 (4): 689–723. https://doi.org/10.1037/0033-295X.99.4.689.

FitzPatrick, Mary, Richard J. Varey, Christian Grönroos, and Janet Davey. 2015. Relationality in the Service Logic of Value Creation. *Journal of Services Marketing* 29 (6/7): 463–471. https://doi.org/10.1108/JSM-01-2015-0038.

Galvão, Marcella Brito, Raíssa Corrêa de Carvalho, Lucas Ambrósio Bezerra de Oliveira, and Denise Dumke de Medeiros. 2018. Customer Loyalty Approach Based on CRM for SMEs. *Journal of Business & Industrial Marketing*, June 4. https://doi.org/10.1108/JBIM-07-2017-0166

Granovetter, Mark S. 1977. The Strength of Weak Ties. *American Journal of Sociology* 78 (6): 1360–1380. https://doi.org/10.1016/B978-0-12-442450-0.50025-0.

Grönroos, Christian. 2017. Relationship Marketing Readiness: Theoretical Background and Measurement Directions. *Journal of Services Marketing* 31 (3): 218–225. https://doi.org/10.1108/JSM-02-2017-0056.

Hakanen, Taru, and Elina Jaakkola. 2012. Co-creating Customer-focused Solutions within Business Networks: A Service Perspective. Edited by Evert Gummesson, Cristina Mele, and Francesco Polese. *Journal of Service Management* 23 (4): 593–611. https://doi.org/10.1108/09564231211260431.

Haythornthwaite, Caroline. 2000. Online Personal Networks: Size, Composition and Media Use Among Distance Learners. *New Media & Society* 2 (2): 195–226. https://doi.org/10.1177/14614440022225779.

———. 2005. Social Networks and Internet Connectivity Effects. *Information, Communication & Society* 8 (2): 125–147. https://doi.org/10.1080/13691180500146185.

Henderson, Conor M., Joshua T. Beck, and Robert W. Palmatier. 2011. Review of the Theoretical Underpinnings of Loyalty Programs. *Journal of Consumer Psychology* 21 (3): 256–276. https://doi.org/10.1016/j.jcps.2011.02.007.

Heskett, James L., Thomas O. Jones, Gary W. Loveman, W. Earl Sasser Jr, and Leonard A. Schlesinger. 2008a. Putting the Service-Profit Chain to Work. *Harvard Business Review*, July 1. https://hbr.org/2008/07/putting-the-service-profit-chain-to-work

Heskett, James L., W. Earl Sasser, and Joe Wheeler. 2008b. *The Ownership Quotient: Putting the Service Profit Chain to Work for Unbeatable Competitive Advantage*. Boston: Harvard Business Press.

Hibbert, Sally, Heidi Winklhofer, and Mohamed Sobhy Temerak. 2012. Customers as Resource Integrators: Toward a Model of Customer Learning. *Journal of Service Research* 15 (3): 247–261. https://doi.org/10.1177/10946705 12442805.

Hooks, Karen L., Steven E. Kaplan, Joseph J. Schultz Jr., and Lawrence A. Ponemon. 1994. Enhancing Communication to Assist in Fraud Prevention and Detection; Comment: Whistle-Blowing as an Internal Control Mechanism: Individual and Organizational Considerations. *Auditing* 13 (2): 86.

Hunt, Shelby D. 1997. Resource-Advantage Theory: An Evolutionary Theory of Competitive Firm Behavior? *Journal of Economic Issues* 31 (1): 59–78. https://doi.org/10.1080/00213624.1997.11505891.

Hunt, Shelby D., and Robert M. Morgan. 1995. The Comparative Advantage Theory of Competition. *Journal of Marketing* 59 (2): 1–15. https://doi.org/10.2307/1252069.

———. 1996. The Resource-Advantage Theory of Competition: Dynamics, Path Dependencies, and Evolutionary Dimensions. *Journal of Marketing*: 107–114.

———. 2005. The Resource-Advantage Theory of Competition. *In Review of Marketing Research* 1: 153–206. Review of Marketing Research. Emerald Group Publishing Limited. https://doi.org/10.1108/S1548-6435(2004)0000001008.

Kaplan, Robert, and Robin Cooper. 1998. *Cost & Effect: Using Integrated Cost Systems to Drive Profitability and Performance*. Boston: Harvard Business Press.

Kegan, Robert, Lisa Lahey, Andy Fleming, and Matthew Miller. 2014. Making Business Personal. *Harvard Business Review*, April 1. https://hbr.org/2014/04/making-business-personal

Kotler, Philip, and Kevin Lane Keller. 2009. *Marketing Management*. Pearson Prentice Hall. https://books.google.pl/books?id=QiTOHgAACAAJ.

Krekel, Christian, George Ward, and Jean-Emmanuel De Neve. 2019. Employee Wellbeing, Productivity, and Firm Performance. *Saïd Business School Research Papers* 4: 1–43.

Ledbetter, Andrew M. 2010. Content- and Medium-Specific Decomposition of Friendship Relational Maintenance: Integrating Equity and Media Multiplexity Approaches. *Journal of Social and Personal Relationships* 27 (7): 938–955. https://doi.org/10.1177/0265407510376254.

Lepak, David P., Ken G. Smith, and M. Susan Taylor. 2007. Value Creation and Value Capture: A Multilevel Perspective. *Academy of Management Review* 32 (1): 180–194. https://doi.org/10.5465/amr.2007.23464011.

Lovelock, Christopher H. 1983. Classifying Services to Gain Strategic Marketing Insights. *Journal of Marketing* 47 (3): 9–20. https://doi.org/10.1177/002224298304700303.

Lovelock, Christopher H., Paul Patterson, and Jochen Wirtz. 2014. *Services Marketing. An Asia-Pacific and Australian Perspective*. 6th ed. Melbourne: Pearson Australia. https://www.pearson.com.au/9781486002702.

Lusch, Robert F., and Stephen L. Vargo. 2014. *Service-Dominant Logic: Premises, Perspectives, Possibilities*. New York: Cambridge University Press.

Lusch, Robert F., Stephen L. Vargo, and Matthew O'Brien. 2007. Competing through Service: Insights from Service-Dominant Logic. *Journal of Retailing, Service Excellence* 83 (1): 5–18. https://doi.org/10.1016/j.jretai.2006.10.002.

Mayer, David M., Maribeth Kuenzi, and Rebecca L. Greenbaum. 2010. Examining the Link Between Ethical Leadership and Employee Misconduct: The Mediating Role of Ethical Climate. *Journal of Business Ethics* 95 (1): 7–16. https://doi.org/10.1007/s10551-011-0794-0.

Miles, Raymond E., Charles C. Snow, Alan D. Meyer, and Henry J. Coleman. 1978. Organizational Strategy, Structure, and Process. *Academy of Management Review* 3 (3): 546–562. https://doi.org/10.5465/amr.1978.4305755.

Montgomery, Cynthia A., and Birger Wernerfelt. 1988. Diversification, Ricardian Rents, and Tobin's q. *The RAND Journal of Economics* 19 (4): 623–632. https://doi.org/10.2307/2555461.

Morrison, Sharon, and Frederick G. Crane. 2007. Building the Service Brand by Creating and Managing an Emotional Brand Experience. *Journal of Brand Management* 14 (5): 410–421. https://doi.org/10.1057/palgrave.bm.2550080.

Mugge, Ruth, Jan P.L. Schoormans, and Hendrik N.J. Schifferstein. 2005. Design Strategies to Postpone Consumers' Product Replacement: The Value of a Strong Person-Product Relationship. *The Design Journal* 8 (2): 38–48. https://doi.org/10.2752/146069205789331637.

Olson, Eric M., F. Stanley, G. Slater, Tomas M. Hult, and Kai M. Olson. 2018. The Application of Human Resource Management Policies within the Marketing Organization: The Impact on Business and Marketing Strategy Implementation. *Industrial Marketing Management* 69: 62–73. https://doi.org/10.1016/j.indmarman.2018.01.029.

Palmatier, Robert W., Rajiv P. Dant, and Dhruv Grewal. 2007. A Comparative Longitudinal Analysis of Theoretical Perspectives of Interorganizational Relationship Performance. *Journal of Marketing* 71 (4): 172–194. https://doi.org/10.1509/jmkg.71.4.172.

Palmatier, Robert W., Cheryl Burke Jarvis, Jennifer R. Bechkoff, and Frank R. Kardes. 2009. The Role of Customer Gratitude in Relationship Marketing. *Journal of Marketing* 73 (5): 1–18. https://doi.org/10.1509/jmkg.73.5.1.

Parasuraman, A. 1988. Servqual: A Multiple-Item Scale for Measuring Consumer Perc. *Journal of Retailing; Greenwich* 64 (1, Spring): 12.

Parasuraman, A., Valarie A. Zeithaml, and Leonard L. Berry. 1985. A Conceptual Model of Service Quality and Its Implications for Future Research. *Journal of Marketing* 49 (4): 41–50. https://doi.org/10.1177/002224298504900403.

Parasuraman, A., Leonard L. Berry, and Valarie A. Zeithaml. 1991. Refinement and Reassessment of the SERVQUAL Scale. *Journal of Retailing; Greenwich* 67 (4, Winter): 420.

Pavitt, Keith. 1990. What We Know About the Strategic Management of Technology. *California Management Review* 32 (3): 17.

Payne, Adrian, and Pennie Frow. 2013. *Strategic Customer Management: Integrating Relationship Marketing and CRM.* Cambridge University Press.

Pervan, Simon J., Liliana L. Bove, and Lester W. Johnson. 2009. Reciprocity as a Key Stabilizing Norm of Interpersonal Marketing Relationships: Scale Development and Validation. *Industrial Marketing Management* 38 (1): 60–70. https://doi.org/10.1016/j.indmarman.2007.11.001.

Peteraf, Margaret A. 1993. The Cornerstones of Competitive Advantage: A Resource-Based View. *Strategic Management Journal* 14 (3): 179–191. https://doi.org/10.1002/smj.4250140303.

Pollack, David M., and Leslie J. Pollack. 1996. Using 360° Feedback in Performance Appraisal. *Public Personnel Management; Thousand Oaks* 25 (4): 507–528. https://doi.org/10.1177/009102609602500410.

Polskie, Radio. 2014. Przeciętny Polak Przeprowadza Się Raz Na 15 Lat. https://www.polskieradio24.pl/42/259/Artykul/1075300,Przecietny-Polak-przeprowadza-sie-raz-na-15-lat

Porter, Michael E. 1979. How Competitive Forces Shape Strategy. *Harvard Business Review*, March 1. https://hbr.org/1979/03/how-competitive-forces-shape-strategy

Reichheld, Frederick. 2003. The One Number You Need to Grow. *Harvard Business Review*, December: 1–11.

Reichheld, Frederick, and Rob Markey. 2011. *The Ultimate Question 2.0: How Net Promoter Companies Thrive in a Customer.* Boston: Harvard Business Publishing. https://books.google.pl/books?hl=pl&lr=&id=e8jhiYjQrU0C&oi=fnd&pg=PR7&dq=reichheld+markey&ots=CC1eQacr8I&sig=iSgh_lWq6TPhrVgOpVEfeP3Hnzw&redir_esc=y#v=onepage&q=reichheld%20markey&f=false.

Reichheld, Frederik, and Thomas Teal. 2001. *The Loyalty Effect: The Hidden Force Behind Growth, Profits, and Lasting Value*, Loyalty-Based Management. Boston: Harvard Business School Press. https://books.google.pl/books?id=D-JlUoXtf-AC.

Robinson, Jennifer. 2008. How The Ritz-Carlton Manages the Mystique. Gallup.com, December 11. https://news.gallup.com/businessjournal/112906/How-RitzCarlton-Manages-Mystique.aspx

Romanowska, Maria. 2014. Bariery Efektywności Badań Naukowych z Zakresu Zarządzania Strategicznego. *Prace Naukowe Wałbrzyskiej Wyższej Szkoły Przedsiębiorczości i Zarządzania* 27 (2): 101–108.

Rossiter, John, and Steve Bellman. 2012. Emotional Branding Pays Off: How Brands Meet Share of Requirements Through Bonding, Companionship, and Love. *Journal of Advertising Research* 52 (3): 291–296. https://doi.org/10.2501/JAR-52-3-291-296.

Rumelt, Richard P., D. Schendel, and David J. Teece. 1995. *Fundamental Issues in Strategy: A Research Agenda*. Cambridge, MA: Harvard Business School Press. https://books.google.pl/books?id=rttTzECN9_YC.

Sasser, W. Earl, Leonard A. Schlesinger, and James L. Heskett. 1997. *Service Profit Chain*. New York: Simon and Schuster.

Schmidt-Subramanian, Maxi. 2019. Forrester Publishes NPS Benchmarks For 260 Brands In 16 Industries. *Forrester Blogs* (blog), November 7. https://go.forrester.com/blogs/nps-benchmarks/.

Schumann, Jan H., Florian v. Wangenheim, Anne Stringfellow, Zhilin Yang, Sandra Praxmarer, Fernando R. Jiménez, Vera Blazevic, Randall M. Shannon, G. Shainesh, and Marcin Komor. 2010. Drivers of Trust in Relational Service Exchange: Understanding the Importance of Cross-Cultural Differences. *Journal of Service Research* 13 (4): 453–468. https://doi.org/10.1177/1094670510368425.

Shostack, Lynn G. 1982. How to Design a Service. *European Journal of Marketing* 16 (1): 49–63. https://doi.org/10.1108/EUM0000000004799.

Slater, Stanley F., and Eric M. Olson. 2001. Marketing's Contribution to the Implementation of Business Strategy: An Empirical Analysis. *Strategic Management Journal* 22 (11): 1055–1067. https://doi.org/10.1002/smj.198.

Slater, Stanley F., Eric M. Olson, and Carol Finnegan. 2011. Business Strategy, Marketing Organization Culture, and Performance. *Marketing Letters* 22 (3): 227–242. https://doi.org/10.1007/s11002-010-9122-1.

Stankiewicz, Marek J. 2000. Substance and Methods of Evaluation of Enterprise Competitiveness. *Gospodarka Narodowa. The Polish Journal of Economics* 161 (7–8): 95–111. https://doi.org/10.33119/GN/113968.

Teece, David J. 1982. Towards an Economic Theory of the Multiproduct Firm. *Journal of Economic Behavior & Organization* 3 (1): 39–63. https://doi.org/10.1016/0167-2681(82)90003-8.

———. 1984. Economic Analysis and Strategic Management. *California Management Review (Pre-1986); Berkeley* 26 (3, Spring): 87.

Uncles, Mark D., Grahame R. Dowling, and Kathy Hammond. 2003. Customer Loyalty and Customer Loyalty Programs. *Journal of Consumer Marketing* 20 (4): 294–316. https://doi.org/10.1108/07363760310483676.

Varelius, Jukka. 2009. Is Whistle-Blowing Compatible with Employee Loyalty? *Journal of Business Ethics* 85 (2): 263–275.

Vargo, Stephen L., Josina Vink, and Kaisa Koskela-Huotari. 2020. ServiceDominant Logic: Foundations and Applications. In *The Routledge Handbook of Service Research Insights and Ideas*, ed. E. Bridges and K. Fowler, 3–23. New York:

Routledge. https://www.researchgate.net/profile/Kaisa_Koskela-Huotari/publication/340777398_Service-Dominant_Logic_Foundations_and_Applications/links/5e9d3f0992851c2f52b288fc/Service-Dominant-Logic-Foundations-and-Applications.pdf.

Walker, Orville C., and Robert W. Ruekert. 1987. Marketing's Role in the Implementation of Business Strategies: A Critical Review and Conceptual Framework. *Journal of Marketing* 51 (3): 15–33. https://doi.org/10.1177/002224298705100302.

Williamson, Oliver E. 1991. Strategizing, Economizing, and Economic Organization. *Strategic Management Journal* 12 (S2): 75–94. https://doi.org/10.1002/smj.4250121007.

Wirtz, Jochen, and Christopher H. Lovelock. 2016. *Services Marketing: People, Technology, Strategy*. 8th ed. Hackensack: World Scientific Publishing Company.

Wirtz, Jochen, Siok Kuan Tambyah, and Anna S. Mattila. 2010. Organizational Learning from Customer Feedback Received by Service Employees: A Social Capital Perspective. *Journal of Service Management* 21 (3): 363–387. https://doi.org/10.1108/09564231011050814.

Wood, Wendy, and David T. Neal. 2009. The Habitual Consumer. *Journal of Consumer Psychology* 19 (4): 579–592. https://doi.org/10.1016/j.jcps.2009.08.003.

Zhang, Mingli, Lingyun Guo, Mu Hu, and Wenhua Liu. 2017. Influence of Customer Engagement with Company Social Networks on Stickiness: Mediating Effect of Customer Value Creation. *International Journal of Information Management* 37 (3): 229–240. https://doi.org/10.1016/j.ijinfomgt.2016.04.010.

Open Access This chapter is licensed under the terms of the Creative Commons Attribution 4.0 International License (http://creativecommons.org/licenses/by/4.0/), which permits use, sharing, adaptation, distribution and reproduction in any medium or format, as long as you give appropriate credit to the original author(s) and the source, provide a link to the Creative Commons licence and indicate if changes were made.

The images or other third party material in this chapter are included in the chapter's Creative Commons licence, unless indicated otherwise in a credit line to the material. If material is not included in the chapter's Creative Commons licence and your intended use is not permitted by statutory regulation or exceeds the permitted use, you will need to obtain permission directly from the copyright holder.

Final Note

The narrative in this book focuses on RM maturity and RM mid-range theory. RM maturity conceptualized as the preliminary theoretical model draws on 13 RM-related themes recurring in the prominent literature of the last 10 years and earlier. The detailed review of 129 papers demonstrated, inter alia, that the traditionally significant sociological references of RM theory are now being supplemented by insights from services marketing, especially from SDL. The core notions of the latter are resource integration and the exchange of services (Lusch and Vargo 2014). In this context, relationships act as a conveyor system, which helps to enhance the value that is (co-)created in these intertwined processes.

The empirical examination of the preliminary RM maturity model exposed the strategic importance of internal relationships. The highest quality of these relationships seems to be the hallmark of an RM-mature firm, along with mastery in managing some distinct customer relationship processes. The co-occurrence of sound internal and external relationships positions an RM-mature firm as a valuable partner capable of co-creating and sharing the added value with all its beneficiaries. The intangibility of this knowledge-based co-creative dialogue perfectly fits into the RBV definitions of VRIO resources and dynamic capabilities. In turn, the empirically verified leverage of these resources and capabilities into sustainable competitive advantage is in line with R-A theory. By bringing these theoretical and empirical insights together, the first goal of this book – to conceptualize and to test the notion of RM maturity and to verify whether

RM-mature firms possess the ability to achieve sustainable competitive advantage over their transaction-oriented rivals – is accomplished.

In addition, the empirical research demonstrated the ascending tendency in proficiency of RM (especially in its strategic and processual dimensions) corresponding with rising levels of competitive advantage (especially its most sustainable elements). Moreover, the association rules/basket analysis of RM activities and approaches across four cohorts of firms shows that moderate proficiency in RM yields no significant advantages and that the relationship between what a company does in terms of RM and achieving a sustainable competitive advantage is nonlinear. These results reinforce the concept of RM maturity and directly confirm the twin theoretic-methodological and empirical hypotheses H1tm and H1e.

Chapter 2 and even more so Chap. 5 discussed the foundations of RM mid-range theory. First, the ontological discourse illuminated the idea of the RM mid-range theory of higher order and the complete system of RM mid-range theories of particular market types underpinned by the R-A theory of competitive advantage. In the course of further elaboration, the adopted epistemological positioning (Bednarek 2006) of the RM upper mid-range theory resembled that of a contingency theory type (Pinder and Moore 1980). However, its general applicability was achieved not by directly introducing moderator variables into the analysis and thus reducing the total domain of the study, but primarily by focusing on the corporate reality immersed in human relationship universals reflected in the final RM maturity proposal. Thus, the whole ubiquitous nucleus of the constantly reproduced relational phenomenon was extracted and analysed. The later discussion on the external factors having an impact on the emergence and the size of a relational niche marks the potential of the complete system of RM mid-range theories to deliver normative guidelines reflecting the specificity of markets and industries. By introducing the proposal of the RM upper mid-range theory and by outlining a solid framework for full-scale studies on RM at the middle theoretical level, the second goal of this book was accomplished.

Put in a nutshell, RM maturity requires raising the HRM process to the top of management's agenda. It starts with fair and inspiring behaviour of the leaders, whose signature is empowering communication. This encourages employees to act attentively and in an engaged way towards their fellow employees, their management, customers and other stakeholders. The end result is a high-performing organization, whose competitive advantage is dynamically stabilized by the idiosyncrasy of its relationship capital. The RM upper mid-range theory requires a company to achieve the state of RM maturity as a sine qua non condition of achieving relationally based sustainable competitive advantage. This superiority is monetized thanks to the differentiating potential of the RM-mature company, which is highly appealing to a limited but abundant niche of customers. The relational niche preserves the position of the company, but simultaneously puts a cap on its expansion. It may well coexist within the larger industry-based market, where dominant corporate strategies are volume-oriented and dominant customer preferences are price-oriented. The size of a relational niche reflects the dialogical knowledge-based co-creative RM capabilities of the company, but also the relative ease in directly accessing customers, the typical transaction value, the potential for creating emotional benefits, and the objective offer characteristics enabling flexible individualization based on intangible service elements.

The research on RM maturity and on the RM mid-range theory should be continued. A significant amount of work should be put into RM mid-range theories of particular market types. Certainly, also the limitations of the research on the RM upper mid-range theory presented in this book imply the necessity for further empirical studies to reaffirm or refute its potential for generalizability on a larger sample of high-achieving companies in international markets. The global COVID-19 crisis has opened up a golden opportunity to put the sustainability of competitive advantage of mature RM companies, in particular, to the test. If these companies suffered less and recovered faster than their transaction-oriented counterparts, RM maturity and RM mid-range theory would gain much credence.

References

Aaker, David A. 1989. Managing Assets and Skills: The Key to a Sustainable Competitive Advantage. *California Management Review* 31 (2): 91–106. https://doi.org/10.2307/41166561.

Abrahamson, Eric. 1991. Managerial Fads and Fashions: The Diffusion and Rejection of Innovations. *Academy of Management Review* 16 (3): 586–612. https://doi.org/10.5465/amr.1991.4279484.

Adèr, Hermanus Johannes. 2008. *Advising on Research Methods: A Consultant's Companion*. Huizen: Johannes van Kessel Publishing.

Adler, Paul S., and Seok-Woo Kwon. 2002. Social Capital: Prospects for a New Concept. *Academy of Management Review* 27 (1): 17–40. https://doi.org/10.5465/amr.2002.5922314.

Aguinis, Herman, Steve Werner, JéAnna Lanza Abbott, Cory Angert, Joon Hyung Park, and Donna Kohlhausen. 2010. Customer-Centric Science: Reporting Significant Research Results With Rigor, Relevance, and Practical Impact in Mind. *Organizational Research Methods* 13 (3): 515–539. https://doi.org/10.1177/1094428109333339.

Aguinis, Herman, Lura E. Forcum, and Harry Joo. 2013. Using Market Basket Analysis in Management Research. *Journal of Management* 39 (7): 1799–1824. https://doi.org/10.1177/0149206312466147.

Ahani, Ali, Nor Zairah Ab. Rahim, and Mehrbakhsh Nilashi. 2017. Forecasting Social CRM Adoption in SMEs: A Combined SEM-Neural Network Method. *Computers in Human Behavior* 75: 560–578. https://doi.org/10.1016/j.chb.2017.05.032.

Ahearne, Michael, John Mathieu, and Adam Rapp. 2005. To Empower or Not to Empower Your Sales Force? An Empirical Examination of the Influence of Leadership Empowerment Behavior on Customer Satisfaction and Performance.

Journal of Applied Psychology 90 (5): 945–955. https://doi.org/10.1037/0021-9010.90.5.945.

Ahn, Jae-Hyeon, Sang-Pil Han, and Yung-Seop Lee. 2006. Customer Churn Analysis: Churn Determinants and Mediation Effects of Partial Defection in the Korean Mobile Telecommunications Service Industry. *Telecommunications Policy* 30 (10): 552–568. https://doi.org/10.1016/j.telpol.2006.09.006.

Aliyu, Olayemi Abdullateef, and Munyaradzi Wellington Nyadzayo. 2018. Reducing Employee Turnover Intention: A Customer Relationship Management Perspective. *Journal of Strategic Marketing* 26 (3): 241–257. https://doi.org/10.1080/0965254X.2016.1195864.

Altuntas Vural, Ceren. 2017. Service-Dominant Logic and Supply Chain Management: A Systematic Literature Review. *Journal of Business & Industrial Marketing* 32 (8): 1109–1124. https://doi.org/10.1108/JBIM-06-2015-0121.

Álvarez, Leticia Suárez, Rodolfo Vázquez Casielles, and Ana María Díaz Martín. 2010. Analysis of the Role of Complaint Management in the Context of Relationship Marketing. *Journal of Marketing Management* 27 (1–2): 143–164. https://doi.org/10.1080/02672571003719088.

Alvarez-Milán, Agarzelim, Reto Felix, Philipp A. Rauschnabel, and Christian Hinsch. 2018. Strategic Customer Engagement Marketing: A Decision Making Framework. *Journal of Business Research* 92: 61–70. https://doi.org/10.1016/j.jbusres.2018.07.017.

Alvesson, Mats, and Stanley Deetz. 2000. *Doing Critical Management Research*. London: SAGE.

Alvesson, Mats, and Kaj Sköldberg. 2009. *Reflexive Methodology: New Vistas for Qualitative Research*. London: SAGE.

Alwin, Duane F. 2007. *Margins of Error: A Study of Reliability in Survey Measurement*. Hoboken: John Wiley & Sons.

Amit, Raphael, and Paul J.H. Schoemaker. 1993. Strategic Assets and Organizational Rent. *Strategic Management Journal* 14 (1): 33–46. https://doi.org/10.1002/smj.4250140105.

Anderson, James C., and James A. Narus. 1990. A Model of Distributor Firm and Manufacturer Firm Working Partnerships. *Journal of Marketing* 54 (1): 42–58. https://doi.org/10.1177/002224299005400103.

Anderson, James C., James A. Narus, and Das Narayandas. 2009. *Business Market Management: Understanding, Creating, and Delivering Value*. 3rd ed. New York: Pearson Prentice Hall. https://www.amazon.com/Business-Market-Management-Understanding-Delivering/dp/0136000886.

Andrews, Kenneth R. 1971. The Concept of Corporate Strategy. In *Historical Evolution of Strategic Management*, 18–46. Homewood: Dow-Jones Irwin. https://doi.org/10.4324/9781315253336-11.

Arli, Denni, Carlos Bauer, and Robert W. Palmatier. 2018. Relational Selling: Past, Present and Future. *Industrial Marketing Management* 69: 169–184. https://doi.org/10.1016/j.indmarman.2017.07.018.

Ashley, Christy, Stephanie M. Noble, Naveen Donthu, and Katherine N. Lemon. 2011. Why Customers Won't Relate: Obstacles to Relationship Marketing Engagement. *Journal of Business Research* 64 (7): 749–756. https://doi.org/10.1016/j.jbusres.2010.07.006.

Aumann, Yonatan, and Yehuda Lindell. 2003. A Statistical Theory for Quantitative Association Rules. *Journal of Intelligent Information Systems* 20 (3): 255–283. https://doi.org/10.1023/A:1022812808206.

Azza, Temessek Behi, and Ben Dahmane Mouelhi Norchene. 2017. Social and Physical Aspects of the Service Encounter: Effects on Trust and Customer Loyalty to the Service Provider. *Advances in Economics and Business* 5 (1): 1–10. https://doi.org/10.13189/aeb.2017.050101.

Bacharach, Samuel B. 1989. Organizational Theories: Some Criteria for Evaluation. *The Academy of Management Review* 14 (4): 496–515. https://doi.org/10.2307/258555.

Badowski, Artur. 2017. Dlaczego i Jak Często Się Przeprowadzamy? *Strefa Biznesu.* https://strefabiznesu.pl/dlaczego-i-jak-czesto-sie-przeprowadzamy/ar/c3-11719258

Bain, Joe Staten. 1968. *Industrial Organization.* 2nd ed. New York: John Wiley & Sons Inc.

Baker, Thomas L., Penny M. Simpson, and Judy A. Siguaw. 1999. The Impact of Suppliers' Perceptions of Reseller Market Orientation on Key Relationship Constructs. *Journal of the Academy of Marketing Science* 27 (1): 50–57. https://doi.org/10.1177/0092070399271004.

Balaji, M.S., Sanjit Kumar Roy, and Khong Kok Wei. 2016. Does Relationship Communication Matter in B2C Service Relationships? *Journal of Services Marketing* 30 (2): 186–200. https://doi.org/10.1108/JSM-08-2014-0290.

Ballantyne, David. 2000. Internal Relationship Marketing: A Strategy for Knowledge Renewal. *International Journal of Bank Marketing* 18 (6): 274–286. https://doi.org/10.1108/02652320010358698.

Banaszyk, Piotr. 2014. Model Biznesu Jako Podstawa Zarządzania Strategicznego Przedsiębiorstwem. *Zeszyty Naukowe Akademii Ekonomicznej w Poznaniu* 43: 7–27.

Baran, Roger, and Robert Galka. 2017. *Customer Relationship Management: The Foundation of Contemporary Marketing Strategy.* 2nd ed. Abingdon: Routledge Publications.

Barner, Robert. 1994. Enablement: The Key to Empowerment. *Training & Development* 48 (6): 33–37.

Barney, Jay B. 1986a. Organizational Culture: Can It Be a Source of Sustained Competitive Advantage? *The Academy of Management Review* 11 (3): 656–665. https://doi.org/10.2307/258317.

———. 1986b. Strategic Factor Markets: Expectations, Luck, and Business Strategy. *Management Science* 32 (10): 1231–1241. https://doi.org/10.1287/mnsc.32.10.1231.

———. 1991. Firm Resources and Sustained Competitive Advantage. *Journal of Management* 17 (1): 99–120. https://doi.org/10.1177/014920639101700108.

———. 1997. *Gaining and Sustaining Competitive Advantage*. Reading: Addison-Wesley Publishing Company.

———. 2001. Is the Resource-Based "View" a Useful Perspective for Strategic Management Research? Yes.

———. 2014. How Marketing Scholars Might Help Address Issues in Resource-Based Theory. *Journal of the Academy of Marketing Science* 42 (1): 24–26. https://doi.org/10.1007/s11747-013-0351-8.

Barney, Jay B., and Asli M. Arikan. 2017. The Resource-Based View: Origise and Implications. In *The Blackwell Handbook of Strategic Management*, ed. Michael A. Hitt, R. Edward Freeman, and Jeffrey S. Harrison, 123–182. Oxford: Blackwell Publishing Ltd. https://doi.org/10.1111/b.9780631218616.2006.00006.x.

Barsade, Sigal G. 2014. What's Love Got to Do with It? A Longitudinal Study of the Culture of Companionate Love and Employee and Client Outcomes in a Long-Term Care Setting. *Administrative Science Quarterly* 59 (4): 551–598. https://doi.org/10.1177/0001839214538636.

Barsade, Sigal G., and Olivia A. O'Neill. 2016. 'Manage Your Emotional Culture'. *Harvard Business Review*, January 1. https://hbr.org/2016/01/manage-your-emotional-culture

Baruch, Yehuda. 1999. Response Rate in Academic Studies-A Comparative Analysis. *Human Relations* 52 (4): 421–438. https://doi.org/10.1177/001872679905200401.

Baruch, Yehuda, and Brooks C. Holtom. 2008. Survey Response Rate Levels and Trends in Organizational Research. *Human Relations*. https://doi.org/10.1177/0018726708094863.

Bass, Frank M., A. Krishnamoorthy, Ashutosh Prasad, and Suresh P. Sethi. 2004. Advertising Competition with Market Expansion for Finite Horizon Firms. *Journal of Industrial and Management Optimization*. https://utd-ir.tdl.org/handle/10735.1/3643.

Baumol, William J., and Sue Anna Bafey Blackman. 1991. *Perfect Markets and Easy Virtue, Business Ethics and the Invisible Hand*. 1st ed. Oxford: Blackwell Publishing Ltd. https://www.abebooks.com/first-edition/Perfect-Markets-Easy-Virtue-Business-Ethics/22861690876/bd.

Bednarek, Monika. 2006. Epistemological Positioning and Evidentiality in English News Discourse: A Text-Driven Approach. *Text & Talk* 26 (6): 635–660. https://doi.org/10.1515/TEXT.2006.027.

Bendle, Neil T., and Charan K. Bagga. 2016. The Metrics That Marketers Muddle. *MIT Sloan Management Review* 57 (3): 73–82.

Bengtsson, Maria, and Sören Kock. 2000. "Coopetition" in Business Networks – to Cooperate and Compete Simultaneously. *Industrial Marketing Management* 29 (5): 411–426. https://doi.org/10.1016/S0019-8501(99)00067-X.

Bernd, Heinrich. 2005. Transforming Strategic Goals of CRM into Process Goals and Activities. Edited by Ilia Bider and Paul Johannesson. *Business Process Management Journal* 11 (6): 709–723. https://doi.org/10.1108/14637150510630873.

Berry, Leonard. 1983. *Relationship Marketing*, 25–80. Chicago: American Marketing Association.

Bharadwaj, Sundar G., P. Rajan Varadarajan, and John Fahy. 1993. Sustainable Competitive Advantage in Service Industries: A Conceptual Model and Research Propositions. *Journal of Marketing* 57 (4): 83–99. https://doi.org/10.2307/1252221.

Bi, Qingqing. 2019. Cultivating Loyal Customers Through Online Customer Communities: A Psychological Contract Perspective. *Journal of Business Research* 103: 34–44. https://doi.org/10.1016/j.jbusres.2019.06.005.

Biemer, Paul P. 2010. Total Survey Error: Design, Implementation, and Evaluation. *Public Opinion Quarterly* 74 (5): 817–848. https://doi.org/10.1093/poq/nfq058.

Bingham, Christopher B., and Kathleen M. Eisenhardt. 2008. Position, Leverage and Opportunity: A Typology of Strategic Logics Linking Resources with Competitive Advantage. *Managerial and Decision Economics* 29 (2–3): 241–256. https://doi.org/10.1002/mde.1386.

Birkinshaw, Julian, Omar Toulan, and David Arnold. 2001. Global Account Management in Multinational Corporations: Theory and Evidence. *Journal of International Business Studies* 32 (2): 231–248. https://doi.org/10.1057/palgrave.jibs.8490950.

Blau, Peter M. 1986. *Exchange and Power in Social Life*. 2nd ed. New Brunswick: Routledge.

Blodgett, Jeffrey G., Donna J. Hill, and Stephen S. Tax. 1997. The Effects of Distributive, Procedural, and Interactional Justice on Postcomplaint Behavior. *Journal of Retailing* 73 (2): 185–210. https://doi.org/10.1016/S0022-4359(97)90003-8.

Bock, Dora E., Stephanie M. Mangus, and Judith Anne Garretson Folse. 2016. The Road to Customer Loyalty Paved with Service Customization. *Journal of Business Research* 69 (10): 3923–3932. https://doi.org/10.1016/j.jbusres.2016.06.002.

Bonner, Julena M., Rebecca L. Greenbaum, and David M. Mayer. 2016. My Boss Is Morally Disengaged: The Role of Ethical Leadership in Explaining the Interactive Effect of Supervisor and Employee Moral Disengagement on Employee Behaviors. *Journal of Business Ethics* 137 (4): 731–742. https://doi.org/10.1007/s10551-014-2366-6.

Bontis, Nick. 1998. Intellectual Capital: An Exploratory Study That Develops Measures and Models. *Management Decision* 36 (2): 63–76. https://doi.org/10.1108/00251749810204142.

Bourdieu, Pierre. 1986. The Forms of Capital. In *Handbook of Theory and Research for the Sociology of Education*, ed. J. Richardson, 241–258. Westport/New York: Greenwood Press. http://www.socialcapitalgateway.org/content/paper/bourdieu-p-1986-forms-capital-richardson-j-handbook-theory-and-research-sociology-educ.

Bratnicka-Myśliwiec, K., M. Kulikowska-Pawlak, and M. Bratnicki. 2018. Contemporary Thinking About Theory Building: A Review of the Concept with Application to Organisational Politics Researching. *Organizacja i Zarządzanie: Kwartalnik Naukowy* 2. https://doi.org/10.29119/1899-6116.2018.42.1.

Bratnicki, Mariusz, and Paweł Brzeziński. 2019. Wykorzystanie myślenia i działania do strategii przedsiębiorczej. *Przegląd Organizacji* 5: 9–15. https://doi.org/10.33141/po.2019.5.2.

Bratnicki, Mariusz, and Wojciech Dyduch. 2020. Understanding Cognitive Biases in Strategic Decisions for Value Creation and Capture. In *Contemporary Challenges in Cooperation and Coopetition in the Age of Industry 4.0*, Springer Proceedings in Business and Economics, ed. Agnieszka Zakrzewska-Bielawska and Iwona Staniec, 359–373. Cham: Springer International Publishing. https://doi.org/10.1007/978-3-030-30549-9_19.

Brodie, Roderick J. 2017. Enhancing Theory Development in the Domain of Relationship Marketing: How to Avoid the Danger of Getting Stuck in the Middle. *Journal of Services Marketing* 31 (1): 20–23.

Brown, Donald E. 2004. Human Universals, Human Nature & Human Culture. *Daedalus* 133 (4): 47–54. https://doi.org/10.1162/0011526042365645.

Buckley, Peter J., Christopher L. Pass, and Kate Prescott. 1988. Measures of International Competitiveness: A Critical Survey. *Journal of Marketing Management* 4 (2): 175–200. https://doi.org/10.1080/0267257X.1988.9964068.

Burt, Ronald S. 2009. *Structural Holes: The Social Structure of Competition*. Cambridge: Harvard University Press.

Butcher, Ken. 2001. Evaluative and Relational Influences on Service Loyalty. Edited by Sparks Beverley. *International Journal of Service Industry Management* 12 (4): 310–327. https://doi.org/10.1108/09564230110405253.

Buttle, Francis, and Stan Maklan. 2019. *Customer Relationship Management: Concepts and Technologies*. London: Routledge.
Cambra-Fierro, Jesús, Iguácel Melero-Polo, and F. Javier Sese. 2016. Can Complaint-Handling Efforts Promote Customer Engagement? *Service Business* 10 (4): 847–866. https://doi.org/10.1007/s11628-015-0295-9.
Cameron, Kim S., and Robert E. Quinn. 2011. *Diagnosing and Changing Organizational Culture: Based on the Competing Values Framework*. 3rd ed. San Francisco: John Wiley & Sons.
Carroll, Archie B. 1991. The Pyramid of Corporate Social Responsibility: Toward the Moral Management of Organizational Stakeholders. *Business Horizons* 34 (4): 39–49.
Carter, Richard, and Geoffrey M. Hodgson. 2006. The Impact of Empirical Tests of Transaction Cost Economics on the Debate on the Nature of the Firm. *Strategic Management Journal* 27 (5): 461–476. https://doi.org/10.1002/smj.531.
Caves, R.E., and Michael E. Porter. 1978. Market Structure, Oligopoly, and Stability of Market Shares. *The Journal of Industrial Economics* 26 (4): 289–313. https://doi.org/10.2307/2098076.
Chamberlain, Edward Hastings. 1962. *The Theory of Monopolistic Competition: A Re-Orientation of the Theory of Value*. 8th ed. Cambridge, MA: Harvard University Press.
Chandra, Yanto, and Ian F. Wilkinson. 2017. Firm Internationalization from a Network-Centric Complex-Systems Perspective. *Journal of World Business* 52 (5): 691–701. https://doi.org/10.1016/j.jwb.2017.06.001.
Chang, Woojung, Jeong Eun Park, and Seoil Chaiy. 2010. How Does CRM Technology Transform into Organizational Performance? A Mediating Role of Marketing Capability. *Journal of Business Research* 63 (8): 849–855. https://doi.org/10.1016/j.jbusres.2009.07.003.
Chang, Song, Yaping Gong, Sean A. Way, and Liangding Jia. 2013. Flexibility-Oriented HRM Systems, Absorptive Capacity, and Market Responsiveness and Firm Innovativeness. *Journal of Management* 39 (7): 1924–1951. https://doi.org/10.1177/0149206312466145.
Chari, Simos, Anssi Tarkiainen, and Hanna Salojärvi. 2016. Alternative Pathways to Utilizing Customer Knowledge: A Fuzzy-Set Qualitative Comparative Analysis. *Journal of Business Research* 69 (11): 5494–5499. https://doi.org/10.1016/j.jbusres.2016.04.160.
Charmaz, Kathy. 2004. Grounded Theory. In *The SAGE Encyclopedia of Social Science Research Methods*, ed. Michael S. Lewis, Alan Bryman, and Tim Futing Liao, 441–444. Thousand Oaks: SAGE Publications, Inc. https://doi.org/10.4135/9781412950589.

Chatterjee, Sayan, and Birger Wernerfelt. 1991. The Link Between Resources and Type of Diversification: Theory and Evidence. *Strategic Management Journal* 12 (1): 33–48. https://doi.org/10.1002/smj.4250120104.

Chatterjee, Sheshadri, Soumya Kanti Ghosh, Ranjan Chaudhuri, and Bang Nguyen. 2019. Are CRM Systems Ready for AI Integration? A Conceptual Framework of Organizational Readiness for Effective AI-CRM Integration. *The Bottom Line* 32 (2): 144–157. https://doi.org/10.1108/BL-02-2019-0069.

Chen, Injazz, and Karen Popovich. 2003. Understanding Customer Relationship Management (CRM): People, Process and Technology. *Business Process Management Journal* 9 (5): 672–688. https://doi.org/10.1108/14637150310496758.

Chen, Tser-Yieth, Tsai-Lien Yeh, and Hsin-Chun Yeh. 2011. Trust-Building Mechanisms and Relationship Capital. *Journal of Relationship Marketing* 10 (3): 113–144. https://doi.org/10.1080/15332667.2011.596471.

Cheng, Lai-Yu, and Chih-Wei Yang. 2013. Conceptual Analysis and Implementation of an Integrated CRM System for Service Providers. *Service Business* 7 (2): 307–328. https://doi.org/10.1007/s11628-012-0160-z.

Chetty, Sylvie, and Desiree Blankenburg Holm. 2000. Internationalisation of Small to Medium-Sized Manufacturing Firms: A Network Approach. *International Business Review* 9 (1): 77–93. https://doi.org/10.1016/S0969-5931(99)00030-X.

Cheung, Mee-Shew, Matthew B. Myers, and John T. Mentzer. 2011. The Value of Relational Learning in Global Buyer-Supplier Exchanges: A Dyadic Perspective and Test of the Pie-Sharing Premise. *Strategic Management Journal* 32 (10): 1061–1082. https://doi.org/10.1002/smj.926.

Chin, Wynne W., Robert A. Peterson, and Steven P. Brown. 2008. Structural Equation Modeling in Marketing: Some Practical Reminders. *Journal of Marketing Theory and Practice* 16 (4): 287–298. https://doi.org/10.2753/MTP1069-6679160402.

Chmielecki, Michał, and Łukasz Sułkowski. 2018. Cultural Factors of Trust in a Public Organization as a Workplace. In *Managing Public Trust*, ed. Barbara Kočuch, Sławomir J. Magala, and Joanna Paliszkiewicz, 99–114. Cham: Springer International Publishing. https://doi.org/10.1007/978-3-319-70485-2_7.

Cho, Jinsook. 2006. The Mechanism of Trust and Distrust Formation and Their Relational Outcomes. *Journal of Retailing* 82 (1): 25–35. https://doi.org/10.1016/j.jretai.2005.11.002.

Chomiak-Orsa, I. 2016. Zarządzanie relacjami w organizacjach sieciowych. *Organizacja i Zarządzanie / Politechnika Śląska* 90: 25–44.

Choudhury, Musfiq Mannan, and Paul Harrigan. 2014. CRM to Social CRM: The Integration of New Technologies into Customer Relationship Management. *Journal of Strategic Marketing* 22 (2): 149–176.

Christopher, Martin, Adrian Payne, and David Ballantyne. 1991. *Relationship Marketing: Bringing Quality Customer Service and Marketing Together*. Oxford: Butterworth Heinemann.

Ciszewska-Mlinarič, Mariola, and Aleksandra Wąsowska. 2015. Resource-Based View (RBV). In *Wiley Encyclopedia of Management*, 1–7. American Cancer Society. https://doi.org/10.1002/9781118785317.weom060174.

Ciszewska-Mlinarič, Mariola, Krzysztof Obłój, and Aleksandra Wąsowska. 2015. Zasobowe i branžowe uwarunkowania wyników polskich małych i średnich przedsiębiorstw. *Marketing i Rynek* 9 (CD): 78–88.

Clarke, Irvine. 2001. Extreme Response Style in Cross-cultural Research. *International Marketing Review* 18 (3): 301–324. https://doi.org/10.1108/02651330110396488.

Coelho, Pedro S. 2007. The Choice Between a Five-Point and a Ten-Point Scale in the Framework of Customer Satisfaction Measurement. *International Journal of Market Research* 49 (3): 313–339. https://doi.org/10.1177/147078530704900305.

Coelho, Pedro S., and Susana P. Esteves. 2007a. The Choice between a Fivepoint and a Ten-Point Scale in the Framework of Customer Satisfaction Measurement. *International Journal of Market Research* 49 (3): 313–39. https://doi.org/10.1177/147078530704900305.

Coelho, Pedro S., and Susana P. Esteves. 2007b. Correspondence Regarding "The Choice Between a Five-Point and a Ten-Point Scale in the Framework of Customer Satisfaction Research", by Pedro S. Coelho and Susana P. Esteves. *International Journal of Market Research* 49 (5): 547–549.

Cohen, Wesley M., and Daniel A. Levinthal. 1990. Absorptive Capacity: A New Perspective on Learning and Innovation. *Administrative Science Quarterly* 35 (1): 128–152. https://doi.org/10.2307/2393553.

Coleman, James S. 1988. Social Capital in the Creation of Human Capital. *American Journal of Sociology* 94: S95–S120. https://doi.org/10.1086/228943.

Colgate, Mark, Vicky Thuy-Uyen Tong, Christina Kwai-Choi Lee, and John U. Farley. 2007. Back From the Brink: Why Customers Stay. *Journal of Service Research* 9 (3): 211–228. https://doi.org/10.1177/1094670506295849.

Collins, Jim, and Jerry I. Porras. 2002. *Built to Last: Successful Habits of Visionary Companies*. New York: HarperCollins.

Colombo, Massimo G., Marco Delmastro, and Larissa Rabbiosi. 2007. "High Performance" Work Practices, Decentralization, and Profitability: Evidence from Panel Data. *Industrial and Corporate Change* 16 (6): 1037–1067.

Coltman, Tim. 2007. Why Build a Customer Relationship Management Capability? *The Journal of Strategic Information Systems* 16 (3): 301–320. https://doi.org/10.1016/j.jsis.2007.05.001.

Coltman, Tim, Timothy M. Devinney, and David F. Midgley. 2011. Customer Relationship Management and Firm Performance. *Journal of Information Technology*, September 1. https://doi.org/10.1057/jit.2010.39.

Comer, Michael J. 1998. *Corporate Fraud*. 3rd ed. Burlington: Gower Publishing, Ltd.

Conner, Kathleen R. 1991. A Historical Comparison of Resource-Based Theory and Five Schools of Thought Within Industrial Organization Economics: Do We Have a New Theory of the Firm? *Journal of Management* 17 (1): 121–154. https://doi.org/10.1177/014920639101700109.

Conrad, Craig A., Gene Brown, and Harry A. Harmon. 1997. Customer Satisfaction and Corporate Culture: A Profile Deviation Analysis of a Relationship Marketing Outcome. *Psychology & Marketing* 14 (7): 663–674. https://doi.org/10.1002/(SICI)1520-6793(199710)14:7<663::AID-MAR2>3.0.CO;2-E.

Cousins, Paul D., Robert B. Handfield, Benn Lawson, and Kenneth J. Petersen. 2006. Creating Supply Chain Relational Capital: The Impact of Formal and Informal Socialization Processes. *Journal of Operations Management*, Incorporating Behavioral Theory in OM Empirical Models, 24 (6): 851–863. https://doi.org/10.1016/j.jom.2005.08.007.

Coviello, Nicole E., Roderick J. Brodie, Peter J. Danaher, and Wesley J. Johnston. 2002. How Firms Relate to Their Markets: An Empirical Examination of Contemporary Marketing Practices. *Journal of Marketing* 66 (3): 33–46. https://doi.org/10.1509/jmkg.66.3.33.18500.

Cox, Eli P. 1980. The Optimal Number of Response Alternatives for a Scale: A Review. *Journal of Marketing Research* 17 (4): 407–422. https://doi.org/10.1177/002224378001700401.

Coyne, Kevin P. 1986. Sustainable Competitive Advantage-What It Is, What It Isn't. *Business Horizons* 29 (1): 54.

Coyne, Kevin P., and Renée Dye. 1998. The Competitive Dynamics of Network-Based Businesses. *Harvard Business Review*. https://hbr.org/1998/01/the-competitive-dynamics-of-network-based-businesses

Crawford, Vincent P. 1990. Relationship-Specific Investment. *The Quarterly Journal of Economics* 105 (2): 561–574. https://doi.org/10.2307/2937801.

Creed, W.E.Douglas. 2003. Voice Lessons: Tempered Radicalism and the Use of Voice and Silence*. *Journal of Management Studies* 40 (6): 1503–1536. https://doi.org/10.1111/1467-6486.00389.

Crosby, Lawrence A., and Sheree L. Johnson. 2004. The Three Ms of Customer Loyalty. *Marketing Management* 13 (4): 12–13.

Crosby, Lawrence A., Kenneth R. Evans, and Deborah Cowles. 1990. Relationship Quality in Services Selling: An Interpersonal Influence Perspective. *Journal of Marketing* 54 (3): 68–81. https://doi.org/10.2307/1251817.

Cross, Kelvin, and Richard Lynch. 1988. The "SMART" Way to Define and Sustain Success. *National Productivity Review* 8 (1): 23–33.

Crowne, Douglas P., and David Marlowe. 1960. A New Scale of Social Desirability Independent of Psychopathology. *Journal of Consulting Psychology* 24 (4): 349–354. https://doi.org/10.1037/h0047358.

Czakon, Wojciech. 2005. Ku Systemowej Teorii Przewagi Konkurencyjnej Przedsiębiorstwa. *Przegląd Organizacji* 5: 5–8.

———. 2011a. Metodyka systematycznego przeglądu literatury. *Przegląd Organizacji* 3: 57–61.

———. 2011b. Paradygmat Sieciowy w Naukach o Zarządzaniu. *Przegląd Organizacji* 11 (5): 3–6.

———. 2014. Szkoły a Mody w Zarządzaniu Strategicznym. *Prace Naukowe WWSZIP* 27 (2): 47–55.

———. 2015. *Podstawy metodologii badań w naukach o zarządzaniu*. 3rd ed. Ed. Wojciech Czakon. Warszawa: Oficyna a Wolters Kluwer business. https://ruj.uj.edu.pl/xmlui/handle/item/85236

———. 2018. Consultation on the applicability of theories during the 24th Nordic Workshop on Interorganizational Research organized by the Vaasa University, Finland, 25–27.04.2018.

Czakon, Wojciech, Patrycja Klimas, and Arkadiusz Kawa. 2019. Krótkowzroczność strategiczna – metodyczne aspekty systematycznego przeglądu literatury. *Studia Oeconomica Posnaniensia* 7 (2): 27–37. https://doi.org/10.18559/SOEP.2019.2.2.

Dalgic, Tevfik. 1998. Niche Marketing Principles: Guerrillas versus Gorillas. *Journal of Segmentation in Marketing* 2 (1): 5–18. https://doi.org/10.1300/J142v02n01_02.

Datta, Deepak K., James P. Guthrie, and Patrick M. Wright. 2005. Human Resource Management and Labor Productivity: Does Industry Matter? *Academy of Management Journal* 48 (1): 135–145. https://doi.org/10.5465/amj.2005.15993158.

Davenport, Thomas H. 2000. *Mission Critical: Realizing the Promise of Enterprise Systems*. Boston: Harvard Business Press.

Davidson, Karina, and Michael William MacGregor. 1998. A Critical Appraisal of Self-Report Defense Mechanism Measures. *Journal of Personality* 66 (6): 965–992. https://doi.org/10.1111/1467-6494.00039.

Davis, Joseph Stancliffe. 2016. *Essays in the Earlier History of American Corporations*. Clark: The Lawbook Exchange Ltd.

Davis, Donna F., and Susan L. Golicic. 2010. Gaining Comparative Advantage in Supply Chain Relationships: The Mediating Role of Market-Oriented IT

Competence. *Journal of the Academy of Marketing Science* 38 (1): 56–70. https://doi.org/10.1007/s11747-008-0127-8.

Davis, James H., F. David Schoorman, Roger C. Mayer, and Hwee Hoon Tan. 2000. The Trusted General Manager and Business Unit Performance: Empirical Evidence of a Competitive Advantage. *Strategic Management Journal* 21 (5): 563–576. https://doi.org/10.1002/(SICI)1097-0266(200005)21:5<563::AID-SMJ99>3.0.CO;2-0.

Davis, Don E., Joshua N. Hook, Everett L. Worthington Jr., Daryl R. Van Tongeren, Aubrey L. Gartner, David J. Jennings II, and Robert A. Emmons. 2011. Relational Humility: Conceptualizing and Measuring Humility as a Personality Judgment. *Journal of Personality Assessment* 93 (3): 225–234. https://doi.org/10.1080/00223891.2011.558871.

Davis, Don E., Everett L. Worthington Jr., Joshua N. Hook, Robert A. Emmons, Peter C. Hill, Richard A. Bollinger, and Daryl R. Van Tongeren. 2013. Humility and the Development and Repair of Social Bonds: Two Longitudinal Studies. *Self and Identity* 12 (1): 58–77. https://doi.org/10.1080/15298868.2011.636509.

Day, George S. 2003. Creating a Superior Customer-Relating Capability. *MIT Sloan Management Review* 44 (3): 77–82.

De Bruin, Tonia, Michael Rosemann, Ronald Freeze, and Uday Kaulkarni. 2005. Understanding the Main Phases of Developing a Maturity Assessment Model. In *Australasian Conference on Information Systems (ACIS)*, ed. D. Bunker, B. Campbell, and J. Underwood, 8–19. Australasian Chapter of the Association for Information Systems. https://eprints.qut.edu.au/25152/.

De Jong, Martijn G., Jan-Benedict E.M. Steenkamp, Jean-Paul Fox, and Hans Baumgartner. 2008. Using Item Response Theory to Measure Extreme Response Style in Marketing Research: A Global Investigation. *Journal of Marketing Research* 45 (1): 104–115. https://doi.org/10.1509/jmkr.45.1.104.

de Ruyter, Ko, Debbie Isobel Keeling, and David Cox. 2019. Customer-Supplier Relationships in High Technology Markets 3.0. *Industrial Marketing Management* 79: 94–101. https://doi.org/10.1016/j.indmarman.2018.11.011.

de Wit, Bob, and Ron Meyer. 2010. *Strategy: Process, Content, Context: An International Perspective*. 3rd ed. Andover: Cengage Learning EMEA.

Delpechitre, Duleeep, Lisa L. Beeler-Connelly, and Nawar N. Chaker. 2018. Customer Value Co-Creation Behavior: A Dyadic Exploration of the Influence of Salesperson Emotional Intelligence on Customer Participation and Citizenship Behavior. *Journal of Business Research* 92: 9–24. https://doi.org/10.1016/j.jbusres.2018.05.007.

Denison, Daniel R., and Aneil K. Mishra. 1995. Toward a Theory of Organizational Culture and Effectiveness. *Organization Science* 6 (2): 204–223.

Deszczyński, Bartosz. 2008a. Customer Relationship Management Gwarantem Bezpieczeństwa Konsumenta. In *Bezpieczeństwo Państw a Procesy Migracyjne*, ed. L. Kacprzak and J. Knopek, 157–167. Piła: Wydawnictwo Państwowej Wyěszej Szkoły Zawodowej (PWSZ) w Pile.

———. 2008b. Zewnętrzne Bariery Wdračania Strategii CRM w Integrującej Się Europie. In *Polityka Unijnej Integracji: Wybrane Relacje Zewnętrzne i Wewnętrzne*, 361–376. Zielona Góra: Uniwersytet Zielonogórski.

———. 2011. *CRM. Strategia. System. Zarządzanie zmianą: Jak uniknąć błędów i odnieść sukces wdročenia*. Warszawa: Wolters Kluwer.

———. 2014. Zasoby relacyjne – konceptualizacja pojęcia w świetle zasobowej teorii przedsiębiorstwa. *Studia Oeconomica Posnaniensia* 2 (11): 25–44.

———. 2016a. The Impact of Opportunity Management on the Relationship Business Model (A Study in the Polish Housing Industry). *Journal of Eastern European and Central Asian Research (JEECAR)* 3 (2): 1–10. https://doi.org/10.15549/jeecar.v3i2.137.

———. 2016b. The Maturity of Corporate Relationship Management. *Gospodarka Narodowa* 283 (3): 73–104. https://doi.org/10.33119/GN/100777.

———. 2017. Word-Of-Mouth in Social Media. The Case of Polish Tourist Industry. *International Journal of Management and Economics* 53 (4): 93–114. https://doi.org/10.1515/ijme-2017-0028.

———. 2018. Empowerment pracowników w przedsiębiorstwach braněy usług biznesowych. *Studia Oeconomica Posnaniensia* 6, no. nr 4 Funkcjonowanie i rozwój sektora usług biznesowych w Europie Środkowej i Wschodniej-aspekty makro-i mikroekonomiczne: 113–143. https://doi.org/10.18559/SOEP.2018.4.7.

———. 2019. The Determinants of Global Account Management (Gam). A Relationship Decision-Making Model. *Argumenta Oeconomica* 2 (43): 233–253. https://doi.org/10.15611/aoe.2019.2.10.

Deszczyński, Bartosz, and Paweł Mielcarek. 2014. The Online/Offline Gap in Lead Management Process. *Przegląd Organizacji* 8: 42–49.

Deszczyński, Bartosz, Krzysztof Fonfara, and Adam Dymitrowski. 2017. The Role of Relationships in Initiating the Internationalization Process in B2B Markets. *Entrepreneurial Business and Economics Review* 5 (4): 91–109.

Dey, Eric L. 1997. Working with Low Survey Response Rates: The Efficacy of Weighting Adjustments. *Research in Higher Education* 38 (2): 215–227. https://doi.org/10.1023/A:1024985704202.

Diefendorf, James M., Erin M. Richard, and Jixia Yang. 2008. Linking Emotion Regulation Strategies to Affective Events and Negative Emotions at Work. *Journal of Vocational Behavior* 73 (3): 498–508. https://doi.org/10.1016/j.jvb.2008.09.006.

Dierickx, Ingemar, and Karel Cool. 1989. Asset Stock Accumulation and Sustainability of Competitive Advantage. *Management Science* 35 (12): 1504–1511. https://doi.org/10.1287/mnsc.35.12.1504.

Dillman, Don A. 1991. The Design and Administration of Mail Surveys. *Annual Review of Sociology* 17 (1): 225–249. https://doi.org/10.1146/annurev.so.17.080191.001301.

do Nascimento, Thaina T., Juliana B. Porto, and Catherine T. Kwantes. 2018. Transformational Leadership and Follower Proactivity in a Volunteer Workforce. *Nonprofit Management and Leadership* 28 (4): 565–576.

Dolata, Ulrich. 2017. *Apple, Amazon, Google, Facebook, Microsoft: Market Concentration – Competition – Innovation Strategies*, Working Paper. SOI Discussion Paper. https://www.econstor.eu/handle/10419/152249

Donaldson, Stewart I., and Elisa J. Grant-Vallone. 2002. Understanding Self-Report Bias in Organizational Behavior Research. *Journal of Business and Psychology* 17 (2): 245–260. https://doi.org/10.1023/A:1019637632584.

Doney, Patricia M., and Joseph P. Cannon. 1997. An Examination of the Nature of Trust in Buyer–Seller Relationships. *Journal of Marketing* 61 (2): 35–51. https://doi.org/10.1177/002224299706100203.

Dörnyei, Zoltán, and Tatsuya Taguchi. 2009. *Questionnaires in Second Language Research: Construction, Administration, and Processing*. Routledge. https://doi.org/10.4324/9780203864739.

Dorotic, Matilda, Tammo H.A. Bijmolt, and Peter C. Verhoef. 2012. Loyalty Programmes: Current Knowledge and Research Directions*. *International Journal of Management Reviews* 14 (3): 217–237. https://doi.org/10.1111/j.1468-2370.2011.00314.x.

Dorsch, Michael J., Scott R. Swanson, and Scott W. Kelley. 1998. The Role of Relationship Quality in the Stratification of Vendors as Perceived by Customers. *Journal of the Academy of Marketing Science* 26 (2): 128–142. https://doi.org/10.1177/0092070398262004.

Doty, D. Harold, and William H. Glick. 1994. Typologies as a Unique Form of Theory Building: Toward Improved Understanding and Modeling. *The Academy of Management Review* 19 (2): 230–251. https://doi.org/10.2307/258704.

Doyle, Peter. 2000. Value-Based Marketing. *Journal of Strategic Marketing* 8 (4): 299–311. https://doi.org/10.1080/096525400446203.

du Toit, Gerard, and Maureen Burns. 2014. How Banks Can Turn the Tide of Customer Defection. *American Banker*, December 24. https://www.americanbanker.com/opinion/how-banks-can-turn-the-tide-of-customer-defection

Dunning, John H. 1993. Internationalizing Porter's Diamond. *MIR: Management International Review* 33: 7–15.

———. 2003. Relational Assets, Networks and International Business Activity. In *Alliance Capitalism and Corporate Management*, ed. John H. Dunning and Gavin Boyd. Cheltenham: Edward Elgar Publishing. https://ideas.repec.org/h/elg/eechap/2550_1.html.

Dwyer, F. Robert, Paul H. Schurr, and Sejo Oh. 1987. Developing Buyer-Seller Relationships. *Journal of Marketing* 51 (2): 11–27. https://doi.org/10.1177/002224298705100202.

Dyduch, Wojciech, and Mariusz Bratnicki. 2015. Tworzenie i przechwytywanie wartości w organizacjach współdziałających w sieci. *Prace Naukowe Wałbrzyskiej Wyższej Szkoły Zarządzania i Przedsiębiorczości* 32 (2): 77–93.

Dyer, Jeffrey H., and Harbir Singh. 1998. The Relational View: Cooperative Strategy and Sources of Interorganizational Competitive Advantage. *The Academy of Management Review* 23 (4): 660–679. https://doi.org/10.2307/259056.

Dymitrowski, Adam, Krzysztof Fonfara, and Bartosz Deszczyński. 2019. Informal Relationships in a Company's Internationalization Process. *Journal of Business & Industrial Marketing* 34 (5): 1054–1065. https://doi.org/10.1108/JBIM-11-2018-0363.

East, Robert, Jenni Romaniuk, and Wendy Lomax. 2011. The NPS and the ACSI: A Critique and An Alternative Metric. *International Journal of Market Research* 53 (3): 327–346. https://doi.org/10.2501/IJMR-53-3-327-346.

Easterby-Smith, Mark, Richard Thorpe, and Paul R. Jackson. 2012. *Management Research*. London: SAGE.

Eggert, Andreas, Wolfgang Ulaga, and Franziska Schultz. 2006. Value Creation in the Relationship Life Cycle: A Quasi-Longitudinal Analysis. *Industrial Marketing Management* 35 (1): 20–27. https://doi.org/10.1016/j.indmarman.2005.07.003.

Eisenhardt, Kathleen M., and Jeffrey A. Martin. 2000. Dynamic Capabilities: What Are They? *Strategic Management Journal* 21 (10–11): 1105–1121. https://doi.org/10.1002/1097-0266(200010/11)21:10/11<1105::AID-SMJ133>3.0.CO;2-E.

Enz, Matias G., and Douglas M. Lambert. 2012. Using Cross-Functional, Cross-Firm Teams to Co-Create Value: The Role of Financial Measures. *Industrial Marketing Management*, IMPASIA 2010, 41 (3): 495–507. https://doi.org/10.1016/j.indmarman.2011.06.041.

Erevelles, Sunil, Nobuyuki Fukawa, and Linda Swayne. 2016. Big Data Consumer Analytics and the Transformation of Marketing. *Journal of Business Research* 69 (2): 897–904. https://doi.org/10.1016/j.jbusres.2015.07.001.

Eshghi, Abdolreza, Dominique Haughton, and Heikki Topi. 2007. Determinants of Customer Loyalty in the Wireless Telecommunications Industry. *Telecommunications Policy* 31 (2): 93–106. https://doi.org/10.1016/j.telpol.2006.12.005.

Eurostat. 2020a. Small and Medium-Sized Enterprises (SMEs) – Eurostat. https://ec.europa.eu/eurostat/web/structural-business-statistics/structural-business-statistics/sme

———. 2020b. Europa – RAMON – Classification Detail List. https://ec.europa.eu/eurostat/ramon/nomenclatures/index.cfm?TargetUrl=LST_NOM_DTL&StrNom=NACE_REV2&StrLanguageCode=PL&IntPcKey=&StrLayoutCode=HIERARCHIC

Eveland, Vicki Blakney, Tammy Neal Crutchfield, and Ania Izabela Rynarzewska. 2018. Developing a Consumer Relationship Model of Corporate Social Performance. *Journal of Consumer Marketing* 35 (5): 543–554. https://doi.org/10.1108/JCM-07-2017-2287.

Falkenberg, Andreas Wyller. 1996. Marketing and the Wealth of Firms. *Journal of Macromarketing* 16 (1): 4–24. https://doi.org/10.1177/027614679601600102.

Feehan, Michael, Cristina Ilangakoon, and Penny Mesure. 2009. Keeping Score. *Marketing Research* 21 (4): 6–10.

Feurer, Rainer, and Kazem Chaharbaghi. 1994. Defining Competitiveness: A Holistic Approach. *Management Decision* 32 (2): 49–58. https://doi.org/10.1108/00251749410054819.

Fink, Arlene. 2010. *Conducting Research Literature Reviews: From the Internet to Paper*. 3rd ed. Los Angeles: SAGE.

Fisher, Nicholas I., and Raymond E. Kordupleski. 2019. Good and Bad Market Research: A Critical Review of Net Promoter Score. *Applied Stochastic Models in Business and Industry* 35 (1): 138–151. https://doi.org/10.1002/asmb.2417.

Fiske, Alan Page. 1991. *Structures of Social Life: The Four Elementary Forms of Human Relations: Communal Sharing, Authority Ranking, Equality Matching, Market Pricing*, Structures of Social Life: The Four Elementary Forms of Human Relations: Communal Sharing, Authority Ranking, Equality Matching, Market Pricing. New York: Free Press.

———. 1992. The Four Elementary Forms of Sociality: Framework for a Unified Theory of Social Relations. *Psychological Review* 99 (4): 689–723. https://doi.org/10.1037/0033-295X.99.4.689.

FitzPatrick, Mary, Richard J. Varey, Christian Grönroos, and Janet Davey. 2015. Relationality in the Service Logic of Value Creation. *Journal of Services Marketing* 29(6/7):463–471.https://doi.org/10.1108/JSM-01-2015-0038.

Foddy, William H. 1994. *Constructing Questions for Interviews and Questionnaires: Theory and Practice in Social Research*. Cambridge: Cambridge University Press.

Fonfara, Krzysztof. 2014. *Marketing Partnerski Na Rynku Przedsiębiorstw*. Warszawa: PWE.

Fonfara, Krzysztof, Miłosz Łuczak, Łukasz Małys, Milena Ratajczak-Mrozek, Robert Szczepański, Marcin Soniewicki, Adam Dymitrowski, and Bartosz Deszczyński. 2012. *The Development of Business Networks in the Company Internationalisation Process.* Wydawnictwo Uniwersytetu Ekonomicznego w Poznaniu.

Fonfara, Krzysztof, Łukasz Małys, and Milena Ratajczak-Mrozek. 2019. *The Internationalisation Maturity of the Firm: A Business Relationships Perspective.* Cambridge: Cambridge Scholars Publishing.

Ford, David. 2011. IMP and Service-Dominant Logic: Divergence, Convergence and Development. *Industrial Marketing Management*, Special issue on Service-Dominant Logic in Business Markets, 40 (2): 231–239. https://doi.org/10.1016/j.indmarman.2010.06.035.

Ford, David, and Håkan Håkansson. 2006. IMP – Some Things Achieved: Much More to Do. Edited by Judy Zolkiewski and Peter Turnbull. *European Journal of Marketing* 40 (3/4): 248–258. https://doi.org/10.1108/03090560610648039.

Ford, David, Lars-Erik Gadde, Håkan Håkansson, and Ivan Snehota. 2011. *Managing Business Relationships.* 3rd ed. Chichester: John Wiley. https://www.wiley.com/en-us/Managing+Business+Relationships%2C+3rd+Edition-p-9780470721094.

Forkmann, Sebastian, Stephan C. Henneberg, Peter Naudé, and Maciej Mitrega. 2016. Supplier Relationship Management Capability: A Qualification and Extension. *Industrial Marketing Management* 57: 185–200. https://doi.org/10.1016/j.indmarman.2016.02.003.

Franklin, Drew, and Roger Marshall. 2019. Adding Co-Creation as an Antecedent Condition Leading to Trust in Business-to-Business Relationships. *Industrial Marketing Management* 77: 170–181. https://doi.org/10.1016/j.indmarman.2018.10.002.

Freng Svendsen, Mons, Sven A. Haugland, Kjell Grønhaug, and Trond Hammervoll. 2011. Marketing Strategy and Customer Involvement in Product Development. *European Journal of Marketing* 45 (4): 513–530. https://doi.org/10.1108/03090561111111316.

Frey, Bruno S., and Margit Osterloh. 2001. *Successful Management by Motivation: Balancing Intrinsic and Extrinsic Incentives.* Springer.

Galvão, Marcella Brito, Raíssa Corrêa de Carvalho, Lucas Ambrósio Bezerra de Oliveira, and Denise Dumke de Medeiros. 2018. Customer Loyalty Approach Based on CRM for SMEs. *Journal of Business & Industrial Marketing*, June 4. https://doi.org/10.1108/JBIM-07-2017-0166

Ganesan, Shankar. 1994. Determinants of Long-Term Orientation in Buyer-Seller Relationships. *Journal of Marketing* 58 (2): 1–19. https://doi.org/10.1177/002224299405800201.

Gentle, Michael. 2002. *The CRM Project Management Handbook: Building Realistic Expectations and Managing Risk*. London/Sterling. http://search.ebscohost.com/login.aspx?direct=true&db=eoh&AN=0658504&lang=pl&site=ehost-live

Geyskens, Inge, Jan-Benedict E.M. Steenkamp, Lisa K. Scheer, and Nirmalya Kumar. 1996. The Effects of Trust and Interdependence on Relationship Commitment: A Trans-Atlantic Study. *International Journal of Research in Marketing* 13 (4): 303–317. https://doi.org/10.1016/S0167-8116(96)00006-7.

Ghemawat, Pankaj. 1991. *Commitment: The Dynamic of Strategy*. New York/Toronto: Free Press.

Giannakis, Damianos, and Michael J. Harker. 2014. Strategic Alignment Between Relationship Marketing and Human Resource Management in Financial Services Organizations. *Journal of Strategic Marketing* 22 (5): 396–419. https://doi.org/10.1080/0965254X.2013.876082.

Giannakis, Damianos, Michael J. Harker, and Tom Baum. 2015. Human Resource Management, Services and Relationship Marketing: The Potential for Cross-Fertilisation. *Journal of Strategic Marketing* 23 (6): 526–542. https://doi.org/10.1080/0965254X.2014.1001862.

Gilley, Otis W., and Robert P. Leone. 1991. A Two-Stage Imputation Procedure for Item Nonresponse in Surveys. *Journal of Business Research* 22 (4): 281–291. https://doi.org/10.1016/0148-2963(91)90035-V.

Gołębiowski, Tomasz, and Małgorzata Stefania Lewandowska. 2015. Influence of Internal and External Relationships of Foreign Subsidiaries on Innovation Performance. Evidence from Germany, Czech Republic and Romania. *Journal of East European Management Studies* 20 (3): 304–327.

Gordon, Ian H. 2001. *Relacje z Klientem. Marketing Partnerski*. Warszawa: Polskie Wydawnictwo Ekonomiczne. https://eki.pl/index.php?br1=30000&page=74&detailed=PWE375&.

Gough, David, and Michelle Richardson. 2018. Systematic Reviews. In *Advanced Research Methods for Applied Psychology: Design, Analysis and Reporting*, ed. Paula Brough. London: Routledge. https://doi.org/10.4324/9781315517971-8.

Gouldner, Alvin W. 1960. The Norm of Reciprocity: A Preliminary Statement. *American Sociological Review* 25 (2): 161–178. https://doi.org/10.2307/2092623.

Gounaris, Spiros P. 2006. Internal-Market Orientation and Its Measurement. *Journal of Business Research* 59 (4): 432–448.

Grace, Debra, and Joseph Lo Iacono. 2015. Value Creation: An Internal Customers' Perspective. *Journal of Services Marketing* 29 (6/7): 560–570. https://doi.org/10.1108/JSM-09-2014-0311.

Grandey, Alicia A. 2003. When "The Show Must Go On": Surface Acting and Deep Acting as Determinants of Emotional Exhaustion and Peer-Rated Service Delivery. *Academy of Management Journal* 46 (1): 86–96. https://doi.org/10.5465/30040678.

Granovetter, Mark S. 1977. The Strength of Weak Ties. *American Journal of Sociology* 78 (6): 1360–1380. https://doi.org/10.1016/B978-0-12-442450-0.50025-0.

Gremler, Dwayne D., and Kevin P. Gwinner. 2015. Relational Benefits Research: A Synthesis. *Handbook on Research in Relationship Marketing*, January 30. https://www.elgaronline.com/view/edcoll/9781848443686/9781848443686.00007.xml

Grisaffe, Douglas B. 2007. Questions About the Ultimate Question: Conceptual Considerations in Evaluating Reichheld's Net Promoter Score (NPS). *Journal of Consumer Satisfaction, Dissatisfaction and Complaining Behavior* 20: 36–53.

Grönroos, Christian. 1990. Marketing Redefined. *Management Decision* 28 (8). https://doi.org/10.1108/00251749010139116.

———. 1996. Relationship Marketing: Strategic and Tactical Implications. *Management Decision* 34 (3): 5–14. https://doi.org/10.1108/00251749610113613.

———. 2004. The Relationship Marketing Process: Communication, Interaction, Dialogue, Value. *Journal of Business & Industrial Marketing* 19 (2): 99–113. https://doi.org/10.1108/08858620410523981.

———. 2009. Marketing as Promise Management: Regaining Customer Management for Marketing. *Journal of Business & Industrial Marketing* 24 (5/6): 351–359. https://doi.org/10.1108/08858620910966237.

———. 2011a. A Service Perspective on Business Relationships: The Value Creation, Interaction and Marketing Interface. *Industrial Marketing Management*, Special issue on Service-Dominant Logic in Business Markets, 40 (2): 240–247. https://doi.org/10.1016/j.indmarman.2010.06.036.

———. 2011b. Value Co-Creation in Service Logic: A Critical Analysis. *Marketing Theory* 11 (3): 279–301. https://doi.org/10.1177/1470593111408177.

———. 2016. *Service Management and Marketing: Managing the Service Profit Logic*. 4th ed. Chichester: Wiley. https://www.wiley.com/en-us/Service+Management+and+Marketing%3A+Managing+the+Service+Profit+Logic%2C+4th+Edition-p-9781118921449.

———. 2017. Relationship Marketing Readiness: Theoretical Background and Measurement Directions. *Journal of Services Marketing* 31 (3): 218–225. https://doi.org/10.1108/JSM-02-2017-0056.

Grunig, James E. 2008. *Excellence in Public Relations and Communication Management*. New York: Routledge.

Guenzi, Paolo, Catherine Pardo, and Laurent Georges. 2007. Relational Selling Strategy and Key Account Managers' Relational Behaviors: An Exploratory Study. *Industrial Marketing Management* 36 (1): 121–133.

Guesalaga, Rodrigo, and Wesley Johnston. 2010. What's Next in Key Account Management Research? Building the Bridge Between the Academic Literature and the Practitioners' Priorities. *Industrial Marketing Management*, Selling and Sales Management, 39 (7): 1063–1068. https://doi.org/10.1016/j.indmarman.2009.12.008.

Gulati, Ranjay, Dovev Lavie, and Ravindranath (Ravi) Madhavan. 2011. How Do Networks Matter? The Performance Effects of Interorganizational Networks. *Research in Organizational Behavior* 31: 207–224. https://doi.org/10.1016/j.riob.2011.09.005.

Gummesson, Evert. 1987. The New Marketing – Developing Long-Term Interactive Relationships. *Long Range Planning* 20 (4): 10–20. https://doi.org/10.1016/0024-6301(87)90151-8.

———. 1999. Total Relationship Marketing: Experimenting With a Synthesis of Research Frontiers. *Australasian Marketing Journal (AMJ)* 7 (1): 72–85. https://doi.org/10.1016/S1441-3582(99)70204-1.

———. 2004. Return on Relationships (ROR): The Value of Relationship Marketing and CRM in Business-to-Business Contexts. *Journal of Business & Industrial Marketing* 19 (2): 136–148. https://doi.org/10.1108/08858620410524016.

———. 2012. *Total Relationship Marketing: Marketing Strategy Moving from the 4Ps–Product, Price, Promotion, Place–of Traditional Marketing Management to the 30Rs–the Thirty Relationships–of a New Marketing Paradigm*. Abingdon: Routledge. https://books.google.pl/books?id=x-iZOqS91eAC.

———. 2017a. From Relationship Marketing to Total Relationship Marketing and Beyond. *Journal of Services Marketing* 31 (1): 16–19. https://doi.org/10.1108/JSM-11-2016-0398.

———. 2017b. *Total Relationship Marketing*. 4th ed. Routledge: Abingdon.

Gummesson, Evert, and Cristina Mele. 2010. Marketing as Value Co-Creation Through Network Interaction and Resource Integration. *Journal of Business Market Management* 4 (4): 181–198. https://doi.org/10.1007/s12087-010-0044-2.

Guo, Lin, Thomas Gruen, and Chuanyi Tang. 2017. Seeing Relationships Through the Lens of Psychological Contracts: The Structure of Consumer Service Relationships. *Journal of the Academy of Marketing Science* 45 (3): 357–376.

Gwinner, K.P., D.D. Gremler, and M.J. Bitner. 1998. Relational Benefits in Services Industries: The Customer's Perspective. *Journal of the Academy of Marketing Science* 26 (2): 101–114. https://doi.org/10.1177/0092070398262002.

Hackman, J. Richard, and Greg R. Oldham. 1976. Motivation Through the Design of Work: Test of a Theory. *Organizational Behavior and Human Performance* 16 (2): 250–279. https://doi.org/10.1016/0030-5073(76)90016-7.

———. 1980. *Work Redesign*. Reading: Addison-Wesley.

Hahsler, Michael, Sudheer Chelluboina, Kurt Hornik, and Christian Buchta. 2011. The Arules R-Package Ecosystem: Analyzing Interesting Patterns from Large Transaction Data Sets. *Journal of Machine Learning Research* 12 (June): 2021–2025.

Hair, Joseph F., Marko Sarstedt, Torsten M. Pieper, and Christian M. Ringle. 2012. The Use of Partial Least Squares Structural Equation Modeling in Strategic Management Research: A Review of Past Practices and Recommendations for Future Applications. *Long Range Planning*, Analytical Approaches to Strategic Management: Partial Least Squares Modeling in Strategy Research, 45 (5): 320–340. https://doi.org/10.1016/j.lrp.2012.09.008.

Hajli, Nick, Mohana Shanmugam, Savvas Papagiannidis, Debra Zahay, and Marie-Odile Richard. 2017. Branding Co-Creation with Members of Online Brand Communities. *Journal of Business Research* 70: 136–144. https://doi.org/10.1016/j.jbusres.2016.08.026.

Hakanen, Taru, and Elina Jaakkola. 2012. Co-creating Customer-focused Solutions within Business Networks: A Service Perspective. Edited by Evert Gummesson, Cristina Mele, and Francesco Polese. *Journal of Service Management* 23 (4): 593–611. https://doi.org/10.1108/09564231211260431.

Håkansson, Håkan. 1982. *International Marketing and Purchasing of Industrial Goods: An Interaction Approach*. Nowy Jork: Wiley. https://books.google.pl/books?id=DEd1AAAACAAJ.

Håkansson, Håkan, and David Ford. 2010. *Accounting in Networks*. Ed. Kalle Kraus, Johnny Lind, and Håkan Håkansson. London: Routledge.

Håkansson, Håkan, and I. Snehota. 1995. *Developing Relationships in Business Networks*. London/New York: Routledge. /paper/Developing-relationships-in-business-networks-H%C3%A5kansson-Snehota/d23b990b4914ac25b889d0cb02c9ec0213038e40

Hallikainen, Heli, Emma Savimäki, and Tommi Laukkanen. 2019. Fostering B2B Sales with Customer Big Data Analytics. *Industrial Marketing Management*, December 24. https://doi.org/10.1016/j.indmarman.2019.12.005.

Hansen, Morris H., and William N. Hurwitz. 1946. The Problem of Non-Response in Sample Surveys. *Journal of the American Statistical Association* 41 (236): 517–529. https://doi.org/10.1080/01621459.1946.10501894.

Hansen, Gary S., and Birger Wernerfelt. 1989. Determinants of Firm Performance: The Relative Importance of Economic and Organizational Factors. *Strategic Management Journal* 10 (5): 399–411.

Harris, Jeanne G., Elizabeth Craig, and David A. Light. 2011. Talent and Analytics: New Approaches, Higher ROI. *Journal of Business Strategy* 32 (6): 4–13. https://doi.org/10.1108/02756661111180087.

Hartline, Michael D., James G. Maxham, and Daryl O. McKee. 2000. Corridors of Influence in the Dissemination of Customer-Oriented Strategy to Customer Contact Service Employees. *Journal of Marketing* 64 (2): 35–50. https://doi.org/10.1509/jmkg.64.2.35.18001.

Harvey, Michael, Matthew B. Myers, and Milorad M. Novicevic. 2003. The Managerial Issues Associated with Global Account Management: A Relational Contract Perspective. *Journal of Management Development* 22 (2): 103–129. https://doi.org/10.1108/02621710310459685.

Hawkins, David, and Bob Little. 2011. Embedding Collaboration through Standards – Part 1. *Industrial & Commercial Training* 43 (2): 106–112.

Haynes, Katalin Takacs, Michael A. Hitt, and Joanna Tochman Campbell. 2015. The Dark Side of Leadership: Towards a Mid-Range Theory of Hubris and Greed in Entrepreneurial Contexts. *Journal of Management Studies* 52 (4): 479–505. https://doi.org/10.1111/joms.12127.

Haythornthwaite, Caroline. 2000. Online Personal Networks: Size, Composition and Media Use Among Distance Learners. *New Media & Society* 2 (2): 195–226. https://doi.org/10.1177/14614440022225779.

———. 2005. Social Networks and Internet Connectivity Effects. *Information, Communication & Society* 8 (2): 125–147. https://doi.org/10.1080/13691180500146185.

HCL Technologies. 2020. *The Employees First, Customers Second Transformation Journey – YouTube*. https://www.youtube.com/watch?v=HmV9dmG1XdY&t=3s.

Heavey, Ciaran, Zeki Simsek, Christina Kyprianou, and Marten Risius. 2020. How Do Strategic Leaders Engage with Social Media? A Theoretical Framework for Research and Practice. *Strategic Management Journal* 41 (8): 1490–1527. https://doi.org/10.1002/smj.3156.

Hedström, Peter, and Lars Udehn. 2011. *The Oxford Handbook of Analytical Sociology*. Oxford: OUP.

Helgeson, James G., and Magne Supphellen. 2004. A Conceptual and Measurement Comparison of Self-Congruity and Brand Personality: The Impact of Socially Desirable Responding. *International Journal of Market Research* 46 (2): 205–233. https://doi.org/10.1177/147078530404600201.

Henderson, Conor M., Joshua T. Beck, and Robert W. Palmatier. 2011. Review of the Theoretical Underpinnings of Loyalty Programs. *Journal of Consumer Psychology* 21 (3): 256–276. https://doi.org/10.1016/j.jcps.2011.02.007.

Hennig-Thurau, Thorsten. 2000. Why Customers Build Relationships with Companies and Why Not. In *Relationship Marketing: Gaining Competitive Advantage Through Customer Satisfaction and Customer Retention*, ed.

Thorsten Hennig-Thurau and Ursula Hansen, 369–391. Berlin, Heidelberg: Springer. https://doi.org/10.1007/978-3-662-09745-8_21.

———. 2005. Managing Service Relationships in a Global Economy: Exploring the Impact of National Culture on the Relevance of Customer Relational Benefits for Gaining Loyal Customers. In *Research on International Service Marketing: A State of the Art*. Ed. P. Gwinner Kevin, K. de Ruyter, and P. Pauwels, Trans. Paul Michael, Advances in International Marketing, 15, 11–31. Emerald Group. https://doi.org/10.1016/S1474-7979(04)15002-3.

Hennig-Thurau, Thorsten, Kevin P. Gwinner, and Dwayne D. Gremler. 2002. Understanding Relationship Marketing Outcomes: An Integration of Relational Benefits and Relationship Quality. *Journal of Service Research* 4 (3): 230–247. https://doi.org/10.1177/1094670502004003006.

Herington, Carmel, Lester W. Johnson, and Don Scott. 2009. Firm–Employee Relationship StrengthA Conceptual Model. *Journal of Business Research* 62 (11): 1096–1107.

Heskett, James L., Thomas O. Jones, Gary W. Loveman, W. Earl Sasser Jr, and Leonard A. Schlesinger. 2008a. Putting the Service-Profit Chain to Work. *Harvard Business Review*, July 1. https://hbr.org/2008/07/putting-the-service-profit-chain-to-work

Heskett, James L., W. Earl Sasser, and Joe Wheeler. 2008b. *The Ownership Quotient: Putting the Service Profit Chain to Work for Unbeatable Competitive Advantage*. Boston: Harvard Business Press.

Hibbert, Sally, Heidi Winklhofer, and Mohamed Sobhy Temerak. 2012. Customers as Resource Integrators: Toward a Model of Customer Learning. *Journal of Service Research* 15 (3): 247–261. https://doi.org/10.1177/1094670512442805.

Hoetker, Glenn, and Thomas Mellewigt. 2009. Choice and Performance of Governance Mechanisms: Matching Alliance Governance to Asset Type. *Strategic Management Journal* 30 (10): 1025–1044. https://doi.org/10.1002/smj.775.

Hogan, Suellen J., and Leonard V. Coote. 2014. Organizational Culture, Innovation, and Performance: A Test of Schein's Model. *Journal of Business Research* 67 (8): 1609–1621. https://doi.org/10.1016/j.jbusres.2013.09.007.

Hollebeek, Linda D., Rajendra K. Srivastava, and Tom Chen. 2019. S-D Logic–Informed Customer Engagement: Integrative Framework, Revised Fundamental Propositions, and Application to CRM. *Journal of the Academy of Marketing Science* 47 (1): 161–185. https://doi.org/10.1007/s11747-016-0494-5.

Holm, Morten, V. Kumar, and Carsten Rohde. 2012. Measuring Customer Profitability in Complex Environments: An Interdisciplinary Contingency Framework. *Journal of the Academy of Marketing Science* 40 (3): 387–401. https://doi.org/10.1007/s11747-011-0263-4.

Holt, D., and D. Elliot. 1991. Methods of Weighting for Unit Non-Response. *Journal of the Royal Statistical Society: Series D (The Statistician)* 40 (3): 333–342. https://doi.org/10.2307/2348286.

Homburg, Christian, Andreas Fürst, and Nicole Koschate. 2010. On the Importance of Complaint Handling Design: A Multi-Level Analysis of the Impact in Specific Complaint Situations. *Journal of the Academy of Marketing Science* 38 (3): 265–287. https://doi.org/10.1007/s11747-009-0172-y.

Hooks, Karen L., Steven E. Kaplan, Joseph J. Schultz Jr., and Lawrence A. Ponemon. 1994. Enhancing Communication to Assist in Fraud Prevention and Detection; Comment: Whistle-Blowing as an Internal Control Mechanism: Individual and Organizational Considerations. *Auditing* 13 (2): 86.

Hooley, Graham, Amanda Broderick, and Kristian Möller. 1998. Competitive Positioning and the Resource-Based View of the Firm. *Journal of Strategic Marketing* 6 (2): 97–116. https://doi.org/10.1080/09652549800000003.

Hooley, Graham, Gordon Greenley, John Fahy, and John Cadogan. 2001. Market-Focused Resources, Competitive Positioning and Firm Performance. *Journal of Marketing Management* 17 (5–6): 503–520. https://doi.org/10.1362/026725701323366908.

Hoppner, Jessica J., David A. Griffith, and Ryan C. White. 2015. Reciprocity in Relationship Marketing: A Cross-Cultural Examination of the Effects of Equivalence and Immediacy on Relationship Quality and Satisfaction with Performance. *Journal of International Marketing*, December 1. https://doi.org/10.1509/jim.15.0018

Hornik, Kurt, Bettina Grün, and Michael Hahsler. 2005. Arules – A Computational Environment for Mining Association Rules and Frequent Item Sets. *Journal of Statistical Software* 14: 1–25.

Horovitz, J. 1979. Strategic Control: A New Task for Top Management. *Long Range Planning* 12 (3): 2–7. https://doi.org/10.1016/S0024-6301(79)80001-1.

Hruschka, Harald. 2019. Comparing Unsupervised Probabilistic Machine Learning Methods for Market Basket Analysis. *Review of Managerial Science*, August 23. https://doi.org/10.1007/s11846-019-00349-0.

Hsu, Li-Chang, and Chao-Hung Wang. 2012. Clarifying the Effect of Intellectual Capital on Performance: The Mediating Role of Dynamic Capability. *British Journal of Management* 23 (2): 179–205. https://doi.org/10.1111/j.1467-8551.2010.00718.x.

Huang, Min-Hsin. 2015. The Influence of Relationship Marketing Investments on Customer Gratitude in Retailing. *Journal of Business Research* 68 (6): 1318–1323. https://doi.org/10.1016/j.jbusres.2014.12.001.

Hunt, Shelby D. 1991. *Modern Marketing Theory: Critical Issues in the Philosophy of Marketing Science*. Cincinnati: South-Western Pub. Co.

———. 1997a. Competing Through Relationships: Grounding Relationship Marketing in Resource-Advantage Theory. *Journal of Marketing Management* 13 (5): 431–445. https://doi.org/10.1080/0267257X.1997.9964484.

———. 1997b. Resource-Advantage Theory: An Evolutionary Theory of Competitive Firm Behavior? *Journal of Economic Issues* 31 (1): 59–78. https://doi.org/10.1080/00213624.1997.11505891.

———. 2000. A General Theory of Competition: Too Eclectic or Not Eclectic Enough? Too Incremental or Not Incremental Enough? Too Neoclassical or Not Neoclassical Enough? *Journal of Macromarketing* 20 (1): 77–81. https://doi.org/10.1177/0276146700201010.

Hunt, Shelby D., and C. Jay Lambe. 2000. Marketing's Contribution to Business Strategy: Market Orientation, Relationship Marketing and Resource-Advantage Theory. *International Journal of Management Reviews* 2 (1): 17–43. https://doi.org/10.1111/1468-2370.00029.

Hunt, Shelby D., and Robert M. Morgan. 1995. The Comparative Advantage Theory of Competition. *Journal of Marketing* 59 (2): 1–15. https://doi.org/10.2307/1252069.

———. 1996. The Resource-Advantage Theory of Competition: Dynamics, Path Dependencies, and Evolutionary Dimensions. *Journal of Marketing*: 107–114.

Hunt Shelby, D., and M. Morgan Robert. 2005. The Resource-Advantage Theory of Competition. In *Review of Marketing Research*, Review of Marketing Research, ed. Naresh K. Malhotra, vol. 1, 153–206. Emerald Group Publishing Limited. https://doi.org/10.1108/S1548-6435(2004)0000001008.

Hwang, Jiyoung, and Jay Kandampully. 2015. Embracing CSR in Pro-Social Relationship Marketing Program: Understanding Driving Forces of Positive Consumer Responses. *Journal of Services Marketing* 29 (5): 344–353. https://doi.org/10.1108/JSM-04-2014-0118.

Ichniowski, Casey, Kathryn Shaw, and Giovanna Prennushi. 1997. The Effects of Human Resource Management Practices on Productivity: A Study of Steel Finishing Lines. *American Economic Review* 87 (3): 291–313.

Jakubów, Leon. 2016. Ewolucja Planowania Rozwoju Przedsiębiorstwa. *Evolution in the Enterprise Development Planning* 444: 211–221.

Jankowska, Barbara. 2009. Competition or Cooperation? (Konkurencja czy kooperacja?). *Ekonomista (The Economist)* 1: 67–89.

Jarratt, Denise. 2008. Testing a Theoretically Constructed Relationship Management Capability. *European Journal of Marketing* 42 (9/10): 1106–1132. https://doi.org/10.1108/03090560810891172.

Jayachandran, Satish, Kelly Hewett, and Peter Kaufman. 2004. Customer Response Capability in a Sense-and-Respond Era: The Role of Customer Knowledge Process. *Journal of the Academy of Marketing Science* 32 (3): 219–233. https://doi.org/10.1177/0092070304263334.

Jayachandran, Satish, Subhash Sharma, Peter Kaufman, and Pushkala Raman. 2005. The Role of Relational Information Processes and Technology Use in Customer Relationship Management. *Journal of Marketing* 69 (4): 177–192. https://doi.org/10.1509/jmkg.2005.69.4.177.

Jelinek, Ronald. 2013. All Pain, No Gain? Why Adopting Sales Force Automation Tools Is Insufficient for Performance Improvement. *Business Horizons* 56 (5): 635–642. https://doi.org/10.1016/j.bushor.2013.06.002.

Johnson, Michael D., and Fred Selnes. 2004. Customer Portfolio Management: Toward a Dynamic Theory of Exchange Relationships. *Journal of Marketing* 68 (2): 1–17. https://doi.org/10.1509/jmkg.68.2.1.27786.

Johnson, Janet Buttolph, H.T. Reynolds, and Jason D. Mycoff. 2019. *Political Science Research Methods*. Thousand Oaks: CQ Press.

Jones, Thomas O., and W. Earl Sasser Jr. 1995. Why Satisfied Customers Defect. *Harvard Business Review*, November 1. https://hbr.org/1995/11/why-satisfied-customers-defect

Jones, Michael A., Kristy E. Reynolds, David L. Mothersbaugh, and Sharon E. Beatty. 2007. The Positive and Negative Effects of Switching Costs on Relational Outcomes. *Journal of Service Research* 9 (4): 335–355. https://doi.org/10.1177/1094670507299382.

Kähkönen, Anni-Kaisa, and Katrina Lintukangas. 2018. Sustainable Supply Management Practices: Making a Difference in a Firm's Sustainability Performance. *Supply Chain Management: An International Journal* 23 (6): 518–530. https://doi.org/10.1108/SCM-01-2018-0036.

Kaidesoja, Tuukka. 2019. Building Middle-Range Theories from Case Studies. *Studies in History and Philosophy of Science Part A* 78: 23–31. https://doi.org/10.1016/j.shpsa.2018.11.008.

Kale, Prashant, Harbir Singh, and Howard Perlmutter. 2000. Learning and Protection of Proprietary Assets in Strategic Alliances: Building Relational Capital. *Strategic Management Journal* 21 (3): 217–237. https://doi.org/10.1002/(SICI)1097-0266(200003)21:3<217::AID-SMJ95>3.0.CO;2-Y.

Kaplan, Robert, and Robin Cooper. 1998. *Cost & Effect: Using Integrated Cost Systems to Drive Profitability and Performance*. Boston: Harvard Business Press.

Kaplan, Robert, and David Norton. 1992. The Balanced Scorecard – Measures That Drive Performance. *Harvard Business Review* January–February: 71–79.

Kaski, Timo, Jarkko Niemi, and Ellen Pullins. 2018. Rapport Building in Authentic B2B Sales Interaction. *Industrial Marketing Management* 69: 235–252. https://doi.org/10.1016/j.indmarman.2017.08.019.

Kazanjian, Robert K., and Robert Drazin. 1989. An Empirical Test of a Stage of Growth Progression Model. *Management Science* 35 (12): 1489–1503. https://doi.org/10.1287/mnsc.35.12.1489.

Kegan, Robert, Lisa Lahey, Andy Fleming, and Matthew Miller. 2014. Making Business Personal. *Harvard Business Review*, April 1. https://hbr.org/2014/04/making-business-personal

Keiningham, Timothy L., Bruce Cooil, Tor Wallin Andreassen, and Lerzan Aksoy. 2007. A Longitudinal Examination of Net Promoter and Firm Revenue Growth. *Journal of Marketing* 71 (3): 39–51. https://doi.org/10.1509/jmkg.71.3.039.

Keiningham, Timothy L., Lerzan Aksoy, Edward C. Malthouse, Bart Lariviere, and Alexander Buoye. 2014. The Cumulative Effect of Satisfaction with Discrete Transactions on Share of Wallet. *Journal of Service Management* 25 (3): 310–333. https://doi.org/10.1108/JOSM-08-2012-0163.

Kelleher, Bob. 2011. Engaged Employees Equals High-Performing Organizations (Achieving Successful Employee Engagement). *Human Resource Management International Digest* 19 (6). https://doi.org/10.1108/hrmid.2011.04419faa.011.

Keramati, Abbas, Hamed Mehrabi, and Navid Mojir. 2010. A Process-Oriented Perspective on Customer Relationship Management and Organizational Performance: An Empirical Investigation. *Industrial Marketing Management, Selling and Sales Management* 39 (7): 1170–1185. https://doi.org/10.1016/j.indmarman.2010.02.001.

Ketokivi, Mikko, and Saku Mantere. 2010. Two Strategies for Inductive Reasoning in Organizational Research. *Academy of Management Review* 35 (2): 315–333. https://doi.org/10.5465/amr.35.2.zok315.

Kihlstrom, John F., Eric Eich, Deborah Sandbrand, and Betsy A. Tobias. 1999. Emotion and Memory: Implications for Self-Report. In *The Science of Self-Report*, ed. Arthur Stone, Christine Bachrach, Jared Jobe, Howard Kurtzman, and Virginia Cain, 93–112. Psychology Press. https://doi.org/10.4324/9781410601261-12.

Killian, Ginger, and Kristy McManus. 2015. A Marketing Communications Approach for the Digital Era: Managerial Guidelines for Social Media Integration. *Business Horizons* 58 (5): 539–549. https://doi.org/10.1016/j.bushor.2015.05.006.

Kim Jean Lee, Siew, and Kelvin Yu. 2004. Corporate Culture and Organizational Performance. *Journal of Managerial Psychology* 19 (4): 340–359. https://doi.org/10.1108/02683940410537927.

Kim, Hyung-Su, and Young-Gul Kim. 2009. A CRM Performance Measurement Framework: Its Development Process and Application. *Industrial Marketing Management*, Impact of Outsourcing on Business-to-Business Marketing, 38 (4): 477–489. https://doi.org/10.1016/j.indmarman.2008.04.008.

Kim, W. Chan, and Renee Mauborgne. 2014. *Blue Ocean Strategy, Expanded Edition: How to Create Uncontested Market Space and Make the Competition Irrelevant*. Boston: Harvard Business Review Press.

Kinard, Brian R., and Michael L. Capella. 2006. Relationship Marketing: The Influence of Consumer Involvement on Perceived Service Benefits. *Journal of*

Services Marketing 20 (6): 359–368. https://doi.org/10.1108/08876040610691257.

Klaus, Philipp 'Phil', and Stan Maklan. 2013. Towards a Better Measure of Customer Experience. *International Journal of Market Research* 55 (2): 227–246. https://doi.org/10.2501/IJMR-2013-021.

Klein, Benjamin, and Keith B. Leffler. 1981. The Role of Market Forces in Assuring Contractual Performance. *Journal of Political Economy* 89 (4): 615–641. https://doi.org/10.1086/260996.

Kogut, Bruce, and Udo Zander. 1996. What Firms Do? Coordination, Identity, and Learning. *Organization Science* 7 (5): 502–518. https://doi.org/10.1287/orsc.7.5.502.

Kotler, Philip, and Kevin Lane Keller. 2009. *Marketing Management*. Pearson Prentice Hall. https://books.google.pl/books?id=QiTOHgAACAAJ.

Kotorov, Rado. 2003. Customer Relationship Management: Strategic Lessons and Future Directions. *Business Process Management Journal* 9 (5): 566–571. https://doi.org/10.1108/14637150310496686.

Kotter, John P., and James L. Heskett. 2011. *Corporate Culture and Performance*. Reprint edition. New York: Free Press.

Krekel, Christian, George Ward, and Jean-Emmanuel De Neve. 2019. Employee Wellbeing, Productivity, and Firm Performance. *Saïd Business School Research Papers* 4: 1–43.

Krosnick, Jon A. 1999. Survey Research. *Annual Review of Psychology* 50: 537–567.

Krupski, Rafał. 2009a. Strategia Jako System UC. In *Koncepcje Strategii Organizacji*, ed. Rafał Krupski, Jerzy Niemczyk, and Ewa Stańczyk-Hugiet, 23–44. Warszawa: Polskie Wydawnictwo Ekonomiczne.

———. 2009b. *Teleologiczny Kontekst Elastyczności Strategii*. Ed. Rafał Krupski, Jerzy Niemczyk, and Stańczyk-Hugiet, 155–68. Warszawa: Polskie Wydawnictwo Ekonomiczne.

———. 2009c. Wstęp. In *Koncepcje Strategii Organizacji*, ed. Rafał Krupski, Jerzy Niemczyk, and Stańczyk-Hugiet, 7–9. Warszawa: Polskie Wydawnictwo Ekonomiczne.

———. 2012. Dwie koncepcje strategii organizacji – razem czy osobno? *Przegląd Organizacji* 1: 3–4.

Kumar, Vineet, and Werner J. Reinartz. 2006. *Customer Relationship Management: A Databased Approach*. Hoboken: Wiley & Sons.

Kumar, Nirmalya, Lisa K. Scheer, and Jan-Benedict E.M. Steenkamp. 1995. The Effects of Supplier Fairness on Vulnerable Resellers. *Journal of Marketing Research* 32 (1): 54–65. https://doi.org/10.2307/3152110.

Kumar, V., Avishek Lahiri, and Orhan Bahadir Dogan. 2018. A Strategic Framework for a Profitable Business Model in the Sharing Economy. *Industrial Marketing Management* 69: 147–160. https://doi.org/10.1016/j.indmarman.2017.08.021.

Kumar, V., Bharath Rajan, Shaphali Gupta, and Ilaria Dalla Pozza. 2019. Customer Engagement in Service. *Journal of the Academy of Marketing Science* 47 (1): 138–160. https://doi.org/10.1007/s11747-017-0565-2.

Kunasz, Marek. 2006. Zasoby przedsiębiorstwa w teorii ekonomii. *Gospodarka Narodowa* 211 (10): 33–48. https://doi.org/10.33119/GN/101446.

L'Etang, Jacquie. 1994. Public Relations and Corporate Social Responsibility: Some Issues Arising. *Journal of Business Ethics* 13 (2): 111–123. https://doi.org/10.1007/BF00881580.

Lacey, Russell, Jaebeom Suh, and Robert M. Morgan. 2007. Differential Effects of Preferential Treatment Levels on Relational Outcomes. *Journal of Service Research* 9 (3): 241–256. https://doi.org/10.1177/1094670506295850.

Lacey, Russell, Pamela A. Kennett-Hensel, and Chris Manolis. 2015. Is Corporate Social Responsibility a Motivator or Hygiene Factor? Insights into Its Bivalent Nature. *Journal of the Academy of Marketing Science* 43 (3): 315–332. https://doi.org/10.1007/s11747-014-0390-9.

Lambe, C. Jay, C. Michael Wittmann, and Robert E. Spekman. 2001. Social Exchange Theory and Research on Business-to-Business Relational Exchange. *Journal of Business-to-Business Marketing* 8 (3): 1.

Lambert, Douglas M. 2008. *Supply Chain Management: Processes, Partnerships, Performance*. Sarasota: Supply Chain Management Institute.

———. 2010. Customer Relationship Management as a Business Process. *Journal of Business & Industrial Marketing* 25 (1): 4–17. https://doi.org/10.1108/08858621011009119.

Lau, Henry, Dilupa Nakandala, Premaratne Samaranayake, and Paul K. Shum. 2016. BPM for Supporting Customer Relationship and Profit Decision. *Business Process Management Journal* 22 (1): 231–255. https://doi.org/10.1108/BPMJ-04-2015-0039.

Laverty, Kevin J. 1996. Economic "Short-Termism": The Debate, the Unresolved Issues, and the Implications for Management Practice and Research. *The Academy of Management Review* 21 (3): 825–860. https://doi.org/10.2307/259003.

Lavie, Dovev. 2006. The Competitive Advantage of Interconnected Firms: An Extension of the Resource-Based View. *Academy of Management Review* 31 (3): 638–658. https://doi.org/10.5465/amr.2006.21318922.

Ledbetter, Andrew M. 2010. Content- and Medium-Specific Decomposition of Friendship Relational Maintenance: Integrating Equity and Media Multiplexity Approaches. *Journal of Social and Personal Relationships* 27 (7): 938–955. https://doi.org/10.1177/0265407510376254.

Lepak, David P., Ken G. Smith, and M. Susan Taylor. 2007. Value Creation and Value Capture: A Multilevel Perspective. *Academy of Management Review* 32 (1): 180–194. https://doi.org/10.5465/amr.2007.23464011.

Levitt, Theodore. 1983. After the Sale Is Over. *Harvard Business Review* 62 (1): 87–93.
Li, Ling, John B. Ford, Xin Zhai, and Li Xu. 2012. Relational Benefits and Manufacturer Satisfaction: An Empirical Study of Logistics Service in Supply Chain. *International Journal of Production Research* 50 (19): 5445–5459. https://doi.org/10.1080/00207543.2011.636388.
Lichtarski, Jan. 2010. Profile Orientacji w Zarządzaniu Przedsiębiorstwem i Kształtujące Je Czynniki. In *Kierunki i Dylematy Rozwoju Nauki i Praktyki Zarządzania Przedsiębiorstwem*, ed. Henryk Jagoda and Jan Lichtarski, vol. 169. Wrocław: Wydawnictwo Uniwersytetu Ekonomicznego we Wrocławiu.
———. 2015. *Praktyczny Wymiar Nauk o Zarządzaniu*. Warszawa: Polskie Wydawnictwo Ekonomiczne.
Lin, Neng-Pai, James C.M. Weng, and Yi-Ching Hsieh. 2003. Relational Bonds and Customer's Trust and Commitment – A Study on the Moderating Effects of Web Site Usage. *The Service Industries Journal* 23 (3): 103–124. https://doi.org/10.1080/714005111.
Lindgreen, Adam, and Valérie Swaen. 2010. Corporate Social Responsibility. *International Journal of Management Reviews* 12 (1): 1–7. https://doi.org/10.1111/j.1468-2370.2009.00277.x.
Lindner, Frank, and Andreas Wald. 2011. Success Factors of Knowledge Management in Temporary Organizations. *International Journal of Project Management*, Complexities in Managing Mega Construction Projects, 29 (7): 877–888. https://doi.org/10.1016/j.ijproman.2010.09.003.
Ling-yee, Li. 2011. 'Marketing Metrics' Usage: Its Predictors and Implications for Customer Relationship Management. *Industrial Marketing Management*, Business-to-Business Marketing in the BRIC Countries, 40 (1): 139–148. https://doi.org/10.1016/j.indmarman.2010.09.002.
Lippman, Steven A., and Richard P. Rumelt. 1982. Uncertain Imitability: An Analysis of Interfirm Differences in Efficiency Under Competition. *The Bell Journal of Economics* 13 (2): 418–438. https://doi.org/10.2307/3003464.
Loufrani-Fedida, Sabrina, Valérie Hauch, and Djamila Elidrissi. 2019. The Dynamics of Relational Competencies in the Development of Born Global Firms: A Multilevel Approach. *International Business Review* 28 (2): 222–237. https://doi.org/10.1016/j.ibusrev.2018.09.001.
Lovelock, Christopher H. 1983. Classifying Services to Gain Strategic Marketing Insights. *Journal of Marketing* 47 (3): 9–20. https://doi.org/10.1177/002224298304700303.
Lovelock, Christopher H., Paul Patterson, and Jochen Wirtz. 2014. *Services Marketing. An Asia-Pacific and Australian Perspective*. 6th ed. Melbourne: Pearson Australia. https://www.pearson.com.au/9781486002702.
Lumley, Thomas. 2011. *Complex Surveys: A Guide to Analysis Using R*. Hoboken: John Wiley & Sons.

Lusch, Robert F., and Stephen L. Vargo. 2014. *Service-Dominant Logic: Premises, Perspectives, Possibilities*. New York: Cambridge University Press.

Lusch, Robert F., Stephen L. Vargo, and Matthew O'Brien. 2007. Competing through Service: Insights from Service-Dominant Logic. *Journal of Retailing, Service Excellence* 83 (1): 5–18. https://doi.org/10.1016/j.jretai.2006.10.002.

Lusch, Robert F., Stephen L. Vargo, and Mohan Tanniru. 2010. Service, Value Networks and Learning. *Journal of the Academy of Marketing Science* 38 (1): 19–31. https://doi.org/10.1007/s11747-008-0131-z.

Lusch, Robert F., James R. Brown, and Matthew O'Brien. 2011. Protecting Relational Assets: A Pre and Post Field Study of a Horizontal Business Combination. *Journal of the Academy of Marketing Science* 39 (2): 175–197. https://doi.org/10.1007/s11747-010-0197-2.

Luu, Ngoc, Liem Viet Ngo, and Jack Cadeaux. 2018. Value Synergy and Value Asymmetry in Relationship Marketing Programs. *Industrial Marketing Management* 68: 165–176. https://doi.org/10.1016/j.indmarman.2017.10.011.

Ma, Hao. 1999. Anatomy of Competitive Advantage: A SELECT Framework. *Management Decision* 37 (9): 709–718. https://doi.org/10.1108/00251749910299129.

Ma, Baolong, Xiaofei Li, and Lin Zhang. 2018. The Effects of Loyalty Programs in Services – A Double-Edged Sword? *Journal of Services Marketing* 32 (3): 300–310. https://doi.org/10.1108/JSM-06-2016-0227.

Macdonald, Emma K., Hugh Wilson, Veronica Martinez, and Amir Toossi. 2011. Assessing Value-in-Use: A Conceptual Framework and Exploratory Study. *Industrial Marketing Management*, Service and Solution Innovation, 40 (5): 671–682. https://doi.org/10.1016/j.indmarman.2011.05.006.

Macintosh, Gerrard. 2007. Customer Orientation, Relationship Quality, and Relational Benefits to the Firm. *Journal of Services Marketing* 21 (3): 150–159. https://doi.org/10.1108/08876040710746516.

Madhavaram, Sreedhar, Elad Granot, and Vishag Badrinarayanan. 2014. Relationship Marketing Strategy: An Operant Resource Perspective. *Journal of Business & Industrial Marketing*, April 1. https://doi.org/10.1108/JBIM-02-2013-0049.

Maher, Patrick. 1996. The Hole in the Ground of Induction. *Australasian Journal of Philosophy* 74(3):423–432. https://doi.org/10.1080/00048409612347411.

Mahoney, Joseph T., and J. Rajendran Pandian. 1992. The Resource-Based View within the Conversation of Strategic Management. *Strategic Management Journal* 13 (5): 363–380. https://doi.org/10.1002/smj.4250130505.

Mäki, Uskali. 2006. On the Method of Isolation in Economics. *Recent Developments in Economic Methodology* 3: 3–37.

Małys, Łukasz, Justyna Światowiec-Szczepańska, and Michał Zdziarski. The Quality of Business Relationships in the Automotive Industry and the Company Performance: The Case of Polish and Brazilian Markets. *Problemy Zarządzania* 3/2017 (70), t.2 (2017): 76–87.

Mangold, W. Glynn, and Sandra Jeanquart Miles. 2007. The Employee Brand: Is Yours an All-Star? *Business Horizons* 50 (5): 423–433.

March, James G., and Robert I. Sutton. 1997. Crossroads – Organizational Performance as a Dependent Variable. *Organization Science* 8 (6): 698–706.

Marcos-Cuevas, Javier, Satu Nätti, Teea Palo, and Lynette J. Ryals. 2014. Implementing Key Account Management: Intraorganizational Practices and Associated Dilemmas. *Industrial Marketing Management* 43 (7): 1216–1224. https://doi.org/10.1016/j.indmarman.2014.06.009.

Marler, Janet H., and Sandra L. Fisher. 2013. An Evidence-Based Review of e-HRM and Strategic Human Resource Management. *Human Resource Management Review*, Emerging Issues in Theory and Research on Electronic Human Resource Management (eHRM), 23 (1): 18–36. https://doi.org/10.1016/j.hrmr.2012.06.002.

Marsh, Herbert W., and Lawrence A. Roche. 2000. Effects of Grading Leniency and Low Workload on Students' Evaluations of Teaching: Popular Myth, Bias, Validity, or Innocent Bystanders? *Journal of Educational Psychology* 92 (1): 202–228. https://doi.org/10.1037/0022-0663.92.1.202.

Martelo, Silvia, Carmen Barroso, and Gabriel Cepeda. 2013. The Use of Organizational Capabilities to Increase Customer Value. *Journal of Business Research*, Strategic Thinking in Marketing, 66 (10): 2042–2050. https://doi.org/10.1016/j.jbusres.2013.02.030.

Martins, Luis L., and Ajit Kambil. 1999. Research Notes: Looking Back and Thinking Ahead: Effects of Prior Success on Managers' Interpretations of New Information Technologies. *Academy of Management Journal* 42 (6): 652–661. https://doi.org/10.5465/256986.

Marzo-Navarro, Mercedes, Marta Pedraja-Iglesias, and Ma Pilar Rivera-Torres. 2004. The Benefits of Relationship Marketing for the Consumer and for the Fashion Retailers. *Journal of Fashion Marketing and Management: An International Journal* 8 (4): 425–436. https://doi.org/10.1108/13612020410560018.

Mauboussin, Michael J. 2012. The True Measures of Success. *Harvard Business Review*, October 1. https://hbr.org/2012/10/the-true-measures-of-success

Mawdsley, John K., and Deepak Somaya. 2018. Demand-Side Strategy, Relational Advantage, and Partner-Driven Corporate Scope: The Case for Client-led Diversification. *Strategic Management Journal* 39 (7): 1834–1859.

Mayer, David M., Maribeth Kuenzi, and Rebecca L. Greenbaum. 2010. Examining the Link Between Ethical Leadership and Employee Misconduct: The

Mediating Role of Ethical Climate. *Journal of Business Ethics* 95 (1): 7–16. https://doi.org/10.1007/s10551-011-0794-0.

McDaniel, Carl, Jr., and Roger Gates. 2015. *Marketing Research*. Hoboken: John Wiley & Sons.

McGahan, Anita M., and Michael E. Porter. 1997. How Much Does Industry Matter, Really? *Strategic Management Journal* 18 (S1): 15–30. https://doi.org/10.1002/(SICI)1097-0266(199707)18:1+<15::AID-SMJ916>3.0.CO;2-1.

Melancon, Joanna Phillips, and Vassilis Dalakas. 2018. Consumer Social Voice in the Age of Social Media: Segmentation Profiles and Relationship Marketing Strategies. *Business Horizons* 61 (1): 157–167. https://doi.org/10.1016/j.bushor.2017.09.015.

Melville, Nigel, Kenneth L. Kraemer, and Vijay Gurbaxani. 2004. Review: Information Technology and Organizational Performance: An Integrative Model of IT Business Value. *MIS Quarterly* 28: 283–322. https://doi.org/10.2307/25148636.

Men, Linjuan Rita. 2014. Strategic Internal Communication: Transformational Leadership, Communication Channels, and Employee Satisfaction. *Management Communication Quarterly* 28 (2): 264–284.

Men, Linjuan Rita, and Katy L. Robinson. 2018. It's About How Employees Feel! Examining the Impact of Emotional Culture on Employee–Organization Relationships. *Corporate Communications: An International Journal* 23 (4): 470–491. https://doi.org/10.1108/CCIJ-05-2018-0065.

Merton, Robert King. 1968. *Social Theory and Social Structure*. New York: Simon and Schuster.

Mettler, Tobias. 2011. Maturity Assessment Models: A Design Science Research Approach. *International Journal of Society Systems Science (IJSSS)* 3 (1/2): 81–98.

Miles, Raymond E., Charles C. Snow, Alan D. Meyer, and Henry J. Coleman. 1978. Organizational Strategy, Structure, and Process. *Academy of Management Review* 3 (3): 546–562. https://doi.org/10.5465/amr.1978.4305755.

Miller, Kent D. 2002. Knowledge Inventories and Managerial Myopia. *Strategic Management Journal* 23 (8): 689–706. https://doi.org/10.1002/smj.245.

Minkiewicz, Joanna, Kerrie Bridson, and Jody Evans. 2016. Co-Production of Service Experiences: Insights from the Cultural Sector. *Journal of Services Marketing* 30 (7): 749–761. https://doi.org/10.1108/JSM-04-2015-0156.

Mintzberg, Henry. 1993. *Structure in Fives: Designing Effective Organizations*, Structure in Fives: Designing Effective Organizations. Englewood Cliffs: Prentice-Hall.

Mintzberg, Henry, and Joseph Lampel. 1999. Reflecting on the Strategy Process. *Sloan Management Review* 40 (3): 21–30.

Miocevic, Dario, and Biljana Crnjak-Karanovic. 2012. The Mediating Role of Key Supplier Relationship Management Practices on Supply Chain Orientation the Organizational Buying Effectiveness Link. *Industrial Marketing Management* 41 (1): 115–124. https://doi.org/10.1016/j.indmarman.2011.11.015.

Mitręga, Maciej. 2019. Dynamic Marketing Capability – Refining the Concept and Applying It to Company Innovations. *Journal of Business & Industrial Marketing* 35 (2): 193–203. https://doi.org/10.1108/JBIM-01-2019-0007.

Mitręga, Maciej, and Gregor Pfajfar. 2015. Business Relationship Process Management as Company Dynamic Capability Improving Relationship Portfolio. *Industrial Marketing Management* 46: 193–203. https://doi.org/10.1016/j.indmarman.2015.02.029.

Mitręga, Maciej, Sebastian Forkmann, Carla Ramos, and Stephan C. Henneberg. 2012. Networking Capability in Business Relationships Concept and Scale Development. *Industrial Marketing Management*, IMP 2011 The Impact of Globalization on Networks, 41 (5): 739–751. https://doi.org/10.1016/j.indmarman.2012.06.002.

Möller, Kristian. 2000. Relationship Marketing Theory: Its Roots and Direction. *Journal of Marketing Management* 16 (1–3): 29–54. https://doi.org/10.1362/026725700785100460.

———. 2006. Role of Competences in Creating Customer Value: A Value-Creation Logic Approach. *Industrial Marketing Management*, Creating Value for the Customer Through Competence-Based Marketing, 35 (8): 913–924. https://doi.org/10.1016/j.indmarman.2006.04.005.

———. 2013. Theory Map of Business Marketing: Relationships and Networks Perspectives. *Industrial Marketing Management*, Theoretical Perspectives in Industrial Marketing Management, 42 (3): 324–335. https://doi.org/10.1016/j.indmarman.2013.02.009.

Möller, Kristian, and Aino Halinen. 1999. Business Relationships and Networks. *Industrial Marketing Management* 28 (5): 413–427. https://doi.org/10.1016/S0019-8501(99)00086-3.

Montgomery, Cynthia A., and Birger Wernerfelt. 1988. Diversification, Ricardian Rents, and Tobin's q. *The RAND Journal of Economics* 19 (4): 623–632. https://doi.org/10.2307/2555461.

Morgan, Robert M. 1994. The Commitment-Trust Theory of Relationship Marketing. *Journal of Marketing* 58 (3): 20–38. https://doi.org/10.1177/002224299405800302.

Morgan, Robert M., and Shelby D. Hunt. 1999. Relationship-Based Competitive Advantage: The Role of Relationship Marketing in Marketing Strategy. *Journal of Business Research* 46 (3): 281–290. https://doi.org/10.1016/S0148-2963(98)00035-6.

Morrison, Sharon, and Frederick G. Crane. 2007. Building the Service Brand by Creating and Managing an Emotional Brand Experience. *Journal of Brand*

Management 14 (5): 410–421. https://doi.org/10.1057/palgrave. bm.2550080.

Mowery, David C., Joanne E. Oxley, and Brian S. Silverman. 1998. Technological Overlap and Interfirm Cooperation: Implications for the Resource-Based View of the Firm. *Research Policy* 27 (5): 507–523. https://doi.org/10.1016/S0048-7333(98)00066-3.

Mugge, Ruth, Jan P.L. Schoormans, and Hendrik N.J. Schifferstein. 2005. Design Strategies to Postpone Consumers' Product Replacement: The Value of a Strong Person-Product Relationship. *The Design Journal* 8 (2): 38–48. https://doi.org/10.2752/146069205789331637.

Mumuni, Alhassan G., and Kelley O'Reilly. 2014. Examining the Impact of Customer Relationship Management on Deconstructed Measures of Firm Performance. *Journal of Relationship Marketing* 13 (2): 89–107. https://doi.org/10.1080/15332667.2014.910073.

Nahapiet, Janine, and Sumantra Ghoshal. 1998. Social Capital, Intellectual Capital, and the Organizational Advantage. *Academy of Management Review* 23 (2): 242–266. https://doi.org/10.5465/amr.1998.533225.

Nayar, Vineet. 2010. *Employees First, Customers Second: Turning Conventional Management Upside Down*. Boston: Harvard Business Press.

Neely, Andy, Chris Adams, and Mike Kennerley. 2002. *The Performance Prism: The Scorecard for Measuring and Managing Business Success*. London: Pearson Education.

Nenonen, Suvi, and Kaj Storbacka. 2010. Business Model Design: Conceptualizing Networked Value Co-Creation. *International Journal of Quality and Service Sciences* 2 (1): 43–59. https://doi.org/10.1108/17566691011026595.

Neslin, Scott A., Gail Ayala Taylor, Kimberly D. Grantham, and Kimberly R. McNeil. 2013. Overcoming the "Recency Trap" in Customer Relationship Management. *Journal of the Academy of Marketing Science* 41 (3): 320–337. https://doi.org/10.1007/s11747-012-0312-7.

Ng, Irene C. L., David Xin Ding, and Nick Yip. 2013. Outcome-Based Contracts as New Business Model: The Role of Partnership and Value-Driven Relational Assets. *Industrial Marketing Management*, Business Models – Exploring Value Drivers and the Role of Marketing, 42 (5): 730–743. https://doi.org/10.1016/j.indmarman.2013.05.009.

Ngo, Liem Viet, and Aron O'Cass. 2013. Innovation and Business Success: The Mediating Role of Customer Participation. *Journal of Business Research*, Recent Advances in Globalization, Culture and Marketing Strategy, 66 (8): 1134–1142. https://doi.org/10.1016/j.jbusres.2012.03.009.

Nguyen, ThuyUyen H., Joseph S. Sherif, and Michael Newby. 2007. Strategies for Successful CRM Implementation. *Information Management & Computer Security* 15 (2): 102–115. https://doi.org/10.1108/09685220710748001.

Niemczyk, Jerzy. 2009. Filozofie i Szkoły Strategii. In *Koncepcje Strategii Organizacji*, ed. Rafał Krupski, Jerzy Niemczyk, and Stańczyk-Hugiet, 11–23. Warszawa: Polskie Wydawnictwo Ekonomiczne.

———. 2015. Metodologia Nauk o Zarządzaniu. In *Podstawy Metodologii Badań w Naukach o Zarządzaniu*, ed. Wojciech Czakon, 3rd ed. Warszawa: Oficyna a Wolters Kluwer business.

Nyaga, Gilbert N., and Judith M. Whipple. 2011. Relationship Quality and Performance Outcomes: Achieving a Sustainable Competitive Advantage. *Journal of Business Logistics* 32 (4): 345–360. https://doi.org/10.1111/j.0000-0000.2011.01030.x.

Obłój, Krzysztof. 1998. *Strategia Sukcesu Firmy*. Warszawa: Polskie Wydawnictwo Ekonomiczne.

———. 2002. *Tworzywo Skutecznych Strategii*. Warszawa: Polskie Wydawnictwo Ekonomiczne.

———. 2007. *Strategia Organizacji*. Warszawa: Polskie Wydawnictwo Ekonomiczne.

———. 2013. *The Passion and Discipline of Strategy*. London: Palgrave Macmillan UK. https://doi.org/10.1057/9781137334947_1.

———. 2019. *Pasja i Dyscyplina Strategii. Jak z Marzeń i Decyzji Zbudować Sukces Firmy*. Warszawa: Poltext.

Oghazi, Pejvak, Fakhreddin Fakhrai Rad, Ghasem Zaefarian, Hooshang M. Beheshti, and Sina Mortazavi. 2016. Unity Is Strength: A Study of Supplier Relationship Management Integration. *Journal of Business Research* 69 (11): 4804–4810. https://doi.org/10.1016/j.jbusres.2016.04.034.

Ohiomah, Alhassan, Pavel Andreev, Morad Benyoucef, and David Hood. 2019. The Role of Lead Management Systems in Inside Sales Performance. *Journal of Business Research* 102: 163–177.

Olson, Eric M., F. Stanley, G. Slater, Tomas M. Hult, and Kai M. Olson. 2018. The Application of Human Resource Management Policies within the Marketing Organization: The Impact on Business and Marketing Strategy Implementation. *Industrial Marketing Management* 69: 62–73. https://doi.org/10.1016/j.indmarman.2018.01.029.

Orr, Linda M., Victoria D. Bush, and Douglas W. Vorhies. 2011. Leveraging Firm-Level Marketing Capabilities with Marketing Employee Development. *Journal of Business Research* 64 (10): 1074–1081. https://doi.org/10.1016/j.jbusres.2010.11.003.

Palmatier, Robert W. 2008. Interfirm Relational Drivers of Customer Value. *Journal of Marketing* 72 (4): 76–89. https://doi.org/10.1509/jmkg.72.4.076.

Palmatier, Robert W., Rajiv P. Dant, and Dhruv Grewal. 2007. A Comparative Longitudinal Analysis of Theoretical Perspectives of Interorganizational Relationship Performance. *Journal of Marketing* 71 (4): 172–194. https://doi.org/10.1509/jmkg.71.4.172.

Palmatier, Robert W., Cheryl Burke Jarvis, Jennifer R. Bechkoff, and Frank R. Kardes. 2009. The Role of Customer Gratitude in Relationship Marketing. *Journal of Marketing* 73 (5): 1–18. https://doi.org/10.1509/jmkg.73.5.1.

Paparoidamis, Nicholas G., Constantine S. Katsikeas, and Ruben Chumpitaz. 2019. The Role of Supplier Performance in Building Customer Trust and Loyalty: A Cross-Country Examination. *Industrial Marketing Management* 78: 183–197. https://doi.org/10.1016/j.indmarman.2017.02.005.

Parasuraman, A. 1988. Servqual: A Multiple-Item Scale for Measuring Consumer Perc. *Journal of Retailing; Greenwich* 64 (1, Spring): 12.

Parasuraman, A., Valarie A. Zeithaml, and Leonard L. Berry. 1985. A Conceptual Model of Service Quality and Its Implications for Future Research. *Journal of Marketing* 49 (4): 41–50. https://doi.org/10.1177/002224298504900403.

Parasuraman, A., Leonard L. Berry, and Valarie A. Zeithaml. 1991. Refinement and Reassessment of the SERVQUAL Scale. *Journal of Retailing; Greenwich* 67 (4, Winter): 420.

Park, Jeong Eun, Juyoung Kim, Alan J. Dubinsky, and Hyunju Lee. 2010. How Does Sales Force Automation Influence Relationship Quality and Performance? The Mediating Roles of Learning and Selling Behaviors. *Industrial Marketing Management*, Selling and Sales Management, 39 (7): 1128–1138. https://doi.org/10.1016/j.indmarman.2009.11.003.

PARP. 2011. *Raport o stanie sektora małych i średnich przedsiębiorstw w Polsce*. Ed. Anna Brussa and Anna Tarnawa. Warszawa: Polska Agencja Rozwoju Przedsiębiorczości.

Paul, Michael, Thorsten Hennig-Thurau, Dwayne D. Gremler, Kevin P. Gwinner, and Caroline Wiertz. 2009. Toward a Theory of Repeat Purchase Drivers for Consumer Services. *Journal of the Academy of Marketing Science* 37 (2): 215–237. https://doi.org/10.1007/s11747-008-0118-9.

Paulk, M.C., B. Curtis, M.B. Chrissis, and C.V. Weber. 1993. Capability Maturity Model, Version 1.1. *IEEE Software* 10 (4): 18–27. https://doi.org/10.1109/52.219617.

Pavitt, Keith. 1990. What We Know About the Strategic Management of Technology. *California Management Review* 32 (3): 17.

Payne, Adrian. 2013. *Strategic Customer Management: Integrating Relationship Marketing and CRM*. Cambridge: Cambridge University Press.

———. 2016. Customer Relationship Management: Strategy and Implementation. In *The Marketing Book*, ed. Michael J. Baker and Susan Hart, 439–466. London: Routledge. https://doi.org/10.4324/9781315890005-28.

———. 2017. Relationship Marketing: Looking Backwards Towards the Future. *Journal of Services Marketing*. 31 (1): 11–15. https://doi.org/10.1108/JSM-11-2016-0380.

Payne, Adrian, and Pennie Frow. 2005. A Strategic Framework for Customer Relationship Management. *Journal of Marketing* 69 (4): 167–176. https://doi.org/10.1509/jmkg.2005.69.4.167.

Payne, Adrian, and Pennie Frow. 2017. Relationship Marketing: Looking Backwards towards the Future. *Journal of Services Marketing* 31 (1): 11–15. https://doi.org/10.1108/JSM-11-2016-0380.

Payne, Adrian, Kaj Storbacka, Pennie Frow, and Simon Knox. 2009. Co-Creating Brands: Diagnosing and Designing the Relationship Experience. *Journal of Business Research*, Advances in Brand Management, 62 (3): 379–389. https://doi.org/10.1016/j.jbusres.2008.05.013.

Penrose, Edith T. 1960. The Growth of the Firm – A Case Study: The Hercules Powder Company. *Business History Review (Pre-1986)* 34 (000001): 1.

———. 2009. *The Theory of the Growth of the Firm.* Oxford: Oxford University Press.

Peppers, Don, and Martha Rogers. 2013. Extreme Trust: The New Competitive Advantage. *Strategy and Leadership* 41 (6): 31–34. https://doi.org/10.1108/SL-07-2013-0054.

Pervan, Simon J., Liliana L. Bove, and Lester W. Johnson. 2009. Reciprocity as a Key Stabilizing Norm of Interpersonal Marketing Relationships: Scale Development and Validation. *Industrial Marketing Management* 38 (1): 60–70. https://doi.org/10.1016/j.indmarman.2007.11.001.

Peteraf, Margaret A. 1993. The Cornerstones of Competitive Advantage: A Resource-Based View. *Strategic Management Journal* 14 (3): 179–191. https://doi.org/10.1002/smj.4250140303.

Peteraf, Margaret A., and Jay B. Barney. 2003. Unraveling the Resource-Based Tangle. *Managerial and Decision Economics* 24 (4): 309–323. https://doi.org/10.1002/mde.1126.

Pfeffer, Jeffrey. 2018. *Dying for a Paycheck: How Modern Management Harms Employee Health and Company Performance—and What We Can Do About It.* New York: Harper Business.

Phillips, Almarin. 1960. A Theory of Interfirm Organization. *The Quarterly Journal of Economics* 74 (4): 602–613. https://doi.org/10.2307/1884355.

Piercy, Nigel. 2016. *Market-Led Strategic Change | Transforming the Process of Going to Market | Taylor & Francis Group.* London: Routledge. https://www.taylorfrancis.com/books/9780203507766.

Pillai, Gopalakrishna Kishore, and Arun Sharma. 2003. Mature Relationships: Why Does Relational Orientation Turn into Transaction Orientation? *Industrial Marketing Management* 32 (8): 643–651. https://doi.org/10.1016/j.indmarman.2003.06.005.

Pinder, Craig C., and Larry F. Moore. 1980. The Resurrection of Taxonomy to Aid the Development of Middle Range Theories of Organizational Behavior. *Middle Range Theory and the Study of Organizations*: 187–211. https://doi.org/10.1007/978-94-009-8733-3_16.

Pingitore, Gina, Neil A. Morgan, Lopo L. Rego, Adriana Gigliotti, and Jay Meyers. 2007. The Single-Question Trap. *Marketing Research* 19 (2): 9–13.

Pluta-Olearnik, Mirosława. 2017. Usługi a wartość poszerzona dla klienta na przykładzie rynku wyposaěenia i dekoracji wnętrz. *Marketing i Zarządzanie* 48 (2): 397–405.

Pollack, David M., and Leslie J. Pollack. 1996. Using 360° Feedback in Performance Appraisal. *Public Personnel Management; Thousand Oaks* 25 (4): 507–528. https://doi.org/10.1177/009102609602500410.

Polskie, Radio. 2014. Przeciętny Polak Przeprowadza Sie Raz Na 15 Lat. https://www.polskieradio24.pl/42/259/Artykul/1075300,Przecietny-Polak-przeprowadza-sie-raz-na-15-lat

Pöppelbuß, Jens, and Maximilian Röglinger. 2011. What Makes a Useful Maturity Model? A Framework of General Design Principles for Maturity Models and Its Demosntration in Business Process Management. In *ECIS Proceedings*, 28, 13. European Conference on Information Systems (ECIS).

Porter, Michael E. 1979. How Competitive Forces Shape Strategy. *Harvard Business Review*, March 1. https://hbr.org/1979/03/how-competitive-forces-shape-strategy

———. 1980. Industry Structure and Competitive Strategy: Keys to Profitability. *Financial Analysts Journal* 36 (4): 30–41. https://doi.org/10.2469/faj.v36.n4.30.

———. 1981. The Contributions of Industrial Organization to Strategic Management. *Academy of Management Review* 6 (4): 609–620. https://doi.org/10.5465/amr.1981.4285706.

———. 1991. Towards a Dynamic Theory of Strategy. *Strategic Management Journal* 12 (S2): 95–117. https://doi.org/10.1002/smj.4250121008.

———. 2008. The Five Competitive Forces That Shape Strategy. *Harvard Business Review*, January 1. https://hbr.org/2008/01/the-five-competitive-forces-that-shape-strategy.

Powell, Thomas C. 1996. How Much Does Industry Matter? An Alternative Empirical Test. *Strategic Management Journal* 17 (4): 323–334. https://doi.org/10.1002/(SICI)1097-0266(199604)17:4<323::AID-SMJ803>3.0.CO;2-5.

Pozza, Dalla Ilaria, Oliver Goetz, and Jean Michel Sahut. 2018. Implementation Effects in the Relationship Between CRM and Its Performance. *Journal of Business Research* 89: 391–403. https://doi.org/10.1016/j.jbusres.2018.02.004.

Prahalad, C.K. 1990. The Core Competence of the Corporation. *Harvard Business Review* 68 (3): 79–91.

Prahalad, C.K., and Gary Hamel. 1994. Strategy as a Field of Study: Why Search for a New Paradigm? *Strategic Management Journal* 15 (S2): 5–16. https://doi.org/10.1002/smj.4250151002.

Preikschas, Michael W., Pablo Cabanelas, Klaus Rüdiger, and Jesús F. Lampón. 2017. Value Co-Creation, Dynamic Capabilities and Customer Retention in Industrial Markets. *Journal of Business & Industrial Marketing* 3. https://doi.org/10.1108/JBIM-10-2014-0215.

Prior, Daniel D. 2012. The Effects of Buyer-supplier Relationships on Buyer Competitiveness. *Journal of Business & Industrial Marketing* 27 (2): 100–114. https://doi.org/10.1108/08858621211196976.

Pukas, Anetta. 2019. *Zarządzanie relacjami z klientem w tworzeniu przewagi konkurencyjnej przedsiębiorstwa: ujęcie dynamiczne*. Wydawnictwo Uniwersytetu Ekonomicznego we Wrocławiu.

Quinn, Robert E., and John Rohrbaugh. 1983. A Spatial Model of Effectiveness Criteria: Towards a Competing Values Approach to Organizational Analysis. *Management Science* 29 (3): 363–377.

Ramani, Girish, and V. Kumar. 2008. Interaction Orientation and Firm Performance. *Journal of Marketing* 72 (1): 27–45. https://doi.org/10.1509/jmkg.72.1.027.

Ray, Gautam, Jay B. Barney, and Waleed A. Muhanna. 2004. Capabilities, Business Processes, and Competitive Advantage: Choosing the Dependent Variable in Empirical Tests of the Resource-Based View. *Strategic Management Journal* 25 (1): 23–37. https://doi.org/10.1002/smj.366.

Reichheld, Frederick. 2001. *Loyalty Rules!: How Today's Leaders Build Lasting Relationships*. Boston: Harvard Business School Press. https://books.google.pl/books?hl=pl&lr=&id=oT3lL0QdWiwC&oi=fnd&pg=PP1&dq=reichheld+2001+loyalty&ots=zD3RjjPbTW&sig=cYD89k0tVodkW2Tc1HhiTuZhacc&redir_esc=y#v=onepage&q=reichheld%202001%20loyalty&f=false.

———. 2003. The One Number You Need to Grow. *Harvard Business Review*, December: 1–11.

———. 2006. The Microeconomics of Customer Relationships. *MIT Sloan Management Review* 47 (2): 72–78.

Reichheld, Frederick, and Rob Markey. 2011. *The Ultimate Question 2.0: How Net Promoter Companies Thrive in a Customer*. Boston: Harvard Business Publishing. https://books.google.pl/books?hl=pl&lr=&id=e8jhiYjQrU0C&oi=fnd&pg=PR7&dq=reichheld+markey&ots=CC1eQacr8I&sig=iSgh_lWq6TPhrVgOpVEfeP3Hnzw&redir_esc=y#v=onepage&q=reichheld%20markey&f=false.

Reichheld, Frederik, and Thomas Teal. 2001. *The Loyalty Effect: The Hidden Force Behind Growth, Profits, and Lasting Value*, Loyalty-Based Management. Boston: Harvard Business School Press. https://books.google.pl/books?id=D-JlUoXtf-AC.

Reid, David Alan, Richard E. Plank, and J. David Lichtenthal. 2004. *Fundamentals of Business Marketing Research*. New York: Haworth Press.

Reimann, Martin, Oliver Schilke, and Jacquelyn S. Thomas. 2010. Customer Relationship Management and Firm Performance: The Mediating Role of Business Strategy. *Journal of the Academy of Marketing Science* 38 (3): 326–346. https://doi.org/10.1007/s11747-009-0164-y.

Reinartz, Werner, Manfred Krafft, and Wayne D. Hoyer. 2004. The Customer Relationship Management Process: Its Measurement and Impact on Performance. *Journal of Marketing Research*. https://doi.org/10.1509/jmkr.41.3.293.35991.

Reynolds, Kristy E., and Sharon E. Beatty. 1999. Customer Benefits and Company Consequences of Customer-Salesperson Relationships in Retailing. *Journal of Retailing* 75 (1, Spring): 11–32. https://doi.org/10.1016/S0022-4359(99)80002-5.

Roberts, Nicholas, and Varun Grover. 2012. Investigating Firm's Customer Agility and Firm Performance: The Importance of Aligning Sense and Respond Capabilities. *Journal of Business Research* 65 (5): 579–585. https://doi.org/10.1016/j.jbusres.2011.02.009.

Robins, James, and Margarethe F. Wiersema. 1995. A Resource-Based Approach to the Multibusiness Firm: Empirical Analysis of Portfolio Interrelationships and Corporate Financial Performance. *Strategic Management Journal* 16 (4): 277–299. https://doi.org/10.1002/smj.4250160403.

Robinson, Jennifer. 2008. How The Ritz-Carlton Manages the Mystique. Gallup.com, December 11. https://news.gallup.com/businessjournal/112906/How-RitzCarlton-Manages-Mystique.aspx

Röglinger, Maximilian. 2012. Maturity Models in Business Process Management. *Business Process Management Journal* 18 (2): 328–346. https://doi.org/10.1108/14637151211225225.

Röglinger, Maximilian, Jens Pöppelbuß, and Jörg Becker. 2012. Maturity Models in Business Process Management. *Business Process Management Journal* 18 (2): 328–346. https://doi.org/10.1108/14637151211225225.

Romanow, Zbigniew. 1997. *Historia Myśli Ekonomicznej w Zarysie*. Poznań: Wydawnictwo Akademii Ekonomicznej w Poznaniu.

Romanowska, Maria. 2014. Bariery Efektywności Badań Naukowych z Zakresu Zarządzania Strategicznego. *Prace Naukowe Wałbrzyskiej Wyższej Szkoły Przedsiębiorczości i Zarządzania* 27 (2): 101–108.

———. 2018. Idea spójności w zarządzaniu strategicznym. *Przegląd Organizacji* 6: 3–9. https://doi.org/10.33141/po.2018.6.1.

Rong, Baiding, and Ian Wilkinson. 2011. What Do Managers' Survey Responses Mean and What Affects Them? The Case of Market Orientation and Firm Performance. https://doi.org/10.1016/j.ausmj.2011.04.001.

Roos, Göran, Alan Bainbridge, and Kristine Jacobsen. 2001. Intellectual Capital Analysis as a Strategic Tool. *Strategy & Leadership* 29 (4): 21–26. https://doi.org/10.1108/10878570110400116.

Rosemann, Michael. 2006. Potential Pitfalls of Process Modeling: Part A. *Business Process Management Journal* 12 (2): 249–254. https://doi.org/10.1108/14637150610657567.

Rosemann, Michael, and Tonia de Bruin. 2005. Application of a Holistic Model for Determining BPM Maturity. *BP Trends* 2: 1–21.

Rossiter, John, and Steve Bellman. 2012. Emotional Branding Pays Off: How Brands Meet Share of Requirements Through Bonding, Companionship, and Love. *Journal of Advertising Research* 52 (3): 291–296. https://doi.org/10.2501/JAR-52-3-291-296.

Rowley, Jenny. 2014. Designing and Using Research Questionnaires. *Management Research Review* 37 (3): 308–330. https://doi.org/10.1108/MRR-02-2013-0027.

Roy, Sanjit Kumar, Gul Butaney, Harjit Sekhon, and Bhupin Butaney. 2014. Word-of-Mouth and Viral Marketing Activity of the On-Line Consumer: The Role of Loyalty Chain Stages Theory. *Journal of Strategic Marketing* 22 (6): 494–512.

Rudawska, Edyta, Ewa Frąckiewicz, and Małgorzata Wiścicka. 2016. Sustainable Marketing as a Response to Contemporary Challenges Facing Companies in Poland. *International Journal of Management Cases* 18 (4): 15–29.

Rudny, Włodzimierz. 2014. Zasoby sieciowe a strategia przedsiębiorstwa. *Studia Ekonomiczne* 202: 23–33.

Rugman, Alan M., and Joseph R. D'Cruz. 1993. The "Double Diamond" Model of International Competitiveness: The Canadian Experience. *MIR: Management International Review* 33: 17–39.

Rugman, Alan M., and Alain Verbeke. 2004. A Final Word on Edith Penrose. *Journal of Management Studies* 41 (1): 205–217. https://doi.org/10.1111/j.1467-6486.2004.00429.x.

Ruiz, David Martín, Dwayne D. Gremler, Judith H. Washburn, and Gabriel Cepeda Carrión. 2008. Service Value Revisited: Specifying a Higher-Order, Formative Measure. *Journal of Business Research*, Formative Indicators, 61 (12): 1278–1291. https://doi.org/10.1016/j.jbusres.2008.01.015.

Rumelt, Richard P. 1984. Towards a Strategic Theory of the Firm. *Competitive Strategic Management* 26 (3): 556–570.

———. 1987. Theory, Strategy, and Entrepreneurship. In *The Competitive Challenge.*, ed. David Teece, 137–158. Cambridge, MA: Ballinger.

———. 1991. How Much Does Industry Matter? *Strategic Management Journal* 12 (3): 167–185. https://doi.org/10.1002/smj.4250120302.

———. 1997. Towards a Strategic Theory of the Firm. In *Resources, Firms, and Strategies: A Reader in the Resource-Based Perspective*, ed. Nicolai J. Foss, 137–145. Oxford: Oxford University Press.

Rumelt, Richard P., D. Schendel, and David J. Teece. 1995. *Fundamental Issues in Strategy: A Research Agenda*. Cambridge, MA: Harvard Business School Press. https://books.google.pl/books?id=rttTzECN9_YC.

Russo-Spena, Tiziana, and Cristina Mele. 2012. "Five Co-s" in Innovating: A Practice-based View'. Edited by Evert Gummesson, Cristina Mele, and Francesco Polese. *Journal of Service Management* 23 (4): 527–553. https://doi.org/10.1108/09564231211260404.

Ryan, Richard M., and Edward L. Deci. 2017. *Self-Determination Theory: Basic Psychological Needs in Motivation, Development, and Wellness*. New York: Guilford Publications.

Sabnis, Gaurav, Sharmila C. Chatterjee, Rajdeep Grewal, and Gary L. Lilien. 2013. The Sales Lead Black Hole: On Sales Reps' Follow-Up of Marketing Leads. *Journal of Marketing* 77 (1): 52–67. https://doi.org/10.1509/jm.10.0047.

Saini, Amit, Rajdeep Grewal, and Jean L. Johnson. 2010. Putting Market-Facing Technology to Work: Organizational Drivers of CRM Performance. *Marketing Letters* 21 (4): 365–383. https://doi.org/10.1007/s11002-009-9096-z.

Samson, Alain. 2006. Understanding the Buzz That Matters: Negative Vs Positive Word of Mouth. *International Journal of Market Research* 48 (6): 647–657. https://doi.org/10.1177/147078530604800603.

Sasidharan Dhanesh, Ganga. 2012. The View from Within: Internal Publics and CSR. *Journal of Communication Management* 16 (1): 39–58. https://doi.org/10.1108/13632541211197987.

Sasser, W. Earl, Leonard A. Schlesinger, and James L. Heskett. 1997. *Service Profit Chain*. New York: Simon and Schuster.

Schein, Edgar H. 1990. Organizational Culture. *American Psychologist* 45 (2): 109–119. https://doi.org/10.1037/0003-066X.45.2.109.

Scherer, Klaus. 1997. Profiles of Emotion-Antecedent Appraisal: Testing Theoretical Predictions across Cultures. *Cognition and Emotion* 11 (2): 113–150. https://doi.org/10.1080/026999397379962.

Schertzer, Susan M.B., Clinton B. Schertzer, and F. Robert Dwyer. 2013. Value in Professional Service Relationships. *Journal of Business & Industrial Marketing* 28 (8): 607–619.

Schmidt-Subramanian, Maxi. 2019. Forrester Publishes NPS Benchmarks For 260 Brands In 16 Industries. *Forrester Blogs* (blog), November 7. https://go.forrester.com/blogs/nps-benchmarks/.

Schmidt-Subramanian, Maxi, Harley Manning, Sam Karpinsky, and Shayna Neuburg. 2019. The Top 10 NPS Questions Answered What CX Professionals Should Know About Net Promoter Score. *Forrester*, November 7. https://

www.forrester.com/report/Executive+QA+Top+10+NPS+Questions+Answered+For+CX+Professionals/-/E-RES60925.

Schoemaker, Paul J.H. 1990. Strategy, Complexity, and Economic Rent. *Management Science* 36 (10): 1178–1192. https://doi.org/10.1287/mnsc.36.10.1178.

Schriesheim, Chester A. 1981. The Effect of Grouping or Randomizing Items on Leniency Response Bias. *Educational and Psychological Measurement* 41 (2): 401–411. https://doi.org/10.1177/001316448104100219.

Schuler, Douglas A., and Margaret Cording. 2006. A Corporate Social Performance–Corporate Financial Performance Behavioral Model for Consumers. *Academy of Management Review* 31 (3): 540–558. https://doi.org/10.5465/amr.2006.21318916.

Schumann, Jan H., Florian v. Wangenheim, Anne Stringfellow, Zhilin Yang, Sandra Praxmarer, Fernando R. Jiménez, Vera Blazevic, Randall M. Shannon, G. Shainesh, and Marcin Komor. 2010. Drivers of Trust in Relational Service Exchange: Understanding the Importance of Cross-Cultural Differences. *Journal of Service Research* 13 (4): 453–468. https://doi.org/10.1177/1094670510368425.

Schumpeter, J.A. 2010 (1950). *Capitalism, Socialism and Democracy: 1st Edition (Paperback)*. Abingdon: Routledge.

Schwalbe, Kathy. 2008. *Information Technology Project Management, Reprint*. 5th ed. Boston: Thomson Course Technology.

Scott, W. Richard. 2002. *Organizations: Rational, Natural, and Open Systems*. 5th ed. Upper Saddle River: Prentice Hall.

Scott, W. Richard, and Gerald F. Davis. 2015. *Organizations and Organizing: Rational, Natural and Open Systems Perspectives*. New York: Routledge.

Sepulveda, Fabian, and Mika Gabrielsson. 2013. Network Development and Firm Growth: A Resource-Based Study of B2B Born Globals. *Industrial Marketing Management*, Business Models – Exploring Value Drivers and the Role of Marketing, 42 (5): 792–804. https://doi.org/10.1016/j.indmarman.2013.01.001.

Shafer, Scott M., H. Jeff Smith, and Jane C. Linder. 2005. The Power of Business Models. *Business Horizons* 48 (3): 199–207. https://doi.org/10.1016/j.bushor.2004.10.014.

Shams, S.M. Riad. 2016. Capacity Building for Sustained Competitive Advantage: A Conceptual Framework. *Marketing Intelligence & Planning* 34 (5): 671–691. https://doi.org/10.1108/MIP-08-2015-0161.

Shapiro, Carl. 1989. The Theory of Business Strategy. *The RAND Journal of Economics* 20 (1): 125–137. https://doi.org/10.2307/2555656.

Sharma, Aran, and Gopalkrishnan R. Iyer. 2007. Country Effects on CRM Success. *Journal of Relationship Marketing* 5 (4): 63–78. https://doi.org/10.1300/J366v05n04_05.

Sharp, Byron. 2008. Net Promoter Score Fails the Test. *Marketing Research* 20 (4): 28–30.
Sheth, Jagdish N. 2017. Revitalizing Relationship Marketing. *Journal of Services Marketing* 31 (1): 6–10. https://doi.org/10.1108/JSM-11-2016-0397.
Sheth, Jagdish N., and Atul Parvatiyar. 2000. *Handbook of Relationship Marketing*. London: SAGE.
Shi, Linda Hui, and Tao (Tony) Gao. 2016. Performance Effects of Global Account Coordination Mechanisms: An Integrative Study of Boundary Conditions. *Journal of International Marketing*, June 1. https://doi.org/10.1509/jim.15.0103.
Shi, Linda H., Shaoming Zou, J. Chris White, Regina C. McNally, and S. Tamer Cavusgil. 2005. Executive Insights: Global Account Management Capability: Insights from Leading Suppliers. *Journal of International Marketing* 13 (2): 93–113. https://doi.org/10.1509/jimk.13.2.93.64858.
Shiri, Soheila, Alireza Anvari, and Hassan Soltani. 2014. An Assessment of Readiness Factors for Implementing ERP Based on Agility (Extension of Mckinsey 7s Model). *International Journal of Management, Accounting & Economics* 1 (3): 229–246.
Shook, Christopher L., David J. Ketchen, G. Tomas M. Hult, and K. Michele Kacmar. 2004. An Assessment of the Use of Structural Equation Modeling in Strategic Management Research. *Strategic Management Journal* 25 (4): 397–404. https://doi.org/10.1002/smj.385.
Shore, Lynn M., Lois E. Tetrick, Patricia Lynch, and Kevin Barksdale. 2006. Social and Economic Exchange: Construct Development and Validation. *Journal of Applied Social Psychology* 36 (4): 837–867. https://doi.org/10.1111/j.0021-9029.2006.00046.x.
Shostack, Lynn G. 1982. How to Design a Service. *European Journal of Marketing* 16 (1): 49–63. https://doi.org/10.1108/EUM0000000004799.
Shott, Michael J. 1998. Status and Role of Formation Theory in Contemporary Archaeological Practice. *Journal of Archaeological Research* 6 (4): 299–329. https://doi.org/10.1007/BF02446082.
Shukla, Mahendra Kumar, and Pinaki Nandan Pattnaik. 2019. Managing Customer Relations in a Modern Business Environment: Towards an Ecosystem-Based Sustainable CRM Model. *Journal of Relationship Marketing* 18 (1): 17–33. https://doi.org/10.1080/15332667.2018.1534057.
Sigalas, Christos. 2013. Developing a Measure of Competitive Advantage. *Journal of Strategy and Management* 6 (4): 320–342. https://doi.org/10.1108/JSMA-03-2013-0015.
Sijun, Wang, Sharon E. Beatty, and Jeanny Liu. 2012. Employees' Decision Making in the Face of Customers' Fuzzy Return Requests. *Journal of Marketing* 76 (6): 69–86.

Simkin, Lyndon, and Sally Dibb. 2013. Social Media's Impact on Market Segmentation and CRM. *Journal of Strategic Marketing* 21 (5): 391–393.

Sin, Leo Y.M., Alan C.B. Tse, Oliver H.M. Yau, Raymond P.M. Chow, and Jenny S.Y. Lee. 2005. Market Orientation, Relationship Marketing Orientation, and Business Performance: The Moderating Effects of Economic Ideology and Industry Type. *Journal of International Marketing* 13 (1): 36–57. https://doi.org/10.1509/jimk.13.1.36.58538.

Singh, Shweta, and Sumit Singh. 2016. Accounting for Risk in the Traditional RFM Approach. *Management Research Review* 39 (2): 215–234.

Slater, Stanley F. 1997. Developing a Customer Value-Based Theory of the Firm. *Journal of the Academy of Marketing Science* 25 (2): 162–167. https://doi.org/10.1007/BF02894352.

Slater, Stanley F., and John C. Narver. 1995. Market Orientation and the Learning Organization. *Journal of Marketing* 59 (3): 63–74. https://doi.org/10.1177/002224299505900306.

Slater, Stanley F., and Eric M. Olson. 2001. Marketing's Contribution to the Implementation of Business Strategy: An Empirical Analysis. *Strategic Management Journal* 22 (11): 1055–1067. https://doi.org/10.1002/smj.198.

Slater, Stanley F., Eric M. Olson, and Carol Finnegan. 2011. Business Strategy, Marketing Organization Culture, and Performance. *Marketing Letters* 22 (3): 227–242. https://doi.org/10.1007/s11002-010-9122-1.

Smith, Timothy M., Srinath Gopalakrishna, and Rabikar Chatterjee. 2006. A Three-Stage Model of Integrated Marketing Communications at the Marketing-Sales Interface. *Journal of Marketing Research* 43 (4): 564–579. https://doi.org/10.1509/jmkr.43.4.564.

Sobczyk, Janusz R. 2010. Kryzys podstaw metodologicznych nauk o zarządzaniu – kryzysem powinowactwa z naukami społecznymi. *Acta Universitatis Lodzensis – Folia Oeconomica* 234: 335–345.

Sopińska, Agnieszka. 2019. Wybór partnerów współdziałania jako jeden z elementów treści strategii relacyjnej. *Przegląd Organizacji* 4: 10–17. https://doi.org/10.33141/po.2019.4.2.

Spake, Deborah F., Sharon E. Beatty, Beverly K. Brockman, and Tammy Neal Crutchfield. 2003. Consumer Comfort in Service Relationships: Measurement and Importance. *Journal of Service Research* 5 (4): 316–332. https://doi.org/10.1177/1094670503005004004.

Spender, J.-C. 1996. Making Knowledge the Basis of a Dynamic Theory of the Firm. *Strategic Management Journal* 17 (S2): 45–62. https://doi.org/10.1002/smj.4250171106.

Sprenger, Jan. 2011. Hypothetico-Deductive Confirmation. *Philosophy Compass* 6 (7): 497–508. https://doi.org/10.1111/j.1747-9991.2011.00409.x.

Sriramesh, K., James E. Grunig, and David M. Dozier. 1996. Observation and Measurement of Two Dimensions of Organizational Culture and Their Relationship to Public Relations. *Journal of Public Relations Research* 8 (4): 229–261. https://doi.org/10.1207/s1532754xjprr0804_02.

Stankiewicz, Marek J. 2000. Substance and Methods of Evaluation of Enterprise Competitiveness. *Gospodarka Narodowa. The Polish Journal of Economics* 161 (7–8): 95–111. https://doi.org/10.33119/GN/113968.

Steel, Marion, Chris Dubelaar, and Michael T. Ewing. 2013. Developing Customised CRM Projects: The Role of Industry Norms, Organisational Context and Customer Expectations on CRM Implementation. *Industrial Marketing Management* 42 (8): 1328–1344. https://doi.org/10.1016/j.indmarman.2012.08.009.

Sterling, Theodore F. 2002. *The Enron Scandal.* New York: Nova Publishers.

Stewart, Thomas A. 2007. *The Wealth of Knowledge: Intellectual Capital and the Twenty-First Century Organization.* New York: Crown Publishing Group.

Stibitz, Sara. 2015. How to Get a New Employee Up to Speed. *Harvard Business Review Digital Articles* 22: 2–5.

Storbacka Kaj, Frow Pennie, Nenonen Suvi, and Payne Adrian. 2012. Designing Business Models for Value Co-Creation. Edited by Stephen L. Vargo and Robert F. Lusch. *Special Issue – Toward a Better Understanding of the Role of Value in Markets and Marketing*, Review of Marketing Research, 9: 51–78. https://doi.org/10.1108/S1548-6435(2012)0000009007.

Storey, John. 2007. *Human Resource Management: A Critical Text.* 3rd ed. London: Thomson Learning. http://edu.cengage.co.uk/catalogue/product.aspx?isbn=1844806154.

Strauss, Anselm L., and Juliet M. Corbin. 1998. *Basics of Qualitative Research: Techniques and Procedures for Developing Grounded Theory.* 2nd ed. Thousand Oaks: Sage Publications.

Struĕyna, Janusz. 2015. Oryginalność w Badaniach Naukowych w Dyscyplinie Nauk o Zarządzaniu. In *Podstawy Metodologii Badań w Naukach o Zarządzaniu*, ed. Wojciech Czakon, 3rd ed. Warszawa: Oficyna a Wolters Kluwer business.

Sulejewicz, Aleksander. 1997. *Partnerstwo Strategiczne: Modelowanie Współpracy Przedsiębiorstw.* Warszawa: Szkoła Główna Handlowa.

Sull, Donald Norman, and Kathleen M. Eisenhardt. 2015. *Simple Rules: How to Thrive in a Complex World.* Boston: Houghton Mifflin Harcourt.

Svendsen, Freng. 2011. Marketing Strategy and Customer Involvement in Product Development. *European Journal of Marketing* 45 (4): 513–530. https://doi.org/10.1108/03090561111111316.

Tadajewski, Mark. 2008. Incommensurable Paradigms, Cognitive Bias and the Politics of Marketing Theory. *Marketing Theory* 8 (3): 273–297. https://doi.org/10.1177/1470593108093557.

Tarhan, Ayca, Oktay Turetken, and Hajo A. Reijers. 2016. Business Process Maturity Models: A Systematic Literature Review. *Information and Software Technology* 75: 122–134. https://doi.org/10.1016/j.infsof.2016.01.010.

Teece, David J. 1982. Towards an Economic Theory of the Multiproduct Firm. *Journal of Economic Behavior & Organization* 3 (1): 39–63. https://doi.org/10.1016/0167-2681(82)90003-8.

———. 1984. Economic Analysis and Strategic Management. *California Management Review (Pre-1986); Berkeley* 26 (3, Spring): 87.

———. 1986. Profiting from Technological Innovation. *Research Policy* 15: 285–305.

———. 2007. Explicating Dynamic Capabilities: The Nature and Microfoundations of (Sustainable) Enterprise Performance. *Strategic Management Journal* 28 (13): 1319–1350. https://doi.org/10.1002/smj.640.

Teece, David J., Richard Rumelt, Giovanni Dosi, and Sidney Winter. 1994. Understanding Corporate Coherence: Theory and Evidence. *Journal of Economic Behavior & Organization* 23 (1): 1–30. https://doi.org/10.1016/0167-2681(94)90094-9.

Teece, David J., Gary Pisano, and Amy Shuen. 1997. Dynamic Capabilities and Strategic Management. *Strategic Management Journal* 18 (7): 509–533. https://doi.org/10.1002/(SICI)1097-0266(199708)18:7<509::AID-SMJ882>3.0.CO;2-Z.

Teneta-Skwiercz, Dorota. 2008. Wymiar Etyczny w Funkcjonowaniu Współczesnego Przedsiębiorstwa. Edited by Jan Lichtarski. *Prace Naukowe Uniwersytetu Ekonomicznego We Wrocławiu* 34: 18–27.

Teo, Thompson S.H., Paul Devadoss, and Shan L. Pan. 2006. Towards a Holistic Perspective of Customer Relationship Management (CRM) Implementation: A Case Study of the Housing and Development Board, Singapore. *Decision Support Systems* 42 (3): 1613–1627. https://doi.org/10.1016/j.dss.2006.01.007.

Terho, Harri, and Anne Jalkala. 2017. Customer Reference Marketing: Conceptualization, Measurement and Link to Selling Performance. *Industrial Marketing Management* 64: 175–186. https://doi.org/10.1016/j.indmarman.2017.01.005.

Thakur, Ramendra, and Letty Workman. 2016. Customer Portfolio Management (CPM) for Improved Customer Relationship Management (CRM): Are Your Customers Platinum, Gold, Silver, or Bronze? *Journal of Business Research* 69 (10): 4095–4102. https://doi.org/10.1016/j.jbusres.2016.03.042.

Toulan, Omar, Julian Birkinshaw, and David Arnold. 2006. The Role of Interorganizational Fit in Global Account Management. *International Studies of Management & Organization* 36 (4): 61–81. https://doi.org/10.2753/IMO0020-8825360403.

Trainor, Kevin J., James (Mick) Andzulis, Adam Rapp, and Raj Agnihotri. 2014. Social Media Technology Usage and Customer Relationship Performance: A

Capabilities-Based Examination of Social CRM. *Journal of Business Research* 67 (6): 1201–1208. https://doi.org/10.1016/j.jbusres.2013.05.002.

Trocki, Michał. 2005. Točsamość nauk o zarządzaniu. *Przegląd Organizacji* 1: 7–10.

Tvede, Lars, and Peter Ohnemus. 2001. *Marketing Strategies for the New Economy*. Hoboken: Wiley. https://books.google.pl/books?id=z_wonQEACAAJ.

Uncles, Mark D., Grahame R. Dowling, and Kathy Hammond. 2003. Customer Loyalty and Customer Loyalty Programs. *Journal of Consumer Marketing* 20 (4): 294–316. https://doi.org/10.1108/07363760310483676.

Urbańczyk, Tomasz. 2012. *Rozwój sieci dostaw poprzez wdračanie koncepcji łańcucha solidarnósci*. Poznan University of Economics and Business.

van de Mortel, Thea F. 2008. Faking It: Social Desirability Response Bias in Self-Report Research. *The Australian Journal of Advanced Nursing* 25 (4): 40.

van den Bosch, Frans A.J. 1997. Porter's Contribution to More General and Dynamic Strategy Frameworks. In *Perspectives on Strategy: Contributions of Michael E. Porter*, ed. F.A.J. van den Bosch and A.P. De Man, 91–100. Boston: Springer US. https://doi.org/10.1007/978-1-4615-6179-8_10.

Van Den Bulte, Christophe, Emanuel Bayer, Bernd Skiera, and Philipp Schmitt. 2018. How Customer Referral Programs Turn Social Capital into Economic Capital. *Journal of Marketing Research* 55 (1): 132–146. https://doi.org/10.1509/jmr.14.0653.

Van Tongeren, Daryl R., Jeffrey D. Green, Timothy L. Hulsey, Cristine H. Legare, David G. Bromley, and Anne M. Houtman. 2014. A Meaning-Based Approach to Humility: Relationship Affirmation Reduces Worldview Defense. *Journal of Psychology and Theology* 42 (1): 62–69. https://doi.org/10.1177/009164711404200107.

Varelius, Jukka. 2009. Is Whistle-Blowing Compatible with Employee Loyalty? *Journal of Business Ethics* 85 (2): 263–275.

Vargo, Stephen L. 2008. Service-Dominant Logic: Continuing the Evolution. *Journal of the Academy of Marketing Science* 36 (1): 1–10. https://doi.org/10.1007/s11747-007-0069-6.

———. 2016. Institutions and Axioms: An Extension and Update of Service-Dominant Logic. *Journal of the Academy of Marketing Science* 44 (1): 5–23. https://doi.org/10.1007/s11747-015-0456-3.

Vargo, Stephen L., and Robert F. Lusch. 2004. Evolving to a New Dominant Logic for Marketing. *Journal of Marketing* 68 (1): 1–17.

Vargo, Stephen L., Josina Vink, and Kaisa Koskela-Huotari. 2020. Service Dominant Logic: Foundations and Applications. In *The Routledge Handbook of Service Research Insights and Ideas*, ed. E. Bridges and K. Fowler, 3–23. New York: Routledge. https://www.researchgate.net/profile/Kaisa_Koskela-Huotari/publication/340777398_Service-Dominant_Logic_Foundations_and_Applications/links/5e9d3f0992851c2f52b288fc/Service-Dominant-Logic-Foundations-and-Applications.pdf.

Vella, Joseph, and Albert Caruana. 2012. Encouraging CRM Systems Usage: A Study Among Bank Managers. *Management Research Review* 35 (2): 121–133. https://doi.org/10.1108/01409171211195152.

Venkatesan, Rajkumar, and Vita Kumar. 2004. A Customer Lifetime Value Framework for Customer Selection and Resource Allocation Strategy. *Journal of Marketing* 68 (4): 106–125. https://doi.org/10.1509/jmkg.68.4.106.42728.

Vij, Sandeep, and Harpreet Singh Bedi. 2016. Are Subjective Business Performance Measures Justified? *International Journal of Productivity and Performance Management*, June 13. https://doi.org/10.1108/IJPPM-12-2014-0196.

Virtanen, Tatu, Petri Parvinen, and Minna Rollins. 2015. Complexity of Sales Situation and Sales Lead Performance: An Empirical Study in Business-to-Business Company. *Industrial Marketing Management* 45: 49–58. https://doi.org/10.1016/j.indmarman.2015.02.024.

Wagner, Janet, and Sabine Benoit (née Moeller). 2015. Creating Value in Retail Buyer–Vendor Relationships: A Service-Centered Model. *Industrial Marketing Management* 44: 166–179. https://doi.org/10.1016/j.indmarman.2014.10.013.

Walker, Orville C., and Robert W. Ruekert. 1987. Marketing's Role in the Implementation of Business Strategies: A Critical Review and Conceptual Framework. *Journal of Marketing* 51 (3): 15–33. https://doi.org/10.1177/002224298705100302.

Wang, Hui-Ling. 2014. Theories for Competitive Advantage. In *Being Practical with Theory: A Window into Business Research*, ed. H. Hasan, 33–43. Wollongong: THEORI. https://ro.uow.edu.au/buspapers/408.

Wang, Yonggui, and Hui Feng. 2012. Customer Relationship Management Capabilities: Measurement, Antecedents and Consequences. *Management Decision* 50 (1): 115–129. https://doi.org/10.1108/00251741211194903.

Wang, Yun, Michel Rod, Shaobo Ji, and Qi Deng. 2017. Social Media Capability in B2B Marketing: Toward a Definition and a Research Model. *Journal of Business & Industrial Marketing* 32 (8): 1125–1135. https://doi.org/10.1108/JBIM-10-2016-0250.

Ward, Scott, and Frederick E. Webster. 1991. Organizational Buying Behavior. In *Handbook of Consumer Behavior*, Ellis Horwood Series in Analytical, ed. T.S. Robertson and H.H. Kassarjian. Upper Saddle River: Prentice-Hall. https://books.google.pl/books?id=dz0fAQAAIAAJ.

Wąsowska, Aleksandra, and Marcin Pawłowski. 2011. Metody pomiaru społecznej odpowiedzialności biznesu – przegląd literatury. *Przegląd Organizacji* 11: 14–17. https://doi.org/10.33141/po.2011.11.4.

Waterman, Robert, Thomas J. Peters, and Julien R. Phillips. 1980. Structure Is Not Organization. *Business Horizons* 23 (3): 14–26.

Watkins, C. Edward, Jr., Joshua N. Hook, Joey Ramaeker, and Marciana J. Ramos. 2016. Repairing the Ruptured Supervisory Alliance: Humility as a Foundational Virtue in Clinical Supervision. *The Clinical Supervisor* 35 (1): 22–41. https://doi.org/10.1080/07325223.2015.1127190.

Wendler, Roy. 2012. The Maturity of Maturity Model Research: A Systematic Mapping Study. *Information and Software Technology*, Special Section on Software Reliability and Security, 54 (12): 1317–1339. https://doi.org/10.1016/j.infsof.2012.07.007.

Wernerfelt, Birger. 1984. A Resource-Based View of the Firm. *Strategic Management Journal* 5 (2): 171–180. https://doi.org/10.1002/smj.4250050207.

Whitlark, David B., and Gary K. Rhoads. 2011. Scoring Success. *Marketing Research* 23 (1): 8–13.

Wiktor, Jan. 2019. Koncepcja Konkurencji M.E. Portera a System Ochrony Rynku Wewnętrznego Unii Europejskiej. *Przegląd Organizacji* 6: 9–16. https://doi.org/10.33141/po.2019.6.1.

Williamson, Oliver E. 1983. Credible Commitments: Using Hostages to Support Exchange. *The American Economic Review* 73 (4): 519–540.

———. 1991. Strategizing, Economizing, and Economic Organization. *Strategic Management Journal* 12 (S2): 75–94. https://doi.org/10.1002/smj.4250121007.

———. 1993. Introduction. In *The Nature of the Firm: Origins, Evolution, and Development*, 3–17. Oxford: Oxford University Press.

Winter, Sidney G. 2003. Understanding Dynamic Capabilities. *Strategic Management Journal* 24 (10): 991–995. https://doi.org/10.1002/smj.318.

Wirtz, Jochen, and Christopher H. Lovelock. 2016. *Services Marketing: People, Technology, Strategy*. 8th ed. Hackensack: World Scientific Publishing Company.

Wirtz, Jochen, and Tomlin Monica. 2000. Institutionalising Customer-driven Learning Through Fully Integrated Customer Feedback Systems. *Managing Service Quality: An International Journal* 10 (4): 205–215. https://doi.org/10.1108/09604520010341654.

Wirtz, Jochen, Siok Kuan Tambyah, and Anna S. Mattila. 2010. Organizational Learning from Customer Feedback Received by Service Employees: A Social Capital Perspective. *Journal of Service Management* 21 (3): 363–387. https://doi.org/10.1108/09564231011050814.

Wirtz, Jochen, Anouk den Ambtman, Josée Bloemer, Csilla Horváth, B. Ramaseshan, Joris van de Klundert, Zeynep Gurhan Canli, and Jay Kandampully. 2013. Managing Brands and Customer Engagement in Online Brand Communities. Edited by Lerzan Aksoy, Allard van Riel, and Jay Kandampully. *Journal of Service Management* 24 (3): 223–244. https://doi.org/10.1108/09564231311326978.

Wirzba, Norman. 2008. The Touch of Humility: An Invitation to Creatureliness. *Modern Theology* 24 (2): 225–244. https://doi.org/10.1111/j.1468-0025.2007.00443.x.

Witek-Crabb, Anna. 2012. Sustainable Strategic Management and Market Effectiveness of Enterprises. *Procedia – Social and Behavioral Sciences* 58: 899–905. https://doi.org/10.1016/j.sbspro.2012.09.1068.

Wong, Amy, and Lianxi Zhou. 2006. Determinants and Outcomes of Relationship Quality. *Journal of International Consumer Marketing* 18 (3): 81–105. https://doi.org/10.1300/J046v18n03_05.

Wood, Wendy, and David T. Neal. 2009. The Habitual Consumer. *Journal of Consumer Psychology* 19 (4): 579–592. https://doi.org/10.1016/j.jcps.2009.08.003.

Wu, Lei-Yu. 2007. Entrepreneurial Resources, Dynamic Capabilities and Start-Up Performance of Taiwan's High-Tech Firms. *Journal of Business Research* 60 (5): 549–555. https://doi.org/10.1016/j.jbusres.2007.01.007.

Xia, Lan, and Monika Kukar-Kinney. 2014. For Our Valued Customers Only: Examining Consumer Responses to Preferential Treatment Practices. *Journal of Business Research* 67 (11): 2368–2375. https://doi.org/10.1016/j.jbusres.2014.02.002.

Yu, Tianyuan, and NengQuan Wu. 2009. A Review of Study on the Competing Values Framework. *International Journal of Business and Management* 4 (7): p37. https://doi.org/10.5539/ijbm.v4n7p37.

Zaglia, Melanie E. 2013. Brand Communities Embedded in Social Networks. *Journal of Business Research*, Thought Leadership in Brand Management II, 66 (2): 216–223. https://doi.org/10.1016/j.jbusres.2012.07.015.

Zairi, Mohamed. 1994. Benchmarking: The Best Tool for Measuring Competitiveness. *Benchmarking for Quality Management & Technology* 1 (1): 11–24. https://doi.org/10.1108/14635779410056859.

Zand, Jafar Danesh, Abbas Keramati, Farzaneh Shakouri, and Hamid Noori. 2018. Assessing the Impact of Customer Knowledge Management on Organizational Performance. *Knowledge and Process Management* 25 (4): 268–278. https://doi.org/10.1002/kpm.1585.

Zawiślak, Andrzej. 2010. *Ekonomia. Nauka Praw Tymczasowych*. Warszawa: Oficyna Wydawnicza Warszawskiej Szkoły Zarządzania.

Zerbino, Pierluigi, Davide Aloini, Riccardo Dulmin, and Valeria Mininno. 2018. Big Data-Enabled Customer Relationship Management: A Holistic Approach. *Information Processing & Management* 54: 818–846. https://doi.org/10.1016/j.ipm.2017.10.005.

Zhang, Wanrong, and Sujit Banerji. 2017. Challenges of Servitization: A Systematic Literature Review. *Industrial Marketing Management* 65: 217–227. https://doi.org/10.1016/j.indmarman.2017.06.003.

Zhang, Jonathan Z., George F. Watson, Robert W. Palmatier, and Rajiv P. Dant. 2016. Dynamic Relationship Marketing. *Journal of Marketing* 80 (5): 53–75.

Zhang, Mingli, Lingyun Guo, Mu Hu, and Wenhua Liu. 2017. Influence of Customer Engagement with Company Social Networks on Stickiness: Mediating Effect of Customer Value Creation. *International Journal of Information Management* 37 (3): 229–240. https://doi.org/10.1016/j.ijinfomgt.2016.04.010.

Zhang, Tingting, Can Lu, Edwin Torres, and Po-Ju Chen. 2018. Engaging Customers in Value Co-Creation or Co-Destruction Online. *Journal of Services Marketing* 32 (1): 57–69. https://doi.org/10.1108/JSM-01-2017-0027.

Zimniewicz, Kazimierz. 2014. *Teoria i Praktyka Zarządzania: Analiza Krytyczna*. Warszawa: Polskie Wydawnictwo Ekonomiczne.

Zineldin, Mosad, and Sarah Philipson. 2007. Kotler and Borden Are Not Dead: Myth of Relationship Marketing and Truth of the 4Ps. *Journal of Consumer Marketing* 24 (4): 229–241. https://doi.org/10.1108/07363760710756011.

Zott, Christoph, and Raphael Amit. 2010. Business Model Design: An Activity System Perspective. *Business Models* 43 (2): 216–226. https://doi.org/10.1016/j.lrp.2009.07.004.

Index[1]

A

Association rules (methodology), 138–141, 144–146, 162, 218

B

Barriers to developing relationships, 195
Basket analysis (methodology), *see* Association rules (methodology)
Blue ocean leadership concept, 40
Business ethics, 89
Business model, vii, 2, 25, 26, 45, 68, 142, 168, 185, 196
Business Process Management (BPM), 68, 82

C

Capability Maturity Model for software (CMM), 68
Chicago school, 3, 4
See also Industrial Organization Economics
Clan culture, *see* Human Relations Model
Cognitive School (strategic management), 4
Commitment-Trust Theory, 44
Competition, 3, 4, 14, 22, 25, 35, 36, 42, 89, 150, 172, 201, 202, 204, 209n2
Competitive advantage, *see* Sustainable competitive advantage
Complaint management (complaints), 96, 97
Configuration School (strategic management), 4
Configuration theory, 168, 170
Corporate culture, 11, 77, 83, 87, 91–94, 101, 166, 168, 183, 185, 207, 208
Corporate Social Responsibility (CSR), 78, 89, 90, 147, 206, 207

---

[1] Note: Page numbers followed by 'n' refer to notes.

CRM systems, 83, 98–101, 175, 176
CRM strategy framework, 82, 89, 96
Cultural School (strategic management), 4
Customer communication processes, 97
Customer feedback, 148, 165
Customer Relationship Management (CRM), 25, 74, 76, 78, 79, 81–83, 89, 98, 100, 142, 143, 149, 180, 195, 196, 201

D
Design School (strategic management), 4
Diversification theory, 169, 170
Dynamic capabilities, 4, 12, 22, 23, 33, 74, 78, 79, 86, 87, 161, 169, 185, 217
Dynamic theory of strategy, 8, 9

E
Emotional culture, 92
Employee empowerment, 92–94, 161
Employee relationship management, *see* Internal relationship management (IRM)
Entrepreneurial School, 3, 4
See also Industrial Organization Economics
Environmental School (strategic management), 4
External relationship management (ERM), 38, 39, 44, 83, 87, 88, 90, 96, 98, 100, 101, 162

F
Five-forces model, 7, 8

G
Global Account Management, *see* Key Account Management (KAM)
Grand theory of competition, *see* Resource-Advantage Theory of Competition (R-A theory)

H
H-D logic, *see* Hypothetico-deductive (H-D) theory confirmation method
Human capital, 33
Human Relations Model (Clan culture), 92
Human resources management (HRM), 40, 78, 87, 94, 95, 100, 218
Hypothetico-deductive (H-D) theory confirmation method (H-D logic), ix, 67–69

I
Idealization strategy (theory building), 67
Industrial marketing, 21, 142
Industrial Marketing and Purchasing Group (IMP), 21
Industrial Organization Economics (IOE), 3, 4, 6, 8, 10–14, 21, 22, 25, 35, 37
Informal relationships, *see* Relationships
Information and Communication Technologies (ICT), 44, 46, 78, 83, 94–101, 149
Intellectual capital, 33
Internal Relationship Management (IRM), 38, 42, 83, 87, 88, 90, 94, 96, 101, 161, 162, 166

INDEX

Isolating mechanism (RBV), 11
Isolating mechanism (theory building), 41–42

K

Key Account Management (KAM), 90
Knowledge, *see* Knowledge management (KM)
Knowledge Management (KM), 8, 11, 25, 31, 33, 78, 86, 87, 90, 91, 93, 96–101, 131, 161, 164, 180, 183, 208

L

Leadership, 40, 94, 147, 161, 166, 184
Lead management, 96, 124, 148, 163–165
Learning School (strategic management), 4
Loyalty management (loyalty), 96, 97

M

Managerial tasks, 186
Media Multiplexity Theory, 174
Mid-range theories, viii, 5, 35, 41, 43–45, 159–209
Monopoly, 6, 205

N

Net Promoter Score (NPS), 97, 134, 135, 167, 168, 209n1
Network approach, 21
Network rent, 13

O

Online relationships, 78, 98, 175, 186, 196
See also Online community
Organizational capital, 33

P

Personal relationships, *see* Relationships
Planning School (Strategic management), 4
Positioning School (Strategic management), 4, 7
Power School (Strategic management), 4
Processes, *see* Process management
Process management, viii, x, 4, 12, 26–28, 33, 68, 77, 78, 81–83, 85, 87–89, 91, 94–98, 100, 101, 124, 161–165, 208, 217, 218

R

R-A theory, 217, 218
Relational assets, 31, 32, 36, 88
Relational benefits, 30, 31, 34
Relational capital, 32, 33, 131, 160, 173, 174, 194, 209, 219
Relational communication, 95, 96, 100, 165
Relational exchange, 21, 30, 34, 44
Relational factors, 34, 38, 45
Relational niche, 166–180, 218, 219
Relational outcomes, 25, 28–32, 34
Relationship capital, *see* Relational capital

Relationship management (RM), vii, viii, x, xi, 21–36, 39, 40, 43–45, 70, 73, 76, 77, 79, 82, 83, 85, 86, 89, 91, 92, 94, 98, 130, 132, 133, 142, 144, 146, 149, 150, 159–209, 217–219

Relationship management business model (RM business model), vii–ix, 26–28, 44–46, 69, 88, 94, 95, 97, 101, 135, 145, 181

Relationship management capabilities (RM Capabilities), 33, 34, 36, 87, 135, 161, 192, 200, 219

Relationship management dimensions, 36, 149, 164

Relationship management maturity (RM-maturity), vii, viii, x, xi, 45, 46, 67–102, 121–150, 160–168, 172, 208, 209n2, 217–219
competence, 149

Relationship management mid-range theory (RM mid-range theory), viii, 13, 21–46, 68, 76, 134, 150, 174, 180, 217–219, x, xi
RM, 159
See also Relationship management upper mid-range theory (RM upper mid-range theory)

Relationship management upper mid-range theory (RM upper mid-range theory), 134, 150, 159, 160, 174, 180, 218, 219

Relationship marketing, viii, 21, 24, 25, 70

Relationship metrics, 27, 97, 134, 135, 169, 170, 213n1

Relationship quality, 28, 29, 217

Relationship rent, 21, 170, 204, 208

Relationships, vii, viii, xi, 4, 13, 22–33, 36–38, 40, 44, 45, 78, 86–90, 94, 95, 97, 98, 101, 148, 150, 160–165, 167, 168, 170, 173–177, 185, 188–192, 194–201, 203–206, 208, 209, 217, 218

Resource-Advantage Theory of Competition (R-A theory), 13, 35, 36, 41, 42, 68, 74, 159, 160

Resource-Based View (RBV), 3, 4, 6, 8, 10–14, 21, 22, 33–38, 73, 86, 160, 161, 169, 185, 197, 201, 217

Resources (RBV), 22, 33, 217

S

Service-Dominant Logic (SDL), x, 26, 27, 77, 78, 82, 83, 85, 86, 88, 92, 93, 97, 161, 167, 177, 178, 217

Service-Profit Chain, 162

Services, viii, 25, 30, 34, 77, 78, 85, 86, 88, 143, 161, 162, 176, 178–180, 194, 196, 199, 217, 219

Social capital, *see* Relational capital

Social-CRM, *see* Online relationships

Social Exchange Theory (SET), 23, 32, 40, 77

Social media, *see* Online relationships

Strategic assets, 10–13

Strategic management, ix, 1–5, 21, 22, 24, 25, 33–35, 38, 160

Structural equation models (SEM; methodology), 25, 137–139

Structure-conduct-performance paradigm (SCP paradigm), 3, 7

Supply Chain Management (SCM), 78, 90, 187

Sustainable competitive advantage, viii–x, 1–14, 21, 22, 34–38, 41–46, 79, 86–88, 92, 99, 101, 130–132, 135, 141, 142, 144–146, 150, 159–161, 163, 165, 166, 170, 172, 197, 203, 217–219

T

Total relationship marketing, 89
Transaction Cost Economics, 3, 4
  See also Industrial Organization Economics

Trust and commitment (RM), 11, 23, 27, 28, 32, 34, 38, 77, 79, 92, 147, 165, 188, 190, 193

V

Value co-creation, 85, 86, 88, 91, 94, 191
  See also Service-Dominant Logic (SDL)
VRIO resources (RBV), 86, 87, 169, 185
  See also Resources (RBV)

The manufacturer's authorised representative in the EU is Springer Nature Customer Service Centre GmbH, Europaplatz 3, 69115 Heidelberg, Germany. If you have any concerns regarding our products, please contact ProductSafety@springernature.com

Printed and bound by CPI Group (UK) Ltd, Croydon, CR0 4YY

23/03/2026

02076663-0008